# The Bridge

J. Nicholas De Bonis

## Race, Rage and Reconciliation in 1960s Iowa

ISBN-10: 198665012X:
ISBN-13: 978-1986650120

# Dedication

Dedicated to my wife, Susan, life partner, best friend, confidante and compass without whose patience, understanding, feedback and support this book wouldn't and couldn't have been written.

And to the East High School Class of 1966, and members of the 1966-1973 classes of East, Central, Columbus, Orange and West High schools who shared their stories, experiences, perceptions and insights that made *The Bridge Between (TBB)* possible.

# Acknowledgements

These acknowledgements can't accurately reflect the amount, quality and timeliness of the assistance provided in the research for and writing of *TBB* or my profound appreciation for each.

My four exceptional editors, Dr. Susan De Bonis, Brian Gruber, Dr. Ellen Hendrix-Erickson and Jennifer Brooks Hope.

The City of Waterloo. – Mayor Quentin Hart, Tim Andera, Noel Anderson, Michelle Westphal, John Dornoff, Wendy Drinovsky and Steve Walker, my "go-to" person for city history.

The Grout Museum – Bob Neymeyer and Sara Nefzger.

The State Historical Library & Archives, State Historical Society of Iowa, Des Moines – Sharon Avery, who fulfilled every request, and the research staff the two days I was there.

The Waterloo Community School District – Superintendent Jane Lindaman, Pam Arndorfer, Crystal Buzza, Lorene Dehl, Katrina Hemann, Sue Liddle, Dr. Beverly Smith, Tara Thomas and Jan Wolf, all of whom responded so quickly and efficiently I became spoiled.

The Waterloo Public Library – Tim Kuhlmann, Susan Harnois and Sue Pearson whose guidance, assistance and interest made the hours there seem like minutes.

Greg Lisby, Georgia State University, my legal scholar and sounding board.

Pat Kinney, *The Courier*, for his support and feedback.

# Preface

*During his 1965 debate with William F. Buckley, (James) Baldwin (broke) down what it's like to be taught all your life that Africans and black people are savages, inferior, and were "saved" by the white man. "Of course, I believed it. I didn't have much choice. Those were the only books there were."[1]*

The class of 1966 at East High School in Waterloo, Iowa, was the 100th in its history. It was racially integrated as all East classes had been for a century. Located on the East Side where virtually all the town's black families lived in a sequestered neighborhood near the railroad yard, it was known as the "black high school," even though the percentage of black students was around 15% that year.

Figure 1 Waterloo, Iowa

*The county seat of Black hawk County in northeast Iowa, Waterloo's estimated population in 2016 was 67,9234. It's just less than 62 square miles in area, slightly smaller than St. Louis Missouri, proper with a population of 315,685.*

The other three public high schools – West, Orange and Central – were on the West Side, comprised of all-white neighborhoods, and had been virtually all white since their openings. Columbus, the Catholic high school, was also on the West Side and virtually all-white.

The year after East's milestone centennial graduation, protests by East students demanding integration and an end to discrimination in both the town and the schools triggered seven years of confrontation, negotiation and compromise that ultimately resulted in the Waterloo Community District (WCSD) school board acknowledging the need for change and committing to a solution.

*The Bridge Between (TBB)* is the story about how the educational experiences and adult lives of Waterloo high school students from

1963-1973 – the 1966 graduates were sophomores in 1963 – were affected by the high schools they attended as 100 years of school segregation unraveled around them, told in their own words.

The 1966 graduates were the last to be untouched by the storm of integration.

Part 1 of *TBB* is Two Tales of a City and contains the first five chapters that provide the essential context for the story.

Part 2 – The Storm Named Integration covers three ERAs. The experiences of the students in each were different and perceptions changed from one *TBB* ERA to the next.

- ERA1 includes the classes of 1963 through the end of the 1966 school year in June.
- The first part of ERA2 begins with the class of 1967 and ends at graduation in June 1970. ERA2 Part 2 is the story of 1968, the most explosive and divisive in the history of the school system and Waterloo.
- ERA3 is 1971-1973 when Central High opened in the fall of 1972 and Orange High that closed that same semester.

Part 3 – The High School Afterparty: Adulthood – is two chapters. One is contributors' perceptions of the effects of high school on their adult lives 50 years later and the Afterword: The More Things Change.

The two questions most asked about *TBB* have been, "Where did the idea come from and why are you writing it?" The answer covers almost decades.

I grew up on the East Side of Waterloo and graduated from East in 1966 at 17. Mentally, emotionally, psychologically unprepared for college, I entered the Air Force delayed enlistment program earlier that spring.

Two weeks after graduation, I took my first airplane ride, from Des Moines, Iowa, to San Antonio, Texas, for basic training. I'd been in school with blacks since the second grade, and had seen bigotry and racism among both blacks and whites on both sides of the Cedar River. But I was unprepared for my first encounters with bigotry and racism in airmen from other parts of the U.S., not just the South. I soon realized it was learned cultural behavior and not something they practiced deliberately or maliciously.

My first duty assignment was Andrews Air Force Base, the president's wing, just outside of Washington, D.C., in Maryland. Our barracks chief and several of the unit's NCOs were black. I was again unprepared by the resentment of some of the white subordinates toward them. We spent a lot of time in D.C. when off duty because the drinking age was 18, 21 in Maryland. I wasn't prepared for the number of restaurants and clubs that were off-limits in certain downtown areas if there were blacks in our group.

In Vietnam in 1969, I lived, worked, hid under bunks and in bunkers from rocket attacks, and became friends with many blacks, some from the most racially torn inner cities in America. I was a grandfathered (accepted) white minority in a barracks which had become black during my last three months, and spent many late nights talking about black and white bigotry and prejudice with Jimi Hendrix and other black artists in the background. Listening to their life experiences gave me lifelong understanding, insight and empathy.

After the service, I attended Flagler College in St. Augustine, Florida. A history buff, I was fascinated by the story of the oldest permanent settlement in North America, but not prepared for discovering its Civil Rights protests just four years before.

In June 1964, Martin Luther King, Jr., was arrested in St. Augustine, and spent a night in jail for trespassing when he and other blacks attempted to eat in the Monson motel restaurant. It was the motel I stayed in the first week I was in the town. King was moved from the St. Augustine jail to one in Duval County/Jacksonville, Florida for his protection. The Monson and St. Augustine were the scenes of several violent confrontations during that time. He'd also been arrested in St. Johns County – the county seat – the year before.

In the mid-1970s, I was working in a small town in Alabama with a young black man colleague my age who went by the nickname "Steady

Eddie." (I've changed his name and some of the identifying details of our employer.) He was the night janitor, the only black at the company, which had some federal contracts that required minority participation. So, he was listed as a vice president of maintenance. I was unprepared for the dual life he lived.

Collectively, these encounters and others enriched racial relationship skills I first acquired at East High School. They also initiated an awareness of how those high school experiences were affecting my adult behavior. It started me wondering how East had influenced classmates and their lives. And how attending one of the white high schools was for those graduates in comparison.

That's the genesis of *The Bridge Between*.

I started making inquiries at the reunions I was able to attend and "the story" began to take form. It got under my skin. At our 40th reunion I made a commitment to do *The Bridge Between*. That's the "why" I'm writing it.

As you read, the focus of *TBB* is the lives of Waterloo high school graduates from 1963-1973, as told by many of them. It's not the story of everyone who attended the five Waterloo high schools during the 10 years. It would have been impossible to account for everyone – as it was even with my own class – much less talk with all of them.[2]

So, these stories aren't representative of Waterloo high school graduates in *TBB's* decade, only those out of the nearly 500 graduates contacted who chose to participate in the story. It isn't an analysis of and offers no interpretation of what was shared. That's up to you, the reader.

*TBB* isn't intended "to pull back the curtain" on the racial tensions, relations and racism that have existed in Waterloo for more than a century. Someone wrote and suggested that should be the book's theme. Those are artifacts of the town's history, aren't a secret and have been dealt with in other articles, papers and books.

It isn't an investigation into or an indictment of the schools, the school board, the city administration or the people.

It's not a story that affixes blame or responsibility, decides right from wrong or singles out the good guys from the bad.

It's a story about the high school as remembered by the people who spoke with me and how those years impacted the following half-century of their lives.

Contributors' perceptions are subjective, not answerable to challenge or dismissal, even if they're based on "alternative facts," in today's idiom. They can't be argued or fact-checked. Perception is, after all, a person's reality.

They were gathered from face-to-face or phone conversations, letters, emails, Facebook, texts or posts on *The Bridge Between* blog from roughly 2015 to May 2018 as I complete the book proof.

The information and data provided are as accurate as they can be, given the 50-year gap between the events and this story. Virtually all of the school system and city records were purged long ago. But archival data exist in the Waterloo Library, Grout Museum, the *Courier,* the library at UNI and the state archives in Des Moines.

The best resource for verification and background was *The Waterloo Daily Courier* archives accessed with a paid subscription to www.newspaperarchive.com. I worked as a stringer in the sports department my junior and senior years in high school, and my sister, Lucy, was the teen correspondent from East High School when she was a senior three years later. I didn't know that until I started writing this book.

Some information has been condensed. Sentences and paragraphs in quotations or italic are verbatim. [Parentheses] mean my paraphrasing.

Letters to the *Courier's* editorial-page forum, "The Public Speaks," adds the community perspective. When reading, keep two things in mind.

First, the editorial staff had its own criteria for selecting which letters are published, and had a policy that allowed it to shorten and edit them.

Its policy was "the correct name and address must be provided to the editor" [for verification of authorship and submission], but readers "may have their names withheld in publication of letters on request."[3] I used the paper; a name on a letter was included; addresses aren't. if the letter was signed (NAME WITHHELD), that's also included

Second, this is a condensed selection intended to offer a balanced sample of what people thought from 1963-1973. Some were shortened or edited when appropriate, but the intent and the tone of the original was retained.

The writing style, while generally correct grammatically, is written colloquially. With incomplete sentences. Sometimes.

Six words are used to describe blacks or African Americans; no hyphen as a noun, except in direct quotes, and hyphenated as an adjective. The other four are "Colored," "Negro" or "Mulatto," and "nigger." Their usage in the book isn't arbitrary. It's based on the context of the source or citation for secondary material. Or the speaker's language when it's a primary source. When "nigger" was used by someone telling a story, the word has been left in. It hasn't been sanitized nor is it used for shock effect. These usages are based on in-depth discussions with several black leaders in Waterloo, friends and other people whose opinions are valued, and secondary sources.[4] Capitalization of the six words is dependent on the source.[5]

The adjective "white-bread" is used to describe environments that are primarily white or Caucasian.

"East Side" precedes "West Side" throughout the book, which neither implies nor from should be inferred my bias from having grown up on the East Side. It's easier to write alphabetically rather than trying to be ludicrously pc by assuring "East" and "West" alternate at each reference.

[Brackets] indicate an author's note, something I've added for explanation, clarification or to expand on the information.

[Sic] means a word, phrase or punctuation that appears odd or erroneous is quoted exactly from the original source and isn't a proofreading error by author or editors.

Who said what isn't relevant. What is are the stories, perceptions and insights of contributors, who are identified only by a [parenthetical] four-part code at the end of each:

1. the high school attended or graduated from – Central [CHS], Columbus [COL], East [EHS], Orange [OHS] and West [WHS]. Columbus, the Catholic high school, was [CHS] long before OHS (Orange High School) and Central became part of the Waterloo Community School District (WCSD). For the sake of continuity, "HS" following either "C", "E", "O" or "W" automatically identifies it as a public school. "COL" is an immediately recognizable designation for Columbus.

2. the two-digit year last year attended or graduation year.

3. ethnicity/race – "AA" is African American, "W" is white.

4. Gender – "M" is male, "F" is female.

For example, the comment code for a white male who graduated from East in 1966 is [EHS 66 WM]. A 1966 East black female would be [EHS 66 AAF].

There may be back-to-back comments with the same ID code. Those are almost certainly comments from two different people; I used the code and not names when I edited and can't guarantee they are.

*The Bridge Between* spans the years from 1963-1973, but there are comments from people who graduated from one of the Waterloo high schools before and after those years. The scope was always "plus or minus" a "few" years when the contributions were relevant.

Finally, the "bridge" in the title has two meanings. One is the physical structure – especially the 4th Street bridge – that connects and separates the East and West communities on the two sides of the Cedar River. The other is the intangible social connection between the two sides, which was tenuous at best from before and through 1973.

*The Bridge Between*. It's a powerful story.

x

Dr. Nick De Bonis
Saint Simons Island, GA
May 2018

# Endnotes

[1] Blay, Z. (02/03/2017 11:59 am ET). 11 James Baldwin Quotes on Race That Resonate Now More Than Ever Black Voices: Huffington Post. Retrieved from http://tinyurl.com/mnoe9nc.

2 There were 160 contributors to The Bridge Between (Table 1). More than half (54.1%) were from East High; 30.5% were from the class of 1966, which was my class. Thirty percent (30%) were West High graduates. There are five unaccounted for in the table. One was from an East High class before World War II who felt compelled to contribute and his comments were not only relevant, but provided some additional framing for the story. Four are in a special "Other" category, including a couple who attended Waterloo schools and all but one or two years one of the high schools. There are also some teachers who graduated between 1963 and 1973 who taught in several of the high schools.

| Table 1 Profile of Contributors to The Bridge Between | | | | | | | | | | |
|---|---|---|---|---|---|---|---|---|---|---|
| | CHS | | COL | | EAST | | ORANGE | | WEST | |
| | B | W | B | W | B | W | B | W | B | W |
| FEMALE | 0 | 2 | 1 | 3 | 4 | 50 | 0 | 6 | 1 | 26 |
| MALE | 0 | 0 | 2 | 7 | 11 | 20 | 0 | 2 | 0 | 20 |
| TOTALS | 2 | | 13 | | 85 | | 8 | | 47 | |

[3] What Do You Think? (August 21, 1968). Waterloo Daily Courier, 4.

4 As an example: African American or black—what's the right term to use? Words Matter: Quartz. Retrieved from https://qz.com/815381/african-american-or-black-whats-the-right-term-to-use/.

5 "Professor Booker T. Washington, being politely interrogated ... as to whether negroes ought to be called 'negroes' or 'members of the colored race' has replied that it has long been his own practice to write and speak of members of his race as negroes, and when using the term 'negro' as a race designation to employ the capital 'N.'" (June 2, 1906). Harper's Weekly, Volume 50, L (2559), 763. Retrieved from http://tinyurl.com/ya7cdzcr.

# Contents

# Part 1 Two Tales of a City

## *TBB* 1: Haves and Have-Nots[1]

*Most residents of Waterloo perceive West Waterloo to be white and affluent. The view of East Waterloo is poor and black. That perception is more valid than non-valid. There is little sense of community. The black community and the economically depressed white community have a feeling of near disenfranchisement.[1]*

The families who settled Waterloo, Iowa, did so on both banks of the Cedar River. They designated the two sides as East and West, even though the river transects the town from northwest to southeast, creating more of a north-south split than east-west. (Figure 1)

Little could they know that "somewhere ages hence. . ." those two decisions where a river wound through a virgin wood "made all the difference."[2]

Blacks migrating to the town in the early 1900s and again after World War II found themselves restricted to living in a segregated neighborhood on the East Side near the railroad yard until into the 1970s.

Not an unusual storyline. Except for the facts that the town was in Iowa, admitted to the union as a non-slave state, and that all black students in the Waterloo Community School System (WCSD) school system in 1963 attended East side schools. And the public schools and Catholic high school on the West Side were virtually all white.

---

[1] The three-part code after each comment by a contributor indicates the high school which the person attended or from which they graduated – Central [CHS], Columbus [COL], East [EHS], Orange [OHS] and West [WHS]; the two-digit graduation year or last year attended the school; ethnicity/race – AA: African American/Black; W: white, and gender – F: female, M: male. For example, a 1996 white male East High grad's comment would be designated [EHS 66 WM].

School segregation was an artifact of the neighborhood schools that was a by-product of the racial segregation in the town enabled by the Cedar River.

East High was the only public high school on the racially mixed East Side. It was known in Waterloo and throughout the state as a "black" high school, because it was the only high school blacks attended. However, East's black student ratio averaged 20% or less from 1963-1973.

West High and Columbus – the Catholic high school – were on the West Side. When the Waterloo and Orange Independent school systems merged in 1964, all-white Orange High became the second West Side high school. In 1972, a third public high school – Central High – was opened, also on the West Side.

Over the years segregation had become a social norm accepted by both blacks and whites in Waterloo. But in the early 1960s, like the nation, the Civil Rights became a priority for the blacks in town. The struggle to find its way as a community

Figure 1 1892 Waterloo Sanitation Planning Map, 1892

*The "East" and "West" side designations are an historical oddity with no verifiable explanation. In fact, there are some odd references to locations "north" and "south" of the river in early anecdotal histories.*

and as a school system from segregation and racism to integration and social inclusive was explosive, confrontational, divisive.

And it affected those of us who graduated from high school in Waterloo from 1963-1973, then and throughout our adult lives.

*The Bridge Between.* One town. Two sides of a river. Two communities. A segregated school system.

A story of the high school experiences, perceptions and insights into race and racial relationships that were affected by the high schools we attended, and the impact on our adult lives shared 50 years later.

## Same River, Opposite Banks

*"If the Cedar River ever runs dry, everyone will know where the town's bodies are buried." Local folklore*

The Cedar River is one of the first Waterloo characteristics of which native-born residents and transplants become aware. The river hasn't been a physical barrier. But it's been a significant, intangible political, social and cultural, socioeconomic and racial divide between East Side and West Side that still reverberates in the town 167 years after it was founded.[3]

The first settlers in Waterloo – originally named "Prairie Rapids" – settled on the East bank of the Cedar River in 1845. It was renamed "Waterloo" in 1851. (Figure 2)

From the outset, Waterloo was a "double city,"[4] a "two-headed town."[5]

The first platting of the Waterloo town site was in the fall of 1853 by the West Side settlers. In February 1854, East Side property owners platted their

| 1845 | Prairie Rapids settled. |
| 1846 | Iowa becomes the 29th state. |
| 1851 | Renamed Waterloo. |
| 1853 | First school opens on the West Side. |
| 1854 | Waterloo is platted. First school opens on the East Side. |
| 1855 | Waterloo replaces Ceda Falls as the Black Hawk County seat. |
| 1858 | East & West residents vote for independent school districts. |
| 1868 | The City of Waterloo incorporated. |
| 1942 | Independent East & West school districts consolidate. |

Figure 2 Waterloo Timeline

section of the town site and organized the Waterloo Township. Parties from both sides of the river joined in June 1854 to file and record with the state a united plat including the land on both sides of the Cedar. (Figure 3)[6]

There was no "East" or "West" designation on the plat. But over the years, this Town of Waterloo plat became known as the "Original Plat of Waterloo East."

In August 1858, Waterloo residents voted on a petition to separate the eastern part of Waterloo township from the west. Eastsiders had petitioned the court for the separation, although they didn't think it would pass.

The day of the election, rain swelled the Cedar River to the point that none of the West Side men voted.[2] Sixty votes were cast, all in favor of the division, and the Township of East Waterloo was formed.

The City of Waterloo was incorporated on June 23, 1868.

Ferries forded the Cedar River near 4th or 10th streets to provide transportation between the East and West Sides. But bridging the Cedar River was essential for the East and West business communities to cooperate to attract new businesses for mutual benefit.

A week after the town was platted in 1854, a crude and rudimentary bridge made of fresh-hewn logs and brush was built, impractical for a permanent structure.

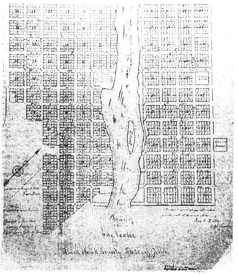

Figure 3 Plat Map of Waterloo
*Waterloo was platted with numbered streets running perpendicularly across the river and named "East" or "West." The grid was like the one used in agrarian Iowa in which county roads ran north-south and east-west every mile. Note the compass arrow on the left which indicates the map isn't laid out north and south.*

[2] Women didn't have the right to vote until 1920.

Severe flooding along the Cedar in 1858 may have been the motivation for the construction of a wooden bridge at 4th Street in 1859. That bridge "succumbed to the river" several times in 1864 and 1865, and was replaced in 1872 by a tubular arch iron bridge. In 1902, a steel and cement arch bridge replaced it.[7]

By the time baby-boomers were born between the end of World War II and the 1950s, there were seven bridges across the Cedar River. An eighth was erected in 1967, the second year of *The Bridge Between* timeline. The final one was built 10 years after the classes of 1973 graduated.

While the bridges provided the ability for the East and West Waterloo sides to interact easily, they couldn't overcome the deep, divisive socioeconomic and racial divisions between the two.

A report on school desegregation in Waterloo by the Iowa Department of Public Instruction in 1973 labeled the river a community divider.

*In fact, in the minds of most people there are two Waterloo's (sic) – one East, one West. The river, instead of being viewed as an asset for recreational and commercial benefits, is viewed as an asset for separation by most west Waterlooians. . . . . almost as if there were no bridges. . . [and] is a mental and emotional barrier, too.*[8]

## A Two-Headed Town

*". . . the Indians [probably] argued about which side of the river was better before the white settlers ever arrived. . . ."*[9]

From its earliest days, there was East Side-West Side competition for government control and buildings, including the library and schools. Businesses, especially the first lumber mills and the railroads later, also participated in crosstown competitiveness.

When Black Hawk County was large enough to set up its own administration in 1853, Cedar Falls was larger than Waterloo and became the county seat. Two years later, Waterloo boosters convinced the Iowa legislature that Cedar Falls wasn't as centrally located as

Waterloo, which was growing more quickly. The legislature permitted a vote in April 1855 and Waterloo was selected as the county seat by a 388-260 vote.

The new county seat needed a courthouse, which pitted Eastsiders against Westsiders over its location. A vote was set up for December 1855 with an odd ballot choice – voters could select either the East Side as the court house site or the side that would pay the most money for the location and erection of county buildings. West Side business interests had been the ones who'd petitioned the legislature for the county seat election and won. In retaliation against and to reduce the West Side influence, Cedar Falls voters formed an almost unanimous voting coalition with East Side, which won the courthouse 467-264 votes.[10]

*The rivalry between east and west side residents manifested itself in parallel development on either side of the river. Both sides felt they must have their own hotels, theatres, industrial districts, prestigious housing developments, and libraries. Announcement of plans to build something on one side of the river frequently prompted a similar declaration on the other.[11]*

When Andrew Carnegie offered Waterloo a $30,000 grant for a library in 1902, the East and West Side factions disagreed on its location for two years. Carnegie heard of the cross-river feud and reportedly suggested the library be built in the middle of the river to resolve the dispute. The mayor proposed building it on the 4th Street bridge, which hadn't been completed. Carnegie increased his donation to allow the Waterloo Public Library entity to build two buildings for $20,000 each. Waterloo was the only city to receive Carnegie funds for two full libraries. Probably not coincidentally, both were dedicated on the same day in February 1906. No record was found that indicates which was first that day.

*The Carnegie libraries were a major resource for students. The East Side library was relatively close to East High and downtown. The West*

*Side library was accessible from West Junior and West High. But they were combined and went into the old post office on the West Side [in 1979]. Now it's not convenient to anyone. [WHS 66 WF]*

*We had a library on each side of the river. In a way, it took away one of the places where you would have intermingled with people from the other side of the river. [WHS 70 WM]*

The competitive East-West rivalry at the core of Waterloo's make-up was evaluated by one source as "healthy."

*While such quarrels may have wasted energy best expended elsewhere, the competition was healthy in other respects. When one side attracted a new business or platted a new housing addition, the other side frequently followed suit with alacrity. The result is that Waterloo enjoyed startling growth around the turn of the twentieth century. The city's population grew from 6,674 in 1890 to 36,230 in 1920. Between 1881 and 1914, the number of factories increased from 28 to 144.[12]*

The competition resulted in a de facto "separate but equal" community code that extended beyond the Carnegie libraries. A railroad for the East Side, a railroad for the West Side. An East Side hospital was balanced with one on the West Side. A community park on one side of town with a swimming pool and tennis courts required a community park on the other. A planned upscale subdivision in Highland on the East Side was matched the Prospect development on the West. A dime store or a movie theater on one side of downtown had its counterpart on the other side of the river.

This unwritten but enduring "separate but equal" code delayed early attempts at desegregation of the Waterloo schools in the mid-1960s, and continued to be an influence as solutions were proposed and implemented in the early 1970s.

*Their business [structures] became identical and the union followed. In as much as goes to make up their business and educational and religious life, [the East and West Sides] are still two identities. They have two separate business organizations, West Waterloo having a Chamber of Commerce, East Waterloo a board of Trade and Commercial Club. Each has a school organization of its own and in many ways of development they are separate. As a result, a spirit of friendly rivalry exists, each side striving to secure the lead of the other in growth, yet determined that, where necessary, joint effort shall secure what divided interest cannot in improvement, location of new enterprises or public benefit.[13]*

## A Blue-Collar Company Town

*Iowans familiar with Waterloo referred to it as a rough blue-collar town. When I was growing up, I assumed that my life was normal. I could walk anywhere I wanted to. I walked to school. I didn't view it as a blue-collar town. I'd never been exposed to professional people. So, when people would call Waterloo "that blue-collar town," I'd just smile and say, "Yah, but it was a great place to grow up." [WHS 67 WM]*

*Waterloo is kind of an anomaly. It's always been a one- or two-industry town. When I got hired by John Deere, it was like being drafted by the Yankees. Insurance. An unbelievable pension. For just working there. [WHS 69 WM]*

Waterloo was a company town during the first two-thirds of the 20th century. The three major employers were the Illinois Central Railroad (IC), the Rath Packing Company and John Deere. Only Deere was on the West Side, upriver from Rath.

The Rath Packing Company opened in November 1891 on the east bank of the Cedar River near what would become 11th Street.

*By [its 50th] anniversary in 1941, [Rath] had grown into the nation's single largest meatpacking facility with branch facilities in 12 states. By the end of World War II, Rath was the fifth largest meatpacker in the U.S. Through two world wars, stock market panics, depression, and drought, the company had failed to show a profit in only four of its years.[14]*

The company would play a major role in black activism and employment gains by blacks in Waterloo when it was struck as part of a nationwide United Packinghouse Workers of America (UPWA) union strike in 1948. Blacks gained access to better job opportunities and leadership in the local union.

By the 1960s and 1970s, meat packing had become a highly competitive, high-volume, low-margin industry that was also was hurt by a decline in per capita pork consumption beginning in 1960. After years of changes in the company's board, employees gained control of the company in 1981, but Rath was finally closed in 1985.

In 1918, John Deere – a global leader in the both the harvesting and tractor business – purchased the Waterloo Gasoline Engine Company. That added the newly designed, all-wheel drive tractor to its product line, which included planters, buggies, wagons, grain drills, and hay and harvesting equipment.

The labor forces at Rath Packing and Deere were unionized in separate efforts in 1942. Waterloo was a strong "union town" through the mid-1970s.

By the early 80s, Deere employed roughly 16,000 people. Economic conditions in the mid-80s and computer technology and robotics reduced that by half.

Parents of many of the high school graduates from 1963-1973 worked for Deere or one of the other companies. Parents and counselors encouraged high school students to pursue educational paths that would result in a job at one of these or other companies, guaranteeing a future with security and a pension.

*Waterloo always protected Deere and Rath. The town made sure they had an available worker supply. And kept out other industries. Most of the other companies in town were subsidiary to John Deere. So, when John Deere went from 17,000 down to 4,000 employees at one point in the 80s, there was no Plan B for Waterloo. [EHS 66 WM]*

*You knew as soon as you could get your diploma, there was a job waiting for you at either John Deere if you were fortunate or at Rath packing if you were not so fortunate. But there were jobs. A lot of students took the job route. You could kind of know where you were going. We were not mentored into seeing something better. And there may not have been anything better. Which was true for both the poorer white students on the east side and the blacks. [EHS 66 WF]*

*My dad worked at Deere until he retired. I swore in high school that I'm not spending my life working for John Deere. [WHS 69 WM]*

*John Deere had been known as a family factory, especially in the operations. In 1982 when the right-sizing started during the fuel crisis, it was being run by the last of the Deere family. Corporate sent a hatchet man. In the next year, 16,000 people got cut to 6,000 people. [EHS 66 AAM]*

The loss of employment at Rath and Deere in the last quarter of the 20th century, and other local manufacturing companies, had a long, lingering impact on the economic health of Waterloo. Hardest hit were the minority groups, as they were in many communities.

## Wrong Side of the River

The enduring local perception that the West Side was more affluent, white collar and professional in *The Bridge Between* decade was based largely on neighborhoods. Company supervisors, managers, executives and professionals lived on the West Side. The blue-collar construction, retail and service industries' workers lived on the East Side.

*I know the West Side of town has its rich section. But there was one on the East Side, too – Highland. With beautiful homes. That was a gorgeous area. [COL 63 WF]*

*There were some houses on the West Side that were nothing outstanding, but we Eastsiders thought they were like castles. The first time I went up Prospect Boulevard when I was 14 or so, I thought, "Holy God, this is like Hollywood." [COL 66 WM]*

*Highland was one of the most affluent neighborhoods in Waterloo at that time. Right in the middle of the black neighborhood, encircled by the black community, on the East Side. It was very, very segregated. [EHS 69 AAM]*

In the early 1900s, Waterloo joined the trend of "specially designed suburbs in America" as its middle-class prosperity grew. The traditional East-West rivalry fostered two prestigious residential developments – Highland on the East Side and Prospect Hills on the West. They were "promoted as automobile suburbs, another indication of the exclusivity each sought to project to prospective home builders."[15]

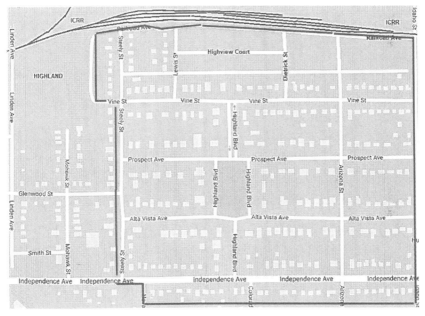

Figure 4 The Highland Community
*Highland became "the first exclusive and specially designed subdivision in the city," the residence enclave for the city's industrial and professional elite.*

The planning for Highland began in 1901 (Figure 4), although filing the plats and building out the houses didn't occur until around 1908.

The Highland development "was conceived of as a separate place, one designed to have a distinct identity. . . . boulevards not mere streets, a central square, and a formal entrance. The Highland Improvement Company installed improvements in advance of settlement totaling over $200,000 by 1909, and this too was a new concept."[16]

By 1945, all but 15 houses were built. Renowned Waterloo architect Mortimer B. Cleveland designed many of the houses and lived in Highland.

The Prospect Hills development was surveyed in 1909 (Figure 5), nearly a decade after the planning began for Highland. Its developers "employed . . . a nationally known Chicago landscape architectural firm . . . to design the curving lanes and boulevards. . . [the] decision to use a professional planner placed Prospect Hills in the midst of the growing national interest in urban planning -and efficient use of space."[17]

As was typical in Waterloo, competition between the two developments "was intense."

*Both were consciously designed as complete districts. Highland developers employed a Chicago landscaper . . . to design plantings for the central square and boulevard. Prospect developers offered P.P. Scheibe, no less than "landscape designer for Kaiser Wilhelm," to provide landscaping plans for lot buyers – at no extra cost. Both sets of developers planted hundreds of trees, built special entrances to set off the districts, and sought and gained streetcar lines. Also, in common with the Highland experience, Prospect Hills promoters built their own homes there in the quest to create an exclusive "country club district" by the Byrnes Park golf course.[18]*

Given the deep-rooted history of East and West Side competition and understanding the developers of Highland and Prospect Hills were targeting the same professionals, successful business people and the town's upper class, it's easy to speculate the Prospect Hills and Prospect Boulevard name was a dig at the Highland investment group. The second Highland plat, filed roughly two years before Prospect

Hills' plat, included a Prospect Avenue – one of the two main east-west streets bracketing the park in the middle of the development.

It's possible the Prospect Hills raised the ante with "Prospect Boulevard."

It's just as probable, however, the Highland developers got wind of the Prospect Hills development, moving in the same social circles with its developers and potential buyers, and "borrowed" the Prospect name for its neighborhood as a preemptive claim to whatever badge value "Prospect" might have had in those days.

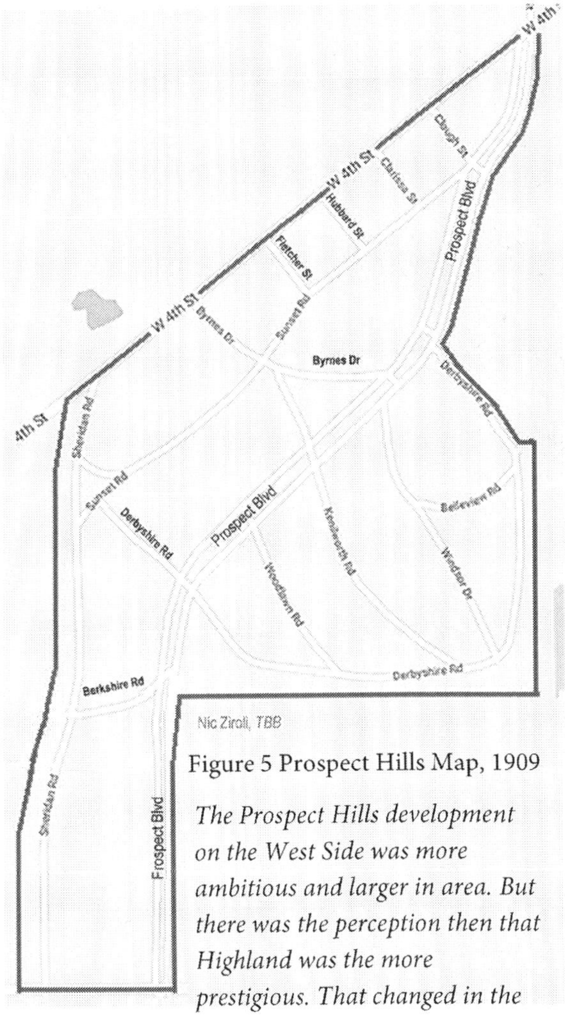

Highland may have been first of the new planned developments in Waterloo, but the Cedar clearly separated the major manufacturing operations on the East Side from the professionals and service industries on the West Side.

As Waterloo grew, "the West Side acquired the cachet of greater affluence, while the East Side attracted

Nic Ziroli, TBB

Figure 5 Prospect Hills Map, 1909

*The Prospect Hills development on the West Side was more ambitious and larger in area. But there was the perception then that Highland was the more prestigious. That changed in the 1970s and 80s when blacks began buying houses in Highland.*

more industrial development and working-class houses."[19]

*The West Side was always thought of in terms of class structure, the people who had money. Lots of big homes, like on Prospect Boulevard, a ritzy area. The separation might have been a balance between race, and economics and social class. The West Side stores catered more to the high-end customer. Once you crossed the bridge, I don't think they catered to one race or the other. But the deeper you went [north] on East 4th Street, the fewer commercial buildings they had compared to West 4th Street. The East Side had fewer dollars than the West. [EHS 68 WM]*

Community social status for families and high school students was also largely a perception based on which side of the river you lived and where.

*People looked down at Eastsiders. You were either black or poor. From the bad side of town, the other side of the tracks. The people on the West Side were more proud of themselves for who they were and where they lived. People on the East Side were a lot more down-to-earth and friendlier. [EHS 67 WF]*

*One was either a professional and lived on the West Side or very poor in horrible jobs like at Rath Packing. There was no middle ground. There was a large group of white John Deere line employees who were able to move into the middle class, though they had limited education. John Deere was considered the best place for someone without much education to become employed and work there all their life. The union was very strong. [WHS 70 WF]*

Not everyone in Waterloo bought into the "East Side poor, West Side rich" mantra.

*I knew both sides of town. The East Side was working class people, not the business owners and the upper class. The only place on the East Side with big homes was Highland, where people thought they were rich, but probably weren't. West Side people were business owners and the upper class, with different areas, like the Prospect Boulevard area and Rainbow Drive. To me, Rainbow Drive was more like the East Side than the East Side. [laughs] You didn't get snubbed until you got to the Prospect area. That was the West Side I stayed out of. [WHS 67 WM]*

*We shopped on the East Side, I went to recreational programs on the East Side, my dad had his office at East High, and we would go there Saturday mornings and roller skate in the car park. There wasn't anything bad about the East Side. It's just where the black people were and I didn't have any contact with them. [WHS 69 WF]*

*West Side was an eclectic mix. I went to school and was friends with kids from wealthy families. I graduated with a girl who had a new Thunderbird and a gasoline credit card. But there were many kids with working-class folks at Deere or Rath's with blue-collar jobs. There was a divide between rich and blue collar on the West Side, but it wasn't as deep a split as the black and white gap. [WHS 69 WM]*

*When I was in high school, Waterloo's segregation was just as much socioeconomic as it was racial. It wasn't the blacks vs. the whites so much as it was the East Side vs. the West side. My dad's feeling was that the racial problems were caused by poverty and the layoffs at Rath. There were a lot of blacks who came into Waterloo to work in the factories. And then there was no work. They found themselves jobless without any other opportunities. We had a segregated poor and black population. It was those people out of work and so down and out and angry about the lack of opportunities in 1968 that stirred up things within the schools. [CEN 73 WF]*

## Eastsider, Westsider

*I have often described myself as "growing up poor on the East Side of Waterloo" and that we had a river in Waterloo instead of tracks. So, I grew up on the wrong side of the river. [EHS 67 WM]*

*There was always a perception that East Side people were a little rougher, not quite as elite socially. [EHS 66 WM]*

*Not to pop anybody's balloon, but I never considered the incidents that occurred in Waterloo [from 1966-1968] as racial. It was primarily East Side-West Side, the haves and have-nots. [EHS 66 AAM]*

Self-identification with the side of the river on which we were raised and went to school influenced both our attitudes and behavior. Some of those still exist today among people who stayed and lived their adult lives in Waterloo.

**'63-'66** *I say this with pride. When somebody asks me where I'm from, I don't say, "Waterloo, Iowa." I say, "East Waterloo, Iowa." People say," There's no such place as East Waterloo." I tell them, if they were from there, they'd know. We had a total disdain for West High. [EHS 61 AAM]*

*Even the society page in the newspaper was biased. It was always geared toward the professional and the wealthy in the community. [EHS 63 WF]*

*I was at Sacred Heart (Catholic 1-8) for 3rd grade, and Friday was communion and the day we always got chocolate milk. That was such a treat in our lives. Sometimes I didn't get any because we didn't have a lot of money. Looking back, I remember how hard that was because I wanted to have chocolate milk like the other kids. My story wasn't unique. There were a lot of kids like that. But you feel so alone on Friday. [COL 63 WF]*

*Growing up, I was proud to be from the East Side. A lot of us felt that we lived on the wrong side of the tracks and the Big Bucks lived on the West. Some of the West High kids had their noses pretty high in the air. They thought they were better because they were from the Big Bucks school or the Big Bucks family. We had the black doctor, Dr. Nash, and black dentist, Dr. Harvey, on the East Side. A lot of the working people lived on the East Side. The owners of the businesses, and the doctors and lawyers lived on the West Side. There were some lawyers in Highland from the Big Bucks family. Old man Black [who founded Black's*

*Department Store] and old man Rath [of the Rath Packing Company]
lived in Highland. There were some Big Bucks on the East Side, but a lot
of them moved to the Prospect area on the West Side. I dated a girl from
West for a while and she could be snobbish, but most of the time, she
was pretty nice. I changed my mind after I graduated, that not all
Westsiders were snobs. [EHS 64 WM]*

*The other [West] side of the river was too rich. I was a poor kid. We
got welfare. I was staying overnight at my friend's place and we were
scouting for food downtown near the fruit market, digging in garbage. I
slipped on a banana, knocked myself out and broke my arm at 10 p.m.
one night. Mom came and got me, took me to the hospital. I was
apologizing all the way there for not having clean underwear on. [EHS
64 WM]*

*I had twin cousins at West High who were a year ahead of me and
they'd take me along to some of their parties. I got the treatment from
their friends for being the "poor cousin from the other side of the tracks."
And, since I went to East High, I was an "easy woman." It worked out
fine once they got to know me. My cousins didn't have any more money
than we did, but I was the poor white girl from the East Side. [EHS 66
WF]*

*The West Side attitude was they were better than us on the East Side.
You'd see it especially in the winter, bad weather. We would have to take
a bus downtown and change buses in front of Woolworth's [on
Commercial Street on the West Side] to get to school. There was about a
30-minute wait. And we'd be standing there, huddled, trying to keep
warm. [laughs] And people walking by would just stare at us blacks
standing there on the West Side. [EHS 66 AAM]*

*It was somehow in our West Side brains that the West Side was better
– more wealth, smarter people, and that everything about being a
Westsider was better. It is embarrassing to admit this, but we thought it
was true. It is especially disturbing because half of our classmates were*

18

*from the East Side. I spent no time on "other side" of town while in high school. [COL 66 WF]*

*I lived on the East side until I was a sophomore at Columbus High in 1962. My parents bought a house on the West Side and I rarely went back to the East side after that. I attended Catholic School all my life, which meant East and West weren't so much divided in my mind because kids from all the parishes were combined at Columbus. [COL 66 WF]*

**'67-'70** *I was in elementary school at Longfellow before lunch programs. You brought your lunch or went home. I never expected to eat unless I stole something. A cupcake or candy from Nelson's Store. I went home for lunch, but I was just biding my time because there was no food there. One day I found a half-eaten piece of liver on the floor. I wiped it off and I ate that and thought I had me the best meal on God's earth. I was so glad and happy I found something to eat that day. And I didn't get sick. [EHS 69 AAM]*

*The family of a girlfriend who lived on the corner a half a block from us moved to the West Side. My mom said, "Well, she's too persnickety to live on the East Side." So, that was the difference I knew. The people on the West Side were wealthy. The East Side wasn't as rich. Prospect Boulevard was the wealthy area on the West Side. But my brother-in-law and West Side friends lived in what were more middle-class or upper middle-class areas. I don't recall any lower-class neighborhoods on the West Side. Highland was the affluent area on the East Side. [EHS 69 WF]*

*My parents were in junior high and high school when their families moved from East to West Waterloo to improve their lives, I assume as part of the white flight. As West Side residents, we thought we were better, black or white. On KWWL evening news, describing events as "in the North End" was code for blacks involved. [WHS 70 WM]*

*My husband wasn't from Waterloo. When we first looked at homes, he found one he wanted me to look at. I told him, "It's a great house, but we could never buy it." And he said, "Why?" "Because our kids would have to go to West High." And he was like, "So?" He didn't understand. [EHS 70 AAF]*

*I went to Lowell Elementary in the 2nd grade, then started at Kingsley in 3rd [both on the West Side] when my parents moved. They were trying to be upwardly mobile. They were both very social, ran with a crowd that generally had more money than they did. There was a socioeconomic change, mild culture shock for me at Kingsley. You had more modest incomes at Lowell. We were comfortable there. I don't think they dressed nicer at Kingsley. But those kids were more socially adept. These were the doctors' and lawyers' kids. I'm shy and an introvert. There was some intimidation factor. I don't know how conscious at the time I was recognizing the difference. But I've always wondered if I would had maintained my comfort level if I'd gone all the way through Lowell. [WHS 70 WM]*

**'71-'73** *We had kids from the West Side who attended our church on the East Side. They were always dressed nicer than we were. It seemed like they came in with new clothes from every store in town. I don't know whether that was true or it was just that I was one of six kids and wore hand-me-downs. One friend's family moved to the West Side and we said, "You traitor, you went over to the other side." [EHS 73 WF]*

*We usually had apples in the car for snacks. My dad made us wait until we'd crossed the bridge to the West Side to throw the apple cores out the window. We were Eastsiders. The whole time we lived on the East Side my dad refused to buy a power mower. He used to push a mower because "I'm an Eastsider." [CEN 73 WF]*

*In Waterloo, you were very aware of who is who. I was very aware of this when I was in elementary school at Kingsley. It had very, very affluent families with very smart kids who are just naturally smart. I was very aware of that. And which kids were characters. I might have learned that from my parents. They were very aware about who was who. My dad picked out a house to move into when I was three years old he liked but my mom didn't, because he wanted to live where the affluent people were. [WHS 74 WF]*

*My father was a surgeon. We lived in a nice house on the far West Side of town, if there was anything intrinsically better about that side of town. And I had every material thing and advantage an upper middle-class kid could want. [WHS 74 WM]*

# Reflections from the Bridge

Charles Mulford Robinson, one of the country's first urban planners, created a career as a "city improver" in the early 1900s.[20] He produced planning recommendations or "wellbeing" [sic] reports for at least 18 cities, including Des Moines, Cedar Rapids and Waterloo in 1910.[21]

One observation in his report was prophetic for the town through the 1960s and 1970s, and today.

*There seems to be only one danger that seriously threatens the advance of Waterloo in municipal aesthetics and effectiveness. That is the lack of complete union between the East Side and the West, [the lack] of the whole souled cooperation which forges itself in the greatness of a common task.[22]*

Black railroad strikebreakers in 1911 were quarantined in a section of the East Side and remained segregated there into the 1970s. This fostered socioeconomic disparity in the town and was a catalyst for later civil unrest in Waterloo like the strike at the Rath Packing plant in the 1940s, and in the late 1960s. Housing covenants and redlining in the 1950s and 60s added to the permanent, scarring dimension of racial separation between the East and West sides.

The passive acceptance of the social, cultural, socioeconomic and racial separation on both the sides of the Cedar River by blacks and whites, the haves and the have-nots perpetuated it.

Few people challenged the century-long status quo of one black high school, even after the 1940s.

Those graduating from high school in Waterloo from 1963-1973 were descendants of 100 years of a "lack of complete union . . . [and] whole souled cooperation."[23]

The racial tension and racial issues that high school students experienced in Waterloo 1963-1973 were fated before and during that decade. Many remain today.

# Endnotes

[1] Technical Assistance Report on School Desegregation in the Waterloo District. (June 11, 1973). Des Moines, IA: Iowa Department of Public Instruction, 6.

[2] Paraphrased from *The Road Not Taken*. (1916). Robert Frost.

[3] For a definitive early resource of Waterloo's history, refer to History of Black Hawk County, Iowa, and Its People, Volume 1. (1915). Hartman, J.C., ed. Chicago, IL: S.J. Clarke Publishing Company. Available as a free Google eBook at http://tinyurl.com/yd54nz5j.

[4] History of Waterloo. (February 11, 1910). Black Hawk County Atlas, Des Moines, IA: The Iowa Publishing Company, 126.

[5] Roosevelt Elementary School, U.S. Department of the Interior, National Park Service: National Register of Historic Places Registration Form, section 8, 10. Retrieved from http://tinyurl.com/ybe8ql4r.

[6] (1) History of Waterloo, 126-127. (2) History of Black Hawk County, 380. (3) History of Black Hawk County, Iowa, and Representative Citizens. (1904). Van Metre, I., ed. Chicago, IL: Biographical Publishing Co., 178.

[7] The Waterloo, Iowa, Flood Control Project: An Assessment & Inventory of Archaeological, Historical and Architectural Resources. (March 1975). Iowa City, IA: Environmental Research Center. In fulfillment of the U.S. Army Corps of Engineers Rock Island District, Purchase Order Number DA CW25-75-M-0479, 37.

[8] Technical Assistance Report on School Desegregation in the Waterloo District. (June 11, 1973). Des Moines, IA: Iowa Department of Public Instruction, 6.

[9] Brief History of Black Hawk County, 2. Retrieved from http://www.co.black-hawk.ia.us/DocumentCenter/View/564.

[10] Veeder, G., County Auditor. (February 2011). Black Hawk County Courthouse History. Retrieved from http://www.co.black-hawk.ia.us/DocumentCenter/View/565.

[11] Historical and Architectoral [sic] Resources of Waterloo. Iowa. National Register of Historic Places Multiple Property Documentation Form. (July 25, 1988).

Washington, D.C.: United States Department of the Interior, National Park Service, E-4,5.

[12] Brief History of Black Hawk County, 2.

[13] Ibid.

[14] Rath Packing Company Records, 1890-1985. Iowa State University: Special Collections Department. Retrieved from http://findingaids.lib.iastate.edu/spcl/manuscripts/MS562.pdf.

[15] Historical and Architectoral [sic] Resources of Waterloo. Iowa, E-7.

[16] Ibid., E-7, 8.

[17] Ibid., E-8.

[18] Ibid.

[19] Roosevelt Elementary School.

[20] Charles Mulford Robinson: A Tribute. Talen, E. Retrieved from http://www.urban.illinois.edu/images/site-content/DURP100essay-1Talen.pdf.

[21] Robinson's two seminal books on city planning in 1901 and 1903 became bibles for the city planning movement which relied on a "commission of professionals" – an architect, a landscape architect, a sculptor, an engineer and "member who [represent] engineering [and] sculpture . . . together and comprehensively. . . ." Improvement in City Life: Aesthetic Progress. (June 1899), *Atlantic Monthly* (83): pp. 771-185. Cited in Urban Planning, 1794-1918: An International Anthology of Articles, Conference Papers, and Reports. (2002). Reps, J.W. Cornell University. Retrieved from http://urbanplanning.library.cornell.edu/DOCS/homepage.htm.

[22] The Wellbeing of Waterloo: a report to the Civic Society of Waterloo, Iowa. (May 21, 1910). Robinson, C.M. *Waterloo Evening, Courier*, 10-12.

[23] Ibid.

# TBB 2: There are Blacks in Iowa?

*"You're from Iowa? Are there any black folks out there?"* – *Rev. Dr. Martin Luther King, Jr., in the late 1950s after meeting Waterloo civil rights activist Anna Mae Weems[1]*

*The Cedar River is as wide as the Pacific. [COL 69 AAF]*

*The Cedar River was as wide as the African diaspora.[2] Especially during the time we were growing up. It was the absolute demarcation. [EHS 69 AAM]*

By the time Waterloo high school graduates of 1963-1973 were in high school, racism and discrimination were embedded in the town's culture. Not because of Jim Crow laws as it was in the South, but as cultural outcomes of the physical division between East Side and West, and history.

Segregation of black workers hired to break a strike at the Illinois Central (IC) railroad in 1911 evolved over the following five decades from de facto to de jure segregation that was mandated, implemented and sustained by the social system in Waterloo.

## Black Heritage in Iowa[3]

*Between 1836 and 1860, most African Americans arrived in Iowa by way of the great rivers: the Mississippi and Missouri. They settled in river communities like Keokuk, Burlington, Clinton and Dubuque, finding work on the docks, riverboats and barges, and as janitors, cooks and waiters. African-American women worked in home-related domestic jobs, such as housekeeping, cooking, and service as chambermaids.[4]*

Waterloo isn't an anomaly in Iowa when it comes to prejudice or racism. But it is unique compared to the other Iowa cities with significant black populations in that it's divided by a river with blacks segregated on one side through the 1970s. It's also the town that had the most significant racial tension and unrest, riots, resistance to school integration and social change than any other in the state during the Civil Rights movement.

Most people unfamiliar with Iowa don't think of it as having black residents, much less overt segregation and the race riots that occurred in the mid- to late-1960s.

Race was an issue in Iowa, however, from its settling as the Iowa Territory in 1838. Part of the Louisiana Purchase of 1803, Congress prohibited slavery in the purchase with the Missouri Compromise of 1820. (Figure

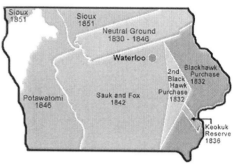

Figure 1 The Iowa Territory
*The Iowa Territory was created out of 6.2 million acres (roughly the size of Vermont) of Indian land confiscated by the U.S. government in 1832 from the Sauk (Sac) and Meskwaki tribes. The only federally recognized Indian tribe in Iowa is the Sac & Fox Tribe of the Mississippi. Its tribal name is Meskwaki ("Red Earth People").*

1) Settlers began arriving in 1833 from Illinois, Ohio, Pennsylvania, Canada, England, Ireland and Germany.

Some of the families who settled the Iowa territory brought slaves with them. Many were "persons from the South. Not all had been slave owners, but they had lived in a community where slavery was considered only the natural order of things. "Thus, it came about that not only were there people in Iowa who openly favored slavery, but there were others who by their passiveness encouraged this sentiment. . . ."5

This sentiment was codified by the first territorial legislature in January 1839 in "An Act to Regulate Blacks and Mulattoes."

It required or allowed by law:

- negroes and mulattoes to obtain from a court a certificate stating they were free.
- posting of a $500 bond as guarantee of their good behavior.

- a fine of $5-$100 to be charged to anyone who hired or harbored a negro or mulatto who had failed to obtain a certificate or post the required bond.
- slaveholders to pass through Iowa with their slaves
- the arrest and return of fugitive slaves.[6]

A law was also passed that said, "A negro, mulatto, or Indian, shall not be a witness in any court or in any case against a white person. [7]

Iowa became the 29th state and the first free state west of the Mississippi River on December 28, 1846.

Voters rejected its first two proposed constitutions in 1844 and 1846. The third, ratified in 1857 as the original state constitution, banned slavery and allowed Negroes to settle in Iowa, but denied them right to vote, serve in the militia or hold legislative office.[8]

In 1854, Congress repealed the Missouri Compromise of 1820 prohibiting slavery west of the Mississippi, permitting people in the Kansas and Nebraska territories to decide for themselves whether to allow slavery within their borders.[9]

*This made western Iowa an important staging area for free-state forces and an area of operations for those engaged in aiding fugitives escape enslavement. . . . Many [Iowa residents] avoided involvement in the slavery issue and wanted to keep black settlement out of the state, while others saw the state standing forth as a beacon of anti-slavery hope.[10]*

On February 4, 1859, abolitionist John Brown and 10 of his men, including three Iowans, crossed into Fremont County in the southwest corner of Iowa with a group of escaped slaves – 12 men, women, and children. (Figure 2)[11] He had been in Iowa many times before.

It's estimated the Underground Railroad in Iowa helped a few hundred black slaves who came from Missouri, Arkansas or Indian Territory [Oklahoma] escape to the north even though it was against the law to do so. "Many . . . were driven by a religious belief that slavery was wrong. . . . [including] anti-slavery Quakers [who] played a leading role."

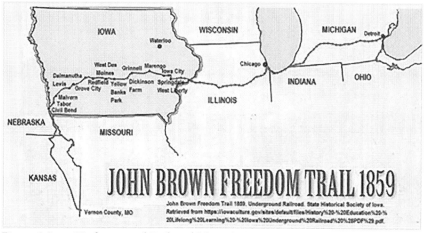

Figure 2 Iowa Underground Railroad Map 1859

*[Iowans] were displeased [that Brown] had gone beyond his regular actions of assisting freedom seekers and had begun to actively free slaves and kill slave owners. Ten months later Brown was dead, having been captured and hung after [he and his followers] attacked the federal arsenal at Harpers Ferry, VA, on October 16, 1859. The brash action ignited great controversy and became a catalyst leading to Civil War.[12]*

As a historical footnote, 76,534 Iowa men served in the Union army in the Civil War that began 14 years later, the highest per capita participation of any state in the Union.

*My dad's father told me that, during the Civil War, our ancestors raised horses in and around Waterloo. And the Union soldiers would come to people's farms in the area, drop off their worn-out horses, and steal people's horses, their pigs, silver and jewelry. My grandfather's grandparents owned slaves, a family of blacks who lived with them. They had their own little house on the property and helped them work the land. Our family posted one of the young black boys at the edge of the woods every day to watch for those soldiers. When they came, he would run back warn everyone. They would hide all their valuables and the black family in this tunnel under their house until they were gone. Grandpa showed me the tunnel. [EHS 66 WF]*

## Black Migration to Waterloo

*The dramatic exodus of African Americans from countryside to city and from South to North during World War I and the decade that followed changed forever black America's economic, political, social, and cultural lives. The Great Migration was, up to that point, the largest voluntary internal movement of black people ever seen.[13]*

The railroad arrived in Waterloo in March 1861 with the Dubuque & Sioux City Railroad,[14] 32 days before the start of the Civil War.

In 1870, the town gave the Illinois Central Rail Road (IC)[15] $23,000 in cash and roughly 70 acres of land on the East Side as an incentive to move its Iowa Division machine shops from Dubuque to Waterloo and not Cedar Falls. The shops opened on East 4th Street employing roughly 160 workers, and included a roundhouse with 14 stalls, and machine, blacksmith, carpenter and paint shops.[16]

By the early 1900s, the IC was one of the town's largest employers with over 2,000 workers.[17]

Native whites comprised 87.9% of Waterloo's population. The minority community included not only blacks, but Greeks, Croatians and Jewish immigrants[18]

*The industrial growth . . . brought waves of immigrants hungry for work. Many of these were Croatians and other eastern Europeans and African Americans from the Deep South. This gave Black Hawk County a diversity of population unusual for mostly homogenous Iowa.[19]*

In 1910, seven million of the nation's eight million African Americans resided below "the Cotton Curtain." During the following 15 years, more than one-tenth – 700,000-plus – of the country's black population would "voluntarily move north"[20] with others from the east "to industrial and/or urban areas such as New York, Chicago, and Detroit, and Waterloo." [21]

*Basically, these people were running away from some things, but [they were] also being pulled by other things. The South was not the best place to live in the early 1910s at all because of lynching and lack of political rights and so forth. Agriculture was in decline because of the boll weevil. Those things were social factors and economic factors that were pushing them out of the South. [And] there was a lure in the North. Businesses and industries were needing workers.* [22]

Waterloo had 29 black residents in 1910. By the end of 1911, there were 395, 13.6 times more. In 1920, there were 856, 30 times as many as there were at the start of the decade.

In June 1911, the IC refused to negotiate a common contract over wages with a federation of unions representing skilled and unskilled workers instead of singly with each as had been the historical protocol. After unsuccessful negotiation, the federation called a strike on the entire IC system for September 30. [23] The Waterloo shops and those throughout the IC system were left at a virtual standstill. [24]

With the Mississippi shops closed, workers were offered free passage and jobs in other IC towns in the north, including Waterloo.

*They were promised better work but were literally "railroaded" into breaking a strike. They were promised homes, but forced to live next to prostitutes, pool halls and bootleggers. Then they were blamed for those activities by the very people responsible. They asked for a voice in their community and received silence in return.* [25]

The IC had prepared for the strike by recruiting professional strikebreakers for its skilled positions, but not for the unskilled, laborer positions that could be filled by blacks.

The railroad nailed posters to tree trunks with large, bold, headlines and placed advertisements in black newspapers along its multitude of branch lines scattered throughout Illinois, Kentucky and the Deep South. [26] The promise was pay seven times what workers made in the

South.[27] It supplied free passes all over the country to anyone willing to move to Waterloo to work and hundreds responded from throughout the country.

*Strikebreakers are expected on every train. No definite statement could be secured from local officials regarding the steps taken to man the shops, but strikers freely predict that another 24 hours will see the city flooded with "scab" labor, as they term them.* [28]

"Hundreds of African American men left their families and made the trip north. . . most of them from towns along the Illinois Central Railroad – Water Valley, Durant, and other places in Mississippi. . ." not aware they were being recruited as strikebreakers.[29] (Figure 3)[30] About 75% of those who migrated to Waterloo came from Holmes County in west central Mississippi where Negroes worked the cotton and soybean fields. In the fall of 1964, the Black Hawk County Branch of the NAACP, the Black Hawk County Conference on Religion and Race, and the Citizens' Committee of Waterloo participated in a proposal to make Holmes and Black Hawk sister counties.[31]

Figure 3 Illinois Central Locomotive Workers Circa 1920

*The Illinois Central went down South and asked people whether they wanted to go to the Promised Land. They got a whole bunch of people, brought them back and unloaded them in the shop yard. – Roosevelt Taylor, grandson of George Martin, strikebreaker from Mississippi*[32]

The IC had planned housing for the influx of strikebreakers in its yards on the East Side. "A number of old boxcars have been pulled in close to the shops and these could be fitted with bunks very easily. Cooking could also be carried on in the yards and thus the necessity for [the public]coming into contact with the strikers would be obviated."[33] As the strike continued, boxcars weren't suitable accommodations. White strikebreakers found lodging throughout the town that was denied to blacks.

*[Housing for strikebreakers was in] what is now known as the "African-American triangle" ["Black Triangle" or "Smokey Row"][34] [Figure 4] – dilapidated, overcrowded housing bounded by Summer and Mobile streets, the Illinois Central Railroad and Fourth Street.[35] [The] laborers are fearful of personal violence. To their uneducated minds their remaining at work will result in their being attacked by the strikers. They have been assured that no harm will come to them, and notice has been served that if they do not work they will have to vacate their bunks in the railroad yards.[36]*

"When someone wanted to go to the store, they'd go out in groups. . . . If [the strikers] got a guy by himself, you wouldn't see him no more after that."

By the end of 1911 the IC had been able to replace the strikers and was operating normally.[37]

The unions didn't capitulate and end the strike against the railroad until June 28, 1915. Many of the European then immigrants left Waterloo while many of the blacks retained lower paying jobs, which provided a better standard of living than what they'd experienced in Mississippi

## SECOND BLACK MIGRATION TO WATERLOO

A second black migration occurred during "the second huge [black] exodus from the South [that] was larger, more sustained, different in character and direction, and precipitated an even more radical and lasting transformation in American life than [the Great Migration during World War I and after]."[38] (Figure 4)

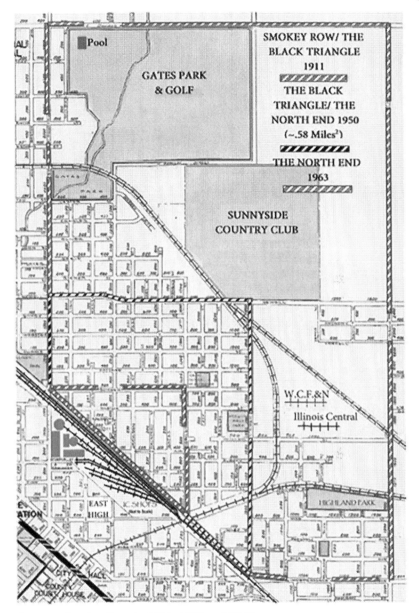

Figure 4 Smokey Row in 1911, 1950 and 1963

*By 1950, blacks were buying homes outside the Black Triangle, north to Newell Street and east to Linden. By 1963, when The Bridge Between story begins, the North End community had expanded north to Donald Street and east to Idaho Street, both near the Waterloo city limit.*

*Between 1940 and 1950, another 1.5 million African Americans left the South. The migration continued at roughly the same pace over the next twenty years. By [the end of the second Great Migration in] 1970, about five million African Americans had made the journey, and the geographic map of black America had fundamentally changed. Roughly one of every seven black Southerners pulled up stakes and headed north or west. In 1970, African Americans were a more urbanized population than whites: more than 80% lived in cities, as compared to 70% for the general population of the United States. . . .* [39]

Waterloo's big upsurge in black residents came because of the town's manufacturing complex during and after World War II, which continued to expand in the 1970s.

"... with the improved labor conditions in the North, wages three or four times those paid in the South and with the more businesslike working atmosphere . . ." black migrants generally experienced "a better and more fulfilling life. . . ." after resettling in places like Waterloo.[40]

Award-winning reporter and writer Nikole Hannah-Jones, who grew up in Waterloo "on the wrong side of the river that divided white from black," humanized the migration to Waterloo in the "Ghosts of Greenwood."

*In 1947, my father, along with his mother and older brother, boarded a northbound train in Greenwood, MS [northwest Mississippi]. They carried with them nothing but a suitcase stuffed with clothes, a bag of cold chicken, and my grandmother's determination that her children – my father was just 2 years old – would not be doomed to a life of picking cotton in the feudal society that was the Mississippi Delta.* [41]

## Segregation & Discrimination: 1950s-1960s

*... he asked me in perfect innocence, "Why don't all the Negroes in the South move North?" I tried to explain what has happened, unfailingly, whenever a significant body of Negroes move North. They do*

*not escape Jim Crow: they merely encounter another, not-less-deadly variety. They do not move to Chicago, they move to the South Side; they do not move to New York, they move to Harlem. – James Baldwin[42]*

*Iowa and most of the Midwest is redneck country. Those are some of the least informed people in the world. So, there are going to be racist attitudes. [COL 69 AAF]*

In the early 1900s, Waterloo segregation was de facto (Latin, "from the fact") – minorities are concentrated in certain neighborhoods as "a result of natural conditions, or due to the gulf between financial classes ... [rather than] be a legal effort to keep the races apart."

*With the climate of intolerance prominent in the country – and Waterloo residents were just as conservative as anyone – restrictive practices occurred, especially in housing. More than any other immigrant or migrant group, blacks were discriminated against in where they could live. The situation was especially unfortunate for the law-abiding, hard-working blacks forced to live . . . in the triangular area termed "Smokey Row" [or the North End] . . . along the north edge of the Illinois Central tracks. . . . Croatians and other immigrants lived in the area in the 1910s, but it increasingly became associated with black settlement in Waterloo as whites withdrew.[43]*

Both black and white strikebreakers in 1910 were housed near the IC railroad yards as a matter of convenience and of safety. Blacks weren't welcome in the white community as the white strikers were, as much for the fact they were taking jobs from residents as their race.

After the strike, the town's unwritten social code restricted them to the black triangle. White homeowners refused to sell their homes to blacks. Real estate agents would only sell homes to blacks in the North End.

In 1916, Waterloo's Board of Realtors asked the City Council to pass an ordinance prohibiting the sale of houses to blacks in white districts. The council refused, but agents continued to informally observe the ban anyway.

By 1920, when Rath Packing Company (Figure 5)[44] began hiring blacks, Waterloo's population had increased 41% overall and from 0.1% black in 1910 to 2.3% black, which created a housing problem.

Figure 5 Postcard of the Rath Packing Company Circa 1935

Breaking the social code and escaping the black triangle was virtually impossible. A 1955 report on Negro-White relations in Waterloo noted, "Although many Negro families have desired and attempted to move out of the deteriorated area, very few have been successful."[45]

"City laws mandated housing discrimination throughout much of Waterloo."[46]

The town's population in the 1960 decennial census was 71,755 (1960) – Negro/Black 0.9%, White 99%. In September 1963, Mayor Ed Jochumsen's Committee on Racial Understanding requested letters from Waterloo industry, real estate and lending agencies about what they were doing about housing and unemployment to "correct the race relations climate here."[47]

Responses to the employment issue were received from Rath, John Deere and Chamberlain.[48]

- Rath reported a 5% Negro workforce: 116 skilled workers, 50 semi-skilled, 46 unskilled and 25 service workers.
- Chamberlain listed 4.5% of its workforce as Negro.
- John Deere said its records weren't set up to "distinguish between race, creed, color or national origin."

Eight major lending institutions replied to the lending and home sales inquiry. They assured the committee "race is no factor in awarding or denying home loans" and such decisions are based on the "individual credit rating of the individual applicant."

The Waterloo Board of Realtors submitted a lengthy response that was printed in full by the *Waterloo Daily Courier,* roughly 25 inches of text; a newspaper column was 29.5 inches long.

The first third was a boilerplate statement assuring the promotion "of discrimination in housing has neither the formal or tacit approval of" the Waterloo Board of Realtors. However, it acknowledged "individual real estate salesmen . . . may have informed colored persons that houses in white neighborhoods were not available. . . ."

The board suggested in the next third "too many laymen [do not understand] realtors are not the persons selling the houses," but homeowners' agents "who choose for themselves to whom they will sell their property." That was followed by a single-sentence paragraph a little more than two inches long.

*Perhaps the individual salesmen who have made the statement [about houses not being available for colored buyers] have only been guilty of trying to protect the feelings of the colored prospect, and avoid the embarrassing situation which was not of his [the realtor's] own making, by telling the colored prospect that the property has been sold instead of bluntly telling him that the owner will not sell to a colored buyer.*[49]

As a remedy, the board noted, "It seems the only thing the realtor can do is to tell the colored prospect the truth – that the owner would not sell to the colored buyer." The realtors asked if the mayor's committee didn't feel that was a solution, what suggestions it had to eliminate the owner's prejudice.

A three-inch lesson in economics in the story explained why the suggestion realtors shouldn't accept listings unless the owner agrees "in writing, to sell to any buyer regardless of color" wasn't feasible.

*To adopt this suggestion would mean that the realtors would thus be applying economic sanctions to force property owners to surrender a property-right [sic] now protected by our American system of law: the right to sell or not to sell to any person at any time, for any price, for any terms, and for any reason.*[50]

Rejecting lawful business wasn't something realtors could do without affecting their livelihoods, the letter continued. Instead of blaming realtors for instances of "prejudice and discrimination" in the residential property sales, the realtor board "respectfully" suggested the committee "direct its attention to removing this prejudice from the property owners who cause the problem."[51]

The committee scheduled a meeting on October 1st at which the various groups would be invited to "explain what they're doing to 'correct the race relations climate [in Waterloo].'"[52] There's no record the meeting occurred.

On Wednesday, November 20, the city council approved an open housing resolution adopted by the Waterloo Committee on Better Racial Understanding at an earlier meeting.

*Be it resolved that this committee recommend to the city council that it declare it to be a violation of public policy to refuse to lease or sell a house to any person solely because of his race, religion or national origin.*[53]

Thirteen days later the committee passed a resolution calling for "a community-wide inter-racial home visitation . . . to provide opportunities for all persons to understand each other through mutual association." It called on all local "churches, social, civic, fraternal, industrial and labor groups" to approve and suggested the holiday season was an excellent opportunity for participation.[54]

*Waterloo was totally segregated. The river separated it. And then the East Side was further subdivided. If you had dark skin, you weren't allowed to live in certain areas of Waterloo. I don't know how that worked. Waterloo didn't have drinking fountains for whites and blacks or like that. Or had to ride in the back of the bus. It wasn't quite as overt. But Waterloo was as segregated as any southern town had been. [WHS 69 WM]*

*When my parents were looking for a house in 1953-1954 outside of the North End, the realtor or seller would make comments on the phone that it was a very nice neighborhood – there were no Negroes and no Jews. Since my mother was born in Waterloo, they couldn't tell over the phone she was black. When they found out, they'd be told it had been sold. Eventually, my grandmother gave them the lot-and-a-half next to hers on the corner. They built a house there. When people found out Negroes were building the house, "For Sale" signs went up all over the neighborhood. Until they realized, "Oh, it's not a Negro, it's Mrs. [so-and-so's] daughter." The sales signs came down. And people didn't move. [EHS 68 AAF]*

Blacks in Waterloo remained socially quarantined in the North End until well into the 1960s, "living in a white man's democracy, and while not legally enslaved, subject to definition by their race."[55]

By then, de facto segregation had evolved into segregation de jure (Latin, "according to the law") – due to "racially-motivated and explicit public policy whose effects endure to the present." Segregation de jure was the basis for government cases and civil law suits against states, cities and school districts throughout the Civil Rights movement.

Housing segregation de jure was achieved in Waterloo as it was other towns and cities throughout the country, by targeted housing ads, redlining and loan refusals, and deed restrictions.

## DISCRIMINATORY HOUSING ADS

The Fourteenth Amendment to the U.S. Constitution says

*No State shall make or enforce any law which shall abridge the privileges or immunities of citizens of the United States; nor shall any State deprive any person of life, liberty, or property, without due process of law; nor deny to any person within its jurisdiction the equal protection of the laws.*[56]

In 1948, the year that many high school sophomores in 1966 were born, the U.S. Supreme Court ruled, "Private agreements to exclude

Figure 6 "Colored Buyer" Real Estate Ads, 1949

persons of designated race or color from the use or occupancy of real estate for residential purposes [standing alone] do not violate [any rights guaranteed by] the Fourteenth Amendment. . . ."[57]

Many real estate ads in the *Waterloo Daily Courier* from 1948 on were headlined, "'Attention Colored Buyer.' . . . The ads for homes in the white sections do not say 'No Negroes Allowed.' However, they leave little room for doubt."[58]

Figures 6 has two examples of realtor and classified ads with stated color preferences that ran in the *Courier* from 1948-1958. Neither color nor race appears as a criterion in real estate ads in the *Courier* after 1958, based on a random stratified sample search through 1963. Nor was a formal policy change by the *Courier* in either the editorial pages or classified ad specifications in 1958.

The "Miller" of Smith & Miller Realtors (Figure 6) was my maternal grandfather, Claude R. Miller.

I never knew much about his business and he died in the spring of my sophomore year of high school. His widow, Ruth, inherited his investment properties, including ones in the North End. A younger sister told me about occasionally going with our mother to collect the rent for Ruth. "We had to go during the daylight time. And she always used the 'n word' when she showed up for supper. When she'd leave, Mom would always say, 'Don't use that word.'"

## "Redlining"

The second method of de jure segregation in Waterloo was "redlining," a discriminatory lending process used by banks that "was almost universal"[59] from the 1930s until the late 1960s.

Federal housing agencies, including the Home Owners Loan Corporation (HOLC) and the Federal Housing Association (FHA), designated areas throughout the country as "deemed unfit for investment by banks, insurance companies, savings and loan associations, and other financial services companies. The areas were physically demarcated with red shading on a map." So, loans denied for property in the red shaded area had been "red-lined."[60]

*Otherwise celebrated for making homeownership accessible to white people by guaranteeing their loans, the FHA explicitly refused to back*

*loans to black people or even other people who lived near black people.
As [the Atlantic author] puts it, "Redlining destroyed the possibility of
investment wherever black people lived."[61]*

Areas were graded from "A" [First Grade/Green] to "D" [Fourth
Grade/Red]. "B" and "C" were Second Grade/Blue and Third
Grade/Yellow, respectively.[62]

Red areas were aging, obsolescent areas in which neighborhood
characteristics were "change of style; expiring restrictions or lack of
them; infiltration of a lower grade population; inadequate
transportation, insufficient utilities, perhaps heavy tax burdens, poor
maintenance of homes and lack of homogeneity."

Red areas had "detrimental influences in a pronounced degree;
undesirable population or infiltration of it; low percentage of home
ownership, very poor maintenance and often vandalism prevail.
Unstable incomes of the people and difficult collections are usually
prevalent."[63]

Loans to blacks seeking to buy a house that they could afford were
denied loans because those properties were generally in a "redlined"
area.

"[Redlining] resulted in neighborhood economic decline and the
withholding of services or their provision at an exceptionally high
cost."[64]

The FHA knowingly subsidized builders who were mass-producing
entire subdivisions for whites – with the requirement that none of the
homes be sold to African Americans [until the Fair Housing Act was
passed in 1968]."[65]

## Deed Restrictions or Covenants

Deed restrictions or covenants was the third method of de jure
segregation in Waterloo.

During the 1950s, government-approved legal contracts in
Waterloo had covenants that restricted where nonwhites could live.
(Figure 7)

# BLACK HAWK COUNTY ABSTRACT CO.
#24

(f) No race or nationality other than the Caucasian race shall use or occupy any building in any lot, except that this covenant shall not prevent occupancy by domestic servants of a different race or nationality employed by an owner or tenant.

(g) No trailer, basement, tent, shack, garage, barn or other out-
. . . .

(h) No old structure shall be moved onto any lot in Hollandale
. . . .

(i) No dwelling, the construction costs of which are less than
. . . .

(j) These covenants shall run with the land and shall be binding
. . . .

(k) If the parties hereto or any of them, or their heirs or assigns shall violate or attempt to violate any of the covenants or restrictions, herein, it shall be lawful for any other person owning any other lot in Hollandale Addition to prosecute any proceedings at law or in equity against the person or persons violating or attempting to violate any such covenant or restriction either to prevent him or them from so doing or to recover damages or other dues for such violation.

(l) Invalidation of any one of these covenants by judgment or court
. . . .

In Witness Whereof, the parties hereto have executed this instrument the 8th day of May, 1941.
Signed:

Signatures of 25 Hollandale Addition
homeowners or their representatives.

Acknowledged: State of Iowa, County of Black Hawk, ss. On this 8th day of May, A. D. 1941, before me C. R. Green, a Notary Public in and for Black Hawk County, Iowa, personally appeared above named parties, who acknowledged said instrument to be their voluntary act and deed. C. R. Green, Notary Public in and for Black Hawk County, Iowa. Notarial seal.

(Original document was shortened by the author due to space considerations.)

Figure 7 1950s Restriction Covenant for Property in the Hollandale Addition on the West Side of Waterloo

These covenants were also used for East Side properties, including the exclusive Highland subdivision that abutted the North End.

Although the U.S. Supreme Court had ruled such "private agreements to exclude persons of designated race or color from the use or occupancy of real estate for residential purposes do not violate the Fourteenth Amendment,"[66] it barred courts from enforcing racial deed restrictions, which "were deemed lawful for another 30 years."[67]

42

Judge William Parker, Iowa's first elected black judge who was voted onto the Waterloo municipal court in 1963, was a mentor of

SOURCE: Jet Magazine, November 21, 1963, p. 3. Retrieved from http://tinyurl.com/j3kgjv6

Figure 8 Judge William Parker
*Judge Parker was Iowa's first elected black judge. He was voted onto the Waterloo municipal court in 1963.*

mine during my final two years in high school. (Figure 8) We had an ongoing conversation about his inability to buy a house on the West Side of town. I was shocked the first time he mentioned it. He admitted being personally frustrated by the social reality of his family's lockout from the West Side that was supported and tolerated by close friends and associates who vocally disclaimed the situation. But he said matter-of-factly "the system" wasn't ready to change.

It was the first time I'd been exposed to the existence such discrimination in Waterloo.

## SOCIAL PREJUDICE AND DISCRIMINATION

More than 1,500 African Americans were living in Waterloo by 1940, many who had followed other family members to employment at Rath and Deere.

"Although many were qualified to work in skilled positions, [jobs for] African Americans were restricted to beef, hog and sheep kills, at lower wages than white workers."[68]

*Black women found employment only as custodians or domestics, and men were limited to laboring and portering jobs in those businesses that would hire them. As in other Midwestern cities, jobs in meatpacking were among the best available for blacks even though they were restricted to only a few departments in the Rath plant.*[69]

There were few black professionals in Waterloo before World War II and into the 1950s. Job discrimination resulted in blacks being assigned the dirtiest jobs at Rath and the hottest jobs in the foundry at the John Deere Tractor Works to African Americans.

*I came to Waterloo the last part of 1948, looking for the promised land. I wasn't quite eighteen years of age and I had been told that I could only come to the Midwest that this was the land of opportunity, and all I had to do was work. I discovered that the land was here, but the promises were little different than those I had just left. Let me hasten to add they were different. It wasn't as obvious, or as pronounced, or as blatant as it was in Mississippi. I well knew where I stood in Mississippi and here I had to be told and reminded.*

*The other thing that so was discouraging to me was how well [Waterloo] had domesticated their black people. They had conditioned most of the blacks who lived here to never look at how well they should be doing to whites who they had gone to school with, but to measure themselves by their country cousin, those of us coming up from the southland. It was amazing how well they taught [the blacks in Waterloo] to measure themselves versus another black person in order to feel good about themself [sic]. – Jimmy Porter[70]*

Blacks faced widespread discrimination in public accommodations, hotels and restaurants, and recreation facilities in Waterloo. A waiter reportedly brought "a raw egg broken on a piece of bread together with the egg shell" when a Negro customer ordered an egg and toast.[71]

*I first really became aware of what it meant to be black in Woolworth's [on Commercial Street on the West Side]. When I was around 10 or 11 [in the mid-50s], they had a soda fountain in there and still had the signs up for colored and white. Potter's [Polar Pantry] ice cream [on Walnut Street on the East Side] had separate windows for blacks and whites. And in many the filling stations. Initially, it made me somber. That's the only word that really comes to mind. [EHS 66 AAM]*

I also have vague memories of separate fountains at the Greyhound bus station on the corner of East 4th and Mulberry across from Lincoln Park in the early 1950s.

## 1948 UNION STRIKES RATH PACKING FOR EQUAL OPPORTUNITY FOR BLACK MEMBERS

For blacks in Waterloo and other Midwestern cities, jobs in meatpacking during and after World War II were among the best available, even though they were restricted to a few departments in the Rath plant.

Black workers at Rath were an integral part of the local United Packinghouse Workers of America (UPWA) union, which secured certification in the early 1940s.

Passage of the Taft-Hartley Act by Congress in 1947 empowered states to decide whether unions could demand a "union shop" provision in labor contracts. Iowa subsequently passed a right-to-work law that prohibited employers and unions requiring union membership or the payment of union dues for workers to get or keep a job.

In March 1948, the UPWA called an industry-wide strike to protest Taft-Hartley and to force wage hikes to keep up with postwar inflation. On March 16, 4,000 Rath employees joined more than 80,000 workers at 65 meatpacking plants nationwide and walked off the job, halting all production.

As the strike lengthened into its third month, peaceful resolve among the union members and financial resources diminished.

Mounting frustration gave way to violence in Waterloo after black strikebreaker Fred Lee Roberts shot and killed white union founder William "Chuck" Farrell on the picket line.

According to Roberts' testimony at his manslaughter trial, he was attempting to go to work, but the strike crowd was at Rath's 18th Street entrance was too large. He drove to the foreman's entrance on Sycamore Street, but when he turned into plant, one of the strikers told him, "You're not going to get through here." Somebody yelled, "Kill him, tip his car over," and the car began to rock. Others yelled, "Kill the jig."[72]

Roberts said he picked up his gun and waved it across the windshield. When he tried to back out, someone said, "We give a . . . [sic] if he has got a gun – kill him."[73] He decided to shoot out the right window, which was open about 10 inches, when he thought the street was clear. According to a police detective witness, Farrell was approaching the car as Roberts fired and was shot in the head, killing him instantly.

Credit: Acme Telephoto. Retrieved from
https://medium.com/@dmegivern/the-10th-worst-city-for-african-americans-in-the-u-s-has-a-story-this-is-how-the-dream-derailed-9a
1e12a8ad41

Figure 9 National Guard Sent in by the Governor

The death precipitated a riot that left the plant in shambles. Gov. Robert Blue sent the National Guard to Waterloo to suppress rioting by union members and escort strikebreakers into the plant. (Figure 9)

Roberts was found not guilty in early February 1949 based on self-defense after the jury of nine women and three men deliberated four hours and 25 minutes for its verdict.[74]

In addition to Roberts' manslaughter charge, a Black Hawk County grand jury indicted 24 others for strike offenses, including charges of conspiracy, assault and malicious mischief.[75] UPWA Local 46 union steward Everett Hopper was acquitted of conspiracy, but two others – Wilbert E. Warren and Russell Edsill – were convicted and were sentenced to three years in prison.[76]

Union members pointed out the riot had been directed solely at the Rath company and not Waterloo's black community.

*If there was a racial break [in Waterloo], it would have been at that time: a black man killing a white man. It never got to the point that someone said, he killed Chuck Farrell because he was white, or because the black man is getting ready to cross the picket line. – Charles Pearson*[77]

The riot reinforced the determination of Rath's management not to negotiate.

Rath and the other meatpacking companies struck by the union eventually defeated the strike. Rath workers returned to the job with a $.09/hour wage increase, exactly what the company had offered at the beginning of the action. It also rewarded non-striking and replacement workers with super-seniority. That resulted in bitterness that "ran deep: it broke up a lot of good friendships" and even divided families. "We had two sisters that used to work right across the table from each other, and one went in and scabbed and the other one stayed out. They wouldn't even speak to each other."[78]

The strike tested Local 46's commitment to the UPWA's racial equality policy and worker solidarity triumphed. Black and white strikers together confronted Iowa National Guardsmen sent to suppress rioting by union members, and black and white union members marched together in the slain worker's funeral procession.[79]

As company-union relations deteriorated in the aftermath of the strike defeat, the growing number of black workers at Rath were able to link their grievances against racial discrimination with Local 46's more confrontational stance toward management. The union had transformed into a dynamic and militant organization and became a springboard to attack established patterns of discrimination in the community.[80]

Many of Local 46's activists were parents of the East High students in the 1950s and 1960s, and were involved in civil rights issues in the public schools as well as the community during the latter half of the 1960s.

This influence was important during the years of upheaval and change in Waterloo that began in the mid-1960s.

## East Side Black, West Side White

*We had our racial problems in Waterloo. But they were very small. Any potential direct confrontation that looked like it was going to occur between blacks and whites in Waterloo was buffered by black senior citizens talking and church leaders telling us, "You have no business doing this," and providing guidance for conduct. [EHS 66 AAM]*

*My sister and I'd always heard about Blood Alley growing up. It sounded terrific. Who would have an alley really named that? It was on the East Side somewhere. It was the talk among kids. You just say, "Blood Alley," and people knew there were shootings there whatever. One Sunday morning my grandpa took us and drove us down Blood Alley. I remember hunkering down in the back seat. It was the most adventurous thing we've ever done. That tells you how it was. [OHS 67 WF]*

*When I was a teenager, I worked for a white guy who was essentially a slum lord. He could buy houses for probably less than $10 grand back in the 1960s. He had 40 or 50 houses before he quit doing it, all on the East Side. And then he would rent them, usually to black people and usually single black women. These were old, two-story houses with attics and basements. You could kind of tell in the North End if someone owned a house. It would have a fence around it and be kind of nicely preserved. The rentals seemed more impoverished and more kind of temporary, more run down. [WHS 69 WM]*

*I became aware of racism in elementary school in Des Moines. The city had a very active NAACP and constantly made everyone aware of the efforts for integration in the school system. As a result, I'd become interested in supporting integration since I was in the third grade and was upset by racism. When we moved to Waterloo, I was very surprised to find differences among people was not allowed. The races were separated by the river. One didn't see anyone but white people on the West Side, never African Americans. The East Side was like a ghetto. And it was white vs. blue-collar. There were also maybe one or two Jewish families. They were owners of the means of production but were treated like second-class citizens. It wasn't a good place to be Jewish. The town had an entrenched racism and division I didn't experience in Des Moines. It led to violence and segregation. Waterloo was a terrible, racist, polluted city. It hardened my attitude towards racists, segregation and the city. I had no desire to ever go back there after high school. And I didn't have to because my family moved to Long Beach, California. I spent the rest of my life working against racism, sexism and working for economic equality. I never went back to Waterloo. [WHS 70 WF]*

*The river area downtown was neutral. It was safe on the East Side, but only to Broadway or the KWWL building. I never ever walked on the East Side except downtown. My parents told me not to travel beyond that. We had an uncle who lived near Rath Packing and we only visited by car. When we were 17 and had access to cars, we drove around more – up East 4th street and in the North End. When the father of my friend found out we were driving over there, he got very angry. [WHS 72 WM]*

Both the East and West Sides also had their subcommunities.

*There wasn't any separation between the North End and the rest of the East Side. It seems like there was a camaraderie, blacks and whites living on the East side got along fine. The attitude was, "We're here and we're going to make the best of it." I don't recall fights or murders. Most of the people took care of their own business. [EHS 60 AAM]*

*I hated living on the West Side because I felt poorer than the rest of the people. People didn't really welcome each other into neighborhoods. [COL 63 WF]*

*When I was growing up, Beech Street [which ran north-south on the East Side of the Black Triangle from Newell, the northern boundary of the triangle, to Independence Ave., the southern boundary] was a black affluent area. It was nice going down that street. The median had grass in it. [laughs] I don't know who took care of all of it, but it was well-kept. [EHS 66 AAM]*

*There were two communities on the East Side – the North End and the rest of the East Side. But there were also two communities on the West Side – the professionals and the non-professionals. [EHS 67 AAF]*

*The black community was more homogeneous in terms of housing; it didn't matter what you did. If you were black, the North End was the only place you could live. The black doctors, dentists, lawyers all lived in the North End. It was always noted when somebody moved to a neighborhood that had been previously been thought of white neighborhood, like north of Newell. [EHS 68 AAF]*

*We lived in Highland, which was an affluent area on the East Side of town where some of the founding fathers of the city lived. The Raths. Mortimer Cleveland, the architect who built some of the most beautiful homes in Waterloo and Iowa. Those names don't resonate with everybody. The police chief lived around the corner. I had three aunts who lived on the West Side, one who just thought Westsiders were better than the East Side because there were "darkies" on the East Side. I couldn't figure it out. We had better houses in Highland. We had the run of the whole Highland neighborhood. It was a wonderful place to grow up. The East Side rocked. We could go everywhere. It had everything. The shops. The movie theaters. Everything. We spent time with our family on the West Side. But they would never come visit us unless they had to. Like Thanksgiving or Christmas. Otherwise, we went there. [COL 71 WF]*

Census data support the "East Side Poor, West Side Rich" mantra in 1963-1973. (Figure 10)

In the 1960 census, the median household (HH) income for the East Side of Waterloo was $5,980. For the West Side, it was $7,003 or 17.1% higher in terms of purchasing power.

In the 1970 census, the median household (HH) income for the East Side of Waterloo was $8,547 and it was $10,732 on the West Side or 25.6% higher in terms of purchasing power.

The purchasing power of the West Side households increased by 4.9% in the 10 years between censuses.

In 1960, the median household income for Census Tract 18 that roughly encompassed the North End was $5,566. By comparison, the median household income for the four highest census tracts on the West Side where a majority of the school board members lived in the Prospect area was $8,450.

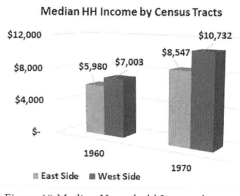

Figure 10 Median Household Income by Census Tracts, 1960 & 1970

*"$-" is the $0 baseline.*

In other words, the households in the four West Side tracts had $23,850 a year or almost $2,000 a month more to spend than did those at the median income level in the North End.

## Waterloo by the Numbers 1963-1973

*When I tell people where I'm from, they imagine a white environment. They shake their heads. "Are there blacks in Waterloo?" If you only knew. Come to my town and see it ain't all white. [EHS 73 AAM]*

Most people outside of Iowa in the 1960s had a perception the state was white. In the 1960 decennial census, 0.9% of the population was black when the national percentage was 10.5%; Iowa ranked 40th out of the 50 states in black population. In the 1970 decennial census, Iowa was still ranked 40/50 with a 1.2% black population.[81]

In 1960, 6.7% of the population of Waterloo was black, the highest percentage in Iowa. Most blacks lived in five East Side neighborhoods called the North End, Smokey Row or the black triangle; the West Side was 99.9% white.

Waterloo was the 5th largest town in Iowa from 1963-1973, but it had the highest percentage of black residents among the state's seven largest towns (Table 1). Its black population was 36% to 54% higher than Des Moines, the city with the next highest percentage. In 1960, 6.7% of the town's population was black;

Des Moines, the state capitol, was second at 4.9%. Ten years later, Waterloo's figure was 8.8%; Des Moines was 5.7% black.

| Table 1 Percentage of Black Population in Iowa's Seven Largest Cities, 1910-1970 | | | | | |
|---|---|---|---|---|---|
| | 1910 | 1940 | 1950 | 1960 | 1970 |
| Cedar Rapids | 0.6% | 1.1% | 0.5% | 1.2% | 1.6% |
| Davenport | 1.3% | 1.2% | 0.8% | 2.0% | 1.2% |
| Des Moines | 3.4% | 4.0% | 2.2% | 4.9% | 5.7% |
| Dubuque | 0.2% | 0.1% | 0.1% | 0.1% | 0.2% |
| Iowa City | 0.6% | 0.6% | 0.9% | 1.5% | 0.1% |
| Sioux City | 0.6% | 1.1% | 0.5% | 1.4% | 1.2% |
| **Waterloo** | **0.1%** | **2.9%** | **2.1%** | **6.7%** | **8.8%** |
| Iowa | 0.6% | 0.7% | 0.7% | 0.9% | 1.2% |
| U.S. | 10.6% | 9.8% | 10.0% | 10.5% | 11.1% |

*These data suggest Waterloo was dealing with racial issues of prejudice and communication between blacks and whites more than the other communities in the state in which a "significant" black population was one percent or less.*

In 2017, Iowa was 30th in population and 35th in percentage of black population at 3.5%. Mississippi was #1 with a black population of 38%. Idaho – where they DO grow potatoes[1] – and Montana were the two states with the smallest percentage of blacks in their respective populations at one percent.[82]

Rapid growth of the black population in Waterloo the decade before 1963-1973 during the early days of the Civil Rights movement created additional pressure on a school system whose school zones were drawn to conform to the segregated community. Rather than implement integration changes that were being legally imposed in the South, the community and the system generally resisted change. It became increasing difficult to thwart the demands of black and white East Side parents and students during the volatile Civil Rights actions in the middle of *The Bridge Between* years. As a result, numerous sources repeatedly noted that Waterloo suffered the most significant racial tension and unrest, riots, resistance to school integration and social change than any other community in the state.

# Reflections from The Bridge

*African Americans in the North lived in a strange state of semi-freedom. The North may had emancipated its slaves, but it was not ready to treat the blacks as citizens. . . or sometimes even as human beings. – Africans in America (PBS)* [83]

*I worked with a guy at UNI, a really nice, enlightened human being, who grew up on a small farm in Washington County. He mentioned many times his dad considered Waterloo to be the armpit of the state. Didn't say it was because of the black people. I met another woman at work who grew up in Vinton. She's scared of Waterloo to this day. These*

---

[1] The reaction of the majority of non-Iowans when meeting someone from the state is, "Oh, that's where they grow potatoes." Iowa – the Hawkeye State – is also known as "The Corn State."

*are college-educated, very intelligent people, but have the "bumpkin bias." [WHS 70 WM]*

It's been easy to point the finger historically at the IC's operational strategy during the 1911 railroad strike as the main contributing cause of racial segregation, and tensions between blacks and whites over prejudice and discrimination in Waterloo. The general perception that Southern blacks were the only strikebreakers hired was and is an artifact of the racial issues between the black and white communities in Waterloo.

In fact, many white "scabs" and their families made their way to Waterloo and onto the company's payroll from the South, the Midwest and the East. Most ended up on the East Side and were the seed generation for the East Side's historically poorer middle-class families.

For high school students in 1963-1973, educational pathways – the schools students attended from elementary through junior high and high school – were defined by the history and pattern of housing and social segregation as they were growing up. The choice of school to attend was dictated by the school system's neighborhood school policy, which had a profound effect on not only students' school and social lives, but throughout their adult lives.

This de jure segregation impacted the generations of Waterloo school students from the black migration during the IC railroad strike in the early 20th century through the mid-1970s. It was difficult at the beginning of *The Bridge Between* decade from 1963-1973 to overcome this history with desegregation strategies to which neither the community or the school system was committed.

# Endnotes

[1] 1960's-1970's: The Civil Rights Movement and Black Protest in Waterloo. Invisible City, Invisible Community 5. Retrieved from https://sites.google.com/site/invcityinvcommunity/home/5.

[2] A diaspora is the movement of a people to several places at once or over time. Defining and Studying the Modern African Diaspora. (September 1998). Palmer, C. Viewpoints: Perspectives on History, American Historical Association. Retrieved from http://tinyurl.com/j6zqjla. For additional information, http://www.africandiasporanetwork.org/.

[3] For a comprehensive Iowa Anti-Slavery Timeline (1839-1854), refer to Iowa and the Underground Railroad. Retrieved from http://tinyurl.com/ybfxz8du.

[4] African Americans. Encyclopedia Dubuque. Retrieved from http://www.encyclopediadubuque.org/index.php?title=AFRICAN_AMERICANS.

[5] Iowa and Slavery. Iowa History Project: Making of Iowa, Chapter XXX. (1900). Sabin. H. & Sabin, E.L. The Making of Iowa, 4th ed. Chicago: A. Flanagan Co. Retrieved from http://iagenweb.org/history/moi/moi30.htm

[6] Blacks and Mulattoes. (1839). The Statutes Laws of the Territory of Iowa. Dubuque, Iowa Territory: Russell & Reeves, 69. Retrieved from http://tinyurl.com/ya99oana.

[7] Practice. (1839). The Statutes Laws of the Territory of Iowa. Dubuque, Iowa Territory: Russell & Reeves, 404. Retrieved from http://tinyurl.com/ya99oana.

[8] Iowa Anti-Slavery Timeline. Iowa and the Underground Railroad. Retrieved from http://tinyurl.com/ybfxz8du.

[9] The Kansas-Nebraska Act. (1996). The History Place: Abraham Lincoln. Retrieved from http://www.historyplace.com/lincoln/kansas.htm.

[10] Berrier, G. Iowa Public Television: Iowa Pathways. Retrieved from http://site.iptv.org/iowapathways/mypath/iowa-and-underground-railroad.

[11] John Brown Freedom Trail Map 1859. Iowa and the Underground Railroad. Retrieved from http://tinyurl.com/ybfxz8du.

[12] Iowa and the Underground Railroad.

[13] The Second Great Migration. In Motion. The African-American Migration Experience. Retrieved from http://www.inmotionaame.org/print.cfm;jsessionid=f83024670315161531970722?migration=9&bhcp=1.

[14] The Early History of Illinois Central Railroad Company in Waterloo (1860-1900). African-American Voices of the Cedar Valley. Retrieved from https://sites.uni.edu/chen/drupal-AA_voice/railroad.

[15] American-Rails.com. Retrieved from http://www.american-rails.com/illinois-central.html.

[16] The Early History of Illinois Central Railroad Company.

[17] Activity #6: Evolutions and Revolutions in Transportation. Cap Silos: Sites & Smokestacks National Heritage Area. Retrieved from http://www.campsilos.org/excursions/grout/two/act6a.htm.

[18] Historical and Architectoral [sic], E-5.

[19] Ibid.

[20] Great Migration Railroad strike 100 years ago.

[21] Black Triangle in Waterloo, Iowa. Scott, M.B. (Wed, 08/24/2011). *African-American Voices of the Cedar Valley: Community.* Retrieved from https://sites.uni.edu/chen/drupal-AA_voice/community.

[22] Great Migration Railroad strike 100 years ago.

[23] *American Labor Violence: Its Causes, Character, and Outcome.* Taft, and Ross, In Industrial Violence 1911-16. (1969). Graham, H.D. and Gurr, T.R., eds. The Illinois Central Shopmen's Strike. *The History of Violence in America: A Report to the National Commission on the Causes and Prevention of Violence.* Retrieved from http://www.ditext.com/taft/violence.html.

[24] A few of the more senior workers stayed on the job to protect pension benefits despite risking incurring "union displeasure" and that of the strikers. Waterloo IC Shopmen Left Places at 8 a.m. (Monday, October 22, 1911). *Waterloo Evening Daily Courier*, 1. Retrieved from https://newspaperarchive.com/waterloo-evening-courier-oct-02-1911-p-1/.

[25] A moment in Black History: Coming to Waterloo. (Feb 1, 2004). Kinney, P. *The Courier.* Retrieved from http://wcfcourier.com/news/top_news/a-moment-in-black-history-coming-to-waterloo/article_699e910e-752e-5eab-aa40-7f8bcffe60b2.html.

[26] The Illinois Central Railroad, Main Line of Mid-America.

[27] *Waterloo Daily Courier* (1933). Cited in 1901-1910: African American Recruitment in the South.

[28] Waterloo IC Shopmen Left Places at 8 a.m.

[29] Great Migration Railroad strike 100 years ago.

[30] African American Railroad Workers. Waterloo's Railroad Development. For Teachers: Industrialization, Student Activities. Waterloo, IA: Silos and Smokestacks. Retrieved from http://www.campsilos.org/excursions/grout/two/act1b3.htm.

[31] Three Lead Drive to Aid Negroes in Mississippi. (September 27, 1964). *Waterloo Daily Courier*, 33.

[32] Great Migration Railroad strike 100 years ago.

[33] Waterloo IC Shopmen Left Places at 8 a.m.

[34] Great Migration Railroad strike 100 years ago.

[35] Black History. Waterloo Homecoming Association. Retrieved from
http://www.waterloohomecoming.com/about-us/black-history/.

[36] Waterloo IC Shopmen Left Places at 8 a.m.

[37] *Without Blare of Trumpets: Walter Drew, the National Erectors' Association, and the Open Shop Movement, 1903-57.* (1995). Fine, S. Ann Arbor, MI: University of Michigan Press. p. 140. Retrieved from http://tinyurl.com/yb9v7oxd.

[38] The Second Great Migration. In Motion. The African-American Migration Experience. Retrieved from http://tinyurl.com/ycrx6em6.

[39] The Second Great Migration. In Motion.

[40] The Maid Narratives: Black Domestics and White Families in the Jim Crow South. (2012). Van Wormer, K., Jackson III, D.W. & Sudduth, C. (2012). Baton Rouge, LA: Louisiana State University Press, 58, 56.

[41] Ghosts of Greenwood. (July 08, 2014). Hannah-Jones, N. ProPublica: Dispatches from Freedom Summer. Retrieved from https://www.propublica.org/article/ghosts-of-greenwood.

[42] Baldwin, J. (July 1960). Fifth Avenue, Uptown. Esquire. Retrieved from http://www.esquire.com/news-politics/a3638/fifth-avenue-uptown/.

[43] Historical and Architectoral [sic] Resources of Waterloo. Iowa. National Register of Historic Places Multiple Property Documentation Form. (July 25, 1988). Washington, D.C.: United States Department of the Interior, National Park Service, E-6.

[44] From the collection of Jan Olive Full. In "Bringin' Home the Bacon." The Rath Packing Company in Waterloo 1891-1985, p.2. Used with the permission of the City of Waterloo. http://www.cityofwaterlooiowa.com/Document_center/Planning/bringinhometheba con.pdf.

[45] Bultena, L. and Reasby, H. (1955). Negro-White Relations in the Waterloo Metropolitan Area. Cited in Munson, K. (July 13, 2015). Waterloo rallies to combat violence, racial divides. The Des Moines Register. Retrieved from http://tinyurl.com/hyuz5sq.

[46] Brief History of Black Hawk County. Retrieved from http://www.co.black-hawk.ia.us/DocumentCenter/View/564.

[47] Realtors Explain Position. Probe of "Race Climate" in Waterloo to Continue. (September 10, 1963). *Waterloo Daily Courier*, p. 19. This was the last classified advertising page.

[48] Ibid.

[49] Ibid.

[50] Ibid.

[51] Ibid.

[52] Ibid.

[53] Council Oks Resolution Calling for Open Housing. (November 20, 1963). *Waterloo Daily Courier*, pp. 1, 3. The word "Better" was incorrectly added to the committee's name in in the story.

[54] Committee Asks Inter-Racial Visits to Homes. (December 03, 1963). *Waterloo Daily Courier*, p. 8. The committee was identified as the Waterloo Committee on Racial Understanding in the story.

[55] Fugitive Slaves and Northern Racism. Judgment Day. PBS: Africans in America. Retrieved from http://www.pbs.org/wgbh/aia/part4/4narr3.html.

[56] Amendment XIV. Citizenship Rights, Equal Protection, Apportionment, Civil War Debt. Retrieved from https://constitutioncenter.org/interactive-constitution/amendments/amendment-xiv.

[57] Shelley v. Kraemer, 334 U.S. 1 (1948). Justia. US Supreme Court. Retrieved from https://supreme.justia.com/cases/federal/us/334/1/case.html.

[58] Walsh, K.C. (2007). Talking About Race: Community Dialogues and the Politics of Difference. Chicago: University of Chicago Press, 90.

[59] Redlining (1937- ). BlackPast.org: African American History. Retrieved from http://www.blackpast.org/aah/redlining-1937.

[60] Ibid.

[61] The Racist Housing Policy That Made Your Neighborhood. (May 22, 2014.) Madrigal, A.C. The Atlantic: Business. Retrieved from http://tinyurl.com/ze963gd.

[62] For additional information, read Federal Lending and Redlining. McGann, S. and Dougherty, J. On the Line: How Schooling, Housing, and Civil Rights Shaped Hartford and it Suburbs (2015 edition). Epress. https://epress.trincoll.edu/ontheline2015/chapter/federal-lending-and-redlining/.

[63] The Racist Housing Policy That Made Your Neighborhood.

[64] Redlining (1937- ).

[65] A 'Forgotten History' of How the U.S. Government Segregated America. (May 3, 2017 12:47 PM ET). Gross, T. NPR: Fresh Air: Race. Retrieved from http://www.npr.org/2017/05/03/526655831/a-forgotten-history-of-how-the-u-s-government-segregated-america.

[66] Shelley v. Kraemer, 334 U.S. 1. (1948). U.S. Supreme Court. Argued January 15-16, 1948. Decided May 3, 1948.

[67] Making the second ghetto: Race and housing in Chicago, 1940-1960. (1993, 1998). Hirsch, A. R. Chicago, IL: University of Chicago Press, 211-212.

[68] Brief History of Black Hawk County.

[69] Meatpackers: An Oral History of Black Packinghouse Workers and Their Struggle for Racial and Economic Equality. (1999). Halpern, R. and Horowitz, R. New York: NY: Monthly Review Press, 120.

[70] Porter was elected a UPWA trustee a year after he went to work at Rath, and served as divisional steward, financial secretary and vice president. In 1973, he left Rath to launch community-based African American radio station KBBG. Meatpackers, 128.

[71] Negro-White Relations in the Waterloo Metropolitan Area. (1955). Bultena, L. and Reasby, H. Cited in *Talking About Race: Community Dialogues and the Politics of Difference.* (2007). Walsh, K.C. Chicago: University of Chicago Press, 90.

[72] Trial Halted. Fred Roberts Case Put Off Until Monday. (January 28, 1949). *Waterloo Daily Courier*, 1.

[73] Ibid.

[74] Jury Frees Roberts. (February 02, 1949). *Waterloo Daily Courier*, Front Page.

[75] Rath Strike Trials Begin Tomorrow. (September 12, 1948). *Waterloo Daily Courier*, Front Page.

[76] Ten Best Waterloo Stories. (December 29, 1949). Editorials, *Waterloo Daily Courier*, 3.

[77] Meatpackers, 129.

[78] Bringin' Home the Bacon. The Rath Packing Company in Waterloo 1891-1985. (2010). Conard, R., 8.

[79] Ibid.

[80] This is the definitive source for the stories of the Baby Boomer blacks' parents who were involved in the 1948 Rath Packing Company strike about what life was like in Waterloo in the 1940s and 1950s. It's a prequel, in a sense, to *The Bridge Between*. Meatpackers, 119-120.

[81] U.S. Census Bureau. Washington, D.C.: U.S. Department of Commerce. Data retrieved from https://web.archive.org/web/20141224151538/http://www.census.gov/population/www/documentation/twps0056/twps0056.html.

[82] Table 1. Annual Estimates of the Resident Population for the United States, Regions, States, and Puerto Rico: April 1, 2010 to July 1, 2017 (December 2017) Washington, D.C.: U.S. Department of Commerce, U.S. Census Bureau, Population Division. Retrieved from https://view.officeapps.live.com/op/view.aspx?src=https://www2.census.gov/programs-surveys/popest/tables/2010-2017/state/totals/nst-est2017-01.xlsx.

[83] Race-based legislation in the North 1807 – 1850. People & Events. PBS: *Africans in America*. Retrieved from http://www.pbs.org/wgbh/aia/part4/4p2957.html. *Africans in America* Narrative Writers. Retrieved from http://www.pbs.org/wgbh/aia/credits.html.

# *TBB* 3: Guess Who's Coming to Class?

*If you don't name something you can act like it doesn't exist. The South had to deal with the heritage of slavery more often, more openly and more publicly than the North did. The North could act like "it's not really happening here." To this day, we're more aware of the heritage of races and Jim Crow racism in the South. I don't know how to compare northern and southern racism. How to rank them. I guess there's some distinctions in terms of their wickedness. [WHS 69 WM]*

*One person told me I couldn't possibly have gone to East High because it was all black. [EHS 68 WF]*

Three facts about Waterloo are central to understanding the community, the school system and its high schools from 1963-1973.

1.  Waterloo was a town separated physically, socioeconomically, socially and racially by the Cedar River virtually from its founding.
2.  Except for less than one percent of the town's black residents, blacks lived on the East Side of Waterloo and were segregated there de jure.
3.  Virtually all black students in Waterloo attended East Side schools.

We're all products of our environments. These interconnected physical, sociocultural, socioeconomic and educational environments had an impact on those of us who graduated from Waterloo high schools, who we are as people and our lives.

The side of the Cedar River on which someone lived in Waterloo meant being assigned a community label of "blue-collar poor Eastsider" or "white-collar rich Westsider." Eastsiders were expected to be less prejudiced, having experienced interracial relationships growing up and in the schools. West Side schools were perceived as academically superior, with better teachers, facilities, equipment and educational materials, which meant students were expected to perform at a higher level.

60

Attitudes, opinions and beliefs are created, shaped and nurtured by parents, family, society, friends and groups. They're also an effect of personal first-hand experiences.

By the time we entered high school in Waterloo, our attitudes, opinions and beliefs about race and ethnicity were already formed.

## *"Daddy, She Has Black Skin."*

*I am a Negro. My skin is white, my eyes are blue, my hair is blond. The traits of my race are nowhere visible on me. . . . I am not white. There is nothing within my mind and heart which tempts me to think I am. Yet I realize acutely that the only characteristic which matters to either the white or the colored race – the appearance of whiteness – is mine. –* Walter White (1893-1955)[1]

Figure 1 Walter White (1893-1955)

*NAACCP Asst. Executive Secretary, 1918-1931, NAACP Executive Secretary, 1931-1955*

Put 10 healthy babies with the same birthdate from 10 different ethnicities and cultures in a row of cribs, and the only differences between them would be physical appearance. The odds any of us could correctly identify the race or ethnicity[1] of any of

[1] The U.S. Census Bureau defines "race" as "a person's self-identification with one or more social groups. . . . White, Black or African American, Asian, American Indian and Alaska Native, Native Hawaiian and Other Pacific Islander, or some other race." Ethnicity "determines whether a person is of Hispanic origin or not. . . . Hispanic or Latino and Not Hispanic or Latino. Hispanics may report as any race." Retrieved from https://www.census.gov/mso/www/training/pdf/race-ethnicity-onepager.pdf. From a sociological perspective, race and ethnicity are a social construct: an idea invented by people who accept it as natural and obvious which may or may not represent reality. A "race" is a group of people grouped by physical appearance and characteristics which usually a result from genetic ancestry, but whose DNA is insignificantly different from any other race. An ethnic group is a population whose

them is infinitesimal. They all make the same noises, the same kinetic movements, their eyes track bright objects in the same way, they respond to tactile and aural stimuli the same way.

*... babies the world over, each exposed to thousands of disparate languages from birth, reward their mothers with roughly the same first word starting with the letter "m". . . .[2] the genetic difference between individual humans today is minuscule – about 0.1%, on average. . . .[3] Ultimately, there is so much ambiguity between the races, and so much variation within them, that two people of European descent may be more genetically similar to an Asian person than they are to each other.[4]*

Babies are race and ethnic and culture and skin-color-blind. They begin to recognize familiar faces and different ones as early as three months old. And by four months, their "brains already process faces at nearly adult levels. . . ."[5]

*When you're a child, it's apparent there are all different shades of people – black, white, yellow, brown. As a child, you don't look at the color of individual skin. [EHS 73 AAM]*

Awareness of differences between self and others is inevitable; humans are different in myriad ways. Recognition of skin-color differences happens at a younger age for some than for others. Many of us remember our first experiences of recognizing these differences and even pointing them out.

We were living in Fullerton, California, when our son – who is Thai by birth – was four and had a part-time Jamaican nanny. While he and I were driving her home one day, he blurted out matter-of-factly, "Daddy, she has black skin." The young woman laughed, unembarrassed. "Uh-huh," she told him. "And you have brown skin, your mommy has white skin and your daddy has olive skin. We all

members identify with each other through common nationality or shared cultural traditions, which is its ethnicity.

have color." He'd already moved on to calling out the names of the various fast-food restaurants we were passing based on their signs.

Exposure to and recognition there a people of different color are the first steps in becoming color blind or prejudiced. For most of us in Waterloo, that occurred at an early age.

Our personal experiences in that recognition are a powerful influence.

*As a young child, I noticed the man who operated the elevator in the department store was black. My mother told me to just thank the gentleman for my ride and always be polite when anyone helped me in any way, such as the black doormen who also were there.* [COL 66 WF]

*The first black person I remember was a black man when I was nine or 10 years old in the elevator at Black's Department store. I remember my mother looking at me with "Don't say anything" in her eyes. The message was you don't look at them, you don't talk to them.* [WHS 68 WF]

*When I was about six years old, my parents hired a black man come to our house to hang wallpaper. I was surprised my parents let a black man come into our house, because I thought black people were bad and scary. It turned out he was exceedingly nice to my younger sisters and me. This really surprised me and confused me because of the negative impressions I had. I'm sure these impressions came from my parents, my neighborhood and my school community.* [COL 66 WF]

*Before we moved to Waterloo, I lived in West Union in northeast Iowa, a town of about 2,500 people [roughly 60 miles to the northeast]. When I was in elementary school, our family would drive to Waterloo to shop. My grandmother said to me "Now when you're in Waterloo, you may see people who look different than you. They have dark skin. You must not stare at them. Do not stare at them."* [EHS 66 WF]

*We lived in a small town about 40 miles south of Waterloo. My first exposure to African Americans was when Mom and Dad took us shopping here. To me they were foreign, not white. My parents said they*

*were from Africa, but they never prejudiced me against black folks.*
*[WHS 69 WM]*

*I knew from the time I was a child about people of color. My parents*
*bought me a black baby doll when I was seven or eight, in the late 1950s.*
*My parents were not at all prejudiced in any way against blacks. I knew*
*there were people of different skins and it never made any difference to*
*me. [EHS 67 WF]*

*We had a housekeeper before kindergarten who was African*
*American. The fact her skin was a different color made no difference to*
*me. When I was older, I realized that other people saw black skin as a*
*negative factor and I resisted that notion. [WHS 68 WM]*

*When I was seven, we would see stuff on TV about the riots and*
*things going on down south in Mississippi. I didn't understand it. I asked*
*my mother, "You mean people really don't like me because of the color of*
*my skin?" I looked at the skin on my arm and it blew me away people*
*wouldn't like me because of my color. [EHS 73 AAF]*

For many *TBB* contributors, exposure to and recognition of people
from different races occurred when we started school.

When my parents bought their first house, I'd completed the first
half of 2nd grade at all-white Whittier Elementary on the West Side.
The house was on the East Side, on Lincoln Street just north of the
Illinois Central (IC) railroad tracks.

My mom enrolled me in Longfellow Elementary about five blocks
south, which was predominantly black. The first couple of weeks was
an adjustment, more because I was the new kid mid-year than the fact
that I was one of the few white students. Friendships developed with
the black kids whose homes were around the school and we even
played together during the summer.

*We didn't know at Longfellow that we [whites] were the minority.*
*We didn't know what minorities were. There were boys and there were*
*girls. And we [girls] had to wear dresses. [EHS 67 WF]*

*Lincoln Elementary [East Side] was all white, but there was one Mexican student who lived 3-4 blocks down from us. It was no big deal. All we knew was his family had a Mexican background and his mom made the best tortillas. He was just one of us, just another neighborhood kid. There was an adjustment going from there to Logan Junior High. The dark skin was something new. But we also had a lot of strange kids to get to know because they came from the other elementary schools. [EHS 63 WF]*

*I was in kindergarten at Hawthorne Elementary [East Side] when I first became aware of differences between me and blacks. A black girl used to walk to school with me and protect me from bullies. My family joked about my little black girl friend. In 4ᵗʰ grade, I asked Mike, a black friend, to join the Cub Scout den my mother was den mother for. I found out what racism was when three members dropped out. And Mike dropped out. [EHS 67 WM]*

In the fall after I'd finished second grade at Longfellow, Mom took me to open house to meet my teacher. But I wasn't on the 3ʳᵈ grade roster. She was told we lived on "the wrong side of the tracks" to attend Longfellow. I was supposed to have been attending Roosevelt Elementary that spring, which was three blocks north and four blocks east of our house. For the second time in less than half a year, I was the new kid. But I wasn't in a white minority; Roosevelt was less than half black.

*There was an adopted student in our 5th-grade class at Roosevelt, and the fact she was adopted was more of a curiosity than race ever was to many of us. [EHS 66 AAF]*

I still remember her name, because in that day "adoption" was not only a curiosity, but carried somewhat of a stigma with it.

For other Waterloo high school graduates, first exposure to someone of another race occurred when their families moved to Waterloo after they'd been in school elsewhere.

*I went to school in an all-white community in southeast Minnesota near the Iowa border until junior high. But I knew about blacks long before I met any of them. My mother was very committed to civil rights. I was a reader. She would give me a book to read about racial issues, and we'd talk about it at bedtime. One time she told me if I was just a little bit older, we would go and ride the buses for civil rights. She wouldn't go alone. But we never did. [EHS 66 WF]*

*I was very good friends with a young black man. Coming from a smaller town and school with no blacks, I didn't have a lot of the baggage about race the kids growing up in Waterloo had. [EHS 66 WF]*

*I lived in Milwaukee until we moved to Waterloo when I was in junior high. The neighborhood there was multiracial, but we were Catholic and attended Catholic school. My younger brother and I were the only blacks. One of my best friends and a young male in school with us were Puerto Rican. Everyone knew your color. So, I knew my race and who I was. We were never treated any differently than any of the other kids. There was no prejudice toward us. [EHS 73 AAF]*

For some, racial awareness didn't occur until junior high – grades 7-9 – when they moved up from an all-white elementary school.

*I remember the first black student who came to West Junior. She sat next to me in the auditorium for some meeting. She was a regular person. I had to reevaluate the fear of blacks that had been put into me. It didn't fit. They're just normal people with different color skin. At that point, I started my broadening my thinking and tried to get my family on board with it. [WHS 68 WF]*

Two people were sensitized to differences between blacks and whites by the book *Black Like Me.*

*My first experience with blacks was in early elementary school. But my most profound experience was in junior high when I read and reported on the book "Black Like Me." I was just so shocked. I had no idea there was that kind of discrimination. I started really thinking about my black classmates and friends. Many their families had moved here from Mississippi and over summer break they would go south to visit family. They were aware of how things were. I wasn't. That book caused me to start to realize how far north discrimination had come. [EHS 68 WF]*

*I read "Black Like Me." It was incredible. Don't remember how I found it. It wasn't a course assignment. But it opened my eyes. I was talking to a co-worker a couple of weeks ago about it. I don't know how it came up, but she'd never heard of the book. [WHS 69 WF]*

Ethnic marketing was a unit in every college marketing class I taught. In the summer 2014 semester, a class was discussing the president of the NAACP chapter in Spokane, Washington, who was white, but had passed herself off successfully for years as African American. She'd been outed by her parents as genetically being and having been raised as white.

The class was roughly 35% white, 65% black, and the students all got into the discussion about whether she should be the head of an NAACP chapter based on her genetics or her performance.

No one had read *Black Like Me*, so I gave a Cliff Notes version of John Howard Griffin's story. A middle-aged white man committed to racial justice, he wanted to experience life as a black to understand the black experience. He had his skin dermatologically altered so he looked black and set out to explore the black community. I related how shocked he was at the depth of the overt prejudice, oppressive behavior and racial slurs he experienced.

One of young black men was a good student, good looking with personality plus to whom both blacks and white responded, and who was a social leader in the school.

He immediately scoffed, rocked his chair back and said I'd made the whole thing up. "There's no white person who would change their skin to black and go into black society." Someone else brought up Michael

Jackson – "He went and turned himself white" – and the discussion
spun off into an entirely new direction. The conclusion was the
woman's genetics in the Spokane case shouldn't be relevant, but the
fact she had falsely passed herself off on job applications as African
American wasn't acceptable.

## Enculturation of Racial Attitudes: Parents and Family

*[Color prejudice] is nothing more than the unreasoning hatred of one
race for another, the contempt of the stronger and richer peoples for
those whom they consider inferior to themselves and the bitter
resentment of those who are kept in subjection and are so frequently
insulted. As colour is the most obvious outward manifestation of race it
has been made the criterion by which men are judges, irrespective of
their social or educational attainments. The light-skinned races have
come to despise all those of a darker colour, and the dark-skinned people
will no longer accept without protest the inferior position to which they
have been relegated.[6]*

"Enculturation" is the $64 word for how we gradually learn the norms
and behaviors of culture as part of the socialization process as we grow
up.

*We're still obsessed with race. People don't look at people as people.
You're stereotyped. And that's who you are. It's not just black and white.
There are a lot of people who make snap judgments and jump on the
bandwagon. It's sad. We don't figure out what really is there before we
decide. We just, "Snap. OK. That's the way it's going to be." [EHS 72
WF]*

These interactions occur in our primary social environments –
family, neighborhood, school, church, synagogue or mosque – with
parents and family, friends and peers, teachers, ministers and lay
leaders, co-workers and others.

Comments of *TBB* contributors are rich in their awareness and
insights of the interactions affected their biases and prejudices about

68

ethnicity and race in high school and, 50 years later, throughout their adult lives.

From birth, parents and family are powerful influencers and role models. We learn from their instructions, guidance, comments and behavior, often couched in "Do as I say and not as I do." Sometimes our biases and prejudices are a modification of or the opposite of what parents and family recommend for whatever reason.

**'63-'66** *My parents were people of character and principle. I was taught God loves everyone and you should treat others like you want to be treated. They taught me not to call people names. [EHS 63 WF]*

*When my brother was very young, he developed a lung infection. This was before penicillin and mother had to take him to Texas where it would be warm all the time. She was about 19 and had family there. When she would walk the town and a black man approached her on the sidewalk, he would step into the street so that she, a white woman, could walk by. When she passed, he'd get back up on the sidewalk. She said it was so hard for her to go through that. I was in junior high before I really understood it. [EHS 63 WF]*

*I knew when you crossed the Mason-Dixon line going from Iowa to Louisiana – you had two bathrooms for men and two for women, one for blacks and one for whites. On the ferry boats, there would be the colored area and a white area. I didn't understand why. Nobody in the family really explained it. They were prejudiced. [EHS 64 WM]*

*When I was seven in 1955, we lived on Iowa Street [in the North End] and a black family moved in next to us with lots of kids. My parents sat us down to tell us we were not allowed to talk or play with them. [COL 66 WF]*

*My dad told me things about being black. Telling me to be careful where you go. Don't talk a lot. Don't look white people in the eye. And I had to tell my younger brothers. [EHS 66 AAM]*

*During the civil rights movement in the 60s, my dad told me, "If I were younger, I don't know I could be just sitting in. I think 100 years after the Emancipation Proclamation, I would probably take it to the streets." He was black and adopted me when he married my mom. [EHS 66 WM]*

**'67-'70** *My parents talked about differences between black and white. "You're just as good as anybody." "Don't let anyone disrespect you." "You're going to have to work 2-3 times as hard to get recognized." "These white kids may be your friends in school, but they're not going to be your friends through life." "You played together in grade school. They won't talk to you when you get to junior high. They talked to you in junior high, they won't talk to you in high school. Some of your friends are going to college with you and they won't have anything to do with you. And those going to other schools, that will be the end of the friendship." There was always an assumption the whites you had known and were friend would abandon you in the different phases of your life. For the most part, that didn't play out. I don't know whether it was because who my brother and I are, our friends are or both. When I talk to my brother, he'll say, "I saw so-and-so," someone I was in KG with, "and they said tell you 'hello.'" One of my closest friends today is the second person I met in kindergarten and I was the only black in the class. I tell her to say "hello" to the whole family. [EHS 68 AAF]*

*I think my parents were a four on a 1-5 scale in terms of racism ["5" being racist.]. When I was younger, I'd gone bowling one night with a friend and a large group of kids, including blacks. I'd been out at events before where a bunch of us, blacks and whites, went out for coffee afterward. She was very disgusted with me that I'd been out with black people in public. "There's nothing wrong with black people. They're just as good as we are. But we don't mix with them socially." I would question that, and she would insist they have their group and we have ours. And they don't mix. I argued that "the Bible says love thy neighbors." And she said, "Oh, they can be our neighbors. But we don't mix with them socially." She kept repeating that phrase. They mellowed. Dad's gone now and Mom's not as strident as she was. [EHS 69 WF]*

*I went to a recreation program when I was in primary school in a community center on the East Side. Every Saturday morning we would drive over there from the West Side. We kids commented about how some of the houses were more rundown and not as well maintained as where we lived. My father said, "Look at the cars. They're newer and fancier." We talked about peoples' values. That their cars and clothing are more important than their houses because they take cars with them in public. It was more of a conversation about why somebody black or white might not take good a care of their house. [WHS 69 WF]*

*My parents taught us all people were God's children and should be treated equally, but there wasn't a single black face in our church or in my Girl Scout troop. My ballet teacher at the YWCA was black. I wonder now years later, whether her being black was why such a talented person was teaching at the YWCA. [EHS 69 WF]*

*The first African-American family moved into our neighborhood in Des Moines in the early 1960s when I was in the 3rd grade. My parents were pro-integration. In our house, the comment was, "This is a great thing. It's about time." [WHS 70 WF]*

**'71-'73** *My brother, sister and I were brought up to look at blacks like they're people just like everybody else, they're part of our society. We just get along. You have to watch what you say sometimes. When you're kidding around, you have to know who you're kidding with. That's like with anybody when you merge with any school. [EHS 71 WM]*

*I was about 10 years old attending a basketball game in Illinois with my family when people in the crowd started yelling "alligator bait" at the black players on the floor. I had never heard that before and didn't understand why they were yelling that. I asked Dad what that meant and he said, "They are yelling at the black players and that is NOT what we do. It is NOT how we talk about other people, no matter how they are different from us." [EHS 72 WF]*

*My dad was a police officer in Cedar Falls. And he would tell me stories about when he would enter a home as a minority police officer. They'd look at him funny, call him the "n" word and tell him to get out of the house. He didn't have a racial bone in his body. And that's the reasons why we kids are the way we are. [EHS 73 AAM]*

*I had a greater rapport with the African American kids than I did some of the white kids in our mixed neighborhood. My mother was married to an African American man. She had a lot of friends who were African American. It seemed to be the natural thing. We gravitated more to some of those people than some of the white people who seemed to be a little snootier. I think the fact I had biracial parents had something to do with it. It seemed like they just didn't want to be bothered with anyone they saw as a lower class than them. That's how it always came across to me as a kid. I never really saw race back then. Years later, you look back and say, "Maybe it was because of race." But my mom and my sister taught me that, regardless of their color, they're still people. [EHS 73 WM]*

Some of what we learn from parents is less of "do what I say" and more of observing what they do.

**'63-'66** *My father was the most non-prejudiced man I ever knew so I never picked up prejudice from him or my mother. They came from dirt poor depression-era people. I never heard a racist term, a racist remark or even criticism of people from my parents. When I heard someone use the "n-word," it shocked me. I wondered how someone could even say that about someone they didn't even know. If you're going to dislike somebody, dislike them because they have lousy personal qualities. Not because by some accident of birth they were born of a certain color or race or sex. [EHS 66 WM]*

*I had really good role models. My parents were big on not being judgmental toward other people. They had a lot of black friends from Rath Packing. During the holidays, blacks were in and out of our house all the time if they didn't have somewhere else to go. One couple among my parents' good friends was biracial, a white woman and a black man, which was extremely frowned upon back in the day. But I could never get either of their boys to talk to me at school and I never knew why. [EHS 66 WF]*

*Because I wasn't exposed to blacks in school and race wasn't discussed in school, my only perspectives were created by my family's values – all people were equal and should being treated as I would want to be treated. That we're all the same – black, brown or other. That's the way we were brought up. I knew about prejudice because of my grandfather's strong dislike of "coloreds," but my grandmother's influence on me never made that an issue while growing up. [WHS 66 WM]*

*It's interesting that, given the way my parents felt about blacks, I married a Jamaican and my brother married a black girl. Kind of weird. My father said, "I'm glad [my daughter] found a man who takes really good care of her and the kids. It's just too bad he had to be black." [EHS 66 WF]*

**'67-'70** *I don't recall conversations with my parents about black-white relations in Waterloo. One time when I was eight or nine, my mother and some of her sisters were discussing a Waterloo Courier article about a farmer from north of Waterloo who'd been arrested in the North End. They were all, "You know what that means." I didn't hear the word "prostitute," but as I got older and learned the North End was primarily the black district, I put it together and knew what they thought. [EHS 68 WF]*

**'71-'73** *My grandfather was grumpy and an equal-opportunity racist who hated everybody. My father, who was a cop, was the antithesis of that. He was more accepting.*

*Gregarious. He'd talk with anyone. And he dealt with all kinds of people.*
*[COL 71 WF]*

"Back in the day" was a frequent expression by *The Bridge Between*
contributors, particularly when setting up a story about being in the
work environment with parents before "Take a Child to Work Day"
became official.

*My father was in business, so I grew up around an environment*
*where he was dealing with adult males. They were all ranges of*
*socioeconomic status, but were white. I saw how people reacted, rich,*
*middle-class or poor. He had no more than two or three colored clients,*
*as they were called in that day. [EHS 63 WF]*

*White truck drivers used to call my dad "Nigger Dan" because he was*
*friends with black drivers. Back in the day, to work on federal projects*
*you had to have two blacks in every 10 drivers. He hired two and never*
*had to hire anyone else. He taught me real young you don't have to be*
*black to be a nigger. To him, it was a matter of attitude. He taught me*
*that, if people treated him decent, he treated them decent. If you come*
*up with an attitude to him, you were going to see an attitude back. He*
*told me, "There are a lot of niggers who aren't black." It was just a*
*derogatory term to him that didn't mean you had to be black. [WHS 64*
*WM]*

*My grandfather owned a poultry business and then a bakery. When I*
*was four or five, he'd take me with him when he made deliveries to the*
*East Side of town. He had stores and restaurants he delivered chickens*
*to. So, I was very aware of people who weren't white. We talked in my*
*family all the time about how we were Indian [Native American] on my*
*grandfather's side of the family. [EHS 66 WF]*

*My father had a Varsity Cleaners route delivering cleaning on the*
*East Side. He was in the black neighborhood a lot and during the*
*summer, when I was younger, I'd sometimes ride along with him. There*
*was one black lady who had two or three kids my age, and her house*

*always smelled so good, because she was always baking cookies. She said her name was "Fannie" and she would always give me a cookie she'd just baked. She was the first black person I ever had an interaction with and it was positive. [WHS 67 WM]*

For some *TBB* contributors, their parents and family members were at the far-right end of the prejudice continuum.

**'63-'66** *I had a black friend I walked to elementary school with and she was so sweet. But when I started junior high, my family wanted me to end the relationship, I am sad to admit. Not because they didn't like her, but because they were afraid some kids would take it the wrong way that I had a black friend. I'm sure it was the way parents of a white girl thought back then. I never said anything like this to my children. Their friends were always welcome at our house, no matter their race. [EHS 65 WF]*

*I had a black friend from the neighborhood who would come into our house. My dad wasn't crazy about my friend, just because he was black. Dad was there when the white guy was killed at Rath's by the black guy [in the 1948 union strike]. He came a long way over the years. We got him to say "colored" instead of the "n" word. My mother wasn't prejudiced. She didn't like the Japanese, but that was because of the war. [COL 66 WM]*

*My parents taught me one thing, but they acted totally the opposite. I went to Grace Methodist [at the head of 5th Street on the East Side at the south edge of the North End] and was always told it doesn't matter what your color is, you love everybody. My parents weren't really like that. I had a number black friends at school. Never had any problems with black kids. But it was understood from the time I was in Logan Junior I didn't bring them home. It wasn't something we talked about, it was just something that was understood. I don't know why. It just was. And I never went to their homes. [EHS 66 WF]*

*My dad was a doctor and he taught us we're all the same – black, brown or other. That's the way we were brought up. But his father was a huge racist. Back in those days, no blacks were allowed to live on the East Side of Logan Avenue. There was a rental house across the street from my grandfather's house. He and the guy who lived next door to the rental house sold it back and forth to each other over the years so they could control who rented it. I looked up to my father more than my grandfather. [WHS 66 WM]*

*One of the black athletes at East watched out for me. One time he called the house to talk. My dad answered and maybe he could tell by his speech he was black. My dad told him never to call the house again. And then he talked to me about it. The boy never called my house again out of respect for my father's wishes. [EHS 66 WF]*

*In junior high, a friend's mother was going to take us to a ballgame, said I could bring a friend and I asked a black one. We were waiting for her after school at the McKinstry parking lot door and the Mom asked who I'd invited. She was shocked when I told her. "She's black." I said, "Yah." She came unglued and said, "You just don't do that." I asked why? "She's black," was the answer. I was appalled and cowed. So, we left without my black friend. The next day my friend I'd invited was mad at me, even though I explained we had waited for her at the parking lot door. She'd misunderstood where we were meeting and had been at the front door of the school. I don't think she believed me. There was a rift for a while. [EHS 66 WF]*

**'67-'70** *In grade school, I walked home with a brother and sister who were black. One day they wanted to see a Christmas present I'd gotten. I brought them home, and went in and told my mom, because I was supposed to say beforehand if I was bringing anybody home. And she told me I shouldn't have brought them to our house. I never ever knew my mom to be prejudiced. She'd always taught us to be respectful and not ever use any words that were against black people. I didn't know what to say. She didn't want me to bring them in.*

*But I always walked home with them and they were my friends. It surprised me. She never explained why to my satisfaction. We talked about it later in life. "I didn't know that about you, Mom." I was embarrassed for her because I'd had to leave them on our steps. She grew up on a farm from way up north in northern Iowa [just south of the Minnesota border]. She wasn't really used to blacks. [OHS 67 WF]*

*One summer I went to North Carolina with another family from the West Side. The mother's father was the mayor of the town. We went to visit him at city hall, and they had a black fountain and a white fountain with signs. I went to use the black fountain and quickly got pulled away. "Don't do that," I was told in a whisper. And then we went to Charlotte to the shopping mall. And they had bathrooms for black women and white women, and black men and white men. I started to go into the restroom for the black women as a protest. A relative of the family put a hand on my shoulder and said, "No, dear, you don't do that." I said, "I don't think this is right." So, my feelings about discrimination started before I ever went to East High. [EHS 67 WF]*

*You could never talk to my dad about the fact I was interacting with African-American students at school and I didn't see anything different about them. I talked to my mom about it. And then she'd say, "Well, you can't date them." [WHS 68 WF]*

*My dad was extremely racist. Mom was much more liberal. But she still had some problems with race. There weren't blacks in Minnesota where my dad grew up, so I think he got it from work at John Deere. How he talked about blacks, used the "n word." Later in life when the first blacks moved into the block, he was very, very upset. And there were so few at West, we just didn't have a chance to associate with them. My dad changed his prejudice later in life, because my sister has two biracial grandchildren and my daughter has three biracial children. It took him a while to have any contact with them. But after he got to know them and saw they were just like the white grandchildren, he did change some. He accepted them, finally, and I think that changed his perception about black people somewhat. He did apologize to some of us kids for some of his earlier behavior. My mom was much a more understanding person, more open. My mom also apologized later for her behavior when we were younger. There really was a change in their beliefs. I didn't take on the same values as my parents. I was more open. And I think it's because I was exposed to segregation living in Waterloo. [WHS 68 WF]*

*I had black girlfriends at East. I could be acquainted with them at school, but that's where it stayed. My parents thought a black friend might have a brother and "you know what those black men are like." So, I didn't bring black friends home. Five years later, when my brother was in high school, he had black friends and brought them home. Because Mom didn't have a girl in the house. One night a large group of black people were marching a half a block down from our house on the East Side in a white neighborhood. My mom called the police and said, "There are 50 niggers running down the street." They went on by and nothing happened. [EHS 68 WF]*

*In the fourth grade, the teacher asked me to copy the names of the kids into her grade book. And she marked "Dark" by all the ones who were black. And the mothers on our block would say, "Oh, so-and-so's kid is in a really dumb class. It's more than half black." Of course, they didn't use the word "black." [EHS 68 WF]*

**'71-'73** *My mom told a story about when she was a little kid playing on her front step on Dawson Street [on the East Side]. Her friend was a little black boy. And my grandmother came out with a broom and shooed him. "Shoo, shoo, run along." Nothing terribly aggressive, but overt. My mom's family would have been glad to move someplace where they would have less contact with African American people day-to-day. [WHS 70 WM]*

*My parents weren't prejudiced. My dad worked with blacks because he was a garbage man. But my grandmother was terribly prejudiced. She lived on Franklin near the railroad tracks [on the East Side] and any time she'd see a black person out her apartment window, she'd go,*

78

*"Damn nigger." And I'd tell her she didn't know them. That came from my Baptist upbringing. I was always "don't condemn somebody until you know about them." That's one thing I can't stand, is when people make judgments before they know the person. Anyone who's lazy and stupid, whether you're white, black or native American or whatever, you're judged a nigger. There are white niggers as well as blacks. My mom's grandmother lived in Cedar Falls, had immigrated from Sicily and was also prejudiced. [EHS 70 WF]*

*My dad was very prejudiced. But I don't remember him ever say anything blatantly racist about blacks. My dad worked with them at Rath's. But he was prejudiced against other groups of people. It was OK to say negative things about Catholics. And the rule was, "You can't marry this boy or that boy unless he becomes a Lutheran. And you can't marry a Catholic." My mom was a typical, stay-at-home mom, baked cookies, was a Girl Scout leader. She was pretty insulated and didn't have opinions about people. The people she went to church with, the girls in the scout troop were all white. She didn't have a lot of interaction with black people. [EHS 70 WF]*

*My dad was very racist; he used the "n-word" all the time. He made it be known that, if I ever dated a black guy, I'd be in big trouble. I ignored what he said. My mom, on the other hand, was quite the opposite. Some of her best friends were black ladies. She was the one that had a blind eye to it. [WHS 71 WF]*

*High school was a confusing time. We were going to school in a high-tension ERAand we needed to be open-minded to very one regardless of skin color. My parents told me, "You have to go to school with them, you have to work with them, but you don't have to be friends with them." I never understood that. If some was my friend in school or work, why they not be my friend away from these settings? Because I grew up on the East Side and attend East High, I'm a more open-minded person. Being my friend has nothing to do with the color of your skin; it's based on how you interact with and respond to me. That's from East High. [EHS 72 WF]*

---

*I was really good friends with a white girl. We were allowed to go to each other's house, but when I went to her house, I was never allowed inside. And I didn't think anything of it. When she came to my house, she'd have dinner with us. And I asked my mother one day why she could come into our house, but I wasn't allowed to go into hers. My mother didn't know that was happening. She must have said something to her parents, because after that, we never went to each other's house. It's never the kids, it's the parents. [EHS 73 AAF]*

---

*My dad would come home and use the "n" word. But never in a mean nasty evil way. It was more of a generational type of thing. After high school, I had a relationship with a guy from Mexico City for almost five years. I remember dreading telling my dad. And when I introduced them, my boyfriend called himself a "wetback," which made my dad laugh, and that's all it took. I told my dad before he died, "One of your grandkids or great grandkids is going to marry a black. It's going to happen. That's just the way it is and the way the world is." And he said, "I suppose so." [CEN 73 WF]*

---

*Dad was more prejudiced than mom was about black people. He grew up in a town with ethnic neighborhoods and would make comments about black people on TV. Mom worked with blacks, had been raised with blacks. My sister wanted to date a black boy. But our parents blew up. Both parents said, "No way my daughter is dating a black guy." [EHS 73 WF]*

---

## Enculturation: First-Hand

### COMMUNITY EXPERIENCES

*When I was walking on campus in college one evening, a bus came by with some white high school kids, and one of them yelled out, "A walking, talking Tootsie roll." [COL 69 AAF]*

*When we get all caught up in this color stuff, we're all mutts, we're all immigrants. Like Rodney King said years ago, "Why can't we all just get along?" [EHS 73 AAM]*

First-hand experiences are powerful influences on our racial biases and prejudices.

Interactions with others result in consequences, positive or negative, which reinforce the adoption or avoidance of biases and prejudices.

We also develop biases and prejudices indirectly, through observation. We watch the interactions of others in a social group, and observe the consequences, which encourage or reinforce the adoption or avoidance of biases and prejudices.

Or we may also develop or modify our biases and prejudices so they're 180 degrees in the opposite direction.

Contributors' first-hand experiences range on the memory spectrum from positive to negative, with some neutrals in between. Which had a more lifelong effect was dependent on the individual. In recalling high school, negative memories surfaced first more frequently.

*I lived in an integrated neighborhood and had white classmates in elementary school. But if they were in the grocery store with their parents and saw me, they would ignore me and wouldn't speak with me. And I wondered why? Had something changed? It puzzled me for years until I finally figured it out. It was a racial thing. But I still don't know why. [EHS 66 AAF]*

The Ideal Dairy at the corner of Columbia and Dawson streets was in the center of the surrounding blue-collar East Side neighborhood. The neighborhood was divided by the Illinois Central railroad tracks that ran behind the dairy. Black families lived on the south side of the tracks toward Virden Creek and Longfellow Elementary. The north side of the tracks up to Logan Junior High was white.

Ideal made its own milk and ice cream from milk collected at area farms delivered every morning to the back of the dairy by big tanker trucks. The dairy's trucks delivered glass quarts to homes throughout the east side. I've never found butter brickle ice cream since. And their malts set the standard for me, which has rarely been equaled, much less surpassed.

The dairy had a small lot beside it where Christmas trees were sold. One year Santa Claus was there and an eight-year-old black girl who lived across the street begged her mother to be allowed to go.

*I was young enough to still believe in Santa and old enough to cross the street. I thought he had candy canes. Mom said "OK" and I was so excited. I ran and put my coat on, and when I got across the street, I kept calling out "Hey, Santa, Hey, Santa." He never acknowledged me. I didn't get a candy cane. It was one of my first experiences in realizing that I was different. [EHS 66 AAF]*

This story bothered me, because my family lived in the block just north of the tracks from Ideal. As the oldest, I became the family store-runner in 4th or 5th grade. I remember black families lived across the street from the dairy, and in the blocks to the south and west. They used the store and were always treated like everybody else.

There is no valid way to infer the relative importance of the positive or "good" high school memories from the negative or "bad" based on where they occurred in conversation with a contributor. Some tackled the easiest questions first – shared the "good" memories, before the bad. Others reversed the strategy and left the "good" memories until the more difficult, uncomfortable ones had been completed. A person could always use the *Family Feud* fast money "pass" option on a *TBB* question and return to it later.

*I first became aware of racial tension when my best friend, his girlfriend and I were in his car going down East 4th Street by the railroad yard. Someone threw a brick through the driver's side window, missed*

*my friend and hit his girlfriend in the side of the head. In broad daylight.*
*[WHS 66 WM]*

When my cousins from a small town near Sioux City came to visit
one time, we took my dad to work. We crossed over the river and were
going up East 4<sup>th</sup> Street. They were looking at the houses and asked, "Is
this where the Negroes live. I said, "Yes. This is the area where more of
them do." They said, "Oh, the poor Negroes." They were insulated in
their town, so I thought it was probably something they'd heard on TV.
There was a stop sign before we turned to go into the IC shop. When
Dad stopped, a black man walked over to the car, got a knife out of his
pocket, came up to my dad's window and was running his thumb over
the blade. My cousins' eyes couldn't have gotten any bigger. My dad
didn't roll down the window. We just went on. If the guy hadn't had the
knife out, my dad might have rolled the window. He worked every shift
there was. And he walked all the time to work. And I walked through
there to East, too. [OHS 67 WF]

When I was older, I listened to KBBG, the black radio station in
town. It was developed to have a black voice in the community. I liked
the gospel music. I would listen to the national news. And I can tell you
the national news on black KBBG was very different than what you
heard on white people TV. The lead story, everything was very different.
It was eye-opening. I never realized how much the news changed based
on who was reporting it. [EHS 74 WF]

## NEIGHBORHOOD EXPERIENCES
Neighborhoods are significant first-hand social learning turfs.

**'63-'66** When I was nine or 10, my family moved from the
West Side back to the East, on Franklin near Irving. It
was a residential area at the time with a lot of neighborhood kids
around. We even played with the kids across the street. There was a mix
of white and black families. Down the street was a black woman named
Jenny. I loved her and everything about that family because, as kind of

*crazy as your own family was, it was just one of those families you walked into and felt so accepted all the time. She would hug you and it was a hug like you never felt in your entire life. And to this day, I don't think I've ever had a hug like that. You just melted. You knew it was a wonderful place to be. So, I gravitated to that family. There was no discrimination in my life at that time. I didn't know what that word meant. I wasn't aware of skin color until I moved back to the West Side. I grew up in a neighborhood where we were all working class families. I think we were all kind of the same. There was no real difference, when I look back on it. I never felt we were different. And there was never a discussion in the neighborhood about black or white. Honest to God. [COL 63 WF]*

*When I lived on Cascaden [Avenue, in the North End that was eliminated in the East High campus project], I'd ride my bike down to the store on East 4th Street and some of the black kids would try to rob me because I had bread money or milk money. And they'd pull a knife on me. So, I ended up getting a bigger knife. That put a stop to that. They didn't bother me anymore. I was probably 12. [EHS 64 WM]*

**'67-'70** *When my friends and I were in junior high, we'd go down to the Cedar River when the water receded from the annual floods and stab the carp. There was a small black café on Independence Avenue [on the south edge of the North End]. We'd go to the back door, the cook would buy the carp for 25 cents each and smoke it. We weren't allowed into the place because we were white. They made us use the back door. [COL 68 WM].*

*When I was a kid growing up, I had friends that were very vocal about how they felt about blacks. Me being a farm kid just off the farm, I thought that was strange. "What did they do to you? Obviously, something bad happened or you wouldn't talk that way. Or use those terms to describe them." I just wanted to be accepted in the group, so I didn't challenge the thinking. As I got older, the vocal expressions and bad terms my friends used became less and less. But it was clear*

84

*segregation was accepted, if not okay. It was certainly tolerated in Waterloo. [WHS 69 WM]*

*In kindergarten, one of my black school friends brought his bike to my home to show me. Our neighbor lady called my mother and asked her, "Do you know your daughter is talking to a Negro boy?" My mother said she did and that he was just showing me his new bike. [EHS 70 WF]*

**'71-'73** *Our neighborhood was white, so we ran around with white kids. Lincoln Elementary [East Side] was almost all white. During the summer, we'd play basketball at Gates or somewhere else and we would see some of the minority kids. But up until we got to Logan Junior, it was kind of our own little white world. [EHS 71 WM]*

*In our neighborhood, we didn't know what color was. We called each other names you can't even use any more. They'd call us things and we'd call them things. I shared that story with my mom this morning [2016] and she said, "Oh, yeah, you guys didn't know you shouldn't use that word. We never told you. Because you were just kids and everybody got along." That's because the house we grew up in was the house my dad grew up in. With a lot of the same families he'd grown up with still there, working at Rath's. [EHS 72 WF]*

## School Experiences

*One of my first, indelibly etched memories of school is the little black boy sitting next to me in kindergarten who cried because he didn't know what scissors were. [EHS 69 WF]*

During our first five years of life, the family is the primary social group. When we start school, it becomes our new social system, and influences our attitudes and behavior. Eligibility criteria for kindergarten was later in the year in the *TBB* decade than it is now. So, students born in September and October, as I was, were able to start kindergarten before we turned five. The question many faced at the end of the day was, "So, how was school today? What did you learn?"

Much of it wasn't from textbooks, but from peer-to-peer and -group interactions.

Some contributors didn't classify first-hand experiences positive or negative, but just simply learning.

**'63-'66** *I first encountered blacks when I went from Jewett [virtually white] to McKinstry Junior. They weren't bad. I had many black friends through sports. I transferred to Logan junior my last quarter of 9th grade. There was a definite difference in the blacks at Logan to the blacks at McKinstry. Logan blacks we're more arrogant and trouble makers. The ones at McKinstry we're just classier and didn't act like they were owed anything. [EHS 64 WM]*

*My first conscious understanding of racism was the one black child who came into Black Hawk Elementary [West Side] in the third or fourth grade. She was in my scout troop. We played together and we were friends, as much as we could be, because she lived on the other side of the school from me. And in the classroom, I never thought of her as black. She wasn't there the next year and we asked the teacher where she was. Her family had decided to move to the East side where there were more black students. We didn't think too much about it, because we were kids. It was okay. I can understand someone wanting to be with people like them. But it wasn't long before it dawned on me what it must have been like for her. And did we do something, say something or something happened in the neighborhood that made it impossible for them to stay? [WHS 66 WF]*

*I'd seen black people at Gates pool in the summer, but I wasn't in school with any until I went to Logan Junior. I remember the first black students I encountered were three guys in crafts class. One was so funny, the class clown. One time early in the 8th grade he called me at home. I thought it was an "I like you call." I was shocked. It wasn't because he was black. It was because I didn't know why he thought I would want to hear from him. He could have been some white guy I didn't care for. It made it uncomfortable in class, because I didn't want him to think I didn't like him. I just didn't want him to call me. I wondered for years if I was prejudiced. And decided, no, he was just someone I didn't care to get a call from. [EHS 66 WF]*

**'67-'70** *When I was in 5$^{th}$ grade at Emerson [West Side], a black family moved into the neighborhood, from the East Side. They had three kids who started school about halfway through the semester. One was in the other 5th-grade class. Our lit teacher was reading us a book called "Mary Jane" about a black girl being integrated into a school in the South. The teacher didn't get to finish the book in the other 5$^{th}$ grade class because of the black girl. So, we didn't get to finish it in our class. There was a lot of talk among the white kids in my class their parents were talking about moving. People on our street were, too. [WHS 69 WF]*

*When I was in the 11th grade, Judge [William] Parker helped fund a program with the collaboration of smaller towns. They sent a bus load of youth to DC and NY. And I got to go. It changed my life. I had never seen brown people in business suits with briefcases. And bunches of them. Going into stores and working in businesses. I'd never seen that. You didn't see it in Waterloo. That was a major life-change for me. In our family, you went to college. But that dream wasn't enough, because I still couldn't conceptualize what the opportunities were. That experience was a life-changer. [EHS 70 AAF]*

A lot of the school stories were still difficult for people to share and evoked emotions a half-century later.

**'63-'66** *Going to Logan [East Side] was different. I came from a white community on the West Side and felt I was as good as anybody else. And I was called the "n word" by some of the whites and looked down on. I felt I was equal and just as good. Not only athletically, but in the classroom. I wanted to excel. I did have some good white friends. But I got involved with the wrong group, I had some things go awry and got in trouble. It seemed like some of my guys, black* *friends had other ideas about school. They didn't care too much about it. They went and wanted to get by, get it over with. I was disciplined when I got into trouble and couldn't participate with the basketball team for a few games. We were under the point system, for being there and participating. And when I couldn't participate, that was a kind of discipline. It set me back. And it kind of hurt. Because I really wanted to do well. [WHS 60 AAM]*

*My early years in school moving back and forth from Catholic school to public school was really hard. The teachers at Sacred Heart were mean. So much meaner than what we came from. Really mean. If you didn't do exactly what you were told to do or you stepped out of line, Sister had a stick. And she would hit you on the legs with a stick. It was really a scary time. [COL 63 WF]*

*I was 105 pounds, taught at an early age you don't back down from anybody and got into a lot of fights, mostly with black people. The last fight I got into was with this black kid in an 8th grade class. I forget the reason we fought. It wasn't racial. Just two guys who sat right next to each other just going at it in class. The teacher sent us down to the principal's office. We never did make it there. Walking down the hallway, we decided to go outside and have a cigarette instead. We went back to the class and the teacher asked if everything was okay. We said, "Fine." He and I became pretty good friends. [WHS 64 WM]*

*I attended Grant Elementary [East Side], which was basically all black, through part of the 6th grade. Then we moved and I finished at Frances Grout [East Side], which was primarily white. So, I had experienced transition from an all-black school before I got to 7th grade at McKinstry Junior. One thing which helped was that there was a summer track and field event in the area. Students would represent their schools there. When my brothers and I showed up, the guys we'd been school with at Grant picked on us because we were there for Grout. My two younger brothers and I got mad, and so, we competed in almost everything. And we took the trophy for Frances Grout. For a small period, our names were on a little-bitty plaque in the middle of Highland. Back during the time where the [Catholic] Bishop had his house there. They had the park there and our name was on a little plaque. [EHS 66 AAM]*

*In elementary school at Longfellow the white kids would hand out invitations for their birthday parties. And I don't remember ever getting one. Then they would talk about the party the next day or Monday. [EHS 66 AAF]*

*I liked elementary school, but we had what we called "old maid teachers." There was one in the fourth grade at Hawthorne [West Side] who was so ornery. One day a black girl brought her a little bouquet of dandelions. The teacher threw it in the garbage and yelled at her in front of the whole class [mimicking a severe voice], "Why would you bring a bunch of weeds to a teacher?" She just went on and on about it, and I felt so sorry for the girl. I thought it was just horrible a teacher would say something like that. The teacher told her not to bring her dandelions ever again. All through school, even high school, the girl never fixed up or dressed nice, was always so bashful, didn't talk to people and didn't have a lot of friends. I always wondered if the teacher just didn't do something to that girl. [EHS 66 WF]*

*I went to Lafayette [East Side], which wasn't integrated. There was my younger sister and myself, a couple of kids from one other family, and a few other African American kids in the remedial class. I fought a lot with people there. Some of it was kids just being kids. Some of it was racial. Some of it was instigated by the white students, but I probably carried a chip on my shoulder also. I wasn't the best student in school and had confrontations with teachers. Sometimes it was the teachers' reactions to my reaction to them. Moving up to McKinstry Junior was a little startling. You go through some identity issues. Most of the blacks lived in the North End and we didn't. I didn't encounter them on a daily basis until junior high. I got pushback all the time from the other blacks because I lived outside the North End. [EHS 66 AAM]*

**'67-'70**   *When I was at Longfellow, a black girl told me she was going to meet me on the bridge over the old Virden Creek, and beat up on me and my black girlfriend. She told us that every day, so, one day, we said "OK, we'll be there." We were scared, but we stayed on the bridge after school and she didn't show up. [Laughs] [OHS 67 WF]*

*In 7th grade, my mom was late picking me up from a basketball game. There were no cell phones. [laughs] My friend and I were sitting in the outer lobby of the gym and a group of blacks started hassling us. Mostly taunting. It was subtle, but the message was, "We should get those white guys' ass." It was said quietly enough so the idea wasn't, "We're going to do this," but to create fear. One of the other black guys I knew was standing off to the side like he wished he wasn't there. He said something to the effect of, "Just leave them alone." That backed them off a little bit. Then mom got there and we got in the car. [EHS 67 WM]*

*The first time I heard the term nigger was in the fifth or sixth grade. The older brother of one of my black friends told me "'Nigger' just means a bad person, it doesn't mean the color of your skin. You could be black or white and still be a nigger." [EHS 68 WM]*

*The typical white person I knew back then was racist. That was just sort of normal behavior. And part of it was anybody who was black was just "other." They weren't part of the West High world. Like in wrestling. If a white kid from West wrestled a black kid from East or any other school, the comment was always the black opponent smelled like an "n-word." [WHS 69 WM]*

*By 10, I was in the process of getting kicked out of all the public schools, because I got in fights when the white kids would call me a "poor nigger" every day. The principal at Longfellow would beat my ass and send me home. I got an ass whipping again when I got home for getting kicked out of school. In 1965, after I'd been kicked out of the public schools, I got transferred to Our Lady of Victory Academy (OLVA). I was one of two black males in the 6th grade. I got in a fight with a white kid and I was on top of him and hitting him, and somebody grabbed me from behind and yelled, "Get off him, nigger. Get off him, nigger." I turned around and it was Sister[Withheld]. I'll never forget her name. It just slammed in my brain, this is a nun calling me this name. I was overwhelmed with emotions and confusion. And I was absolutely devastated. Totally devastated. [EHS 69 AAM]*

**'71-'73** *My brother was walking home one day from Roosevelt Elementary [East Side], a little kid wearing penny loafers. He was attacked by three girls from Logan who wanted the pennies, but he couldn't get them out. So, they beat him over the head with a [soda] pop can. He had to go to the hospital and had stitches put in. My folks pulled me out of Logan and my brother out of Roosevelt, and we didn't finish the school year on the East Side. [CEN 73 WF]*

## On the Job Experiences in

As high schoolers entered the work force, first-hand learning experiences represented another level of influence and influencers on our biases and prejudices.

*The summer before my senior year, I worked at the Paramount Theater. One day, a group of black guys snuck in a back door and surrounded me. They were probably junior high age. They started coming at me, and I started swinging and screaming. It didn't take long for the ushers and manager to get upstairs. I was pretty rattled. We ended up in court because the manager pressed charges. One of the boys testified they came after me because I had called them black bastards or something to that effect. I testified I never called them any such thing. Another employee who was a year older testified she was the one who had called them names, and I was too nice and would never call anyone names like that. I felt very vindicated and was happy my mom heard the truth. One of the boy's mom came up to us afterwards and apologized for her son's actions. She made a very good impression on me. [EHS 66 WF]*

Est Fourth Street, Waterloo, Iowa

photolibrarian. https://www.flickr.com/photos/photolibrarian/8537692204/in/pool-505639@N21

Figure 2 The Paramount Theater

*The Paramount Theater opened at the east end of the 4ᵗʰ Street Bridge in 1927 as the Riviera Theater, renamed in 1929. A fire destroyed the landmark's stage area in 1972, but even though the rest of the theater was spared, it was ultimately demolished. The site is now a riverfront park.*

**'67-'70**  *I've seen good and bad on both sides of race. In Waterloo, there were certain places I knew if I was walking down the street I'd get beat up because I was white. But I ran across a lot of really good black people, too. I worked at a gas station across from Rath Packing. Friday mornings my boss would cash checks for Rath Packing employees if they bought a tank of gas. The first Friday I was there, four car loads of big black men pulled in and I was a little scared. They were extremely big men working third shift at Rath as slaughterers. Over time, I got to know some of them and they were really nice guys. I was 18 and all these big men were calling me "sir." That really surprised me. One day a lady came in with a bunch of kids in her car and didn't have money for gas. And she wanted to know if I could give her a dollar's worth. I didn't know her and said, "No, I can't do that." She said she'd give me a tire for a down payment or security for* the $1. I told her "no," but gave her a dollar's worth of gas and took it out of my own pocket. About three days later she tracked me down at work and gave me my dollar back. That surprised me. [COL 68 WM]

I worked part time at Penney's for a year while in high school. The store picked one girl employee from each high school to be on the teen board. I was from West, and there was one from Orange, Cedar Falls and Northern University High in Cedar Falls. But there were two from East – one white and one black. I got along better with the black girl than I did the white. I never thought of her as black, just a good friend. [WHS 69 WF]

**'71-'73** I was in the co-op program working at Allen Hospital when I was in high school. If I stayed on Highway 63, I didn't have any concerns about driving from the West Side to Allen on the East side. I was scared to death to go off 63. All I heard was, "Don't go on East 4th Street." I was always afraid to go to the East Side. I don't remember anybody ever sitting down and telling me to be afraid. The race riots happened when I was young, which is a bad memory. The East Side is scary. But if I stayed on 63, I was fine. [WHS 74 WF]

## EXTRACURRICULAR & CHURCH EXPERIENCES

Recreation and sports are fertile environments for learning about others, whether it's in the neighborhood, a park or a program. Waterloo had two swimming pools – the Byrnes Park pool (opened on the West Side in 1908) and the Gates Park pool (opened on the East side in 1928). Byrnes wasn't legally segregated in the 1960s but wasn't frequented by blacks because they didn't live on the West Side. Black-white relationships occurred at Gates.

**'63-'66** I used to play basketball all the time at St. Mary's [East 4th Street] with the black guys because there was a light. Or we played at Logan because there was a light on the back of the gym. We didn't care where you were from. We got along. [EHS 64 WM]

*I always had cordial relations with most of the black people I knew. We lived on the edge of the "ghetto" and I delivered the Waterloo Courier and the Des Moines Register into the 'hood. I worked in a Conoco station there. Played basketball and football with several black students. I can only remember two times that anything racial happened. A bunch of us, whites and blacks, were playing a pick-up game of basketball one day, and I beat one of the black players to the basket. He called me on it. "Your daddy's black. Blacks don't beat blacks." My stepfather was black. I didn't pay any attention to it. Another time at Sullivan Brothers Park [on East 4th across the tracks from the IC railroad yard], one of the black players said I was so well liked by other black kids "because your daddy is a nigger." At first, I was taken aback by his comment until he explained it was a positive comment. Black people refer to each other as "my nigger." I understood where he was coming from. [EHS 66 WM]*

*Gates Park [on the northern city limit of the East Side of Waterloo] seemed to be kind of like a neutral zone where the rules about races not getting along got bent. Especially when it got really hot. [EHS 66 AAM]*

*I was from a small town with no black people. When I was five or six at Gates pool, I was talking with a little black girl about the same age in the shower. She was telling me about how Negroes in the South weren't allowed to drink out of certain fountains or eat at certain counters. I was appalled and asked why. She told me, "Because we are Negroes." I told her I thought that wasn't fair. Mom and I talked about it on the way home. She said some people thought the white race was better than the Negro race. My dad commented onetime color didn't matter, you have good and bad people of all colors. [EHS 66 WF]*

*I took a cousin of mine who lived in the country to the Gates pool one time and she'd never seen a black person. She said, "Look, there's black kids over there." I told her it was OK, they swim here all the time. "Don't say anything." I didn't want to be embarrassed. I think it was just unusual to her. [EHS 66 WF]*

**'67-'70**      *I was probably in elementary school when I became aware of blacks at the Gates Park swimming pool. I had an incident, which probably didn't happen to most people, that made an impression on me. There was a little group of black kids who were in the upper elementary grades swarming, milling around me and my younger sister. And they started coming over and started grabbing at our crotches. I was too young to know what that was about. They pawed at us like that for a little while, and we moved away from them, tried to avoid them. I told Mom and Dad about it at supper, and I think back to how horrified, angry they must have been. But I don't remember they did anything about it except tell us to stay away from the black people. [EHS 69 WF]*

**'71-'73**      *I was in the Chevaliers Drum and Bugle Corps. There were black kids in it and we all hung out together. When the drum corps was on a trip, some of us would take some extra snacks because we knew some of our black friends couldn't afford them. So, we'd share. We were more aware of someone's income or lack thereof, not their color. I just don't remember ever being in a group growing up that was segregated. [WHS 71 WF]*

*The summer before 9th grade at Logan Junior, I was hanging out at the Gates Park swimming pool with my sister and friends one evening. We were horsing around and my friends pushed me into the pool. I landed on or near a black girl. I got out of the pool and don't remember if I apologized or not, it was so long ago. But she wanted to fight with me. A black lifeguard got between us, and the manager kicked her and her friends out. I stayed until my parents came to pick me up, because the manager didn't want the situation to escalate. The next day, the story in the black newspaper, The Defender, reported I'd injured her arm, which was supposedly in a cast or a sling, but she'd been the one kicked out of the pool and the white girl wasn't. The article called it just one more example of discrimination in Waterloo, which was frankly ridiculous. That's when my mother said, "We're moving." Our house*

*sold, but my folks said I could finish at Logan where I had a great group*
*of friends and my older sister could finish her senior year at East. [CEN*
*73 WF]*

Both black and white churches, their pastors and congregations on
both sides of the Cedar River were often community activists during
*The Bridge Between* decade. Their influences were acknowledged by
the respondents

*My religious background was Church of Nazarene. There was no*
*smoking, drinking or dancing. And we were to be friends with and kind*
*to everyone. No people were off limits. I've kept philosophy for a long*
*time, even after I became a Baptist in the military. [EHS 66 WM]*

*Our church hosted a youth exchange with a black church to talk*
*about things. It was interesting because the visiting youth sat in the pews*
*one side of the middle aisle and we sat on the other side. The other*
*pastor had schooled his students on how to speak publicly. And they did*
*beautifully. And then it was our turn, and we all sat like a bunch of*
*dummies on our side. Because of my parents teaching me so much, I did*
*the speaking for our group. I didn't know I had those words myself. But*
*it worked. [EHS 66 WF]*

*When I was in the youth group at Grace United Methodist, our youth*
*director had the idea of holding dances in the fellowship hall for the*
*community. We had tons of kids [including blacks who lived in the*
*neighborhoods around the church] at the dances and a couple*
*subsequently came to church on Sunday mornings. When the church*
*administrative board found out there was dancing in the church, they*
*had a conniption and demanded it stop. In those days, Methodists didn't*
*drink or dance. We told them we weren't dancing in the sanctuary, but*
*in fellowship hall. The board said we could invite the blacks to our youth*
*fellowship meetings, but there would be no dances. It was the dances that*
*were bringing these kids in off the streets. We were reaching out and*
*argued it was a great way to connect with the kids in the church*

*neighborhood. If we'd been able to keep that up, we'd have been doing a great service to the area. [WHS 66 WF]*

*I was around 10 when my father took us as a family several times to a black church in Waterloo to hear the music and particularly to hear a preacher. We were warmly welcomed by the minister and other people, and I was there as part of a family, so I didn't feel uncomfortable. [WHS 69 WF]*

*I didn't really have much interaction with people of color except, occasionally, my grandma, who was a minister, would take me to what she called the black church. The thing I remember most was you put your finger in the air, raised your hand, if you were going to walk out. It was "excuse me." But I loved to go to those churches with grandma. We didn't go that many times, but she loved to go. With grandma, we didn't have the racial issues at all. [WHS 70 WF]*

## Toto, I've a feeling we're not in Waterloo anymore

Memorable first-hand racial experiences for Waterloo high school students was seeing the racial grass on the other side of someone's fence when traveling outside of the town/county and particularly Iowa home neighborhoods.

**'63-'66** *I moved back and forth between Iowa and Louisiana when I was a kid. My grandmother ran a family store in a small town in Louisiana that had been there 100 years and was postmaster. It was all black down there, with a few white people. My grandmother had a black nanny, Lizzie. My grandmother would give Lizzie and her family food and rice, and let them get into the big ceramic vat she had. That's how my grandmother paid her. I was eight or nine and all my friends there in Louisiana were black. When I got off the school bus, I'd change my clothes, and run down the lane to Lizzie's and Gunn's. They had six or seven children and sometimes I'd be down there playing all day. Sometimes Lizzie would fix something to eat.*

*Their parents had been sharecroppers after the civil war. They were really nice people. [EHS 64 WM]*

*I went on vacation to Florida with my aunt and uncle when I was a junior in high school, and experienced segregation. I was shocked. It never occurred to me that Waterloo might be that way. I was aware that the black people were kept within their boundaries in Waterloo. And I think now how sad it is that someone doesn't have the opportunity to live where they want to live and have the freedom of choice. In my mind, black people are still looked down upon. [EHS 66 WF]*

**'67-'70** *My folks were from a small town in Missouri. We were visiting one time and I asked my mom about the little brick building behind the school. She said it had been the black school at one time. The kids could go kindergarten through 8ᵗʰ in the town, but if they wanted to go to high school, they had to live 20 miles away from home, if their parents were wealthy enough to pay room and board. [EHS 68 WF]*

**'71-'73** *We were on an orientation tour at UNI and the group went into the student union. There were some black students sitting at one of the tables. And I heard a mother behind me, I think she was from Charles City, say, "I wonder how many of THEM [emphasized] are here?" And I thought, "What's the big deal? What's your problem? They're probably just kids from Waterloo." When I sold candy in high school, I had one lady who said, "No, if I buy candy, I'm going to buy it from West High kids." And I thought, "Yeah, you don't want to buy it from a [Catholic] fish eater." We got more of that type of stuff from the West kids than the East kids. [COL 75 WM]*

# Reflections from the Bridge

A community's public schools are an extension of the relationships among and between the community and its citizens, the city administration, and the board of education (BOE) and school system.

Those relationships in Waterloo were virtually unchanged between the union strike at the Rath Packing Company in 1948 and 1963-1973.

Waterloo had only two mayors in that time, who were elected for two-year terms.

The second Waterloo school district superintendent since it was formed in 1942 took over the summer before the 1966 school year.

The East high principal first appointed in 1941 retired at the end of the 1965-66 school year. His replacement taught at East for two years following World War II and was an assistant principal there since 1948.

The Waterloo Independent and Orange Consolidated school districts merged in July 1964. The principal of Orange High continued in that position until the school was closed at the end of the 1971-72 school year. West High's principal, first appointed in 1928, would retire in 1968 at the start of the second *TBB* era.

But Waterloo high school graduates from 1963-1973 would experience the effects of destabilized relationships between the community, community administration and the school district – the triarchy responsible for governing the town – largely due to increased black civil rights activism in the community. The impact affected the students differently in the three *The Bridge Between* eras.

# Endnotes

[1] Wright, W.F. (1948) A Man Called White: The Autobiography of Walter White. New York: Viking Press, p.3. Retrieved from http://tinyurl.com/h4wxd7k. PHOTO: Stakeman, J. and Stakeman, R. Walter White at Atlanta University. The Walter White Project: Walter White Biography, 4. Retrieved from scalar.usc.edu/nehvectors/stakeman/walter-white-at-atlanta-university. Bill Nye: Race is a Human Construct. Big Think: Think-Tank. Retrieved from http://bigthink.com/think-tank/bill-nye-race-is-a-social-construct.
2 Why every baby around the world's first word starts with the letter M. (September 16, 2016). Quartz: Tongue Ties. Retrieved from http://tinyurl.com/y9shreo8.

3 Genetic Evidence: DNA. What does it mean to be Human? Human Evolution Research. Washington, D.C.: Smithsonian Museum of Natural History. Retrieved from http://humanorigins.si.edu/evidence/genetics.

4 How Science and Genetics are Reshaping the Race Debate of the 21st Century. (April 17, 2017). Chou, V. Science in the News. Harvard University: The Graduate School of Arts and Sciences. Retrieved from http://sitn.hms.harvard.edu/flash/2017/science-genetics-reshaping-race-debate-21st-century/.

5 Infants process faces long before they recognize other objects, Stanford vision researchers find. (December 11, 2012). McClure, M. Stanford University: The Stanford Report. Retrieved from http://news.stanford.edu/news/2012/december/infants-process-faces-121112.html.

6 Colour Prejudice. [1948]. Sir Alan Burns. London: Allen and Unwin, 16.

*Copyright © 2018 Marvitz Photography. Used with permission.*

# Part 2 Educational Pathways: No Shades of Gray

## *TBB* 4: The Waterloo Triarchy

*Segregation in Waterloo was de facto. But it was just as overt in Waterloo as it was in the South, more so than in other northern cities. It was as clear as night and day there was a black space and a white space in Waterloo. And when you get out of your space, there are going to be consequences on somebody. And you have to respond. [EHS 69 AAM]*

*The school board was a bunch of white guys who all lived within a square mile of one another in the Prospect Boulevard area, the richest neighborhood in Waterloo. – Community Folklore*

Three facts about Waterloo and its schools have been shared.

1. Waterloo was a town separated physically, socioeconomically, socially and racially by the Cedar River virtually from its founding.
2. Except for less than one percent of the town's black residents, blacks lived on the East Side of Waterloo and were segregated there de jure.
3. Virtually all black students in Waterloo attended East Side schools.

There is a fourth fact – a community's public schools are an extension of the relationships between the community and its citizens, the city administration, and the board of education and school system. These three form a sociopolitical triarchy which collectively govern and influence a community. It's often difficult to separate their influences, especially in Waterloo.

It was a unique period of shifting, confusing, frustrating and confrontational political, social and educational environments. It's impossible to separate these influences on the adult lives of high school students during this period. It's a cliché: you can take the graduate out of Waterloo, but you can't take Waterloo out of the graduate.

This was evident when the stories about experiences, perceptions and insights from the 1963-1973 graduates separated almost naturally into three distinct *TBB* eras.

# Triarchy 1: The Community and Its Citizens

Most people associate the beginning of the Civil Rights Movement with the U.S. Supreme Court's 1954 ruling *Brown v. Board of Education* [of Topeka, Kansas] in which it unanimously ruled racial segregation of children in public schools was unconstitutional. Or the Montgomery, Alabama, bus boycott in 1955-1956 that

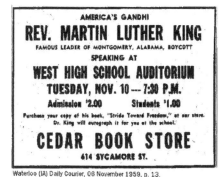

Waterloo (IA) Daily Courier, 06 November 1959, p. 13.

Figure 1 Ad for MLK Appearance in Waterloo, 1959

resulted in Martin Luther King, Jr., being elected president of the group formed to support the boycott.

Until then civil rights hadn't been a major national agenda item. Nor was it on the agenda in segregated Waterloo. That changed following *Brown* and Montgomery.

Invited to Waterloo by local activist Anna Mae Weems, King spoke at West High School on November 10, 1959, four years after he led the non-violent boycott of the segregated bus system in Montgomery. (Figure 1) He challenged the audience to work "not just for the progress of one race but for all humanity."

*. . . whenever anything new came into history there have been new responsibilities and new challenges. It would be tragic indeed if we stood in the midst of the promised land and followed the old. We must rise from the narrow confines of individualism and emerge to the broader sense of humanity of the whole human race.*[1]

He spoke the following morning to a student and faculty assembly at the Iowa State Teachers College in Cedar Falls (now the University of Northern Iowa) and the University of Iowa that night in Iowa City. In October 1962, King made a second Iowa visit to Cornell College in Mount Vernon and Coe College in Cedar Rapids. "I Have a Dream," his most famous speech, was given 10 months later at the Lincoln Memorial in August 1963 during the "March on Washington for Jobs and Freedom."[2] Two black members of the UPWA union at Rath Packing in Waterloo were there.[3]

On September 15, 1963, four young black girls – an 11-year-old and three 14-year-olds were killed in a bombing by white supremacists while attending Sunday school in Birmingham, Alabama, at a church that had been used for civil rights meetings.

Little more than a month later, Waterloo held a memorial service for the girls at Grant Elementary School that was attended by a group from Birmingham, including one of the girl's parents. Waterloo churches paid for their transportation.

The Birmingham bombing and other incidents in 1963 inspired local activism "to integrate and stop injustice in Waterloo schools in subsequent years."[4]

*1963 had great impact. It was one of the toughest years we went through in the civil rights struggle. . . [It] made people more aware of who they are, and where they are, and to try to get a road map of where they're going.*[5]

In June 1964, two months after King was assassinated, the NAACP organized a "March for Freedom" through downtown Waterloo as black activists and many whites began to demand the end to discrimination in housing and employment, and desegregation of the schools.

A Selma civil rights sympathy march in March 1965 sponsored by the Waterloo ministerial association drew 300-500 people. About 100 people "bundled up against 30-degree weather and wind"[6] marched in a re-enactment on March 25, 2018.

The death of a black man at the city jail the following summer resulted in rioting.

*There was an incident in which a black guy got arrested and the police basically killed him. Then they tried to make it look like he hung himself in the jail cell. But the cells were constructed where you couldn't commit suicide. There was a sheet tied around some bars, but his feet were still touching the floor. And basically, they got away with it. Racial tension was very high then. [EHS 66 AAM]*

The Waterloo Human Rights Commission was started in the summer of 1966.

In July 1967, a protest and riot broke out in the town over alleged discrimination in a state- and federally funded program for unemployed blacks.

From 1967-1970, race riots and segregated Waterloo schools thrust the town into national spotlight at times.

The community and its people had changed in their awareness of and willingness to passively accept segregation and racial inequality, as had the nation. This change was one source for conditions that contributed to the formation of the perfect storm affecting Waterloo, its schools and its high school students through the end of *The Bridge Between* story.

# Triarchy 2: Waterloo City Administration

The second source contributing to the forming of the perfect storm of unrest was the city's administration. The mayor's office and the police were faced dealing with and controlling unstable racial tension and violence that mirrored what was happening throughout the nation in the middle of the 1963-1973 *TBB* decade.

Waterloo had two mayors during the 10 years from 1963-1973. (Figure 2) Ed Jochumsen was first elected in 1958 and served seven two-year terms, including 1963-1966. He left office before Waterloo started to burn.

Dissatisfied with Jochumsen's administration, Waterloo elected Lloyd Turner in 1966, who served seven terms, including the explosive years of local civil rights conflicts.[7]

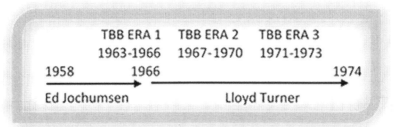

Figure 2 Waterloo Mayors During *The Bridge Between* Story

Employment and real estate discrimination in Waterloo, and desegregation of the schools were at the top of the black community's agenda during his tenure.

Five months after Turner was sworn in as mayor, he "had an opportunity to see virtually every one of some 200 Negro pickets who [literally] paraded through his office" while he worked at his desk during a three-hour protest.[8] His "the buck stops at my desk" actions, accessibility to the community and commitment to bringing all parties in the civil rights issues to the table to find a consensus was highly visible.

Frequently caught between protestors and the police, Turner held the latter accountable for participating in solutions and not just law enforcement.

## VIGILANCE

*Waterloo is the only city that the police ride around in cars with a red dragon on them. You never see any type of an animal on police cars. Okay? (laughs) I know what "vigilant" means. But I don't know what "vigilance" on the police cars means. Waterloo is the only police department that has some type of symbol like that on its cars. [EHS 74 AAM]*

The relationship between the black community and police in Waterloo had been strained – an understatement by all accounts – for decades, certainly since post-World War II.

The long-time folklore in the black community of Waterloo is the police department's patch and patrol cars with a distinctive red "dragon" and the word "Vigilance" is a code for a covert policy that over-polices the blacks in the North End. (Figure 3) The "dragon," as it's usually described, was considered a fire-breathing, armor-scaled reptilian, symbolically prepared to wreak havoc on the black community.

Figure 3 The Police Department Griffin & "Vigilance" Logos

The proof often cited is that Waterloo has the highest per capita of black men incarcerated in the state and that the 123-member department today has only two black officers (1.6%) in a town with a 15.7% black minority.

The slogan and "dragon" design was implemented in 1964 when chief Robert Wright wanted to replace the triangular patch embroidered simply with "Waterloo Police Department" for something that was not only unique, but symbolic of police work.

The "dragon" he selected is actually a griffin – also called "griffon" or "gryphon," the symbol of "vigilance" in Greek mythology. It has the head and wings of an eagle, the king of birds, for vigilance, and the body, tail, and hind legs of a lion, the king of the beasts, for strength. In

Greek mythology, a griffin pulled the chariot of Apollo, the Greek sun god.

*Waterloo Courier* artist Jack Bender designed the patch using the griffin at Chief Wright's request.

*The Waterloo police weren't known to be nice back then. I've seen them beat people with billy clubs, blacks and whites. They thought they were judge and jury. One time I was at my mother-in-law's house with four or five friends and the police pulled up in four squad cars. They jumped out and ran up behind the house. We went to see what was going on and they're clubbing this white guy. Another one was kicking him. We told them to stop. One turned around said, "You don't know what he did." I said, "That doesn't give you the right to knock the hell out of him because we don't know what he did." They told us to get out of there or they'd arrest us, too. We had to go back to the house. [EHS 64 WM]*

*I emulated my father, and my husband and I had the same discussions with our kids as they were growing up. We let them know it's not always safe out there for black people, black men in particular. The cops stopped my husband one time near our house and they beat him. Our sons were in the car. They must have been about 3 and 5. Our youngest son got physically sick and grew up with animosity toward the police. I had to tell him what they did was wrong, but you can't put yourself in danger by hating them and letting them know, because they will kill you. I told him just like that. My husband's always been a very decent person. He's never been in trouble. He's just a good man. But they stopped him because they could. I think it was just some rotten cops they had. And their excuse was "we were fearful for our lives." It's the same thing today. It hasn't changed, really. [EHS 69 AAF]*

# Triarchy 3: The WCSD System

The Board of Education was the third triarchy member contributing to the perfect storm through which high school students lived from 1966-1973.

The East-West competition in Waterloo affected the town's education system from its founding. The first school was built on the West Side in the spring of 1853. (Figure 4) East-Side started its first school the next year. The first bridge across the Cedar River was built in 1859, but children were still schooled on their own sides of it.

| | | 1st East Side School Opened | | East, West Schools Split | | East, West Districts Merged | | 1st Black Teacher Hired; 2nd in Iowa |
|---|---|---|---|---|---|---|---|---|
| Waterloo Settled | | | | | | | | |
| 1845 | 1853 | 1854 | 1859 | 1866 | 1911 | 1942 | 1945 | 1952 |
| | 1st West Side School Opened | | 1st Permanent Bridge Over Cedar River | | Black Migration to Waterloo | | 2nd Black Migration | |

Figure 4 Waterloo School System History, 1845-1952

"The location of neighborhood schools thus became an issue more politically charged than usual."[9] A large three-story brick school was built on the West Side in 1860 even though the East Side school was overcrowded due to the population growth in the industrial sector on the East Side. ". . . the affluent West Side received the new facilities, it seemed."[10] A new school was built on the East Side four years later.

In early 1866, East Side residents petitioned "for a school district of their own, independent from the existing, west-dominated district." West Side citizens opposed the split, but the day of the vote, heavy rains and flooding on the Cedar River prevented most of the Westsiders from reaching the polling place on the East Side. The measure passed overwhelmingly. The East Side became the East Waterloo Independent School District and the West Side became the Independent District of Waterloo.[11]

The two districts operated autonomously, side-by-side for 76 years before rejoining in 1942 as the Independent School District of Waterloo (ISDW).[12]

In 1952, Lily Williams Furgerson was the first black public-school teacher hired in Waterloo, the second in Iowa, just 10 years before *The Bridge Between* timeline began in 1963. She taught at Grant

Elementary, the predominantly black school on the East Side, and in the Bridgeway Project in the late 1960s.

In 1963-1973, no school boundary crossed the river. That school separation affected not only academic lives in Waterloo, but students' social lives as well.

In July 1964, the ISDW merged with the East Waterloo Township (EWT) and Orange Consolidated school systems. The merger expanded the Waterloo school district to the south and east of the town. The boundary change and school reorganization laws required the expanded district change its name to the Waterloo Community School District (WCSD); it became the third largest school district in Iowa.[13]

In 1967, 81% of white students attended schools at all levels which were at least 90% white; 30% of black students attended schools which were at least 90% minority.[14]

Of the 33 Waterloo schools, only 11 percent had black students, all of them on the East Side. Two-thirds [66 percent] of Waterloo's black students attended schools with black majorities.[15]

## The WCSD Board of Education (BOE)

The school board was slow to respond to the demand for equal educational opportunity in the 1960s, and found the schools and its superintendent literally under attack.

One of the persistent perceptions East High students shared was that it, and the East Side junior high and elementary schools, were treated unequally by the BOE, especially when it came to budgets and hiring of teachers.

The general perception was that West High received new textbooks, science equipment, learning support materials and East received the hand-me-downs. That West sports teams had the best equipment; East equipment was held together with baling wire and bubblegum. That the best teachers were hired for West High; less qualified ones taught at East because the more qualified wouldn't teach there.

Cited as proof?

---

*At that time, all but one of the school board members were white guys who lived within five blocks of each other on Prospect Boulevard on the West Side. The other one lived in Highland on the East. The two richest neighborhoods in Waterloo. [EHS 67 WM]*

---

This perception offered by more than a dozen contributors isn't totally myth.

In 1963, five members of the school board did live within less than roughly a half-square mile of one another near West High (Figure 5), but not on Prospect Boulevard. The other two were East Side residents who lived across or a block from East High School, not in Highland.

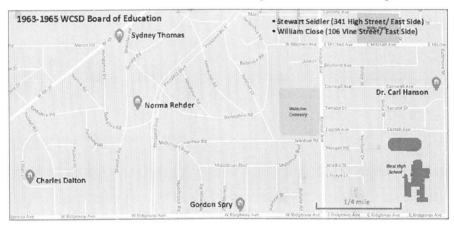

Figure 5 Board of Education (BOE) Homes, 1963

---

The perception that the WCSD school board was dominated by the West Side voters doesn't match the reality. In 1963, four of the seven members lived on the West Side. (Table 1) In 1969, the year after the 1968 riots at East High School, the first black member of the board was elected and tipped the BOE member balance 4-3 for the East Side. After several years of failure to develop a viable and acceptable desegregation plan, the board elected in 1972 had only one representative from the East Side, six from the West.

The composition of the Waterloo board of education from 1963-1969 reflected the same stability it had virtually since the IDSW was formed in 1942. (Table 1)

| YR | West Side^W | Table 1 WCSD Board of Education Members 1963-1973 | | | | | | |
|---|---|---|---|---|---|---|---|---|
| '63(2) | | | | | | | | |
| '64 (3) | 4/7 | | | CH^W | | ST^W | SS | GS |
| '65(2) | | | | | | | | |
| '66 (2) | 4/7 | WC | | | | | | |
| '67(3) | | | CD^W | | NR^W | | | |
| '68(2) | | | | | | | | |
| '69(2) | | | | RW^W | | RH | | |
| '70(3) | 3/7 | | | | | | | |
| '71(2) | | | | | | | JS | KG |
| '72(2) | 4/7 | TL | | | | WK^W | | |
| '73(3) | 6/7 | | | | | | EM^W | MM^W |

*WCSD board of education members from 1963-1973 who resided on the West Side are indicated by an asterisk. The first column is the school year in which the members were elected and the number of seats open. Some of the BOE members served before 1963 and after 1973. The school board was elected at large until the early 1990s when board districts were established. In the early part of the TBB decade, the trend was multiple terms for board members. By the end of the decade, the churn was much more frequent.*

| | |
|---|---|
| CD: Charles Dalton* [1st term 1956] | RH: Dr. Robert Harvey [Black] |
| CH: Dr. Carl Hanson* [1st term 1957] | RW: Dr. Richard Wells* |
| EM: Eugene Mixdorf* | SS: Stewart Seidler [1st term 1945] |
| GS: Gordon Spry [1st term 1962] | ST: Sydney Thomas* [1st term 1957] |
| JS: James Sage | TL: Thomas Lind |
| KG: Rev. Kenneth Gamb | WC: William Close |
| MM: Mrs. Thomas McKernan* | WK: William Kammeyer* |
| NR: Norma Rehder* [1st term 1949] | *West Side resident |

Six of the seven board members from 1963-65 had served three or more terms. Seidler and Rehder were on their sixth and fifth terms, having been on the board since 1945 and 1949, respectively. Seidler is credited with a third of a term, having been appointed for one year in 1945 to complete an unexpired term.

There were eight candidates for three open positions in 1964, which was unprecedented in a board election, which had a history of incumbents running unopposed. The longstanding incumbent BOE membership started to change in 1969 following three years of racial disturbances in the schools

The most significant change on the BOE occurred in 1969 when Dr. Robert Harvey was the first black elected to the board. In the 1968 board election, 2,300 ballots were cast. In 1969, 3,397 residents voted, an almost 50% increase.

Harvey received 46.9% of the votes, 104 ahead of incumbent Dr. Richard Wells. He carried the East Side, Wells the West. A respected East Side dentist and community activist, Harvey was a member of the NAACP, East Waterloo Citizens Committee that was active in school issues after 1966 and the Waterloo Fair Employment Practices Committee. He was elected as the board vice president in 1971, the last year of his term.

The number of students in the Waterloo schools was roughly 15,000 students in 1963. By 1969, the number had grown to 19,729. In 1962, one school board vote was cast for every 10.1 students. In 1969, it was one vote for every five students.

As the schools headed into the decade of the 70s, the driving force for voters was the lack of viable solutions proposed and implemented by the BOE to resolve the school segregation that had been the status quo since the beginning of the 20th century.

Two new board members replaced nine-term incumbent Stewart Seidler and six-term member Gordon Spry in 1970 in the "largest voter turnout for a Board of Education election in the history of Waterloo."[16] The 5,529 turnout was 1,592 more than the previous high recorded the year before. The voting site at West High accounted for 31% of the votes.

James Sage, part owner and operator of a 470-acre farm on the northern edge of East Side Waterloo, was selected by 44.7% of the voters among the eight candidates for the three open positions. Rev

Kenneth Gamb was also elected to his first term, having failed to win one of the two open seats in 1969. A resident of Elk Run Heights on the southeast side of the city north of the Cedar River, he was pastor of the Prince of Peace Lutheran Church in Evansdale and vice president of the Waterloo Ministerial Association. The group was involved in school issues in the late 1960s. Mrs. Norma Rehder won her 8th term with the second highest vote total, having been elected every three years since 1946.

Thomas Lind joined the board in 1971. Athletic Director at Columbus High, he had campaigned on the failure of the superintendent and the school board in their intent to be "advocates of alert cooperation with the whole Waterloo community."[17] He specifically cited the example of BOE election voting reminders that weren't provided to people with no children in school, including 18-year-olds (who were given the right to vote in July by the 26th Amendment), and parents and students of non-public schools whose tax money is spent on public education.[18] Excess brochures were printed by the school system and distributed to Catholic churches and organizations during the weekend prior to the vote. Lind had 3,997 votes to school board president Charles Dalton's second-place 1,710 votes.[19]

Harvey was defeated in 1972 by roughly 2,500 of 7,500 votes cast in another record election turnout. The previous record was in 1970. Harvey carried only two of the 12 precincts, Grant and McKinstry, which are in or near the North End. He was replaced by William Kammeyer, a West Side resident who was the second-highest vote getter. Two-term incumbent Dr. Richard Wells was the highest with 5,790 votes and won the other 10 precincts.

Harvey declined to comment about the election. "The people of Waterloo made their choice and showed their wishes when they cast their ballots."[20]

Harvey had received endorsements from the NAACP, the Citizen's Committee of East Waterloo, SHARE[21] and WEPACE (Waterloo

Educators' Political Action Committee for Education). The Citizens' Committee was incorporated in early 1966 "to engage in activities for the general good of its members and the citizenry; to promote greater interest in politics among Negroes.[22] WEPACE was the political arm of the Waterloo Education Association (WEA).

Kammeyer, a 1956 East High graduate and supervisor at John Deere Waterloo Traffic Works, cited his support for busing "only on a voluntary basis"[23] as a factor in his win. He was endorsed by the NSA (Neighborhood School Association).[24]

By the end of 1973, other Eastsiders were elected to the three-year BOE terms.

The record voter turnout trend continued in 1973 when 9,064 cast ballots for three seats, a 25% increase from the previous year when only two seats were open. Each vote represented 1.83 Waterloo students.

Newcomers Gene Mixdorf and Mrs. Thomas McKernan defeated one-term board president Sage and one-term member Gamb. Mrs. Rehder won her 9th election.

All three had been endorsed by the NSA. Their election was, "In effect . . . a repudiation of the adoption of [desegregation] Plan A, voted in by the present board to help desegregate the Waterloo schools and accomplished by some involuntary busing of students. The closing of three elementary schools because of declining enrollments was another factor."[25]

In 2018, the Waterloo BOE has seven members, each elected for four years or to complete an unexpired term of a regularly elected member. Four members are elected from director districts and three are elected at large.[26]

## WCSD School Superintendents and Principals

The school district's superintendent and its principals were integral participants in creating or participating in the conditions that helped formation of the perfect storm. (Figure 6)

114

Jack Logan was the first superintendent of the Independent School District of Waterloo (ISDW) formed in 1942. He had been superintendent of the East school district for nine years before its merger with the West district. Logan served until 1961 when he resigned to comply with the system's age 70 retirement policy.

| TBB ERA 1 | | | | TBB ERA 2 | | | | TBB ERA 3 | | |
|---|---|---|---|---|---|---|---|---|---|---|
| 1962 | 1963 | 1964 | 1965 | 1966 | 1967 | 1968 | 1969 | 1970 | 1971 | 1983 |
| Dr. George Hohl | | | | | | | | Dr. Gene Lubera | | |
| | | | | | | | | | | George Diestelmeier |

Figure 6 WCSD School Superintendents, 1963-1973

There were three Waterloo school superintendents from 1963-1973.

To replace Logan, the BOE appointed Dr. George Hohl, a former teacher and administrator in Des Moines who had been the superintendent in Passaic, N.J. for the previous two-and-a-half years. A graduate of Drake University in Des Moines, he earned an M.A. and Ph.D. at Northwestern in Chicago.[27]

Hohl was superintendent during *The Bridge Between* ERAs 1 and 2, fulfilling the community's expectation for Logan-like continuity in that position.

Hohl resigned in late March 1970 to take a teaching position in education at Iowa State University and the board began a search for his successor.

In June, a letter to the *Waterloo Daily Courier* made a pitch for the assistant superintendent, George Diestelmeier.

*[The BOE hopes] to find someone with experience in school administration . . . has an understanding of physical facilities to ours . . . who works well not only with his immediate staff but with principals and classroom teachers as well . . . can establish rapport with our community . . . who works with leaders of our city to problem-solve, coordinate plan . . . so qualified he can make the transition between the former superintendent and himself unnoticeable.[28]*

The letter writer challenged the Ph.D. criterion that Diestelmeier didn't hold. "That degree DOES [sic] entitle one to a greater salary, but does not mean the bearer is more intelligent or would perform more outstandingly in the position than one which has by experience shown himself more than capable."[29]

Diestelmeier had submitted a letter to the BOE at Hohl's resignation that he was not a candidate for the position. "The response to this decision when made known," according to the letter to the editor, "was so overwhelming that Mr. Diestelmeier was prevailed upon to reconsider . . ." and his name was re-submitted. It cited Diestelmeier's qualifications as ". . . Waterloo-born, Waterloo high school graduate, Waterloo teacher and administrator, and completely Waterloo community-oriented. . . ."[30]

The board hired "outsider" Dr. Gene Lubera in October 1970 from the Ohio school district where he'd been superintendent for a year. His one-year contract wasn't renewed because of his confrontational relationships with the BOE and the community. Lubera resigned and the board initiated a second superintendent search in less than 18 months.

Parents and the community were shaken and angered at the board for its poor decision in hiring Lubera, and for failing to back and even undermining him.

Three changes in superintendents in less than two years affected school policies and procedures, but generally wasn't something on students' minds until it affected our personal lives. That would become a major problem in *TBB* ERA3.

In 1971, the board hired Diestelmeier, who had formally announced his candidacy for superintendent when Lubera quit. In hindsight, his experience and community relationships proved to be the perfect qualifications for dealing with the changes necessary for shepherding Waterloo and the schools through the slowly progressing desegregation process, including being held hostage in his office by black protestors in 1972, the final school year in the *TBB* story.

# Educational Pathways

*In the mid-1960s, you didn't cross the river to go school. There wasn't open enrollment. If you lived on the East Side, you went to East High. For most of the kids who grew up on the East Side, a racially mixed school was no big deal. The same kids I went to elementary school and junior high with were now in high school with me, and it was OK. Where I lived, we were surrounded by black people and it was OK. We just couldn't play with the family next door because they were Catholic, went to St. Mary's. [EHS 67 WF]*

*When I started at Roosevelt Elementary in 1955, it was 90% white. By the time I left in 1962, it was 50-50 black and white. It eventually became about 90% black before it was closed. [EHS 68 WF]*

For Baby Boomers who started high school in Waterloo in 1963, the educational pathways in the public school system were essentially the same as they had been since 1942, with school boundaries adjusted occasionally to accommodate population shifts. The mantra seemed to be, "It ain't broke, so we don't need to fix it."

Eastsiders went to public school on the East Side of the Cedar River, Westsiders to school on the West Side. East Side schools were biracial, a number were heavily a majority black or white. West Side schools were white with very few minority students. (Figure 7)

School zones superimposed on neighborhoods which were residentially inevitably results in school segregation or provides a means for deliberately protecting certain neighborhoods from minority enrollments.

These disparate East-West high school educational pathways had an influence on our experiences and perceptions and insights, and throughout our adult lives.

The public school educational pathways shifted slightly in the summer of 1964 when the Waterloo Independent (ISDW), East Waterloo Township (EWTSD) and Orange Consolidated (OCSD) school districts merged, expanding the Waterloo district to the east and south. Iowa law required the new district change its name and it became the Waterloo Community School District (WCSD), its current name.

The new district had to "assimilate 3,700 additional students, 130 new teachers, two [white] school districts, a new administration building, and begin operation of a bus system for the first time. . . ." before school started in the fall.[31] (Figure 8)

## East Side, West Side Educational Pathways

*The mantra was, "West is Best, East is least, Columbus doesn't rate." They made us snobs. They told us we were at the best high school there is. It's tribal. Everyone believes their school is the best. West had won the Bellamy Award a few years earlier. They really held that up. [WHS 70 WM]*

*A lot of the kids from the West Side went straight from high school to college because their parents could afford it. Some of the East Side kids did, but usually with scholarships. Education wasn't important to my parents. They even told me I didn't have to go to high school. [EHS 70 WF]*

Figure 7 provides a visual context for the public and parochial schools in Waterloo in 1964 reflecting the relative balance between the former on both sides of the Cedar River. *TBB* begins in 1963 when the school system was the Independent School District of Waterloo. It merged in 1964 with the East Waterloo Township and the Orange Consolidated schools and became the Waterloo Community School District.[32] The schools that became part of the WCSD are included in the map.

There were 18 public schools on both the East and West Sides in 1964, and four Catholic schools on each side. Immanuel Lutheran was also on the East side. (Table 2)

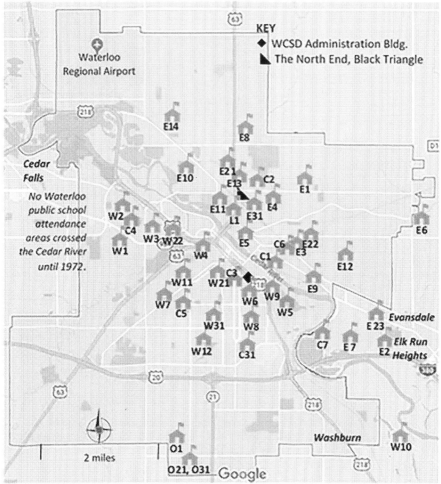

Figure 7 Waterloo Schools Map, Public & Parochial, 1964

*Public and parochial (Catholic & Lutheran) schools in 1964 after the three-district merger into the WCSD. The school name key is in Table 2 below. Elementary schools are numbered from "E/W1" (East/West) and up. Junior high schools are "20s" starting with "E/W21." High schools are "30s" starting with "E/W31." Catholic schools (grades 1-8) numbered from "C1" and up, and Columbus High (grades 9-12) is "C31." "L1" is Immanuel Lutheran (1-8).*

| Table 2 Key to Schools in Figure 7, Waterloo Schools, 1964 | | |
|---|---|---|
| East Side Public (18) | West Side Public (18) | Catholic Schools (8) |
| Elementary | Elementary | Grades 1-8 |
| E1 City View Heights | O1 Orange Elem | |

| | | |
|---|---|---|
| E2 Elk Run | W1 Black Hawk | C1 Our Lady of Victory |
| E3 Frances Grout | W2 Castle Hill | Academy (OLVA) |
| E4 Grant | W3 Edison Elem. | C2 St. Mary |
| E5 Hawthorne | W4 Emerson | C3 Sacred Heart |
| E6 Hewitt | W5 Nellie Garvey | C4 Blessed Sacrament |
| E7 Jewett | W6 Irving | C5 St. Edward |
| E8 Krieg | W7 Kingsley | C6 St. John |
| E9 Lafayette | W8 Kittrell | C7 St. Nicholas |
| E10 Lincoln | W9 Lowell | High School |
| E11 Longfellow | W10 Washburn | C31 Columbus High |
| E12 Maywood | W11 Whittier | School |
| E13 Roosevelt | W12 Cresthaven | |
| E14 Van Eaton | **Junior High** | **Lutheran School (1-8)** |
| **Junior High** | O21 Orange Jr. | L1 Emmanuel Lutheran |
| E21 Logan Jr. | W21 West Jr. | |
| E22 McKinstry Jr. | W22 Edison Jr. | |
| E23 Bunger Jr. | **High School** | |
| **High School** | O31 Orange High | |
| E31 East | W31 West High | |

## Chips on High School Shoulders

The rivalries between multiple high schools in any town are inherently intense, even without a physical separator like the Cedar River that makes schools' turf finite and definite. (Figure 8) Bragging rights are balanced on everything from academic performance to marching bands in the 4th of July parade, exaggerated by sports, the most visible image of a school.

Sports arouses school allegiance, and flaunts the school's initial, colors, nickname and mascot in the best tradition of heraldic symbolism during the Crusades. (Table 3)

*The cheerleaders from East and West highs would meet at the old Bishop's Cafeteria on East 5th Street. The West high kids were very stand-offish and communicated that attitude. There weren't a lot of friendships between East and West high kids, spending time together outside of the formal groups. At least that was my experience. But I dated some guys from West High. [EHS 63 WF]*

*And look out when East High played West High in sports – there were sure to be some fights before, during or after the game. [EHS 66 AAF]*

*We didn't have a lot at East and West did. For example, when I ran track and field, we had some new hurdles in good shape. Others we had to get nuts and bolts and screws and put them together. Our stuff was run down. And when we'd have a track meet at West High, all the hurdles were brand new and all their equipment was brand new. And we'd go, "Oh, boy, you guys got it made. It's not going to help you win, but you've got nice equipment." It was a big deal to them. And they'd really try and show off during football season. They had newer equipment than we did. The attitude was, "We got all this, and we use it well and we're going to show you we use it well. You're going to lose. And we're going to try and drive you right back across the river." [EHS 66 AAM]*

| Table 3 The Five Waterloo Highs Schools, Logos/Mascots | |
|---|---|
|  | East High – The Halls of Troy. Orange & Black. The Trojans. East Side High School opened on High Street between Lime and Vine in 1874. East High, without the "Side," opened at Mulberry and East 6th streets, the intersection where city hall is today. The building burned in 1915 and was re-opened as East High School in 1919 at the High & Vine street location of the original East High. |
|  | Central High – Light Blue & Gold. The Chargers. Opened in 1972 on the southwest side of Waterloo as part of the school district's long-term integration strategy. |
|  | Columbus High – Green & White. The Sailors. Established in 1959 at its current West Side location. *The Columbus mascot is a sailor, which in my day looked like Popeye on steroids and I guess it still does. [COL 69 AAF]* |

Orange High – Orange & Black. The Tigers. It was closed after the June 1972 graduation before Central High opened in the fall.

*People in Waterloo thought of Orange High as a "country school," especially the Columbus kids I met at UNI [The University of Northern Iowa]. [OHS 68 WF]*

West High – Old Rose & Black, the only school in the country with "old rose" as a color. Opened in 1922 on West 4th Street, the current facility was opened in 1955.

The Wahawks ["**WA**terloo" and "Black **HAWK** County.]" The original mascot was an Indian chief, later changed to a hawk-like character named "Westy" and the Indian head was changed to a spear.

A number of East athletes talked about learning more about the West High Booster Club after high school, and its tremendous commitment to Wahawk teams and the school, which they recognized fostered the disparity. West athletes talked about how the club helped fund equipment, athletic bags and gear, for example. East High's Booster Club was no less committed, but didn't have the financial resources or demographics on the East Side for fund-raising. This was an issue even when some of the East *TBB* athletes' kids played for the Trojans.

*Orange had been an independent school district. There was a lot of pressure when we came into the Waterloo school system. Most people saw it as a take-over rather than a merger. There was a vote [to merge], but we felt we got treated as the stepchildren. Everything had to go through the Waterloo school board. That's where all the decisions were made. We got all the used buses and books and desks. [OHS 68 WF]*

*I remember folklore and conversations about how West supported and trained its athletes. My family was all wrestlers. And the coaches from West would pay our wrestlers to go over on the weekend and wrestle their kids in practice. As a student, I believed West and Orange got more than East did. [EHS 70 AAF]*

*The first time I really recognized the differences between East and West High was we had a swing show and West had a variety show. They had real costumes ordered from New York for their variety show. They had the best of the best. We were making our own costumes and pulling things together from here and there for the swing show. [EHS 70 AAF]*

*When you're talking East Side versus West Side kids, you're talking about the river. The divide started right off the bat in junior high school. The white kids from Lincoln merged with the integrated kids from Roosevelt and Longfellow into Logan Junior. We'd play Edison and West Junior on the other side of town, which were white schools. It was a prelude to what we were going to experience in high school. [EHS 71 WM]*

*There wasn't just a black issue between the East and West Sides. There was a white issue from the West Side to the East Side. The West Side kids had the air that they were a better white person than I was because they lived on the West Side. Three middle schools fed West High. Edison, which I thought was more blue-collar. West Junior was upper middle class. And then you had Hoover, which was kind of like the junior high Taj Mahal. That was where doctors', lawyers' and businessmen's kids attended. As a white football player at East, I had the biggest chip on my shoulders about West and wanted to beat them because of their arrogance, who they thought they were. [EHS 71 WM]*

*At West, there were kids of doctors, lawyers, judges, council members. The assumption was they had more money and so they were expected to be smarter. [WHS 74 WF]*

EDUCATIONAL PATHWAYS FOR CATHOLIC SCHOOLS

The educational pathway in Waterloo for Catholic students grades 1-8 was also well-established since the first school – Our Lady of Victory Academy (OLVA) – was founded in 1872 on the East Side. (Figure 8)

Columbus High (9-12)
West Side

(K/1-8)

OLVA (East Side)
St. Mary (East Side)
St. John (East Side/SE)
St. Nicholas (East/Evansdale)
Blessed Sacrament (West Side)
Sacred Heart (West Side)
St. Edward (West Side)

Figure 8 Catholic Educational Pathways,
1963-1975

The pathway was extended when Columbus High opened in August 1959 to serve the needs of the eight Catholic parishes in Waterloo, Evansdale and Cedar Falls, which shared the school's cost. There were 901 students at Columbus the first year, which was a 38% increase over the number students at OLVA, Sacred Heart and St. Mary Catholic high schools the previous year. The staff included 16 priests, four of whom were full-time faculty, 18 religious and 10 lay instructors. In 1964, there were 1,241 students with 61 faculty, 3 clerical staff and a part-time worker.[33]

In 1969, "Based on the $640 per pupil cost of the National Education Association . . . Waterloo's Catholic school enrollment of 3,800 results in a savings of $2,432,000 to [the city's] taxpayers in annual operating costs."[34] Conversely, the Waterloo school district's budget would be affected in the coming years when public school students enrolled in Catholic grade schools and Columbus High due to busing.

# Busting Perceptions: Waterloo Schools by the Numbers

Dallas Cowboy star running back Don Perkins is known in Waterloo as the first black student to attend West High in the mid-1950s, although people still believe he lived on the East Side. The generally accepted story is that the BOE allowed him to attend West because of his athletic ability. He was elected student council president his senior year. People again believe he was elected because he was a star athlete at West.

None of these perceptions are based in fact. Perkin's family lived on the West Side in Riverview.

*I met some kids at West Junior from Riverview, sort of a shanty-town neighborhood by the river on the West Side. There were a lot of salvage yards and lower income people like the East Side. They didn't have indoor plumbing. I'd never run up against like that before. Nobody really wanted to be around them. [WHS 67 WM]*

His three older siblings, among other blacks, had attended West Side elementary and junior high schools and West High school before him. When Perkins' mother died, his father moved the family to the East Side. He was allowed to finish at West where he was already attending.

A good student and active in the school, Perkins was elected vice president of the student government as a junior, before his athletic reputation had been fully established in his senior year at West.

The Perkins story is relevant, because of the accepted myth he broke the barrier at West High when he graduated in 1955.

East High is on the side of town at the southern edge of the North End. Known as the black high school in the 60s and into the early 70s, *TBB* participant's estimates of racial balance at East from 1963-1973 ranged from 25-30% black to 100%, even among East graduates.

The actual percentage was between 18-20%.

*TBB* contributors' estimates of black-white or other ethnic student percentages at West were consistently 100% white in 1963 to less than five percent by 1973 since there were no blacks on that side of town.

Many people were surprised when I mentioned FIVE high schools. Unless they were involved in sports, they didn't know or remember Orange High. It was a little sibling to its bigger Waterloo schools, having merged into the WCSD in 1964. Those who did know Orange perceived it as a farm school with no blacks, who didn't farm.

Central High –opened in 1972 as Orange was closing – was perceived by as a racially balanced school with an equal number of black and white students who attended from the East Side due to forced busing.

Two percent (5/242) of the first Central graduating class in 1973 – drolly promoted as the school's "biggest ever" – were black students, based on a count of the senior class in the yearbook.[35] The second graduating class in 1974 was 0.9% black students (2/211). The class of 1975 – the first group of students to have attended Central all three years – was comprised of 10.2% black students (17/166). Central High closed in 1988, re-opened as a junior high school and was converted to a middle school in 1996.[36]

Columbus has always been considered a white school because of the belief tuition would be too expensive for black families. Estimates of black students at Columbus were zero percent in 1963 to less than five percent in 1973.

Among people who attended the five Waterloo high schools from 1963-1973, racial mix perceptions were based not only on whether the school was on the East Side or West, but through observation and socialization at sports competitions, local activities like parades, community band and chorus, drum & bugle corps, church attendance, parties hosted by the YMCA or in Cedar Falls, cruising the strip and in other formal and informal groups.

People's perceptions of the percentage of blacks in Waterloo and the racial composition of East High from 1963 to 1973 are not close to the reality. Perception of the percentage of black students at Central was closer. The perception that West, Orange and Columbus were white high schools was spot on.

# Reflections from the Bridge

People and communities are change aversive. There is fear of loss of control and self-determination. "Better the devil you know than the devil you don't know." The outcome is social inertia, status quo; changes aren't made in the absence of a compelling reason to do so.

The triarchy accepted an inertia that hampered, if not thwarted, desegregation of Waterloo's schools, maintained the status quo.

Their inaction left the students caught in the crossfire from 1963-1973 between the local human rights commission, the Kansas City office of the U.S. Civil Rights Commission (USCRC) and the Iowa Department of Public Instruction (DPI), and the philosophically polarized Citizen's Committee of the East Side and the Neighborhood Schools Association.

The students in *TBB* were, in a sense, an embodiment of Waterloo itself for two reasons – the high-profile, state-wide success of the high school sports teams, and the student walkouts, riots, protests and battles over school integration during the latter part of the Civil Rights movement.

The smoldering frustration of East Side and pro-Civil Rights West Side parents resulted in the upheaval of change from 1963-1973.

# Endnotes

[1] Work for Humanity, Dr. King Advises. (November 11, 1959). *The Waterloo Daily Courier*, 3.

[2] MLK Day – Martin Luther King Jr.'s Eastern Iowa visits in 1959 and 1962. (Jan 20, 2014). Dorman, T. *The Cedar Rapids Gazette*. Retrieved from http://www.thegazette.com/2014/01/20/mlk-day-martin-luther-king-jr-s-eastern-iowa-visits-in-1959-and-1962.

[3] Civil rights Activists recall watershed year in civil rights struggle. (February 3, 2013). Kinney, Retrieved from http://wcfcourier.com/news/local/activists-recall-watershed-year-in-civil-rights-struggle/article_a8b56418-a64f-5020-bdbf-efe87d474ec9.html.

[4] Activists recall watershed year in civil rights struggle. (Feb 3, 2013). Kinney, P. Waterloo-Cedar Falls Courier. Retrieved from http://wcfcourier.com/news/local/activists-recall-watershed-year-in-civil-rights-struggle/article_a8b56418-a64f-5020-bdbf-efe87d474ec9.html.

[5] Ibid.

[6] Civil and Human Rights March commemorates Selma march, stresses voting rights. (March 26, 2018). Steffen, A. Retrieved from http://wcfcourier.com/news/local/civil-

and-human-rights-march-commemorates-selma-march-stresses-
voting/article_86279c7d-3535-59d4-aefc-edd86b0a4082.html.

[7] Jochumsen and Turner provided stability in the mayor's office. The last mayor to have served more than seven terms was Ralph Slippy, who was elected nine times from 1936-1945. Leo Roof followed Turner and also served nine terms.

[8] Negro Pickets March At City Hall 3 Hours. (June 03, 1966). *Waterloo Daily Courier*, 1.

[9] Roosevelt Elementary School, U.S. Department of the Interior, National Park Service: National Register of Historic Places Registration Form, section 8, 11. Retrieved from http://focus.nps.gov/pdfhost/docs/NRHP/Text/04001402.pdf.

[10] Ibid.

[11] History: Waterloo Schools. Retrieved from http://www.waterloo.k12.ia.us/history/.

[12] Roosevelt Elementary School, 10.

[13] (1) East Twp. Schools in City District. October 15, 1963). *Waterloo Daily Courier*, Front Page. (2) History. Waterloo Schools.

[14] Ibid.

[15] School Desegregation in Waterloo, Iowa. (August 1977). A Staff Report of the United States Commission on Civil Rights, p. 5.

[16] Sage, Mrs. Rehder, Gamb Elected to School Board. (September 15, 1970). *Waterloo Daily Courier*, Front Page.

[17] Public School Pupils Used to Distribute Voting Data. (September 12, 1971). *Waterloo Daily Courier*, 17.

[18] Ibid.

[19] Linn Wins at Waterloo. (September 14, 1971). *The Des Moines Register*, 7.

[20] Kammeyer, Wells Elected to Board. (September 12, 1972). *Waterloo Daily Courier*, Front Page.

[21] SHARE was a Waterloo organization formed in 1972 to "promote quality integrated education, i.e., cultural, economic and racial integration, for every child in the public-school system, and to the acquisition and dissemination of full knowledge on those issues pertinent to making the community a united, progressive city with equal opportunity for all citizens." 'Quality' Schools Group is Formed. (May 09, 1972). *Waterloo Daily Courier*, 3.

[22] Citizen's (sic) Committee of East Waterloo, Iowa, Inc. (March 02, 1966). Articles of Incorporation. *Waterloo Daily Courier*, 2.

[23] William Kammeyer Files for School Board Post. (August 04, 1972). *Waterloo Daily Courier*, 3.

[24] School Board Election. (September 10, 1972). *Waterloo Daily Courier*, 13.

[25] NSA-Backed Slate Sweeps Election. (September 12, 1972). *Waterloo Daily Courier,* Front Page.

[26] Role of the Board. Waterloo Schools. Retrieved from http://www.waterlooschools.org/board/role-of-the-board/.

[27] George Hohl Is Appointed School Superintendent. Takes Position on July 1. Jack Logan Retiring Then. (January 21, 1962). *Waterloo Daily Courier,* 1. Waterloo Daily Courier

[28] The Public Speaks. Backs Diestelmeier for Superintendent. (June 18, 1970). Pieters, J.S. *Waterloo Daily Courier,* 4.

[29] Ibid.

[30] Ibid.

[31] School Board Will Study Oversize Class Problems. (September 20, 1964). *Waterloo Daily Courier,* 13.

[32] History. WCSD Home. Retrieved from http://www.waterlooschools.org/history/.

[33] *Go Forth and Teach: Continuing the Challenge. A sequel to With Faith & Vision.* (2001). Toale, Rev. Dr. T.F., exec. Ed., Casey, C, ed. & Beckett, L, ed. Dubuque, IA: Loras College Press, 222-223.

[34] Comprehensive Plan Depends on Bus Bill. Close a2 Catholic Schools. (February 10, 1969). *Waterloo Daily Courier,* 2.

[35] A count of yearbook photos doesn't represent precise data; not every student has a photo taken or submitted or photos are lost. Yearbooks don't usually list those students who aren't pictured.

[36] For a complete historical timeline of the Waterloo Community School District, see the Waterloo Schools History at http://www.waterloo.k12.ia.us/history/.

Sunrise Downtown Waterloo. Black Hawk County, IA. Retrieved from https://www.co.black-hawk.ia.us/.

# TBB 5: High School Is Black & White

Figure 1 The 1960s

*There has never been a decade quite like the Sixties; the diversity, conflicts, hope, anger, the music, the dance crazes and the fun. . . . [It] was a decade of change. . . . that resulted in the most significant changes in our [country's] history. . . . [in] one of the most turbulent decades in modern history. . . . [It was a] time of turmoil. . . racial unrest. . . social injustice . . . our involvement . . . Vietnam [resulted in] violence in the streets of U.S. cities as well as on college campuses in protest of the War in Vietnam [that] was unprecedented in our history.*

*[It was also] was a great decade to have grown up in. . . . just ask anybody who was a baby boomer [including high school graduates from 1963-1973]. . . . life seemed so much more carefree and slower. . . . We knew all our neighbors on the street where we lived. Innocent fun was the game not violence against our fellow man.*

*. . . We all believed in Make Love, Not War. We were idealistic innocents, despite the drugs and sex.[1]*

Going into the 60s, the triarchy relationships among the community, its government and the school board had been relatively stable and unchallenged since the Waterloo Community School

District [WCSD] was formed in 1942. That changed in the 60s and early 70s.

The status quo of the Waterloo school system and the schools was replaced with unfamiliar storming in ERA1, school years from the fall of 1963 to graduation in 1966. Having a new superintendent office disrupted the traditionally stable high school setting for 1963 graduates, many of whose parents and older siblings had attended the same school. Population shifts from 1960-63 affected minority enrollments in the East Side schools, from elementary through high school.

Graduates of ERA2 school years, 1967-1970, were buffeted by changes in the superintendent's office and on the WCSD Board of Education (BOE), and challenges to the segregation of community schools. Metaphoric horizontal wind shears included student walk-outs at East, riots and protests, hostile confrontations with the principals and the BOE.

The storm continued somewhat abated into ERA3, 1971-1973, as the school board and administration, and the community sought for an acceptable solution for integrating all Waterloo schools. At the end of 1973, there was a plan – a tenuous one – but one that could be achieved at the time.

## High School's a Brand-New Game

By 1964, 10 years after the U.S. Supreme Court struck down the separate but equal doctrine in American public schools, just one in eighty-five Southern black children attended an integrated school.[2]

In Waterloo in the early 1960s, one in 10 students attended an integrated school. There were virtually no black students at West, Orange or Columbus high schools on the West Side.

For many East Side students, the transition from elementary to junior high school included their first exposure to black classmates, adjustment students from the biracial schools on the East Side had already made.

According to the majority of *TBB* respondents, the transition to East High was easier for Logan students than those from McKinstry given the respective ratio of blacks and whites in the junior highs.

The Catholic schools in Waterloo had very few black students, although there was a Spanish surnamed [the term used then] minority in the system. Catholicism is the major religion of Hispanics or Latinos. (Figure 2)

*I was in the first pool of blacks to go through all four years of high school at Columbus. There had been blacks at Columbus before who only went a year or two. It was just me, and my sister and brother. So, I recruited two other black students to come to Columbus. The church helped financially with people coming from their parishes to Columbus, both black and white. And they paid monthly, which helped a lot.*

*The people I knew valued education. If you value something and it's worth achieving, then you have to pay for it. The reason my mom was so heart-strong on Catholic school was so we got a good education and had discipline. My family believed in discipline. We had a thing where you had to be in the house by 10 pm, no "ifs, ands or buts." My mom believed in studying. Her folks were the first blacks to have a car in the Mississippi town she grew up in and she had a college degree. [COL 64 AAM]*

The decision to attend Columbus was also an issue for white students on the East Side because of the tuition. Not attending Columbus but switching to public school in the 9th grade – the last year of junior high – was a difficult transition. Many classmates who had been in the parochial schools together for eight grades opted for public schools. They had to seek and forge new social, study group and other relationships with a smaller core of support than the students who attended Columbus. While Columbus students also had to establish new friendships, their environment contained a larger core support group of long-time friends, and people who shared a similar religion and/or desire for and ability to have a private school education.

*When I was at Columbus High, I thought I was better than the white kids. Based on me being a basketball star and lean and tall. I thought I was all that and a bag of chips. I never had a problem with prejudice. Father Walter Brunkan was the most important influence in my years at Columbus. An assistant principal, he was promoted to principal and remained in that role for over 20 years. Brunkan could look through me. And I never had another person in my life who could do that, even my mom and dad. They knew when I lied, but they couldn't look through me. He could look through me and tell me I was lying. So, I have a problem with people lying because of what he did to me. [laughs] [COL 64 AAM]*

*When it was time to decide about public or Catholic high school, our priest and my parents wanted me to go to Columbus. Some of my Catholic friends couldn't go to Columbus because it cost a lot of money. And I didn't want to put that hardship on my dad. That was the main reason I went to East. And because my friends from junior high were going there. [EHS 66 WF]*

*Going to Columbus, the "fish-eater" and "cat-licker" name-calling came up every occasionally in jest from kids at the other schools. My mom said that was a big deal when she was in school. We used to jibe the Protestant kids that, "Too bad you won't go to heaven." We had a lot of humor in the neighborhood. We weren't too pushy. [COL 66 WM]*

## Faculty Transitions to East High School

White faculty at East High also had adjustments to make, especially if they weren't a product of the East Side schools or other racially mixed communities, even if the college or university attended was multicultural.

*I openly congratulated a white quarterback for his success. Other football players, some of them black, were in the room and*

*said nothing. But one uttered a comment to let me know it
wasn't appreciated. A lesson for me on handling race relations in
class at East. [EHS teacher]*

*An incident has stuck with me to this day. A black male in
class had misbehaved or at least did something I thought he
shouldn't. I don't recall exactly what. When I started to verbally
discipline the young man, he became very withdrawn, said
nothing and displayed wide fearful eyes. I stopped my verbal
correction and never again tried to correct the behavior of black
students. I felt like Simon Legree [the cruel slave owner in "Uncle
Tom's Cabin"] talking to him and didn't want that feeling again.
I decided at that point to let these little errors slide and refer
major problems to the office. [EHS teacher]*

*It was probably 1965 when a black female student asked me
after American history class one day why I never taught any
black history or mentioned the contributions of blacks. I didn't
have an answer. I told her I didn't know any black history, I
hadn't been taught that aspect of American history and asked if
there were any significant contributions to American history
made by blacks I should cover. She told me the first traffic light
had been developed by a black and mentioned Crispus Attucks,
the first to man to fall at the Boston Massacre in 1770. I then
mentioned the conversation to other social studies teachers in the
hall, but no one had advice on how to handle that situation. One
asked, "Are there any contributions made by blacks?" EBONY
magazine was running a series on black history at the time,
which the student mentioned. All I could tell her was I hadn't
read and didn't read that magazine. [EHS teacher]*

*The women teachers had a reputation, even the smaller ones,
for not having a problem even facing guys down. It was a
learning thing. My cousin was an aide at East after we
graduated. She talked with the new white teachers and told them*

*what she had been told when she started. "You cannot show
weakness. If you believe a situation has to stop, you have to
stand your ground. Stand your ground and earn the reputation
of holding that ground, and the students will respect you. They
may say a lot of things, but you have to stand your ground." The
teachers were taught that. But they were also taught, "You can't
touch them." It was passed on from teacher to teacher to teacher.*
[EHS 66 AAM]

## The Black Experience in High School 1963-1973

There was a gulf between blacks and whites in Waterloo when we
were in high school in 1963-1973. We whites didn't understand what
the black community and our classmates were experiencing. We were
like John Howard Griffin in *Black Like Me* – empathetic with blacks
and their civil rights, but with absolutely no idea what it was like being
black. Our black classmates masked most of what they were feeling,
but it could have been discovered with deeper communication with
them.

That's not an indictment; it's the way it was. Teenagers – black and
white, brown, yellow, purple – live myopic lives, self-centered, focused
on what's important to them. It's also a defense mechanism against
stresses from the demands and expectations of others and life.

My "ah-hah" moment came in the downtown market in Danang,
Vietnam, in 1969 when I realized I was the only Caucasian and my
assistant was the only black anywhere within probably more than five
square miles. We were a head-and-a-half taller than the Vietnamese,
our eyes were a different shape and our skin colors were different.
There was no hiding, no blending in. I the other airman if that's how
he felt being black in America. He said "yes,' except the Vietnamese
avoided us, head and eyes down, patronizingly deferential. Not what
blacks experienced in a white crowd back home in "the real world."

**'63-'66**  *I recognized I was black early on in life as a
youngster growing up in Riverview on the west side*

*and going to Riverview Elementary. It was a poor area, mostly white with a few blacks. I didn't have a problem with being black until I started getting called the names. I started to see it's a different world, that some whites thought they're better. And we got looked down upon as if we were worse. When I looked at it, I realized there are some whites that were in worse shape than we were. And I had no problem realizing who I was. I had no problem. And I didn't have a problem with people looking down on me, because I felt I was good as anybody. I could compete in the classroom and, for that reason, I felt I was just as good. [WHS 60 AAM]*

*I lived on Beech Street and the whites would pass by the house going to Porky's at the [Sunnyside] country club. A white lady passed in a new fancy convertible one day when I was talking to my girlfriend, loudly, having fun. The woman thought I'd said something to her, got out of her car and approached us. She accused me of saying something out of place to her. I asked what she was talking about. She said she came through the neighborhood all the time and nobody ever said anything to her. And I said, "Nobody said anything to you this time." She said she was going to call the police. That's my most vivid memory of racism that was happening in Waterloo. [EHS 61 WM]*

*We were living on the West Side when I was in high school. But my brother and I had black friends from the East Side who went to Columbus with us. You didn't see a lot of blacks in any of the Catholic schools unless you're talking St. Mary's out on East 4th Street where my cousins lived. We carpooled to school so sometimes they'd pick us up or drop us off. There was a woman living across the street from us who knew everything that went on in the neighborhood, always looking out the window, watching everything. One time when our black friends were dropping us off, she opened her door and stood on the porch screaming she didn't want niggers in our neighborhood. To "get out of our neighborhood. Get Out. I don't want you here. I don't want to look at you. I don't want to see you." My mom happened to be home and my mom had a lot of balls. And she was irate. She stood in the middle of the street and defended our black friends being on our street. She told the woman they were welcome any time. The woman wasn't the only person on the street who complained. They still came by our house; our mom was adamant things weren't going to change. We were young. We were aware there were sensitive racial issues in town. We heard about it, we read about it. But it's not really touching your personal life in a personal way until something personal like that happens. It opened a lot of discussion about how sad it was for them. I didn't understand it, because I didn't have to feel it personally. They felt every minute of it. How do you verbalize all of that? It was a hard time. It didn't affect our friendship. We remained friends well past our high school years. But we weren't accepted in that neighborhood for a long time. It pitted us against some of the other families on the block, some of whom wouldn't speak to my mother. [COL 63 WF]*

*I always knew there were different people. From when I was very small and started school. Between Cottage and Oneida Street where I grew up, there were whites, Native Americans, mulattos. There was a mixture, but it was predominantly black. It was like a family almost. Most of us couldn't afford to have locks on our doors. Everybody knew everybody. We could be somewhere else and do something and get in trouble. Strangers would say, "I'm going to tell your dad." [laughs] There were women in the neighborhood that would light you up with a strap. And "I'm telling your dad." And you'd get home and he'd know about it. And he'd light you up, too. It was family. [EHS 66 AAM]*

*Judge William Parker moved into Highland Park [on the East Side] where the builders and professionals of Waterloo lived in 1964-65. Crosses were burned on his front lawn one night. My father walked down there and sat with him until late in the night. [EHS 66 WF]*

*I lived in Mason City, Iowa, – the north central Iowa All-American setting for Meredith Wilson's "The Music Man" – until the 9th grade. There weren't many minorities. I remember two black brothers in school* with me, the Brown brothers. I had a paper route. And there was a woman on my route who had two mixed-race boys. She was always terrified to open the door when I collected. Her husband was black, a really good friend of my father when he was growing up. For a white woman to be married to a black person in the early 60s in Mason City was terrifying. [EHS 66 WM]

**'67-'70** My folks talked to us about diversity issues starting in elementary school all the way through. They would always tell us basic, common sense things. "Do what you're supposed to do. Follow the rules. We're not third-class citizens." [EHS 67 AAM]

I was very fortunate. We were never told by our family being black meant something. Our dad never said it outright, but in some ways, he let us know, didn't let us forget we were black and have a black heritage. For example, I was in gospel choir at one of the Protestant churches, even though I went to Columbus. There were black kids in my kindergarten. But at St. Mary's Elementary there were only two or three black families. About the same at Columbus High. I knew there was a difference in color. It never really bothered me and I never thought about it. It wasn't important because our family didn't focus on it. When I started to look back, I'd remember incidents and I think, "Ah-ha, it was because I was black." For example, I wasn't invited to parties by the white girls at Columbus. [COL 69 AAF]

There was one black family my whole neighborhood and one of their kids was in my class. One year the family went on vacation and while they were gone, their house burned down. Rumors in the neighborhood was it was white teenagers, but nobody was ever caught and charged. They didn't move back. After that were no black people in my neighborhood. It was very segregated in those days and I lived in the same neighborhood all the way through high school. [WHS 69 WM]

I don't remember ever not knowing black wasn't better. My mother was on welfare. And to make sure there were no black men in the house, the welfare people would come through our house. I saw fear in my *mother's eyes and I'd ask what the matter was. And her whole vernacular would change when interacting with these people. She'd start speaking proper, as we'd say. And they'd come in, and look under the bed and in the closets. It was totally dehumanizing and humiliating at every level. It had gotten to the point they wouldn't send her welfare check directly to her. She had an overseer in an office downtown next to the Strand Theater. My mom wasn't comfortable talking to him. I was the second oldest, in grade school, but the most capable. And when it was time, I had to go downtown and ask her overseer for shoes or clothing. And he would talk to me like I was the lowest thing on the planet earth. And he said, "Why did your mother send you down here? She knows she doesn't have any money." And I would say, "She just got her check and she didn't buy any groceries. You got the check, I need some shoes." They stole 80% of her check on a regular basis. So, I started stealing and robbing at an early age. I don't recall any memories where my black wasn't an issue or a concern or something I had to be conscious of all the time. [EHS 69 AAM]*

*I got placed on probation at a very young age for breaking into everything in the neighborhood, every store. I took pride in the fact I never robbed anybody black or stole anything from a black business. That was a badge of honor for all of us young black kids. Our motto. There were the stores on East 4th street – D&M Market, Neubauer & Crow, Cal & Art's Pool Hall, Webbeking Bakery, the record store near the alley – and we would have some good schemes to go in stealing for food at a very young age. There was the Piggly Wiggly [on Logan Avenue] on the way to school, and we'd go in every morning and steal our breakfast. We'd steal donuts from the Hostess truck at the loading dock and sometimes there'd be a bag of money in there. It was a matter of survival. When I was at Logan Junior High, I had to go to the head of the CETA [Comprehensive Employment and Training Act] program in Waterloo, who was a coach at Logan, to get a summer job. I was one of the "bad kids" so I didn't get a job easily. I had to grovel and beg. He* *hired me at $1.25 back in those times, but he worked me like [pauses] . . . worse than a field hand. [EHS 69 AAM]*

*I remember when I was a kid hearing one out of three black people in Iowa lived in Waterloo. I thought the only place there were murders in Iowa was Waterloo. That wasn't literally true, obviously. [WHS 69 WM]*

**'71-'73** *I grew up in a diverse environment. My dad married a Caucasian woman who became my stepmother and her son became my brother. My aunt was white, my first cousins are mixed. That's what Waterloo was made of. Dad owned a jazz club. He was a percussionist, played the drums. And a lot of the guys in his groups were Caucasian. So, I grew up in a multiracial environment. [EHS 73 AAM]*

*My parents were golfers, probably one of the first black families in Waterloo who golfed. They came home one time from a party at the Gates Country Club where my mom and some white woman had gotten into it because she called my mom a nigger. And my mom hit her over the head with a bottle. [EHS 73 AAF]*

*In Waterloo, when I went for a job, I knew I was going to stand in front of a Caucasian interviewer. So, I would have to project myself, in a way, as if it's a show. [EHS 73 AAM]*

## 1968 The East High Campus Plan

The Waterloo Urban Renewal Board petitioned on behalf of the Board of Education (BOE) for a U.S. Department of Housing and Urban Development (HUD) federal open-spaces grant in 1968 to develop a campus around East High comparable to the one at West High. (Figure 2)[3] East had a brief front lawn, a small parking lot behind and a crumbling concrete stadium a block from the main building.

Long-time board member Stewart Seidler – one of the two East Side residents on the seven-member board – noted, "Why should West

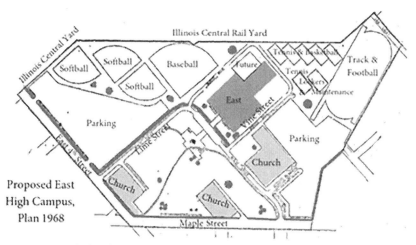

Figure 2 Proposed Plan for the East High Campus, 1968
*The U.S. Department of Housing and Urban Development appropriated
$1.15 million under the Open Spaces Program to help fund the costs of the
East High campus expansion.*

High have a campus and not East? Why should one school be deprived
and not the other?"[4]

The plan would include recreation areas, green spaces and parking
lots for three churches around the school. According to several
sources, the campus was also intended to eliminate a residential area
from which attacks had made been during riots in 1967 and 1968, and
was to elude and hide from authorities.

Cascaden Place and Pierce Street were also eliminated in the plan to
make way for the softball and baseball fields.

The grant would provide 50% reimbursement to the city and BOE
for 162 parcels of land and 100% reimbursement for the relocation of
35 families.[5]

The $5.8 million bond required was passed by 73.7% in late October
1968, carrying all 10 precincts; a 60% favorable vote was required. It
was approved by 84% of East High-area voters.[6]

Its passage permitted the BOE to budget and plan for a new high
school to "relieve pressure on East and West Highs and permit the

conversion of Orange High to an elementary and junior high center. . .
."[7] The site of the new school hadn't been selected at the time, but it
was opened as Central High on the West Side in 1972, ERA3 in *The Bridge Between.*

Before it agreed to allocate the funds Open Spaces Grant funds,
HUD required assurance that there would be adequate relocation
housing for displaced residents. That responsibility was assigned to the
relocation section of the Waterloo Urban Renewal Department.[8]

Waterloo received the grant on April 16, 1970, and the school board
began to clear the project area by buying and razing houses of owners
who agreed to sell.

Figure 3 East High Campus, 2018

By the fall of 1971, the school looked the same, but it was "for the first
time clearly visible from . . . East Fourth Street [its western boundary
three blocks away]."[9] (Figure 3)

## Reflections from the Bridge

*On 1 February 1960, 17-year-old Franklin McCain and three black
friends went to the whites-only counter at Woolworths in Greensboro,
North Carolina, and took a seat. "We wanted to go beyond what our
parents had done. The worst thing that could happen was that the Ku
Klux Klan could kill us ... but I had no concern for my personal safety.*

142

*The day I sat at that counter I had the most tremendous feeling of
elation and celebration. . . ."*[10]

At his inauguration as Alabama governor in January 1963, the year
*The Bridge Between* begins, George Wallace shared his belief there was
a "deep-seated aversion to racial integration among Northerners as
well as Southerners" when he stated, "In the name of the greatest
people that have ever trod this earth, I draw the line in the dust and
toss the gauntlet before the feet of tyranny . . . and I say . . . segregation
today . . . segregation tomorrow . . . segregation forever."[11]

As we finished junior high, the spring of 1963 was marked with
Civil Rights marches, black voter registration drives, sit-ins and
protests, Wallace blocking the door at the University of Alabama to
prevent two black students from enrolling and President Kennedy's
nationwide address that evening: "For the first time he unequivocally
condemns segregation and racial discrimination, and he announces his
intention to submit to Congress a new, effective, civil rights bill."[12]

*. . . in 1963 the number [of blacks] who were prepared to commit
[active] resistance [to segregation] reached a critical mass. "In three
difficult years. . . the southern struggle had grown from a modest group
of black students demonstrating at one lunch-counter to the largest mass
movement for racial reform and civil rights in the 20th century".*[13]

Rev. Martin Luther King, Jr., proclaimed, "1963 is not an end, but a
beginning," in his acclaimed "I have a dream speech" at the August
March on Washington for Jobs and Freedom.

His prophecy would play out over the next 10 years in an unlikely
location to outsiders – a Midwestern Iowa town named Waterloo in
which blacks and whites had been segregated by a river for since the
turn of the 20th century.

# Endnotes

[1] The 60s Official Site. Retrieved from http://www.the60sofficialsite.com/.

[2] Millhiser, I. (May 14, 2014). 'Brown v. Board of Education' Didn't End Segregation, Big Government Did. Activism: The Nation. Retrieved from https://www.thenation.com/article/brown-v-board-education-didnt-end-segregation-big-government-did/.

[3] Modified sketch from Proposed East High Campus Plan. (January 19, 1969). *Waterloo Daily Courier*, 35.

[4] East High Cut Questioned. School Bond Vote to be in October. (August 13, 1968). *Waterloo Daily Courier*, 8.

[5] 29 Parcels Purchased. Report Progress on East Project. (April 21, 1970). *Waterloo Daily Courier*, 6.

[6] East High Sets [sic] in New Surroundings. (July 11, 1971). *Waterloo Daily Courier*, 15.

[7] School Bond Issue Passes by 73.7%. Proposal Carries All Precincts. (October 22, 1968). *Waterloo Daily Courier*, Front Page.

[8] More to Relocation of Families from Open Spaces than Moving. (July 12, 1970). *Waterloo Daily Courier*, 20.

[9] Ibid.

[10] 1963: the defining year of the civil rights movement. Younge, G. (May 07, 2013). *The Guardian*. Retrieved from https://www.theguardian.com/world/2013/may/07/1963-defining-year-civil-rights.

[11] (1963) George Wallace, "Segregation Now, Segregation Forever." BlackPast.org. Retrieved from http://www.blackpast.org/1963-george-wallace-segregation-now-segregation-forever. Wallace ran for President four times between 1964 and 1976 – three as a Democrat and once as an Independent.

[12] Kennedy's Civil Rights Speech. CRMVet.Org. Retrieved from http://www.crmvet.org/tim/timhis63.htm#1963jfks.

[13] Race, reform, and rebellion: the second Reconstruction in black America, 1945-1990. (1991). Marable, M. Jackson, MS: University Press of Mississippi, 69.

# Part 2 The Storm Named Integration

Almost everyone with whom I had contact while researching, talking to the graduates and writing *The Bridge Between* said he or she couldn't wait to read the book.

My honest response was, "Neither can I." Because even though I knew the book's theme, I had no idea what I would find in talking with them. There wasn't even a draft of an outline. There couldn't be.

Threads from the contributors' memories, perceptions and insights essentially wove themselves into a colorful, retrospective story across three distinct ERAs from 1963-1973.

## *TBB* 6: ERA1 1963-66 – The Calm Before the Storm

*When we went to [East High between 1954 and 1960], you didn't hear of a Negro making a fuss over everything he didn't like. We all got along just fine. Some of them were our friends and held offices in the homerooms and school committees. . . . Letter to The Public Speaks, Waterloo Daily Courier, September 16, 1968.[1]*

*We were in the locker room at West when we played them for the first time that season. I had just moved to Waterloo and joined the team. There was some commotion outside. They had a stuffed effigy with an East High shirt and pants hanging there. This was before we played the game. I never will forget what coach said to me after we lost the game. "You didn't have that energy out there the other guys have. Probably because this is your first year playing against West. And this is the type of stuff that happens." I told him "with my dying breath, I will always try and beat their brains out." That lit the fire underneath me. [EHS 61 AAM]*

> *We didn't have violence at East when I was in school, other*
> *than the boys puffing up with their testosterone. There wasn't*
> *what was coming. The clouds were growing in 1963. But we just*
> *didn't recognize it. [EHS 63 WF]*

The 1963 graduating classes at East, West and Columbus high schools lived through significant transitions in the U.S. and the world during their high school years.

President Dwight Eisenhower and Vice President Richard Nixon were finishing their second term in the White House in 1960. In May, an American U-2 spy plane was shot down over Russia and the pilot captured. In November, Americans elected its first Catholic president amid worries he would be subservient to the Pope. A coalition of Communists and insurgents emerged in Vietnam causing the buildup of American forces in 1961 with John F. Kennedy's presidency. In October 1962, the U.S. and Russia went the brink of nuclear war on live television.

The national backdrop continued to change dramatically during 1963 in ways that affected those of us who would graduate in the next 10 years.

Civil Rights leader Medgar Evers was killed in June, shot in the back in the driveway of his home in Jackson, Mississippi. It was the first in a string of assassinations that shocked America and resulted in the Sixties being remembered as, among other things, "The ERAof Assassination."

The end of August, Martin Luther King, Jr., co-founder and president of the Southern Christian Leadership Conference (SCLC), made his "I have a dream speech" during The March on Washington.

On November 22, 1963, President John F. Kennedy was assassinated in Dallas, Texas. Most of us who were in first grade or higher can tell you exactly where we were when we heard the news. Within an hour of the shooting, 68% of Americans knew; within two hours, 92% had heard, primarily from TV or radio.[2] We watched with the world "that long weekend of shock and mourning made a lasting impression on countless [us] young people just coming of age . . . ."[3] Until the 9/11 terrorist attacks on the World Trade Center in New York City, the assassination "was the longest uninterrupted news event in TV history. . . ."[4]

*In a very real sense, the Kennedy assassination produced a national sense of vertigo with Americans, regardless of age, race or background, questioning the very meaning of citizenship, freedom, security and justice.*[5]

## High School by the Numbers

At the start of the 1966 school year, Dr. George Hohl was the superintendent of Waterloo public schools, appointed by the Independent School District of Waterloo (ISDW) in 1962, only the second superintendent in the district since it was formed in 20 years earlier.

Charles Hoffman was principal at East High and had been since 1941. (Figure 1) He would retire at the end of the 1965-66 school year. His replacement, Lawrence Garlock, taught at East for two years following World War II and had been an East assistant principal since 1948.

West High principal Bill Gibson, first appointed in 1928, would retire in 1968 at the start of the second *TBB* era.

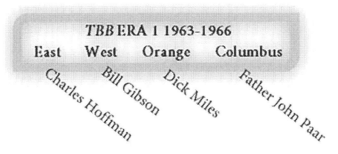

Figure 1 ERA1 High School Principals

| Table 1 Percentage of Blacks in Waterloo & Its High Schools | | | | |
|---|---|---|---|---|
| | ERA1 1963 | ERA 2 1967 | ERA 3 1970 | Central 1972 |
| Waterloo | 6.7%** | | | |
| East | 15.0% | | | |
| West | 0.0% | | | |
| Orange | | | | |
| Central | | | | |
| Columbus* | 0.0% | | | |
| *Estimates only. **From the U.S. Census Decennial Census, The Bureau didn't start issuing updates between each census until 1990. | | | | |

*Table 1 shows the percentage of Waterloo's black population in TBB ERA1 and the percentage of black students in East, West and Columbus high schools at the beginning of the ERA. The Orange Consolidated School District merged with the ISDW district in 1964, adding Orange High to the roster of WCSD high schools, the second on the West Side. Central High didn't open until the 1972-73 school year, the last year in the TBB decade. It*

Despite perceptions that East was the "black high school," only 15% of the study body was black in 1963. (Table 1)

Black students only attended East Side schools in 1963 at the start of *The Bridge Between* story. (Figure 2) Four of the 12 elementary schools had no black students, three others had below 15 percent. The others ranged from 23 percent to 99 percent. For half of the elementary students, junior high would be their first experience in a biracial school environment.

Two of the five elementary schools that fed into Logan Junior in 1963 had black students. Logan was 28% black. (Figure 2) Krieg, Lincoln and Van Eaton were white. McKinstry Junior had a 13.0% black enrollment that year. There were no black students at Lafayette, and only nominal numbers at Maywood and Frances Grout whose students moved up to McKinstry.

In 1964-1965, the Waterloo school system "ranked among the best in the nation" in academic accomplishment and administration

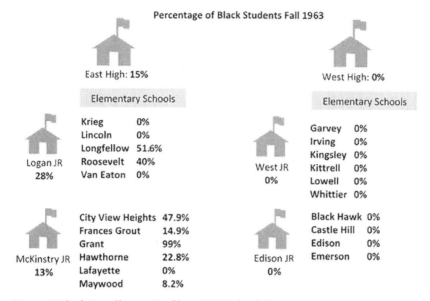

Percentage of Black Students Fall 1963

East High: 15%    West High: 0%

Elementary Schools    Elementary Schools

Logan JR
28%
Krieg       0%
Lincoln     0%
Longfellow  51.6%
Roosevelt   40%
Van Eaton   0%

West JR
0%
Garvey    0%
Irving    0%
Kingsley  0%
Kittrell  0%
Lowell    0%
Whittier  0%

McKinstry JR
13%
City View Heights  47.9%
Frances Grout      14.9%
Grant              99%
Hawthorne          22.8%
Lafayette          0%
Maywood            8.2%

Edison JR
0%
Black Hawk  0%
Castle Hill 0%
Edison      0%
Emerson     0%

Figure 2 Black Enrollment Profiles, 1963 School Year

effectiveness. Thirty-six (36) per 1,000 students ranked at the 98th percentile or above in the National Merit Scholarship Qualifying tests, "the highest for any of the metropolitan areas in Iowa and 14th in the nation. . . ." Among the 21 largest Iowa school districts, only four had a higher percentage of teachers with bachelor's degrees. It had the highest ratio of noncertified personnel to staff, which indicated "that a maximum effort is being made to free teachers of 'housekeeping' chores so they may concentrate on instruction." The system had a high pupil/teacher ratio of 26.4; the range was 21.2 to 21.6.[6] That had been reduced by 1969.[7]

Twenty-six percent (26.1%) of East High students, 28.9% at Orange High and 36.1% and 31.6% at West High expected to earn a bachelor's degree.[8]

## High School's a Brand New Game

*When people ask me about East over the years, they're surprised we started with around 650 kids our sophomore year and 200 or so were gone by graduation, most in the first year or so. I don't know whether that dropout rate was proportional for the number of black kids and white kids in our class. [EHS 66 WM]*

*I went to West my sophomore year for one semester. It was a big daycare. The faculty didn't care. "Don't come to school or take the test, it's no skin off my back." At Columbus, it was "nose to the grindstone 24/7." [COL 67 WM]*

Figure 3 East Waterloo High School
*Copyright © 2018 Marvitz Photography. Used with permission.*

Moving up to high school was different for students each year from 1963-1973. Not more difficult, just different.

*The black students had stronger personalities and stood up for themselves more than the white students did. They weren't low on self-esteem. They were forthright. And their habits were completely different than a lot of white people. They'd be trying to put the make on somebody in the classroom. You didn't see white dudes running around pimping. There were no Justin Biebers back then. [laughs] [EHS 64 WM]*

*Coming into East High from all-white Evansdale, my major adjustment was to be sensitive to race issues in my interactions with others, both black and white. After immersion into East, it became apparent to me we are all more alike than we are different. We have similar motivations and desires. And the many different personalities, morals and behaviors among us are less a characteristic of race than being humans. [EHS 66 WM]*

*I was used to going to school with black kids at Francis Grout and McKinstry. I never really realized East was different than the other high schools. I've had black friends my whole life. The racial mix never affected me in any way. I never had problems with anyone. [EHS66 WM]*

## Racial Relationships

*When I was at Logan Junior, this black kid stole my new suede jacket and transistor radio out of my locker. He came up and was talking to me not realizing he was wearing my coat. I got it back, but that incident carried into gym class when we were at East. We were doing relays and the same kid kept taking our ball and throwing it across the gym. I told him to leave it alone. He was way bigger than me, and he hit me in the shower and knocked me out. He threatened to come after me where we lived. I had many, many black friends that vowed to protect me, big name athletes. This kid was a troublemaker from the word "go." But there were just as many white kids that were big trouble makers, too, and went around to see who they could pick on and start fights with. [EHS 64 WM]*

*Everybody seemed to get along at East. We had camaraderie. Especially in the band. The Beatles were getting going. We had a pretty good football team just getting ready to start that long winning streak in the late 60s. We had the great basketball team with Gaylen Tann and Don Ross and Duane St. John. The athletics and the band and the camaraderie with the students. And I think we had great teachers as well. Those were pretty good times. [EHS 65 WM].*

# Racial Division in High School

*For the student council election in the spring, I filled out the form all candidates had to file showing interest in running for treasurer. Candidates were selected by the teachers or someone in the administration or both. I never knew how. But seven black students didn't register for the election; they just nominated themselves. I was shocked because I never thought someone would be nominated just because they were black. They were allowed to make speeches in the auditorium before the election. But none of them won. I didn't understand it at all. Why didn't they like us whites and felt they had to be a separate black group of nominees? Something's not right. [EHS 63 WF]*

The categorization of people by social strata occurs in all societies and social groups, and high school is no different.

Very few black friends attended our first class reunion five years after graduation from East. That continued to be the rule for several of the subsequent reunions I could attend. No rhyme or reason has ever been agreed to as to why, even by black students on the reunion committees who had commitments from other black alumni to be there, but weren't.

It caused me to reflect on black friendships, some since elementary school. It didn't take long to grasp that I'd never been invited to their homes. Or that I'd never extended that invitation either. Which became one of the *TBB* topics. The responses made it clear I wasn't alone.

*There was a definite racial separation at East. There were two different cultures, a sort of self-imposed segregation between blacks and whites. I was part of the white culture, whether it was my choice or not. I wouldn't be welcome in the black culture and I really didn't seek that. But I also realized black students wouldn't be able to be fully participate in my white culture. It's just the way it was. Not my rules, but I sensed I needed to comply with the system that was in place. [EHS 66 WM]*

*I went to a black friend's house a couple of times. We had "rolled steak." Hot dogs. They had the best hot dogs at his house. [EHS 66 WM]*

*Although I knew some of the blacks in our high school, I didn't interact with them that much. There wasn't conversation about what matters. There was sexual banter – which matters. [laughs] But not about how we hoped to mature as people and leave our mark in the world and what we care about deeply and what's not working. [EHS 66 WF]*

*My biggest sadness was I had a chance in homeroom to talk to a wonderful black woman of color and her best friend. I remember talking to them about what it was like to be black and to be white, and becoming friends. But after the after the Watts riot in 1965, all conversation was cut off. If a black person was seen talking to a white person and they were friends, then they were "Oreos." There was this whole about needing to know who you were as a black person. I thought, "Here, we die if we can't talk to each other and yet I was powerless." [EHS 66 WF]*

*When I was a senior I took a black friend from my house over to hers in the black community. And had to drop her off on a corner. Because if she was seen being dropped off by a white person, she would have been ostracized. [EHS 66 WF]*

*Friendships with blacks outside of school was difficult. They had their own things they did and we had other things we did. Transportation was a problem. We didn't all have a car back then. Bus service was limited. It was hard to get together. And I suppose a lot of people didn't have black students as friends like I did. [EHS 66 WF]*

*During my first year or two at East, I went to several school dances held in the student union. The black students stayed together and danced together at one end of the union, and whites were at the other end. There wasn't much interaction between the two groups socially. [EHS teacher]*

*My sister was at East in 1968. For a while, white girls couldn't bend over at a water fountain without one of your friends right behind you. One of the black boys would come up behind you and put his hand up your skirt. There wasn't any discipline. One of her first days at East, the teacher wasn't in the room before class started. My sister was one of the few whites in the class. The black guys got up and started sitting around her, putting their hands down her blouse. She got up, left the room, went to the office, sat down and said, "I'm not going back to that class." And nothing was done about it. [EHS 66 WF]*

*I had white friends in school and socialized with some outside of school. At parties and stuff. Basement parties in the North End like we used to have. [Black students] would invite one of the white athletes. He'd show up. Sometimes certain people didn't like him being there. Someone would walk up and confront him. When they did, another black guy would step in and defend, protect him. I never went to parties at the white kids' houses. I didn't know anyone who did. [EHS 66 AAM]*

*I had good relationships with the other athletes at East. I remember a lot of them [rapidly named a half-dozen East football players]. In track many times, when there was a larger meet like the Drake Relays, there wouldn't be enough competitors from either East or West to travel alone, so we'd travel together. [East star] Bob Tyson and I had a great relationship in the 100- and 200-sprints, trading off who won. We were color blind. We competed against each other, but there was never any racial judgment on either part. My perception was not only grounded in sports, but also socially. There would be a community dance at times and players from East, black and white, would be there. So, we occasionally interacted on the social plane. I wasn't oblivious to the riots and the upheaval on the East side, but I never personally had that kind of experience. [WHS 67 WM]*

*There was an intense rivalry between East and West. We hated to lose, but we weren't going to beat East in football. Obert Tisdale [later an Iowa State University academic all-conference player] was the*

154

quarterback and 1967 Iowa All-State 1ˢᵗ team Tom Smith [future Miami Dolphin] was in the backfield, and they could run like bullets. East would literally walk up to the line of scrimmage and call out the play. It wasn't a number they called out. They'd call out a name. And the coach asked us, "What are they telling you out there?" And we told him they were telling us where they were running. It wasn't arrogant. Half of the touchdowns East scored were called back because of penalties. [WHS 67 WM]

To a certain extent, at least at East, racial tension was somewhat of a joke. When there was rioting going on at various places around the country, my friends who were black would joke around and laugh and say, "We'd better hurry up and get home, there's going to be a race riot." And they'd laugh. It was kind of like, "This is ridiculous." The idea of a race riot in Waterloo. [EHS 67 WF]

It's remarkable how little interaction there was between the whites and the blacks in high school, given the plays, band, sports and everything else we shared. Mixed-race kids were neither fish nor fowl back then. Nobody quite knew who they were, including them. That had to be a really tough thing. I would guess the people who didn't go to East High would guess the percentage would be 50% to 75% black. Which would be an emotional guess from seeing the East football or basketball teams. If you looked in the stands, that wasn't the ratio. [EHS 67 WM]

People at East were more socially advantaged. I had some black friends when I was there and there was more diversity. A lot of things which could be called racist or indicated you weren't tolerant of the races wasn't because you didn't like them or thought anything bad about the blacks. It was you were scared. I felt scared from the time I was threatened by a black student at Longfellow. I was afraid a lot of the time. And I wasn't that I thought blacks were bad people. Because I know everybody has bad people and good people. [OHS 67 WF]

The only thing I ever did down on 4ᵗʰ Street was cruise. Or we would ride around the West Side, to see the other side of town. There were *boundaries. We knew where we could go and where we shouldn't go. We often went where we shouldn't go . . . Prospect Boulevard. [laughs] I remember cruising the strip the first night back from playing pro baseball. I had a 1967 Ford like in the movie "Bullitt," Steve McQueen's car. [EHS 67 AAM]*

## BLACK SELF-SEGREGATION AT THE 3$^{RD}$ FLOOR LOCKERS

I could count on both hands the number of black and white East grads who didn't talk about the 3$^{rd}$ floor with a finger or two left over. The black lockers were on the 3$^{rd}$, where the black students congregated and controlled the bathrooms for boys and girls.

*That's the way it was. We didn't ask questions about how it got that way. That's just the way it was. [EHS 60 AAM]*

*We blacks all congregated on the third floor. The lockers weren't segregated. There were whites there. But that's where we met with each other. [EHS 61 AAM]*

*We went in a few days before school for the social ritual of putting locks on lockers. When I started my sophomore year, my friends and I were told the seniors have the main floor lockers. The popular kids get the ones in the middle under the clock. The juniors could possibly be on the main floor, but on the side hallways and the second floor. The 3$^{rd}$ floor was for the colored kids. It's just the way it was. I just thought that's where the colored kids wanted to be. I wanted to be where my friends were. [EHS 63 WF]*

*If you were a girl, you wanted a locker on the main hallway on the first floor under the clock, because that's where the popular girls had theirs. Two of us got right around the corner off the main hallway our junior years and on the main hallway our senior year. [EHS 66 WF]*

*The whites were on the first and second floor, the blacks were on the 3$^{rd}$ floor. I knew because that's where my homeroom was. They segregated themselves. They wanted to be with their friends, just like I* *wanted to be with my friends. That was their choice. Things changed radically after we graduated in 1966. [EHS 66 WF]*

*There was no written rule for blacks that, when you come to school, you have to go to the 3rd floor until the bell rings. But it was understood [that's the way it was]. New blacks would come to East and, just because their friends and everyone they knew gravitated to the 3rd floor, it just became natural. When I came in as a sophomore, I didn't really notice there was something unusual about that. If you wanted to talk and be with your black friends, everybody was going to go to the 3rd floor. My brother, who was four years older, didn't notice it either. It was just accepted. [EHS 66 AAM]*

*We had de facto segregation at East High school. For example, there was no rule the black kids had to be on the 3rd floor, but it was that way for a long time and was socially acceptable. For our 25th reunion memory book, there was a comment from one of the black classmates remembering "the good times on the third floor." I was a little taken aback and wondered how many of the black students really resented that, even though it was an established practice. That wasn't too many years before the problems at East in 1968. [EHS 66 WM]*

*I was told repeatedly not to get a locker on the 3rd floor. Because all the black kids had their lockers on the 3rd floor. That will stand out in my mind forever. It didn't matter, because I was in the band and the band lockers were assigned by the band room. [EHS 66 WF]*

*I was on the 3rd floor for homeroom. It's where one of the black girls stabbed another girl in the bathroom with a fingernail file. That scared the buns out of me. I never went into the bathrooms on the 3rd floor. There was the black boy who stabbed his girl with the ice pick. I remember one of the teachers carrying her down and she was bleeding all over everything. [EHS 66 WF]*

*Most of the black people had their lockers on the 3rd floor. I knew there was tension. But I didn't think about it that much. I can't remember people using the "n-word" back then. Black people were part of the community and part of the school. I didn't know they were a problem. [EHS 66 WM]*

*I always felt guilty I was able to do things the black students weren't able to do, like move among the floors in the school. But if you look at it in reverse, I wasn't able to go to the 3rd floor because of the situation with the blacks and their lockers. [EHS 66 WF]*

*The bathrooms on the 3rd floor were off-limits to whites. I assumed it was originally institutional racism. But the blacks all had their lockers there. You picked your locker. So, by the time we got there in the mid-60s, it was self-segregation. I know a couple of the black kids who were in band – our lockers were down by the band room – and got hassled because they didn't have their lockers with the rest of the black kids. [EHS 67 WM]*

## BIRACIAL DATING

Interracial dating was a taboo in the early 1960s in Waterloo and most of the rest of the United States. And it wasn't just blacks and whites, but interracial dating and marriage were forbidden in many cultures and ethnic groups.

*My brother was dating a Catholic and, for my mother, that was just as bad as if he'd been dating a black. [EHS 66 WF]*

*My youngest brother liked a girl from Panama when he was in high school. Mom said not to date her. In her mind, she was black. My brother stopped dating her because he got punished all the time for continuing to do so. Then he left home, went into the Air Force and married her. Mom didn't say much to another brother's wife who was Icelandic or my second wife, who was Asian. [EHS 66 WM]*

There was biracial dating at East in the late 1950s and early 1960s. But it was very concealed, out of sight.

*There was some biracial dating. We really didn't go anywhere together socially after school. My basketball coach found out when I was dating a white girl and he said, "I'm ok with it. But our society isn't ready for it." [EHS 60 AAM]*

By the mid-60s, biracial dating had become slightly more prevalent and not as underground. But there was tremendous pressure on the couple, the need to be secretive beyond discreet. For both people, the reactions of peers and parents was rarely neutral or positive. And then there was the school administration with which they had to deal.

*When I was a sophomore at East in 1963, I learned first-hand about black/white dating. The older sister of a friend of mine was secretly dating a black guy. When it became public, she was disgraced by her parents and classmates. My friend was so upset about the reaction to her sister it affected her as well. It wasn't accepted at all. Which is why my friends stayed in the white group of friends, and only interacted with the blacks in class and extra-curricular activities in school. [EHS 65 WF]*

*A girl in high school I'm still friends with was deeply in love with a black guy I ran around with, a super athlete. Her dad wasn't into that. They had to keep it a secret from both parents. My friend's dad was black, his mother was Mexican, I think. I was never invited into the house to meet her. He always asked, "Can you just wait outside here a minute while I go in?" [COL 66 WM]*

*There were a few bi-racial couples when we were in school. The ones people found out about, there was usually some flak which resulted. There was one biracial situation where the teachers ostracized the students in the relationship – meaning they were discouraged from associating with each other in that way. It was an athlete and a student class president. There was a teacher-counselor who constantly discouraged that relationship. At the time, I didn't know or have an opinion about whether was to protect them or the school. Or whether it was the counselor's prejudice. It was interesting because the counselors were involved in rather dubious relationships with students. Today I'd probably say it was racially motivated. [EHS 66 AAM]*

*There was a girl a year ahead of me who had a black boyfriend and it was the talk of the school. People went on and on about what a terrible person she was. She was poor, but intelligent. The reaction was, "What do expect from white trash like that?" And there was a girl in my class who had a black boyfriend. A good friend of mine who worked at the East Side library told me she and the black boy would meet there in the book stacks. That became a huge deal. She was middle-class, attractive, smart. My friend didn't tell anyone else, but the library was used by other students to do research. So, it became well-known throughout the school. The other girls in our class were horrified. "How could she, a boyfriend-girlfriend thing? Going together?" Although they may not admit it today. I wasn't horrified. Maybe because of my family experiences. I've always been kind of, "So what?" [EHS 66 WF]*

The relationship was in reality "a close personal friendship which gave me insight and formed some values in my mind I wouldn't have gotten any other way," according to one of the pair. The girl's parents knew, because he visited their home. There initially was a bit of disapproval from them, because "the friendship wasn't something they'd ever considered, was different." It didn't stay that way; they liked him and he liked them. She visited his family as well. The friendship continued after high school, and he continued to visit the parents on several occasions even after she was gone and married.

Biracial dating was a shrouded part of the culture even at Columbus.

*I was dating a white girl when I was 17 or so. She and her cousin, who was dating my buddy, picked us up a couple of times and we'd go to her dad's office when it was closed, and sit and drink a beer. I didn't drink beer. But they drank beer and smoked, and we thought we were doing something big. We never had sex because I was Catholic and didn't believe in sex before marriage. And my mom didn't believe in mixed-race dating. She believed in black-and-black and white-and-white. [COL 64 AAM]*

*There was one biracial couple who were underclassmen during my senior year. They really stood out. The black boy was an athlete, and she was pretty, and so it was accepted on the surface, but most people disapproved and quietly whispered about it. [COL 66 WF]*

*My friend's sister dated a black young man. I remember her parents forbade it, so she would sneak out with him. It wasn't very acceptable. [COL 67 WF]*

There were some of us who were interested in seeing someone of the other race, but who never acted on it for myriad reasons. The primary one was fear of the experiences from friends and family just related.

*I sat beside a black male student in science class my junior year. He was popular, cute, well-liked, involved as much as I was in school activities and smart. I love smart guys. I never thought of dating black guys. It was hard enough to find smart guys, period. We talked about school and things, and we enjoyed each other's company. I said one day I'd like to keep the conversation going and he said he'd like to, too. We both knew it meant we'd like to know each other a little more. But he stopped and then said, "I don't think it would be a very good idea." It put me back, because in my mind it was just a boy and a girl. I didn't date anybody on a more serious level. Then I realized, "Gee, he's right." We stayed friends and continued to talk, but that was the last time we talked about anything more than the in-class friendship. [EHS 63 WF]*

This topic came up at one of our later 1966 class reunions. I told one of the black women I'd been interested in seeing her in high school. She asked why I hadn't told her that, made a move. Because she probably would have said "no," which she confirmed, laughing. "But it would have been nice to know."

There was also a social protocol for biracial couples. A white girl dating a black boy was more acceptable than a black girl dating a white boy.

*When I was a sophomore, I was coming out of the 3rd floor cafeteria and heard a commotion by the blacks' lockers. There were never loud voices in school and commotions like that. A group of black girls had surrounded the cheerleader captain. Everyone knew her. And, of course, she was white. She was in her uniform which caught my eye, otherwise I probably wouldn't have noticed. I stopped and a black girl was yelling at the cheer captain about a boy. Something to the effect of "you keep your hands off him, he's mine and he doesn't know you." The black girl was really aggressive, not physically, but really yelling. The white cheerleader responded quietly and slowly, like, "I'm not going to talk about or have anything to do with this." I didn't like the way it was going and left. I didn't know what happened. The cheerleader and the senior athlete the girl was yelling about stayed together, married and had a family. [EHS 63 WF]*

*A black guy who was a couple of years older dated white girls. I walked by his house one day. The front door opened and a white girl walked out. The girls would go into the black community, but not vice versa. And the couple didn't prance around us at school. [EHS 66 WM]*

## Racial Bias in High School

*There were three blacks in my homeroom. And I wondered then what they must have felt like. [EHS 66 WF]*

While the average academic performance for Waterloo schools was better than the national norm on standardized tests, scores for students in predominantly "Negro" schools indicated they weren't learning as well.[9]

An accelerated curriculum was approved by the BOE in early March 1963 that offered "superior students . . . in the top 10% of their class" an educational pathway through which a he or she could move through traditional curriculum at rates faster than typical based on his/her ability. The program had been launched in the system five years earlier in 1958 as an experimental one.[10]

Students selected for the accelerated program could complete both the 7th and 8th grade math courses in the 7th grade, permitting them to take algebra and geometry in the 8th and 9th grades instead of in the 9th grade and sophomore year of high school.

The creation of the high-ability accelerated student grouping resulted in two other clusters in the Waterloo schools – classes with medium- and low-learning ability students. This was in addition to special needs students.

The accelerated curriculum is different from one with classes that include students at all three ability levels. The argument for that heterogenous model is it "allows students to learn from each other's' differences and actively interact with diverse individuals, while at the same time sharing their unique abilities and interests."[11]

One of the common perceptions expressed 50 years after graduation was the stratification of classes by ability was a disadvantage to the black students, because their educational pathways had taken them through less academically rigorous elementary schools making them less likely to qualify for accelerated classes.

*The [accelerated program] is a long-standing educational issue. The argument is that, if you don't divide the classes, you keep the brightest students down and the lower students shooting for the middle. It started in junior high, with four divisions of academic levels. I think you're more intellectually stimulated with that strategy. I think there was one black in the accelerated civics class, and a few in math and chemistry. [EHS 66 WM]*

*There were some black kids in the upper level classes, but not a lot of them. You had some blacks who were extremely bright and were allowed in the door. Tracking was a form of segregation and I think there was a lot of that going on all over the country. It was a disadvantage for the black kids and I'm very sure it was deliberate. Another indication tracking was deliberate was classes were offered at West High they didn't have at East. For example, I wanted to take psychology and sociology which were offered at West. When I asked, I was told I had to have a car and the time to drive to West High during the day. I didn't have a car and there wasn't time between classes to make the trip. I ended up having to take them in summer school. [EHS 66 WF]*

*I had a whacked out reading class in the 10<sup>th</sup> grade. It was supposedly an advanced English class. Not a single black student. Blacks just weren't in my classes. Where were they? They were in the building, in band and choir. But not in chemistry or in math. [EHS 66 WF]*

*I didn't take Latin at Logan because I wanted to take Spanish. That put me out of classes with the accelerated group. Out of advanced math, science and English class. I landed in an English class with a new teacher and 29 classmates that were very different from me. I didn't know anyone; they were the motorcycle crowd and the smokers, but only a few blacks. I was very worried and nervous at first, and wondered how I was going to get along with them. So, I made a plan to make friends with the guys sitting in front and back of me. Which I did. But I never saw them outside of class. The teacher always put our scores on the board. I was always in the high 90s. Everyone else was in the high 60s. Made me uncomfortable and I told him about it. And he said, "Well, that's the way I like it. So, I'll lower the curve so the person next to you will get an 'A' also. And the next three will be 'Bs' then 'Cs.'" He did that, but still kept putting our scores on the board. [EHS 66 WF]*

*The American history we were taught was so white-washed. I'm a huge history buff. And everything we learned was wrong. We were just one step beyond Washington threw the apple across the Potomac and couldn't tell a lie, everybody was wonderful and there were all these heroes of the 50s. The books hadn't evolved much beyond that. [EHS 66 WM]*

*The year we graduated, West High had 10 straight-"A" students. I think we had one at East, our valedictorian. And I remember seeing in the Courier several years later West had 40 or so 4.0 graduates. One of our teachers at East who'd spent more time teaching at West said, "You're going to have to earn what you get here. Not like West because their daddies are rich." [EHS 66 WM]*

## RACIAL BIAS IN THE CLASSROOM

There were very few black teachers in the Waterloo school system in the early 1960s. The first one hired in Waterloo and only the second in Iowa was Lily Williams Furgerson in 1952 two years before the landmark U.S. Supreme Court ruling in *Brown v. Board of Education* forced the nation to integrate its schools. Teachers encountered by black students were white.

*For me, teachers were the indicators. They didn't really engage the black students that were in my classes. [EHS 66 WF]*

*A disadvantage of being black at East High was counselors told me I wasn't college material. And I know quite a few blacks who heard the same thing They encouraged us instead to pick up a labor skill. But there were some black students they obviously couldn't pitch that to. They were academically in the upper echelon in their classes and the counselors couldn't ignore the fact these were going to be high achievers. [EHS 66 AAM]*

*One of my teachers, I think it was in a college prep class, didn't tell me not to worry about trying to go to college. But she discouraged me. I got the impression it was because she assumed I was probably going to drop out anyhow. [EHS 66 AAF]*

*I'm sure the curriculum was biased. Everything was biased – that's how it was. In elementary school, every single one of our reading books featured only white children. It was as if black people were invisible. [COL 66 WF]*

One of the most important high school experiences which affected my life was when one of the science teachers [they were all white] took a personal interest in me. He saw a potential in me, not just as an athlete. He was pushing me to be the best I could be. He gave me more confidence in myself. When I first started in his class, my grades weren't much too talk about. After he helped me, gave me encouragement, stayed on my butt, my grades went up by multiple points. He went further than any teacher helping me out with my academics. That helped me out with the other classes. He gave more of his time for me. And I saw him work the same way with other students. *[EHS 67 AAM]*

As Table 2 indicates, neither the majority of black or white students in Waterloo high schools had the opportunity to interact with black teachers, especially in *The Bridge Between* ERA1.

| Table 2 ERA1 Black & White Faculty at East & West High Schools | | | | |
|---|---|---|---|---|
| FACULTY PROFILE | East High School | | | |
| | Female | | Male | |
| | Black | White | Black | White |
| 1963 | | 18 | | 34 |
| 1964 | | 25 | | 39 |
| 1965 | | 24 | 1 | 41 |
| 1966 | | 28 | 1 | 41 |
| FACULTY PROFILE | West High School | | | |
| | Female | | Male | |
| | Black | White | Black | White |
| 1963 | 1 | 23 | | 33 |
| 1964 | 1 | 27 | 1 | 37 |
| 1965 | | 35 | 1 | 45 |
| 1966 | | 35 | | 48 |

The second semester of my senior year, my friend insisted I take mechanical drawing with her. She told me I'd love it. Mr. Lowe, the teacher, was black. And he was the only instructor at East High who said to me, "You need to go to college." The only one. I always knew I was smart. But in all my time in school up to then, he was the only teacher or counselor who told me I should go to college. I know part of the reason I was successful in life was due to intelligence. But nobody saw that aspect of me when I was in high school. Due to lack of money and no support from my environment, I wouldn't have considered college except for John Lowe. I've persevered and worked for all I have because of him. I often think of [where I could have ended up] and it's not appealing. East made a difference for me in being able to communicate with African American people in my life. I'm sure Mr. Lowe had many things happen to him because he was black. He didn't have to say encourage me, he didn't hesitate to tell me. It made a big difference to me and I've never forgotten it. [EHS 66 WF]

## Socioeconomic Division in High School

Socioeconomic status was a separator in Waterloo and in the schools, real or perceived. There were some "haves" on the East Side, but the social classes on the East Side were primarily middle-middle class and below, with the curve shaped heavily toward the bottom of the middle class and into the lower classes. The West Side curve was skewed to the upper middle class and upper class.

Race was less of a divider on the East Side than economics. A lot of kids who went to East High didn't feel they were any better than a black person because our economic circumstances weren't any different. My mom, especially, was in the same position as a black person, cleaning houses or being a maid. The only the difference was skin color. Because of that, I don't think we blacks and whites on the East Side struggled against each other so much. I felt more prejudice against the higher economic people on the West Side than any black person on the East Side. I didn't know any of the West Side kids, but I thought they were rich, snooty kids. [EHS 66 WF]

*I shined shoes from the time I was 11 years old until I was 16. I started out with a cardboard box one color polish on brush and rag, went to all the blue-collar bars in downtown Waterloo. I used to make $5 a night shining shoes. My brother started doing it when I got too old. I don't know what the West-Side rich kids were doing. [EHS 64 WM]*

*It's not really funny, but there were frequent confrontations between the white and black girls. Because black kids seem to have so little. And there was a perception the little white girls would come to school and their hair would be all done up and they would go home to their little houses. Some of the black girls would look at them and go, "Oh, you know you think you're something" and hit them. I was really shy then. I worried about the black girls confronting me. I wasn't worried about the white girls. [EHS 66 AAF]*

*I went to Edison Junior High [on the West Side]. That definitely put me from the wrong side of the tracks at West High, which had its own kind of bigotry. There were foreign exchange students and students from East who came to take courses they couldn't get there. But West was divided between the Prospect kids, the rich kids in town, and the rest of us.[12] If you went to West Junior where these kids went, you were part of the "in crowd." If you went to Edison, you had a terrible time getting any social purchase from those Prospect Boulevard kids. No one was overtly mean to us, but you just weren't part of the crowd. There was one kid from Edison who was sort of accepted because her mother was from one of the prominent Waterloo families. West was a great school academically, but if you lived in the wrong part of town, it was socially a nightmare. For the West Side kids, we were asked to submit a brief bio for, I think, our 5th reunion booklet. I focused on the great education I'd received and what I was doing. When I got the booklet and read it, I literally started banging my head. It was clear there were more people who had been more "out" than "in" when we were in high school. And you never knew it. I had friends from the Prospect Boulevard area and am in contact with one of them even today. But she didn't participate in*

168

*the "in" crowd even though she lived on Prospect and had grown up with those kids. [WHS 66 WF]*

*There was kind of a smugness at Columbus. And I had somewhat of a chip on my shoulder, because there were some really rich people whose kids went there. Men didn't have uniforms, but we did have to wear dress pants and a dress shirt. Clothes were really big. A lot of people had really good clothes. Those of us from the East Side didn't dress so well. Some of the kids from St. John's and St. Nick's in Evansdale were at a disadvantage. They just didn't have the money. [COL 66 WM]*

## Athletes Were Elites

Athlete or non-athlete was another division in our high school social relationships.

*We were kind of looked up to as athletes. We may have been black, but students had a certain respect for us. Idolized us. We got treated better as an athlete in my ERAthan one who didn't participate. We had special privileges. Athletes didn't have to go to gym class. Didn't have to go to swimming, got automatic "A's." I guess they figured we were already equipped, we were physically able and well-fed. Even in the lunch room, we could go at off hours, get a sandwich from the cafeteria. [EHS 60 AAM]*

*One time I had to go drop something off to one of the teachers' rooms on the 3ʳᵈ floor. I was lamenting how scary it would be, because it was like walking through a gauntlet. One of the white football players who went to our church said he'd walk with me. I've been to his house. It was about the size of a garage. One bedroom with a blanket for a doorway. It was out in Maywood, the poorest, poorest area in town and on the East Side. Much poorer than probably the homes of the blacks on the team. And I could not believe the respect he had among black students as we walked through the 3ʳᵈ floor hallway. Amazing. Just amazing. I thought first the black respect was racism; he was a white guy who was a captain of a black team. It wasn't that. He and I had a few discussions about what respect was like. One time I said something about the glory of being on the winning team. He said, "No. It's all pain. We're doing it because it's our only chance to ever get higher education, to go to college. And that's the only reason. All day, every day, on the weekend, I am in pain." It did open my eyes. [EHS 66 WF]*

*McKinstry where I went and Logan were opponents in sports. But when we got together at East, it was good because – for football and the other sports – it made us a more powerful team. McKinstry had as dynamite right running back. Logan had a really dynamite left running back. [EHS 66 AAM]*

*Westsiders had an attitude, but so did we Eastsiders. As a guy, when it came to East High, it was always sports. That was the mentality ingrained in me from my older brother and everybody he knew. And sports proliferated everything. "We're East High Trojans and we can take anybody." Especially the West Side. We not only beat them, but we dominated them. [EHS 66 AAM]*

## Pregnant and Unmarried

Being unmarried and pregnant in high school wasn't permitted in the early 1960s.

*I got pregnant in my junior year and got married – you had to get married to stay in school if you were pregnant. I missed the second semesters of both my junior and senior years due to pregnancy, but was able to catch up in summer school and still graduate with my class. [EHS 66 AAF]*

East High basketball player Ron Green was married in August 1965 and was dropped from the team because of the school district's rule excluding married students from participating in extracurricular activities. He sued so he could play during his senior year and the trial court issued an injunction in January 1966 restraining the school board from enforcing the rule.[13] Green played.

In January 1967, after Green had graduated, the Supreme Court of Iowa reversed the district court ruling and set a precedent that "barring married students from participating in extracurricular activities is neither arbitrary, unreasonable, irrational, unauthorized, nor unconstitutional [under the Fourteenth Amendment]."[14]

*One of my friends got pregnant and my mom didn't want me running around with her. I said, "Mom, she's my friend." When she came back after having the baby, she was a different person. I wanted to be her friend, but it was like she'd left us behind. I was never able to talk to her about it. I remember seeing one of her notebooks on the study hall table when she'd gotten up. On the back page she'd just written the baby's name over and over and over. I thought, "You're hurting over this but not talking to anybody about it." I think I grew up a lot then. [EHS 66 WF]*

## The High School Experience

Outside the school environment, cruising 4th Street from the East to the West Side and back – or the reverse – was a social activity for high schoolers in Waterloo during the *TBB* decade. More so on Friday and Saturday nights. The route went from Lincoln Park and Franklin Street on the East Side of the Cedar River to the JC Penney parking lot on Commercial on the West Side and back, roughly a mile and a half.

Social status was based on whether you had your own "wheels" or whether it was "daddy's car," an "all show and no go" or a "circus wagon," a "souped or hopped up" machine with "glass packs" or a "crop duster," "jacked up" or "lowered." And how many of the opposite sex could be picked up by either gender.

Like George Lucas's *American Graffiti*, there were very few, if any, blacks in the slow-moving queue of cars on Waterloo's strip.

*We blacks were into cruising. We just didn't go downtown. We felt we weren't welcome. We would cruise further up East 4th Street north of the ICC tracks up to Newell or Gates Park. And we would drag race out on the Willow extension to Idaho. The cars were souped up like the white kids', many of them even nicer. I knew some black guys who would come in from Des Moines to drag race. They didn't race for pinks [the winner gets the title to the loser's car.] For blacks, it was for money. [EHS 66 AAM]*

I never knew any and wish I'd been able to experience it.

## EAST HIGH WAS A TOUGH SCHOOL

East High's reputation as being a tough school in the perceptions of most was baggage sophomores had to pick up and carry each school year. When gauged with objective, factual data, the reputation was largely undeserved. East graduates who contributed tended to rate the issues of confrontation or violence in the range of one to two a month. The perceptions of graduates of the other Waterloo high schools and outsiders were in the one-to-two-a-week range.

*There were fights occasionally when I was in school in the early 60s. After 1966, the blacks were trying to run the school and were getting away with it. And that's where the tough reputation came from. But after [black educator and administrator] Walt Cunningham took over at East [in 1976], fights went way down. He had big assistants who would drag you to the office. If you mouthed off, he'd have you hauled off to jail. His attitude was, "I may act white, but I'm black and you're not going to pull that 'You're prejudiced' stuff on me. People think I'm awful tough on my own race. But they've gotten by with so much stuff for so many year, I'm tired of it. They're not going to do that." [EHS 64 WM]*

*I thought East High was a rough school. We had all the black students in Waterloo. We had the poor students, living in poverty, more than they had on the West Side. I remember a couple girls from McKinstry who lived in Highland Park, both of their parents had money. One came to East and the other was sent to boarding school out of state instead. Eventually, the other girl was sent away, too. [EHS 66 WF]*

One of the black girls in my homeroom didn't like that I talked to the other black girls. She was a little resentful or something. One day we were going up the stairs and she told me I was up white motherfucker. And I just said to her, "Well if I'm a white one, then you're a black one." That was it. She never said anything again. [EHS 66 WF]

The only time I really felt uncomfortable with black people was in gym class. We were playing basketball. This one black girl was being really pushy and stuff. And I wondered, "Why, why can't you just play nice?" But that could have been the way she played on the schoolground, at home, or she might have had brothers or something. So, I just stayed away from her. [EHS 66 WF]

There was a lot of fear and violence at football games which I never realized, because I always sat with the band. But one time when the band wasn't playing, I asked a friend of mine who was a blonde to go to a home game at Sloane Wallace with me. She went down to the concession stands and when she came back, she'd had hair yanked out of her head. By the black girls. [EHS 66 WF]

East wasn't a violent school. [laughs] I think people try to perpetuate a single incident. Like I'd see two guys get into it, black and white. There's a scuffle. One of the teachers would break them up. They'd go to the office and everything would be straightened out. The next week, you'd hear, "Oh, man, these guys just beat each other and the janitor had to clean up the blood all over." A week later, a knife and a stabbing were included in the story. [EHS 66 AAM]

Teachers never broke up the girls' fights because they were smart. [long laugh] You step in the middle of a girls' fight, you're really risking it. I'm not sure why. The girls have access to more utensils in their purses? Whereas guys only had what was in their pockets. Girls carry ink pens, pencils, cosmetic things, rat tail combs which can become weapons real quick. And you're going to step in? No!! [laughs] [EHS 66 AAM]

There was always a rumor there was going to be a fight out by the tracks. Half the time nobody showed up. I know this from personal observation. There was a certain amount of entertainment value to those. *[EHS 66 WM]*

I always thought we had the right principal at the time, Mr. Hoffman. I remember some disturbances in the hallway and he'd come out of his office. Saw what was happening. Walked up to it. Had it calmed down. Was fair to everybody, didn't jump the gun. And I think it helped back then that you couldn't tell from the way he dressed he wasn't a doctor or a lawyer. He commanded respect and had an element of fairness that carried over. For years, he sat in the back pews of the church I attended and I never picked up on it. *[EHS 66 WM]*

I had a confrontation with another white girl on the bus. She came after me when we got off because she thought her boyfriend was talking to me and started swinging. I'm meek, don't stand up for myself. But I just grabbed her hair while she was swinging and she couldn't hit anything. It was a heart-throbber for me, but everybody else was laughing. The bus driver had to come out and stop it. *[EHS 66 WF]*

When people found out I went to East High, they thought I went to the slum school. It was like, "Ooh, you went to East?" "Yah." They never really said anything, but you could tell by the looks on their faces. And they would cringe a little bit that you went to East High. *[EHS 67 WF]*

I heard it was a tough school and believed that. My cousin from East said their goal was to not get pregnant before they got out of school or got married. At West, ours was to go to college. *[WHS 65 WM]*

We always heard East High was a very tough school. I have no idea whether that was true. I think the reputation came about because most of Waterloo's blacks and more of the poor went to school there. *[COL 66 WF]*

East did have a bad rep. There seemed to be a lot of violence on the East Side. I remember my brother and his friends were involved in a

*rumble after a football game. I believed what I heard, deserved or not.*
*[COL 67 WF]*

One of the major pieces of East High cultural folklore to come out of the 1966-1968 ERA was "The Fight" that took place in study hall sometime between in the 1966-67 academic year.

Who was involved in the fight depends on who's telling the story.

*The big thing in study hall was no noise. If you wanted to visit with somebody, you had to get permission and you had to be quick. Smith got up to talk to a girl. Holmes said, "You gotta sit down." Pretty soon Smith was saying, "Make me." They got into a pretty good fight, tumbled over a couple of desks, scrapping, smacking each a couple of times [EHS 66 WM]*

Or it was Smith monitoring the study hall and Holmes was the protagonist.

There's no disagreement one of the combatants was East football star running back Tom Smith, who was a standout for the Miami Hurricanes in college. He was drafted in the 7th round by the Miami Dolphins in 1973 and was on the team's second straight NFL championship team.

Each witnesses was adamant about the identity of the second participant, most often identified as Mike Allen, although Denman Phillips and Mannie Holmes were also choices.

Allen played football and wrestled for East, and at the University of Northern Iowa. He's a member of the National Wrestling Hall of Fame. Holmes played football and wrestled for the Trojans. The Mannie Holmes Cultural Diversity Center in Waterloo is named in his honor for his community involvement as an adult. Phillips was a successful contractor in partnership with his brother Waterloo before his death at age 51.

To set the record straight, Smith shared how it had been told at several of the class's reunions over the years.

Howie Vernon, the head football coach and faculty member in charge of study hall on the 3rd floor, had a riser with a desk on it. This was so he or whoever was acting as monitor if he was out the room could see the entire study hall, from front to back.

*When I was a sophomore, I was in charge of study hall for some reason one day. The desk was up on a platform. Mr. Vernon would leave and I'd sit there on a kind of power trip. And Allen was making some racket or doing something and I told him to shut or be quiet or something. He came running up toward the desk, jumped up on the raised platform and took a swing at me or maybe I swung at him. We knocked the desk onto the floor. We're on the 3<sup>rd</sup> floor and it crashed down. And the school came to a crashing halt. Everybody down below thought the school was being torn down. All the teachers came running upstairs to see what had happened. We're rolling around the floor in a fight. People are screaming and yelling. It was a big deal. I think Mannie intervened after the scuffle. I think we both got suspended for three days from school. And after a few years it really got blown out of proportion into a pretty big thing.*

The two all-star athletes met the first week at East. Smith had gone to Logan and Allen to rival McKinstry junior high. "When we met at East it was like two bulls in room together," Smith recalls. "'What are you looking at?' you know. I think it was being a tough kid or something. Turns out we turned out to be great friends."

*The people I hung around with didn't get into fights. At one of our reunions, the story was told by Michael Allen and Tom Smith about the fight they had in study hall. Michael thought this white boy was a patsy and Tom Smith basically wiped up the floor with him. I thought Smith was a young jock and I didn't like him until after we'd graduated. I found out at college he did have a brain and thoughts worth listening to. [EHS 68 AAF]*

A second frequent story shared to illustrate East's violent conditions was the ice pick stabbing of a student in April 1966. A 15-year-old girl

East student suffered three stab wounds in her chest and two in her left hand when she was attacked by a 17-year-old male in the corridor outside a classroom. She was treated and recovered.[15] Her stepfather said the young man had attempted to date the victim, but "she did not like him and had repelled his attention."[16]

The assailant gave himself up four days later to police in Detroit where he had fled to relatives in a stolen car. He was charged with assault with intent to commit murder.[17]

The initial municipal court hearing for the young man was continued a week until the judge decided whether he should be charged as a juvenile or an adult. There were no further newspaper reports about his case through May 1968 and juvenile records are sealed.

## ADVANTAGE/DISADVANTAGE OF HIGH SCHOOL ATTENDED

Was the high school someone attended a life advantage or disadvantage? Responses were not only insightful, but reflect awareness and thought which suggest, in and of themselves, the answer is "yes."

*I wrestled at East, but didn't play basketball because I didn't know how. My mom died when I was about 12-13, and I had to be home and take care of and watch my brothers instead of being at the playground learning to play the game. And I don't have the skill even now. I don't regret it. I'm much more proud and happy to have taken care of my brothers. [EHS 66 AAM]*

*I moved to Waterloo when I was 15-16, spent a couple of months at Logan Junior and then started at East in the fall of 1963. Very few students in the state of Iowa are ever going to experience a mixture of different people and different races and attitudes than we had at East. I didn't have a lot of black friends. But it exposed me to a part of the world other people don't have a clue about. And it changed me. It made me quite a bit less parochial. To grow up in the world where everybody's exactly like you, the same background, the same interests, the idea anyone deviates from that must be wrong – it's not who I am. [EHS 66 WM]*

Having the opportunity to go to school with the kids I did in a racially mixed environment made me a much more rounded person. I realized a black person can be just as good as a white. If you treat everybody with respect and kindness, most of the time they'll treat you that way back. To this day, I don't feel I'm a prejudiced person. It bothers me when people use the "n-word," but the "f bomb" agitates me just as much. When I was younger, I wouldn't have reacted like I do today. Becoming a born-again Christian six years ago has made all the difference. *[EHS 66 WF]*

Frankly, I went to school because I had to. I was more interested in boys than getting a higher education, so I didn't focus a lot on race and diversity. Remember the pimp walk the black guys did? Oh, honey. And some of the older boys would pick up some of the girls after school. They would let you into East then even if you didn't go to school there. *[EHS 66 AAF]*

I was very advantaged for attending East because I learned about lifestyles I wouldn't have learned at West. Someone's color never stopped me from communicating with and trying to learn from them. I liked that. *[EHS 66 WF]*

Attending East helped me to see both races had good people and bad. Most white kids were taught prejudice growing up. It was my generation that learned open-mindedness, and began to change that and become accepting. We taught our kids the color of skin does not determine merit or values within a person. *[EHS 66 WF]*

Kids who attended all-white high schools didn't have the knowledge of other cultures. No way to repudiate anything you're being taught is God's truth from a racial perspective unless you have a way to challenge it. When the dynamics include different cultures, what you're being taught has to be acceptable to all. This was evident in some of the kids at NIACC *[North Iowa Area Community College in Mason City]* from *these small towns without diversity. They didn't know how to deal with us blacks. There was a confrontational bull-in-the-ring attitude from the males. And from the females, it was totally different. We were a social and dating curiosity for them. [EHS 66 AAM]*

*Those of us at East got a better start in life by learning how to interact with people and be sensitive to others. To a certain extent, a little self-preservation; you learned how not to poke the bear. There was always a certain element you had to be aware of, you had to know how to handle yourself and how to deal with people to avoid problems. You learned how to observe. And that added a lot to our character. A lot of that carried over into the rest of our lives. [EHS 66 WM]*

*My memories of East are mostly happy and a good part of my empathy for all people comes from going there. It changed me for the better. Interracial relationships were still regarded as not good when we went to school. I never did anything when I was younger to help, but as I got older I feel I have helped in small ways. [EHS 66 WF]*

*I'm glad I attended East High School, had interactions with black students. I feel like they're my brothers and sisters, too. They're not different just because of skin color. Everybody has their stories. I wouldn't look down on somebody because of their race or nationality. When I see people, I smile at them. Lots of times blacks would smile back and you could get a dialogue going with him. It's not so much that way anymore. [EHS 66 WF]*

*We students at West were disadvantaged because the school wasn't biracial. It was too comfortable. It was a disservice in that we were insulated from a broader view of the world, a broader view of people. The kids at East got to deal with the interracial environment every day. We graduated without that. [WHS 66 WF]*

*My whole sophomore year, all I wanted to do was be a cheerleader, run around with the cheerleaders, to be one of the "Big Shots" people we thought were better than the other girls. And when I didn't get to be a cheerleader or on the junior varsity squad, I was heartbroken. Then I tried out in my junior year and saw how catty the cheerleaders were, how silly the peer groups were. After that I didn't care whether I was a Big Shot or not. [EHS 66 WF]*

---

*Someone asked me at the 10-year reunion who I went to prom with and I told them I hadn't gone to prom. No one had asked me. And he said, "If I'd known that, I would have asked you." [laughs] It was water under the bridge. I didn't feel sorry for myself because of those things. [EHS 66 WF]*

---

*My friendship with black male student was my major advantage. I had acquaintances with black students and I've worked with blacks over the years. I've not had a closer black friend. It was a close personal friendship which gave me insight and formed some values in my mind I wouldn't have gotten any other way. People are people. We're all the same. We have the same feelings as people, skin color makes no difference. We want the same things for our kids. There is more common between us than there are differences. [EHS 66 WF]*

---

*When I went to the State College [now UNI] as a naïve 18-year-old with not a big world view, I seemed to know more of the real world than the guy who came from Grinnell or this girl from Sheldon. At East, I encountered people that were different from me. And I put a human face on them. I didn't just use a stereotype, they're "this or that" or "a welfare fraud." Dealt with them as friends, except maybe for a couple of them who beat me up, which happened with whites, too. When I went to college, I realized there were a lot of people who don't know anything beyond their little hometown. That may seem a little snobbish. But I felt I knew a little bit more about the world. And I thought we got a great education at East. [EHS 66 WM]*

---

*Attending Columbus allowed a lot of the racial tension in Waterloo to be ignored and it was never discussed in any of my classes. A personal disadvantage was I was clueless as to what was occurring in the Sixties as far as civil rights. [COL 66 WF]*

180

*I've lived in seven states and traveled the world as a representative for [a global Fortune Top 15 company] and worked with people from over 100 different countries cultures and backgrounds. Being Catholic with an overall moral compass on loving all people and treating them with respect has helped me tremendously in being successful in society, and in making great friendships. [COL 66 WF]*

*Columbus taught me compassion courage strength kindness and faith in myself and others [COL 66 WF]*

*Going to Columbus provided no advantages in adapting to the multi-racial, multi-ethnic world of my adult life. It was a disadvantage. [COL 66 WF]*

*Nothing was done at Columbus to show us black people were just like white people. There was an undercurrent of racism that was passed on to students from elementary school on. [COL 66 WF]*

About 10% of the district's school population was Negro, but from the 1963 to 1966 school years, Negroes accounted for 40.5% of high school dropouts, "consistently higher proportionately than that of their white counterparts. . . ."[18]

## Storm Warnings

From the start of the fall 1960 school year to June 1967 high school graduations, racial tensions in Waterloo intensified as demands for change moved to the forefront of the black community's agenda. Extending the storm metaphor, clouds were beginning to form over the long-time acceptance of status quo. (Figure 4)

*I applied and was hired for a part-time job at AT&T my senior year. A black girl in a couple of my classes called, asked if I'd applied and learned I gotten the job. She was upset and said she would have to report it to the NAACP, because she applied, too, and didn't get hired. I didn't know what she was talking about. This was a major company with tough requirements. I was an honor student with 3.5 GPA who had to get special permission to even apply. This girl had a "C" average and*

181

*wasn't in any honor classes. I was upset she was attacking me for being an accomplished student and wanted to try to take something away from me. How did she even know my business? [COL 66 WF]*

We didn't seem to be paying much attention in school or in our social groups to the Civil Rights movement. We knew racism and civil rights existed when we were in school. But it didn't seem to be part of what was going on in Waterloo. We had racial tension. We were very aware of that. But it was more isolated. *[EHS 66 AAM]*

Figure 4 Five major events were produced by the growing Civil Rights movement within Waterloo in *TBB* ERA 1.

*Two of the first three were peaceful marches in support of Civil Rights actions in other U.S. cities. The third was establishment of a local Human Rights Commission. But the death of Terry Sallis, a young black man in police custody, arguably put the match to the long-simmering racial tensions in the town. A year later, the North End was on fire.*

## JUNE 1964 NAACP MARCH FOR FREEDOM

The Waterloo branch of the NAACP and the Citizens' Committee organized a "March for Freedom" in downtown Waterloo on Saturday, June 27, for the "non-violent protest against discriminatory practices in the city of Waterloo."

Leaders had expected some 1,000 demonstrators. An estimated 450 Negroes and whites participated, marching five abreast in a two-block line in complete silence. They left the football practice field at East High at 10 a.m. and walked 10 blocks through downtown on 5th Street to Commercial Street on the west side of the Cedar River. The march then turned up 4th Street to Mulberry Street and ended at City Hall eight blocks farther at 11:30 a.m.

182

Mayor Ed Jochumsen was presented with a list of grievances, which included "discrimination in jobs, housing and law enforcement in the Negro community." The group pressed "the need for a solution" that would include the city council commission setting up a local "Human Rights Commission with a budget so adequate attention may be given to civil rights for minority groups."

Jochumsen commended the group for "the way you have conducted this demonstration." And stated some of the grievances were being addressed by "urban renewal to improve housing, through the Fair Employment Practice Commission and through conferences on law enforcement. . . ." [19]

## JANUARY 1965 WATERLOO HUMAN RIGHTS COMMISSION COMMITTEE FORMED

*In January 1965, Mayor Jochumsen formed a committee to begin working on buffering race relations in Waterloo. Over the next 18 months, thirteen concerned citizens and two mayors drafted the blueprint that established the Waterloo Commission on Human Rights. Under Mayor Lloyd Turner, Resolution No. 16909 was approved on July 7, 1966, establishing the Waterloo Commission on Human Rights. On July 28, 1966, the Commission hired its first staff.[20]*

## MARCH 1965 SELMA SYMPATHY MARCH

On Sunday, March 14, 300-500 people – about two-thirds of them Negroes – marched peaceably in Waterloo in sympathy with the civil rights movement in Selma, Alabama. Organized by the Waterloo Ministerial Association, Negro and white clergymen led the group on the 10-minute walk from Grace Methodist Church at the head of East 5th Street to the Black Hawk County courthouse parking lot three blocks away. A series of prayers, and a brief presentation by the senior pastor at Grace preceded a short talk by civil rights activist Rev. Jack Hanford of the Wesley Foundation at the State College of Iowa [later UNI]. Hanford noted that the rights of people in Waterloo were being denied as they were in Selma, but "with polite words." He related that he had received a death threat for his civil rights work in a letter postmarked in Waterloo. Citing the Revolutionary War rallying cry, "Give me liberty or give me death," he stated that many people "were given bondage instead. Give us liberty. We've had enough death." The event took 30 minutes altogether.[21]

## JUNE 1966 DEATH OF TERRY SALLIS

On Wednesday, June 1, Eddie Sallis, a 23-year-old black man, was found hanging in his Waterloo police station jail cell and died, despite efforts by police and firemen to revive him. He was alive at 6 a.m., but a fellow prisoner found him about 6:15 with his trousers tightly twisted around his neck. Sallis and another man had been arrested an hour before for intoxication, but were also suspected of a break-in at a local restaurant earlier that morning.

A complaint on behalf of Sallis's family was filed with the Waterloo Human Rights Commission the following day with 35 Negroes in attendance. The family's representative told the commission "a medical practitioner here in the city said this could be foul play . . . . [The investigation should explain] how could a man hang himself in the city jail when he is only wearing jeans." She said the other suspect arrested claimed Sallis had been beaten after being brought to the police station. A community meeting was scheduled for that evening in the North End to prevent violence.[22]

The police chief reported the person arrested with Sallis had been given a physical examination as soon as he made accusations of brutality, but there was no evidence of any injury. The accusation was also reported to the FBI.[23]

On Friday, June 03, a picket line of 200 Negroes, including an estimated 100 Negro students who walked out of classes at East High, peacefully walked through the Mayor Lloyd Turner's office and around his desk for roughly three hours. The protest was called off when the mayor agreed to meet with the demonstrators that afternoon.

The group asked for a complete investigation of Sallis' death by the county attorney, a funded commission be established to study civil rights problems and some members of the police force be removed. The president of the Waterloo Human Rights Commission organized the previous year then submitted his resignation from the commission, he said primarily due to a lack of appropriate funding.

Saturday morning the Black Hawk county attorney reported the death of Sallis was a suicide based on the autopsy performed on Friday. It presented "no evidence . . . to show [Sallis] was struck, kicked, or in any way mistreated." And that "Sallis was legally and medically intoxicated at the time of his death." The president of the Black Hawk County chapter of the NAACP, physician Dr. Warren Nash, was present at the autopsy, and concurred with the medical examiner's and pathologist's reports. He told a meeting of Negroes on Friday night the death was a suicide.[24]

"Sworn statements [made by] three other prisoners in jail" at the time of Sallis' death made to the county attorney and two agents of the Iowa Bureau of Criminal Investigation also factored into the finding.[25]

That night, "Roving bands of Negroes throwing rocks, whiskey bottles and at least one piece of pipe, damaged numerous cars on the East side . . . and injured at least four persons. . . . in spite of appeals for non-violence by leaders of [Negroes protesting] in city hall demonstrations." Some of the leaders worked through the night "to head off the missile-throwing youths."[26]

The next day, Sunday, June 05, graduation ceremonies for Waterloo's four high schools in 1966 started at Columbus. West, Orange and East graduations were Tuesday-Thursday, 07-09 June, respectively.

*Waterloo was a powder keg for a long time, ever since blacks came to Waterloo in the early 1900s. Pressure had been building since then. I remember blatant racism when I was a kid. There were places in town that wouldn't serve blacks. There were white-owned businesses on East 4th Street south of the tracks in which blacks weren't welcomed. There was an unwritten rule blacks weren't allowed on the West Side after dark. They were contained within the North End. As an adult, I understand now there was a lot of subtlety to the racism then. [EHS 66 AAM]*

*The national racial stuff had been going on for a long time. The quiet populace was waking up, becoming more radical. It was a rise in radicalism across the country which hit a town like Waterloo. Probably more than any other town in Iowa because we had the largest black population. We had a large African American community, and they had been segregated into a certain part of town and their kids had been segregated into certain schools. Kids going off to college and coming back with new ideas. Instigators were coming in. I remember going to Cedar Rapids with someone who said, "You have to understand my mom's married to [lowers voice] a black guy." It was like it was a big deal. "The black people in Cedar Rapids are different, not like the black people in Waterloo," she told me. [EHS 66 WF]*

## Reflections from the Bridge

*We went to high school in a fairly good time. When Kennedy was killed [in 1963], it was a big thing in our heads. During Civil Rights, had someone said, "I'm really being mistreated," I would have said, "Really, you are?" Until those civil rights workers were killed. And then I thought, "My gosh, this is really happening. This is really happening." [EHS 66 WF]*

The U.S. was a "confident nation"[27] in 1963. But we high schoolers were becoming more cognizant of world events that impacted lives everywhere in the country the murder of civil rights leader Medgar Evers in June, Martin Luther King, Jr.'s "I have a dream speech" during The March on Washington for Jobs and Freedom in August, the assassination of president Kennedy in November.

Conformity and passivity were waning as options among the blacks in the Waterloo. The general response by school and community officials was a hardline, no-compromise strategy, supported by many of the citizens, especially those on the West Side.

Riots in Waterloo in 1966 and 1967 gave impetus to social activism, considered as catalysts for the second *TBB* ERA, the school years from the fall of 1967 to graduation in 1970.

It was no cliché; a racial storm was brewing in Waterloo that would unsettle the status quo in the community and for its high school students during *TBB* ERA2.

# Endnotes

¹ The Public Speaks: Plead, East Students Wake Up. (September 16, 1968). Waterloo Daily Courier, 4

2 How John F. Kennedy's Assassination Changed Television Forever. (Nov. 14, 2013, at 1:25 p.m.). Sneed, T. U.S. News & World Report. Retrieved from http://tinyurl.com/ybrfsfrk.

3 JFK assassination: When a nation coming of age lost its youth. (November 17, 2013, 12:51 PM). Flanagan, B. CBS News. Retrieved from https://www.cbsnews.com/news/jfk-assassination-when-a-nation-coming-of-age-lost-its-youth/.

4 5 Ways JFK's Assassination Changed America Forever. (Nov. 22, 2013). Giokaris, J. Mic. Retrieved from http://tinyurl.com/y8bpurnj.

5 Kennedy's legend lives on. Joseph, (November 21, 2013). PBS NewsHour: What the Kennedy assassination meant to us. Retrieved from http://www.pbs.org/newshour/multimedia/jfk-essays/.

6 Teacher Retention Here Ranked. Sixth Among 21 Largest Districts. (March 30, 1969). Waterloo Daily Courier, 15.

7 Editorials. Waterloo Leads Iowa Cities on School Test. (April 03, 1969). Opinion Page. Waterloo Daily Courier, 4.

8 Ibid.

9 Ibid., 5.

10 Policy Adopted for Best Scholars in the System Here. (March 12, 1963). Waterloo Daily Courier, 3.

11 What is the Difference Between Heterogeneous and Homogeneous Grouping? (January 29, 2015). Alstad-Davies, C. A+ Teachers' Career Edge. Teacher Job Interview Questions and Answers. Retrieved from http://tinyurl.com/y8bnzpyh.

12 Prospect Boulevard is on the West Side of town near West High and major hospital complexes. There is also a Prospect Circle in a lower socioeconomic area of the West Side and a Prospect Avenue in the North End on the East Side.

13 School Board to Appeal Married Student Ruling. (January 25, 1966). Waterloo Daily Courier, Front Page.

14 Board of Directors of the Independent School District of the city of Waterloo v. Green, 147 N.W.2d 854 (Iowa 1967). (January 10th, 1967). Supreme Court of Iowa. Retrieved from https://www.courtlistener.com/opinion/1580949/board-of-dir-of-ind-sch-dist-of-waterloo-v-green/.

15 1) Youth Is Nabbed for Stabbing. (April 17, 1966). Waterloo Daily Courier, 27.

16 Girl Stabbed During School. (April 26, 1966). Des Moines Register, 8.

17 1) Extradition Waived in Stabbing. (April 29, 1966). Waterloo Daily Courier, 3. 2) Suspect in School Attack May Face Federal Change. (April 28, 1966). Waterloo Daily Courier, 26.

18 Hearing. Waterloo Commission on Human Rights. (September 07, 1967), 26. Cited in School Desegregation in Waterloo, Iowa. (August 1977). A Staff Report of the United States Commission on Civil Rights. Kansas City, MO: USCCR Midwestern Regional Office, 5.

19 1) Freedom March Planned by NAACP Downtown. (June 15, 1964). Waterloo Daily Courier, 19. 2) 1,000 Marchers, Leaders Predict. (June 26, 1964). Waterloo Daily Courier, 1. 3) Rights Marchers Air Grievances. (June 28, 1964). Waterloo Daily Courier, 13.

20 History. Waterloo Commission on Human Rights. Retrieved from http://www.cityofwaterlooiowa.com/residents/human_rights/history.php.

21 Sympathy March in Waterloo Peaceful. Event Takes 30 Minutes Altogether. (March 15, 1965). Waterloo Daily Courier, 3.

22 Plan Probe of Sallis' Jail Death. (June 02, 1966). Waterloo Daily Courier, 21.

23 Negro Pickets March at City Hall 3 hours. (June 03, 1966). Waterloo Daily Courier, 1, 2.

24 No Question that Sallis Killed Self, Says Martin. (June 05, 1966). Waterloo Daily Courier, 14.

25 Ibid.

26 Rocks and Bottles Fly in Outbreak. (June 05, 1966). Waterloo Daily Courier, 13.

27 The JFK assassination: When America lost its innocence. (November 11, 2013). Schieffer, B. CBS News: Face the Nation. Retrieved from https://www.cbsnews.com/news/the-jfk-assassination-when-america-lost-its-innocence/.

# *TBB* 7: ERA2 1967-70 – The Perfect Storm Takes Shape

By the summer of 1967, the response of the black community in Waterloo to racial inequity and injustice was escalating from civil-mannered marches, and numerous non-productive meetings with city officials to four years of confrontation and violence. Much of it was focused on East High and the school system.

The second ERAof *The Bridge Between (TBB)* picks up in the summer of 1967 with two events that forecast the volatile and unstable 1968 – riots protesting discrimination in a state-funded on-the-job (OJT) training program for unemployed blacks and the Board of Education (BOE) implementation of a voluntary open enrollment program, a strategy to avoid more formal integration policies and actions.

In September 1967, the multiracial Waterloo Commission on Human Rights (WCHR) conducted a hearing on the issues facing Waterloo. Housing was predominant as an influence on the community and ultimately the school system in that it forced busing as a requirement to desegregate its schools.

*. . . housing is the major problem [sic] in the field of human relations facing the city of Waterloo. . . . There is little in the experience of a Negro reared in a ghetto to escape it – least of all to walk uninvited into a real estate office to buy or rent a home in some distant part of the community. West Side and Cedar Falls whites are not likely to act as individuals to invite unknown Negroes to become their neighbors, nor are the likely to depart, from their comfortable surroundings to seek a home in the ghetto.*[1]

# High School by the Numbers

Dr. George Hohl's tenure as superintendent of Waterloo public schools continued into the 1967 school year, which was considered by most to be a positive stability in that position. However, principal changes occurred at three of the four high schools during *TBB* ERA2. (Figure 1).

East High principal Lawrence Garlock, who became principal in 1966 after 18 years as assistant principal, dealt with the disturbances and disruptions of the 1968 protests. In February of 1969, he asked the board of education (BOE) to be re-assigned.

Howard [Howie] Vernon, East's head football coach and assistant principal for the previous two years, was named principal at the beginning of April.[2] He assumed the position in the summer of 1969 as the third principal at East in four years.

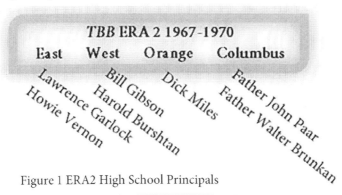

Figure 1 ERA2 High School Principals

West High principal Bill Gibson retired in 1968 after 39 years. His replacement was his administrative assistant, Harold Burshtan.

Columbus principal Rev. John Paar left in February 1968. The new head was Father Walter Brunkan who served through 1973, the end of *TBB ERA3*

Dick Miles started his 10th year as principal of Orange High and would remain in that position until the school was closed at the end of the 1971-72 school year.

The percentage of blacks at East and West had changed from *TBB ERA1* (1963-1967) to ERA2 (1967-1970), and would continue to do though all three ERAs. (Table 1)

| Table 1 Percentage of Blacks in High Schools, 1963 & 1967 | | | | |
|---|---|---|---|---|
| | 1963 | 1967 | 1970 | 1972 |
| Waterloo | 6.7%** | | | |
| East | 15.0% | 20.8% | | |
| West | 0.0% | 0.5% | | |
| Orange | N/A | 0.0% | | |
| Central | Opened 1972 | | | |
| Columbus* | 0.0% | 0.0% | | |
| * Estimates only. ** From the U.S. Census Decennial Census, The Bureau didn't start issuing updates between each census until 1990. | | | | |

The black student population at East grew 5.8% to 20.8% fueled by increases in the middle and elementary schools. (Figure 2) Logan's black student percentage increased 2.1%, with a growth of 8.0% in black students at Roosevelt and 10.9% at Longfellow. McKinstry's black enrollment nearly tripled due to a 65.1% black enrollment at the six elementary schools that fed into it. Maywood was the only the only elementary school to have a black population decline at -2.2 %.

There were no official black student data reported for the West Side schools. Two new elementary schools were opened: Westridge on the West Side in 1968 and Greenbrier on the East in 1969. (Figure 2)

## High School's a Brand New Game

The transitions for students from junior high to high school in ERA2 were similar to those shared by ERA1 graduates.

*My introduction to blacks was at Logan Junior. Lincoln Elementary was a great school. There were just no blacks. But I participated in a lot of summer sports stuff and track even in elementary school. I met a lot of black kids even though I didn't go to school with any. It gave me a competitive edge, because I was always going against kids who were fast*

*and in high jump and so forth. I was big for my age. So, I could compete
with just about anybody. [EHS 68 WM]*

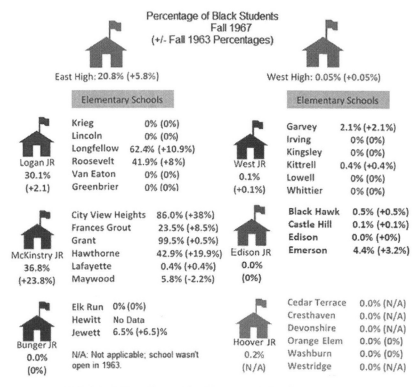

Figure 2 WCSD Black Enrollment Profiles, 1967 School Year
*The shifting minority enrollments in the East Side schools required shifting
students, sometimes to three schools in as many years, according to some
parents. Graduates reported that, in many cases, they were able to catch up in
high school with displaced friendships from elementary or junior high school,
which helped make transitions to the "big campus" easier.*

When you got to East High, you knew certain of the old-school
teachers were going to be prejudiced. And you had to deal with that. It
wasn't a secret in the black community. [EHS 68 AAF]

Our grade schools and middle schools in Elk Run and Evansdale were
all white. I never was around African Americans until I went McKinstry
Junior for 9th grade. So, segregation wasn't only because of the Cedar
River, but also by the smaller rural areas [around Waterloo] which were

*completely segregated – Gilbertville, Dunkerton, etc. And Evansdale people were looked down upon by students at East and West due to their economic status. [EHS 68 WF]*

*There was one good teacher at Logan Junior, the wrestling coach. He was a huge positive influence in my life, the first time I had a positive impression of anybody white. I'd never met anybody white with whom I had a relationship that could be construed as positive by any stretch of the imagination. All their actions were negative. I didn't like them, I didn't like being around them, I didn't trust them. Especially older white men. There was anger and fear bound all up in one. As a kid, the best description is you're always like you've got PTSD [post-traumatic stress disorder]. You're anxious, always on your toes when you're around white people. [EHS 69 AAM]*

*Most McKinstry students had very little multiracial experience when they got to East High. A lot them didn't adjust well. They didn't want to be associated with most blacks. And Evansdale was part of that. They called themselves the "E'dales," so everyone started to refer to them as that. Some of my white friends did try to help the McKinstry kids in their own way, not with deep discourse. They didn't try to mentor. They would just say, "You know, [name] is a good kid. She's ok. I went to school with her. We did these things together." [EHS 69 AAF]*

*There were no blacks in my grade school. So, Logan was my first exposure and it wasn't a good one. I always carried my books from class to class. One day I walked around a corner, and a black girl and I ran into each other. My books went all over the floor and she said, "I'm going to see you after school." I wondered which door she would be at. My dad always picked me up from school and I knew where he'd be in the parking lot. If I didn't come out right away, he'd get mad and I'd possibly get a hit or whatever. He was abusive. I went out the door, and the girl and a friend were there. She pushed me, and I socked her in the nose and was suspended for two weeks. It was a stupid fight. We didn't even know each other. After that, we tried to avoid one another. But I went to YMCA camp the next summer, and she was there and chased me around camp with a knife. [EHS 70 WF]*

*The only thing that made East a workable situation was when the athletics were nailed together. I've always said athletics is probably the best bridge there is even though it causes complications in other places. When people work together, play together and win together . . . [paused] We won so much at McKinstry, I was used to that when I got to East High. But they didn't have athletics for girls. I was a heck of an athlete. I was an excellent swimmer and won medals in the 50- and 100-yard dash at the end-of-the-school-year races at Longfellow. And I was the chin-up champion. I know a lot of young women my age who were involved in sports; we just couldn't compete in high school. We would have been stars, too. [EHS 69 AAF]*

*Going from [private Lutheran] Immanuel to Logan was a culture shock for me. It was unbelievable. We were all white at Immanuel, so I wasn't exposed to any differences in people through 8th grade. Most of my friends from Immanuel went to West Junior. Only one of the girls came with me to Logan. I had no idea what public school was like. I didn't have any friends. I had to make friends at Logan. And I was sad. It was a different world. I didn't know any of the rules or customs. I got beat up because I used the sidewalk in front of Logan instead of the field to go home after school. The unspoken rule that blacks used the sidewalk and the whites used the grassy field. I didn't know it. I was approached by two black girls. And they said they wanted whatever was in my purse. I stood my ground. They tried to grab my purse and pulled me around by it. I really couldn't tell you how I got away. [EHS 70 WF]*

*A lot of blacks had a tough time because of family. Some felt like something was owed them. The blacks were a little more aggressive at times. A little angry. Some of the white students were afraid of the blacks. But the white people were a little more arrogant at times, thought they were perhaps a little more special. So, yes, there was some push and shove. [EHS 68 WM]*

**Student transitions at West and Columbus were based more on socioeconomic status rather than race.**

*Edison was a small, white junior high, 300 or so kids. We were mixed in at West High with a much bigger group of probably 500 kids from West Junior. I went to church at a downtown church, so I knew a lot of the West Junior kids from Sunday school and youth group. I didn't socialize with them. There was a group of rich, wealthy kids from Prospect Avenue most of my friends and I had no contact with. They'd say "hi" to me, but I didn't socialize with them, even though some of us went to church together. [WHS 69 WF]*

*My Westsider friends who went to Columbus would joke I was going to the pagan high school. [EHS 69 WF]*

*When I was at Columbus, I wished at times I was going to East, because they were probably having more fun and there were more black people. But Daddy sent us to Columbus, so that's where we were going to go. [COL 69 AAF]*

*The tension at Columbus was between the poor and the rich. Students came from five different parishes, which meant more Westsiders than Eastsiders. I was kind of lucky because I'd gone through seven years at St. Mary's and a year at St. John's [on the East Side], so I knew kids from both the East Side parishes. All the parishes were more financially stable than St. Mary's parish where I lived. When I went to school, I had patches in my shorts and pants, and shoes that were too small because we were poor. I didn't realize it at the time, but I had the same chip on my shoulder a lot of the black kids did. The bullies and kids I got into arguments or fights with in school were West Side kids that came from complete families and had more money. The Westsiders didn't really tell you they were better by talk, but you could tell when you came into the room they looked down on you. They stayed in their own groups. And the East Side kids did, too. [COL 68 WM]*

## Racial Relationships

*I thought I was black until I was a freshman in college. I hung around with blacks and I'd talk like them. You could take three Englishmen with the heaviest English accents and put them into a room with some black guys, and after an hour they'd walk out talking like blacks. The blacks were more hip, had such a good sense of humor. They were always messing with each other. I always had so much fun in school with them. It turns you black. After school, they'd go in their social direction and I'd go in mine. It just so happened that their friends were black and mine were white. [EHS 68 WM]*

*I inadvertently let the "N" bomb fly during a casual wrestling match with a black classmate. I apologized, but of course we could not be friends after that. I deeply regret that. [EHS 68 WM]*

*I was once called a nigger-lover by a classmate. It was a "name-calling thing" at the time. And said, "Yes, I AM and proud of it. And, you idiot, you're missing so much by not being one." [EHS 69 WF]*

*I once described a friend to a group of white friends and was chastised later for never mentioning he was black. I didn't because I honestly and genuinely didn't think designating race was important. After knowing a person for a length of time, it just didn't register any longer that they were black or white. [EHS 69 WF]*

## Racial Division in High School

*By the 1970s, blacks had the ability to live anywhere in Waterloo they chose. However, middle class blacks comprised the majority moving out of the East Side into the more expensive homes of the West Side or Cedar Falls. Low-income blacks lacked the financial capabilities to take advantage of the freedom to move, and were therefore left stranded on the East Side, unable to take advantage of these new freedoms.*[3]

Data from a 1969 study of East, West and Orange high school students reported relatively few unpleasant experiences with other students. Ninety percent (90%) of the black students surveyed had "none, very few or not very many" unpleasant experiences. It was the same for 95% of West students, 94% at East[4] and 93% at Orange. The data were "quite reassuring for school people to know such a large percentage of today's students – from all groups – consider themselves to have had such a limited number of unpleasant experiences at school."[5]

*I had a diverse set of racially diverse friends, which wasn't that common. I'm not sure how diverse we were socioeconomically. There was a perception among us there was a divide. My white friends at East were from my classes in elementary and junior high school. But I had black friends from my neighborhood and church. [EHS 68 AAF]*

*Being involved in sports, I hung out with black guys in school, not so much away from school. We sat next to each other in classrooms and were always talking football or about a game. It seemed like we were having more fun than anybody else. Socially, I didn't hang out with black people outside of school except walking home and "see you tomorrow." Never had any of my black friends over for dinner and didn't go to their houses, unless dropping them off after practice. We went about our business and they went about theirs. Then we'd get up the next day, see them in school and you were best friends. Occasionally I'd go by black friends' parties – they always had the best music. [EHS 68 WM]*

*Being in sports, I had a lot more black friends than most of the other students. In team sports, you're relying on another person to do something and they're relying on you. When we'd see each other outside of school, we'd just launch right back into talking about the common denominator – the sports experience. I always looked at sports as a means without an end. It was always open doors and upbeat. Blacks dominated sports. I was lucky to be able to excel along with them. I look back at my senior year especially as being fun since we never lost. The closest anybody ever came to beating us was a 20-point margin. I got upset or mad, because we'd be up five or six touchdowns in the first half and I'd get taken out, had to sit on the bench so we didn't run up the score. [EHS 68 WM]*

*We went to a church on the West Side and were friends with a number of families. When blacks went marching through West High, one of my friend's dad got all over me. "What do they think they're doing?" I didn't know, other than protesting black people couldn't go there. Which they proved by his reaction. [EHS 68 WF]*

No reliable sources were found for the "marching through West incident" among the contributors or the *Waterloo Daily Courier* archives. All that can be said is "perception is reality."

*I worked at a drug store on West 5th street when I was 17 and a senior at East. There was an old, gross fart who delivered cigarettes. I took him up to shelve the cigarettes in the storeroom one day and he tried to kiss me. He was feeble, so I brushed him off with my forearm. A woman walking by saw it and I turned bright red. I told my boss and he said, "Oh, he would never do that." Well, he did. A black guy had been asking me out all senior year. I was working one night, and he came in and was talking to me. It was a short conversation. When he left, the boss came running up, "Is everything all right, is everything all right?" He wouldn't believe me about the old white guy. But when a black guy came in, he thought something might be wrong. The young man called the house one day and mom answered the phone. When she handed it to me, she said, "Get rid of him." Because he was black. I've always felt bad about that, because he was a nice guy and I liked him. He was smart. An athlete. His family was respected in town. But he was black. [EHS 68 WF]*

*Our West Side Baptist Church girls' circle took baskets to a family near East High at Christmas. Our counselors thought the West Side girls should see what poverty looked like. When we arrived, police cars with lights flashing were sitting in the street. All the neighbors were on their porches watching. It was humiliating and unkind to the family. The counselors had called the police to inform them a group of white girls were going to be there at night. The police showed up to protect us. I and the other girl from East were totally disgusted. I walked by that house every day without police protection. [EHS 68 WF]*

*Black and white students were under the same pressures, rubbing shoulders every day, involved in the same activities at East. But the white and black student communities inside East were just about as segregated as Waterloo was. Part of it was attitudes people got growing up and part of it was where you went to elementary or junior high. There wasn't a lot of interaction before high school between kids who went to McKinstry Junior and Logan Junior, with a couple of exceptions. One would be athletes and cheerleaders at the two schools. You stayed friends with the people you grew up with, unless you wound up dating somebody from one of the other schools. A couple of my girlfriends at McKinstry dated boys from Logan and one of the boys dated a girl from Logan. Those interactions wound up linking the two communities. Interestingly, those were white kids. And part of it was where you went to church. For example, there weren't a lot of Lutheran Churches on the East Side; there was Immanuel and First Lutheran. So, if kids from McKinstry and Logan went to those churches, they had a chance to get to know each other from the time they were little. For blacks, it really was a matter of church and neighborhood. Kids who went to McKinstry went to churches with kids from Logan. The black community was much more homogeneous than the white community was. Especially from a religious standpoint. Catholic kids tended to interact with Catholic kids and Protestant kids tended to interact with protestant kids. [EHS 68 AAF]*

*We weren't allowed to go to games on the East side. We weren't allowed to cross over the river, so I never went to an East High athletic event. We were allowed to go to the West High games, which I did fairly frequently. And my perception was the East football team was mostly black and the West team was mostly white. [WHS 68 WF]*

*After the race riot in 1967, we had a lot of tension at East. And we had meetings in the gymnasium about blacks and whites. One black kid stood up and said, "I'm not black, I'm brown." That's when we were first starting to call them black. [EHS 68 WM]*

*There was a great deal of racial tension at East starting in about 1968. It was attributable in part to the civil rights movement in general. It was about a half-dozen to a dozen black kids, some of whom I knew, who were really the radicals only because they're the ones who made their presence known. And they were advocating for changes to be made in the system in general. Not just the school system. But Waterloo and the United States in general. [EHS 69 WM]*

*I was working at Penny's in the late summer, early fall of 1968, one selected from the different high schools to work there. We were also the store's the teen fashion board and occasionally we'd do modeling or a little fashion show. One time they took us in two cars from Penny's on the West Side to KWWL-TV on the East Side, about a half-mile away, to shoot a TV commercial. One of the cars left right after we were dropped off, so there wasn't room in the remaining car for everybody to ride back to the store. The other girls had jumped in the car and so I said I'd walk back. The only other one who wasn't in the car was the black member of the fashion board, the second representative from East. The other high schools only had one, all white. I told her, "You can walk with me. We'll just walk back." We got to Kresge's [dime store on East 4th Street], and I asked if she was thirsty and wanted a Coke. We went in, sat down at the lunch counter and ordered Cokes. It didn't dawn on me until later maybe that wasn't such a hot idea. We got served eventually. But they weren't busy. And there were several white waitresses just standing there looking at us like, "What in the heck is this?" [WHS 69 WF]*

*Most people not from Waterloo thought East High was the black school. Their exposure to East was limited to the very good black athletes being written up in the newspaper sports section. "Oh, yeah, that's where*

*Jerry Moses went to school or Don Ross." Famous athletes. In those days, a basketball team was 15 kids. There were probably four blacks on the East teams. But they were the good ones. Very good athletes. The black kids I became familiar with through other student council or through sports were high-potential. They were destined to be successful. I didn't have a lot of exposure to those who were at risk at that time. The ones I did know were all good guys. [WHS 69 WM]*

*I had black friends at East High. And we would socialize occasionally. Go bowling or sometimes church activities. And I was able to go at least once, maybe twice, on integrated, week-long bus trips to New York City for the UN thing. {EHS 69 WF]*

*Waterloo was totally segregated when I was in school. There were very few black white friendships. You just didn't have black-white male bonding relationships. As a matter of fact, there was a white kid . . . [paused] we probably could have been friends from a distance. We'd talk and laugh in class. And I'd throw him a piece of candy sometimes or he'd throw me one. When the bell rings you go your separate ways. The blacks with blacks and whites with whites. There was a mutual distrust. The whites didn't trust us either. [EHS 69 AAM]*

*I never went to anyone's house in the North End. But to give friends from the West Side a thrill, we'd drive to Blood Alley there. [laughs] I wouldn't have taken that drive with blacks. Because it was dangerous. You never knew what might be going on in the North End. There were shootings and robberies. None of my black friends ever said, "Don't go or stay out of there." I couldn't drive you to where it was it now. [EHS 69 WF]*

*The year before we graduated [fall of 1967], Charlotte Roberts was homecoming queen, a black, and there was such a fuss about it. The E'dales [students from Evansdale] started it and kept the mess going. Because they didn't want any nigger queen representing them. But the administrators weren't far behind. They should have been leading them. No black at East could get elected queen without the Caucasian students*

*voting for you, too. There weren't enough of us. The following year when*
*I graduated, East wouldn't do a homecoming queen. They had*
*Homecoming princesses. I think there were six of us. [EHS 69 AAF]*

Memory is unreliable, regardless of age. Memories aren't like data stored on a computer, which don't change.

The Homecoming Queen story recounted by several people is an example. The perceptions are different than the facts.

A photo of the six 1967 East High homecoming queen candidates, including Charlotte Roberts, appeared on The Teen Page in *Waterloo Daily Courier* on East's Homecoming day, Friday, October 6.[6] The following Friday, there was a photo of Sandy Brackin in the East High news on The Teen Page that identified her as East High's Homecoming queen.[7]

In 1968, six Trojan princesses were presented at the Homecoming game, including two African Americans. No Homecoming Queen was chosen.[8] In 1969, the East homecoming halftime included a parade of seven princesses and the crowning of three queens, including one African American.[9] This protocol was followed through Homecoming 1972, when three queens, including one black queen, and four princesses were crowned.[10]

Across the Cedar River, West High presented four 1968 homecoming princesses chosen out of 10 senior nominees at the Wahawk Homecoming Pow Wow on Thursday night.[11] The four were pictured the next day on the Teen Page in the *Courier*. The election of four Wahawk princesses out of 10 nominees was followed for West's Homecoming from 1969[12] to 1972.[13]

Orange High selected a queen in October 1968[14] and again in 1969.[15] The high school closed in the spring of 1972. Columbus also had a homecoming queen in 1969[16] and continued to do so through the fall of 1972.

A reverse discrimination experience was shared by one contributor who graduated from West.

*I was in the chorus at West and we had a combined concert with all the area public high schools – East, West and Orange. One of the songs required a soloist. It wasn't a Negro spiritual. But it was a black piece of music, a "call-and-response" in blues terminology. The soloist sings a line and the chorus responds. But we never rehearsed a soloist. East had a black soloist, Orange had a white soloist, of course, and we [West] had nobody. The more I thought about it, I realized there was no reason for us to have a soloist. The black guy from East is the one who has to sing the song. And he did. And that was probably a decision of the three directors. But we never rehearsed the soloist. [WHS 69 WM]*

The social environment at Columbus was understandably different than East when it came to social relationships between blacks and whites.

*The African-American kids we had at Columbus were high-level, college-bound kids. Most of the black kids I met there fit right in, were really good people. Good athletes, but good students. You had to be committed to being a good student at Columbus. The Eastsiders had a higher-end socioeconomic status than some of the other minority kids. There were better jobs for people then. Deere, Rath, Chamberlain. Better lives for those people. [COL 69 WM]*

*I don't ever recall going to a party given by one of the white students at Columbus. There were a couple of people who were very friendly. But the majority of friendships were during school time. That was it. [COL 69 AAF]*

*We didn't have the experience of whites driving through the neighborhood when I was growing up on the East Side. It was different at that time. People were more polite. Everyone sort of knew their place. I never remember a situation where the whites were harassing blacks until the thing at the football game in 1968. I wasn't there. The games were switched to the afternoon instead of nighttime. [COL 69 AAF]*

# BIRACIAL DATING

*Friendships in high school with black students started in elementary school. I tried to get up the courage to date a black girl once. I wasn't ready for that kind of social ostracism. I would have been ostracized by both whites and blacks. Because that's the way it was in 1966-67. She worked with me. Beautiful, beautiful girl. We went out for a coffee once. I was interested, but I'm not sure she was. [EHS 67 WM]*

*The administration made biracial dating an issue. [EHS 67 WM]*

Biracial dating at East and the administration's attempt to aggressively discourage, if not prevent it, became a major issue of contention between it and the students in 1968. It was one of the 12 grievances which would be raised by black students at the beginning of the school in the fall when black activism exploded on the East Side: "Teachers should not interfere with the personal lives of students." "Interference" referred specifically to parents being notified by the administration if their student was involved biracial dating.

*I didn't date white boys, although one asked me to prom. My parents had a hissy. Because they were absolutely against interracial dating, particularly if it was their daughter. There was a much worse stigma against black girls dating white boys back then in the black community. It was bad enough black guys would ask white girls out, but the stigma of a black girl going out with a white boy was beyond the pale. And a lot of it had to do with how black slave women were treated by their masters. My brother didn't date white girls in high school. That didn't happen until after he completed community college. My parents never particularly liked it. And my mother never liked his white wife. [EHS 68 AAF]*

*I had a good friend who liked a black boy, but we didn't ever consider them to be a couple. I would have known if there was more than that. I didn't ever think about dating or date one of the black boys. But there were a couple [names withheld] who were very good looking. And very nice men. It wouldn't have flown with my family anyway. [EHS 69 WF]*

*I don't remember biracial couples in school. Which I had always considered kind of a problem, because there were a couple of black gals I really liked. But at that particular time, it never even occurred to me to invite them out. [EHS 69 WM]*

*Biracial dating? Oh, my God, back in the sixties? No way. That was just wrong. I never said that, but I thought that. I never knew an interracial couple. But in my mind, I thought, "That's just not God's way. It's not right." When I look back, I wasn't really a racist. But some of my ideas and thoughts and positions were racist by today's standards. [WHS 69 WM]*

*There were a few black guys going around having sex with a few white girls, but those weren't relationships. Those were girls with what was called "jungle fever." [EHS 69 AAM]*

Athletes were a primary target of the administration's effort to contain biracial dating. The resulting eruption wracked the basketball coach's life and family, and resulted in an East administrator-counselor being targeted as a bigot responsible for the campaign.

*One of the black athletes was dating a white girl. I happened to be walking into the new wing and a basketball coach had this person cornered back behind the stairwell. He was going at him hook and tong. Because he was dating a white girl. And he shouldn't be doing that. He was going to ruin his chances for college and scholarships. The same old crap. Nothing was done overtly by the administration, but everyone knew. [EHS 67 WM]*

*We had a black basketball player who was dating a white student. The coach was up in arms about it. In a team meeting in the locker room, he said it wasn't right, it wasn't going to work and we shouldn't be doing that. The black basketball players decided among ourselves that, if he couldn't go along with what was going on, we were going to quit, and the white players were right with us. We knew what he was talking about. It was something he wasn't going to tolerate. [EHS 67 AAM]*

Head basketball coach Murray Wier – who also the school's athletic director, tennis and a history teacher – detested the administration biracial dating policy. He didn't approve of his athletes dating at all. He didn't want girlfriends or cheerleaders distracting the guys.

During the 1968 riot, in which East High was a target and the national guard was patrolling the North End, Wier and some of the other history teachers were being threatened. There was conjecture it was because they weren't including black history in their classes, but there was no district black history curriculum at that time, which wasn't the teachers' responsibility.

Someone drew a noose on the blackboard in Wier's class and wrote his wife's name under it. Authorities suggested he keep a shotgun by the front door of his home near the North End during the disturbance, which he did. His children weren't allowed outside by themselves for over a week.

A number of the basketball players Wier coached at East were illiterate kids from very poor families with nothing going for them. He mentored them, kept them in school and they respected him. The parents of those kids were at the Wier house frequently. One player's dad would visit frequently and the two would write, talk, all night. On Sundays after church, the coach drove around the East Side to see his students and players.

One biracial player wasn't accepted as black by the blacks or the white as white. They called him "half breed" because biracial kids weren't very common back then. Wier "felt horrible for him and blamed his parents for what they put him through," according to a reliable source.

Another explained the relationship between the coach and his players this way.

*He cared about his guys. He wanted them to win, because he saw what it did for them as people.[1] He wanted them to go on, and have good lives and be good fathers. He talked to them about that ad nauseum. Some of the players' fathers came to the game drunk, and made fools out of themselves and embarrassed their kids. And coach would take them aside, talk to them and talk to the kids. It really hurt him. He was very protective of his players.*

When Wier first used five black starters on his team for out-of-town games, he required they wear sport coats and bought them for a few. He was uncomfortable taking the players out for restaurant meals in other towns that didn't welcome integrated teams. So, he would buy buckets of chicken to eat on the bus back to Waterloo.

Eating with family members in basketball rival Marshalltown on one occasion, Wier was recognized and a couple of guys at the counter started talking loudly about the East Waterloo basketball team and using racial slurs. He finally walked over and challenged them to take it out into the parking lot.

When his family moved to the West Side following the 1968 riots, Wier was heavily recruited by West High to coach, where his son played basketball. But he remained at East as a teacher and athletic director, coaching until 1974, and retiring after 39 years at the school.

Jim Sullivan of the *Waterloo Courier* wrote of the coach, "Murray Wier always did things his way. He lived with a quick wit and a fierce desire to win. He lived to coach, to teach, to succeed."[17]

I knew Coach Wier not only at East, but our families attended Grace United Methodist Church two blocks from the high school and

---

[1] Wier's basketball teams were 372-149 in his 24 seasons as head coach, during which he coached 26 all-state players. The Trojans played in the state tournament eight times, but didn't win the state title until his final season as head coach in 1974 and was named Iowa State Coach of the Year. He was the school's athletic director for 34 years (1955-89) and spent 10 seasons as a tennis coach. He's a member of the Iowa High School Athletic Association's Halls of Fame as a player (1969) and a coach (1983).

he was my Sunday school teacher for several years. I also interacted with him as a student council leader, and as a sports stringer for the *Waterloo Daily Courier* in my junior and senior years. His comments to any black athlete or student involved in biracial dating would have been made from his concern for how that person would be affected by the ensuing fallout and drama, not his personal beliefs.

*One black athlete, a junior, dated a senior white girl as a junior. He didn't really care. Because he was such an athlete, people didn't say a whole lot. There was some muttering under people's breath, especially white guys. And black girls. The black boys were, "Wow, how does the do that?" She was tall, nice-looking and smart. [EHS 68 AAF]*

*There was interracial dating at East. But the black boys were always ostracized, pulled into the office, told this interracial dating isn't going to go on. [EHS 69 AAF]*

*One of the big problems one administrator had was with [a student athlete]. He was with a white girl and her parents were raising holy hell. He came into East High from Kansas City, I think. He was used to dating white girls and it was no big deal to him. But the parents complained. And the administration got on him, riding him, trying to get rid of him. That had nothing to do with his education. Two other black girls and I decided to find out what the administrator would do if we went with white guys. We didn't really go with them – I was dating my future husband. But we created the perception we were involved with the whites. And the administrator never said a word. To me, that followed the whole pattern of, "Caucasian men can do whatever they want whenever they want to black women." But black men cannot touch a white woman. That's part of the heritage we grew up in. Bringing attention to the racism at East meant the boy didn't get put out of school. Black parents were against interracial dating, too, because the whites will kill you. My parents experienced that firsthand in the south. Every parent tries to protect their child. And mine came straight out and said, "These white folks will kill you as black men over these white girls.*

*And if they get caught, they girls are going to say they were raped." Both sets of parents objected, whites and blacks. [EHS 69 AAF]*

*When I was a junior at West High, we went on a campus visit at Iowa State. They took us through the student center to eat at the cafeteria. I saw a white girl and a black guy sitting together. The way they were sitting, they were "together." And I just went, "Whoa." That was shocking. I'd not seen that before. [WHS 69 WF]*

## Racial Bias in High School

*The first year Nativity at East High had a black king was 1965 [the 40th year of the Christmas tradition]. The first time we had a black angel was in 1966. So, we were making some progress and some barriers were coming down back then. [EHS 67 WM]*

*Outside of Waterloo particularly, East was perceived as a black school. The other perception was West High was a better school academically. The year I graduated, that wasn't born out by the standardized test results. [EHS 68 AAF]*

Very little had changed in the school system or the high schools between the fall of 1963 and the start of the school year in the fall of 1967.

*Gifted white students at East were often sheltered and encouraged, at least academically. They were more advantaged, generally given the benefit of doubt. But the assumption was that, if you were black and had gone to Grant or Longfellow or Roosevelt or even Lafayette elementary schools, until proven otherwise, you weren't as smart as the other students. Lafayette wasn't a wealthy school, but it was good academically. If you lived in Highland or were from Lafayette, the assumption was you were smart, knew your academics. The white students at Roosevelt were smart, the blacks not so much. So, starting in junior high school, kids from those schools seemed to be shunted into the non-college track. I supposed it was probably based on testing. But the fact of the matter was that, when you look through the yearbooks, there* are very few black students in Olympiad honor society or other similar clubs. [EHS 68 AAF]

Our classes at West were separated by academic ability: upper, middle and lower. And my circle of friends was in our accelerated classes. It was a segregation not based on race. [WHS 68 WF]

Black students at East High were, in general, counseled away from college prep courses unless they were identified as gifted. I was told I wasn't very good in math and science even though my ITBS (Iowa Test of Basic Skills) and ITED (Iowa Tests of Educational Development) scores were in the low-mid 90s. And I was in a program for gifted students in science and math my junior and senior years of high school. Those messages made me think I wasn't very good, which was much more important than test scores. If I knew then what I know now, I likely would have gotten a science – physics, geology, earth sciences – or engineering degree. As an aside, I scored higher on the quantitative portion of the GREs than I did the language portion. [EHS 68 AAF]

They divided us up into sections for classes at Orange, those of us who were probably going to college and those who weren't. In the end, it didn't make a difference to the students. We all graduated in the same class. And many of us had been together since kindergarten. [OHS 68 WF]

We were tracked in junior and high school, but there were just as many bright, intelligent blacks enrolled in my college-bound track as was proportionate to the population of the school. I'm still surprised when people say tracking is a way of keeping blacks down. [EHS 69 WF]

The principal [at East] was a racist. When we were organizing a walkout to have a black history course, he was adamant about, "No, we're not having that." We kind of tore it up. [EHS 69 AAM]

There was a racial bias and discrimination in high school. I was one of the top students academically at East and got very few scholarships. And many of the black students who didn't do nearly as well *academically as I had done got LOTS [emphasized] of scholarships. Got full rides because of affirmative action. And, yes, I was resentful about that. If my skin had been black, I would have gone to college free, too. [EHS 69 WF]*

A continuing problem for the WCSD school system was the number of its "minority isolation" schools. Under 1972 federal guidelines, a "minority isolation" school had more than 50% minority enrollment.

In 1972, the Iowa State Board of Education issued nondiscrimination guidelines designed to help school districts end racial isolation and imbalance in many of Iowa's urban communities. Any building with a minority population in excess of 20 percent over the district's overall minority population would be deemed "out of compliance." That school district's board of directors would then be required to take action to reduce the minority percentage or defend the imbalance as nondiscriminatory [e.g., a planned "magnet school" or "50-50" school]. In the 1972-73 school year, eight Waterloo school district buildings were out of compliance, which added an additional factor in the system's attempt to desegregate.

Minority isolation schools in Waterloo weren't the result of school boundaries being set to maintain black students in schools in the black community on the East Side. They were the consequence of a neighborhood school system preferred by both black and white parents in a community that was segregated.

Regardless, "minority isolation" would become a major issue in the middle of *TBB* ERA2.

The other two issues that would have a long-term effect on racial bias in Waterloo's high schools were black history classes, and the lack of black faculty and counselors.

RACIAL BIAS IN THE CLASSROOM

*My perception when I was at East was black athletes won games for us. And you're not going to tell a black athlete you didn't pass this test and so you can't play tonight. [EHS 67 WF]*

Teachers encountered by black students in the Waterloo schools had always been white. Many had gone to schools in small communities in Iowa that had no blacks. The state colleges and universities they attended had few, if any, black students. Their first encounter with black students was in their first teaching position after graduation, which sometimes made relationships with students difficult.

The other side of the coin was that students often had little in common with middle-class white teachers, no common frame of reference that would permit them to be relevant role models. (Table 2)

| Table 2 ERA1 & ERA2 Black & White Faculty at East & West High Schools | | | | |
|---|---|---|---|---|
| FACULTY PROFILE | East High School | | | |
| | Female | | Male | |
| | Black | White | Black | White |
| ERA 1 1963 | | 18 | | 34 |
| 1964 | | 25 | | 39 |
| 1965 | 0 | 24 | 1 | 41 |
| 1966 | 0 | 28 | 1 | 41 |
| ERA 2 1967 | | 29 | 1 | 53 |
| 1968 | | 33 | 1 | 53 |
| 1969 | 2 | 14 | 1 | 42 |
| 1970 | 4 | 28 | 1 | 42 |
| FACULTY PROFILE | West High School | | | |
| | Female | | Male | |
| | Black | White | Black | White |
| ERA 1 1963 | 1 | 23 | | 33 |

| 1964 | 1 | 27 | 1 | 37 |
|---|---|---|---|---|
| 1965 |  | 35 | 1 | 45 |
| 1966 |  | 35 |  | 48 |
| ERA 2 1967 | 1 | 36 |  | 60 |
| 1968 | 1 | 38 |  | 61 |
| 1969 |  | 39 |  | 66 |
| 1970 | 1 | 45 |  | 72 |

*GPA was always a monkey on my back. I was having a problem with my grades, and my basketball coach brought me into the office and really told me royally, "Hey if you want to stay in sports, you better get the grades." There were a couple of teachers who seemed like they didn't care whether we graduated. Those were the ones with the monkey. A counselor flat out told us males, as minorities, you "don't have to worry about GPA, you're going to be working in the foundry at John Deere. And the girls are going to be a maid or cleaning houses." I'll never forget that. We black students talked about it afterward, in the cafeteria. [EHS 67 AAM]*

*One of the most important high school experiences which affected my life was when one of the science teachers took a personal interest in me. He was driving me to be the best I could be. He gave me more confidence in myself. He went further than any teacher helping me out with my academics. I think he saw a potential in me, not just as an athlete. When I first started in his class, my grades weren't much too talk about. After he helped me, gave me encouragement, stayed on my butt, my grades went up by multiple points. That helped me out with the other classes. He gave more of his time for me. And I saw him work the same way with other students. [EHS 67 AAM]*

*After [predominantly black] Longfellow Elementary, I was very comfortable [with the racial mix] at Logan Junior. I was in an accelerated track and felt like I was given a chance to be really better at Logan for the most part. Except for my algebra teacher. I couldn't do algebra the way the teacher taught it or the way it was in the book. But I would always get the answers right. This was long before STEM and trying to get girls into those kinds of programs. And he would always say I was cheating. I would say, "Well, how could I be cheating if you can't figure it out my solution?" He was just horrible to me. And he would never give me an "A." I ended up with a "B" in algebra. Because he couldn't solve my problems and he couldn't figure out how I did it. A greater person would have recognized that talent in me and supported me and nurtured me. He turned me against math. For a long time. [EHS 69 AAF]*

*It was important to me that I got "As." I could never get an "A" in one teacher's class, so I decided I would never miss a problem or a miss a question in her class. I got every question right, every homework assignment was done perfectly. When I got my report card, I got a "B" from her. And I asked her, "I didn't get nothing wrong, how come I got a "B." She said, "Because I don't give niggers 'A's.'" [EHS 69 AAM]*

*My favorite teacher at East was Mr. Jesse High, one of the black teachers imported into Waterloo. He taught African history. I think he designed the African-American history program. I was bound to him because he was reinforcing all the things my dad had told me. [EHS 69 AAF]*

*I had a black friend who was a very bright student. He chose not to do a term paper and he still got an "A" in English class. I did the term paper and didn't get an "A." And I confronted the teacher and asked her, "What would the administration say?" My grade was changed. One summer I ran into her when I was at UNI. And she remembered me. She asked me what I was studying. English. [EHS 70 WF]*

*When I was in the black history class, I felt sorry for the black students. They were under a certain social pressure from other black students not to socialize with the white students. They were being forced to take sides, to side with the black people or participate in the white community. [EHS 70 WF]*

In the fall of 1968, the BOE adopted open enrollment as the principle means to integrate, allowing children to attend any school in the system that had space.

A school board member observed at the time:

*The intent of the school administration and the school board is to proceed very gradually and with great caution. The Waterloo school district will probably do only a little more than it is forced to do to achieve desegregation of its schools. The school system has no plan for desegregating its schools, nor is it trying to develop one. Now, this system buses something less than 300 children to white schools in what is called "voluntary open enrollment:" the children only go to schools where there is available space – and only those who volunteer to participate.*[18]

This repudiates the 1969 BOE policy statement committing the district to eliminate schools with high proportions of minority and disadvantaged children, and provide a maximum educational opportunity for all. It wasn't reported whether the statement was made by a member who was on the school board in 1969.

Students had been bused in previous years, but it was so East High students could take electronics and auto mechanics courses offered at West. In 1967, parents at Roosevelt elementary convinced the school board not to bus students to Longfellow to ease overcrowding; the board opted to purchase three relocatable classrooms instead.[19]

Busing would continue to be a solution proposed to desegregate the schools through the early 1970s as the school board sought ways to avoid being forced to make changes by state and federal authorities.

## The High School Experience

*My perception of high school is different from perceptions other people have of me. I thought people didn't like me. Other black students would taunt me about being an "Uncle Tom" or a goody two-shoes. Some of the girls told me, "You just think you're all that." Other black students said, "Oh, you're just trying to be white, because you talk all proper and you hang out with those white kids." Many of those white kids I'd known since kindergarten or junior high. I gravitated toward the people who did the things I did, like anybody else. They were friends who cared and shared my interests. The criticism from other black students give me a sense of being apart from them. Years after high school, some of those same people said, "You were so amazing, I was just in awe." Really? It's all a matter of perspective. [EHS 68 AAF]*

*The only time I remember a racial episode at Columbus was after MLK died. I was walking down the corridor between classes with my friend Frank. We were seniors, his brother was in the 9th grade. A kid came running up and told Frank his brother was in a fight. He took off running. He was kind of a heavy kid, but he ran so fast I couldn't keep up with him. By the time I got to where the fight was, Frank and his brother were gone. I went to the Dean's office and heard them talking. The secretary and a couple of priests wouldn't let me in. I said, "That's my friend. What the hell's going on?" And they told me to mind my own business and just go back to class. I was pissed because I didn't know what was going on with my buddy. After school, I had track practice. I was in the locker room changing and found out the fight had something to do with the black kids, including Frank's brother, wearing arm bands after the assassination. We didn't have any black kids on our track team, because there weren't many black Catholics in Waterloo at that time. Some of the kids around me were saying those niggers needed to be taught a lesson. That pissed me off. I was a little guy wrestling 120 pounds. I told them straight out, "Frank and his brother are my friends." I'd known Frank since the fourth grade. Then I got real mad and raised my voice and told them, "If any of you mothers hurt or go after those guys, you'll have to deal with me and my people." They couldn't understand why he was wearing a black band mourning Martin Luther King. These were rich kids from the West Side. I wasn't quite sure about the arm bands myself at first. It was the same way when JFK was killed. A lot of non-Catholics didn't realize the relationship Catholics had with JFK. [COL 68 WM]*

*When people at UNI learned I was from Waterloo, they wanted to know if I went to "West High or Hershey High?" That's one term for East popular in the late 1960s from people only knew what they heard on TV or read the newspaper. [WHS 69 WM]*

## EAST HIGH WAS A TOUGH SCHOOL

East's reputation as a tough school had been magnified not only in Waterloo, but had spread throughout the state and even nationally. The students were aware of the reputation that extended into their adult lives when people wanted to know how they survived, whether they carried a gun or saw someone killed.

*There was a fight in the lunch room once and I'm lucky to still be alive. Two black girls were in a fight all over the place. As they went past our table, one of them kicked it and I picked my tray up just in time to save my food. And I said something like "dirty nigger," but they apparently didn't hear it, because I'm still alive. [EHS 68 WF]*

*In study hall one time, two black girls whose babies had the same daddy got in a fight right over the desk of a friend of mine, over the top of her. One lost a wig and the other had her dress pulled off. One pulled out a straight razor. The male teachers were standing in the hall just watching and didn't do anything to stop it. No one was apparently injured. Our chemistry teacher was an older woman who'd gone back to school to become a teacher. One day a black student wouldn't do anything she said. She told him, "I'm not afraid of you." It was the women faculty who stood up to the students. [EHS 68 WF]*

*Two guys got into a fight with a knife in front of the lockers going to the student lounge. A friend got blood all over his locker. At our 45th reunion, he said, "I just kept my head down while I was here at East, just waiting to get out of here." I did pretty much the same thing. I didn't want to participate in things at school; I kept jobs so I couldn't. [EHS 68 WF]*

*There were isolated incidents in school, but they were usually blown out of proportion. Fights weren't a daily occurrence by any means. It was so outrageous when it did happen, the story exploded and people wouldn't just forget it. When school got out, sometimes there'd be kids on one side of the street yelling at kids on the other side of the street and throwing rocks or something. [EHS 68 WM]*

*Fights were almost a daily event. Mostly blacks, boys and girls. The girls had the best fighter reputations. The best fights were a black girl on a black boy. [EHS 70 WF]*

*I was aware of fights at East High, which was a big school. The male teachers wore ties and suitcoats. And you knew there'd been a fight, because they would immediately take off their suit coats in case a girl needed to be covered up. If someone ripped their clothes up. It was usually girl fights I was aware of. They would rip the earrings out of the ears. They were really violent. That was the most prevalent kind of fighting – black girl on black girl. [EHS 70 WF]*

*East High had two reputations. It was known as a tough school, but it also had a reputation as an athletic school. The period of so many years of not losing a football game. Unfortunately, in our society, people pick up that if you attended an integrated school, it was a tough one. [EHS 70 WF]*

Incidents involving East students outside of school only added to the perception of toughness.

On a football Friday night in November 1970, the center of the West High football team was beaten with a tire iron in the school's parking lot by Eastsiders after the East-West football game. West lost 20-9.

The player and a teammate left the West dressing room after changing into street clothes, accompanied by their girlfriends, when three carloads of black youths pulled into the lot. People from two of the cars started a shoving match with the West players that escalated into a fight.

The West players were attacked as they were trying to get the girls to one of their cars. The injured player suffered cuts on his back and an arm, and was hit on the head with the tire iron. He was listed in "fairly good" condition after being admitted to the hospital and was released the next day.

Three 17-year-olds were arrested and charged with assault, and a 16- and 15-year-old were charged with "affray." All had addresses in the North End. Tried in juvenile court, the judgments in their cases were sealed.[20]

On the following Monday, two white 18-year-olds and a 17-year-old were arrested on a complaint of assault after the same game filed by a black East High student. The incident took place a couple of blocks from the stadium just before the end of the game. All three lived on the West Side.[21]

The traditional intracity rivalry game was played at Sloane-Wallace Stadium, the site of the 1968 disturbance that spread to three days of rioting on the East Side.

## ADVANTAGE/DISADVANTAGE OF HIGH SCHOOL ATTENDED

Responses in ERA2 about whether the high school attended was a life advantage or disadvantage were similar in insight to those in ERA1.

*Oh, man, was I very advantaged for having attended East. It helped me to cope in life after I graduated. East taught me how to relate and interact with people different than me. How to respect, how to cope with difficult cultures. When I was in Salt Lake City, Mormons had their own way of thinking. It was a great help then and even for me today. [EHS 67 AAM]*

*When you grow up in a household with a manufacturing mindset, the hope is that, when you finish high school, you can get a job at John Deere or Rath Packing Company. Two or three of the teachers at West helped drive me, got me to focus more on the importance of study and math, for example. The teachers were instrumental in the development of my mindset beyond that expectation. They told me, "You've got the skill set and we'll help you, but you've got to be the driving force." And the counselors were very helpful. All the way through Edison Junior High and West High, there was a wide variety of courses and opportunities.* [WHS 67 WM]

*As an adult, one of my greatest joys in my working life was my nonwhite co-workers. I was allowed to be part of their various cultures. I didn't know anything any different in high school. As an adult, I wish I would have had. But back in the 60s, I don't know how many black friends I would have had. Allen nursing school wasn't interracial. Hawkeye Tech was just starting with a campus out on the south side of Waterloo. I was looking at an early yearbook. When I looked at some of the early programs, automotive and nurses aid, I realized Hawkeye was integrated.* [OHS 67 WF]

*We had qualified teachers at Orange High who provided a good education. Orange had real sense of community. We had pride. Community pride and school pride. I didn't experience any bullying. I knew I needed an education. And I had a work ethic instilled in me.* [OHS 67 WF]

*Attending East helped me, and in turn, it helped my daughter. It developed in me a tolerance for people who are not like me, don't necessarily look like me or think like me or believe like me. So, my daughter grew up basically with a very good relationship with the black people she went to school with. She had sleepovers at friends' homes who were black. Black kids came and had sleepovers at our house. Came for lunch from school. That's just the way we raised her. I'm sure my couple of years at East had some impact. But I think it actually started before that.* [EHS 67 WF]

*I saw a fight one time started by some stupid white guy who was parroting something he heard his parents say. To my regret I didn't say anything. I was 16 or 17, but I wish I'd known better. I used to tell some jokes I wish now I hadn't. Especially now that I have a black grandchild. [EHS 67 WM]*

In 1966, the white students had an advantage at East. I remember being embarrassed in the 5$^{th}$ or 6$^{th}$ grade for my friend who was the only black at Francis Grout. He played trombone, I played trombone and we sat together. Which is sort of how we became friends. I regarded us as friends. I'm not sure how he regarded as. But I can remember being embarrassed for him when we talked about slavery in class. Just the fact his ancestors had been slaves. We hadn't seen "Roots" and "12 Years a Slave." And even after seeing those, we whites only have a limited idea what slavery was all about. [EHS 67 WM]

There were disadvantages attending East in terms of money spent in the schools. West High was a brand-new building. They had an excellent football field and track. We had the crumbling concrete ashtray [stadium] behind the school. We did have a new basketball arena. Their auditorium was where the Waterloo Symphony performed. East High's auditorium was cracked seats. The light board was put in by the WPA in the 1930s. That wasn't a joke. I saw the plaques. Better and more senior teachers moved to West and Orange schools before and during time at East. West Junior got better teachers than either McKinstry or Logan Junior, I'm sure. Looking back on it, knowing what I know now, give me the diversity. Attending East absolutely made me a better person. Just being able to embrace difference. The important thing is not how we're alike, but how we're different. [EHS 67 WM]

Dad died when I was 13 and my mom remarried when I was a sophomore at East. We built a house on 9th Street. I was registered at West for the next year and went on the orientation. Then we were called at 5:30 that evening and told I was actually in the Orange District. I went from a class of 300 to one of about 90 in one day. [OHS 67 WF]

I had black friends at Roosevelt Elementary. I just thought of my black classmates as other children. I don't recall thinking in terms of color. There was a little girl in kindergarten or first grade I would play *on the playground and we would have great fun. And I remember telling my mother I wanted her to come home for a play day. And I think my mother probably said, "Okay." But it never happened. I just didn't really understand why. As I got a little older, I thought about it. Even though Roosevelt was biracial, there was still a very clear-cut separation the population. The white kids lived west of East 4th Street and the black children lived east of East 4th. At East, it also seemed to me both black and white students were most comfortable with the segregated lives we lived outside of school. While we were all part of the same East Side community, we never intermingled in our East Side neighborhoods. In school we would laugh and talk and enjoy one another's company. There was more white participation at social events in high school than there was black. But once you left the building, that was it. Neither the white nor the black students were comfortable socializing outside of school. I thought that was very sad. Even now, at our most recent class reunion, only a few of our black classmates attended. The reunion committee did its very best to reach everybody. A number of black class members confirmed they were coming. I think three did. There were over 100 of us there. We were really taken aback, mystified the blacks didn't come. The ones who did had a wonderful time. [EHS 68 WF]*

*Attending East High School was an advantage. It made me aware of the fact my world was bigger than just white. My mother and a sister were the only family left in Waterloo when I was growing up. We lived on the East Side, the cousins lived on the West. And my aunt would always say to my mother, "How do you do it, living on the East Side?" They had this image there was crime, that it was less than a desirable place to live. So, other than shopping for clothes at JC Penny just across the river or going to the doctor a little further up on West 4th Street, my life was on the East Side. [EHS 68 WF]*

*When I was a junior or a senior, [name withheld] was running for class president. He was white, a skinny little guy. He gave his speech and told everything that was wrong with the administration. He called one of*

*them "the Big Kahuna" and hinted one of the male counselors was gay.*
*Before we could vote, the teacher told us his speech was inappropriate*
*and his name was removed from the ballot. We said we'd write it in.*
*And the teacher said, "I'd think very carefully about it." So, I took my*
*pen and wrote in his name. All the kids were excited about the write-in*
*and someone called KWWL. And they said it was too hot a story for*
*them to handle. They didn't want to report anything like that. It was a*
*lesson in a democracy; you did what you were told. [EHS 68 WF]*

*East parents were called to a meeting at school by the administration*
*to discuss controlling violence. One of the proposals was having parents*
*volunteer as hall monitors. My mom said, "Give me a gun and I'll take*
*care of it for you." [EHS 68 WF]*

*I had conflict with another black student until we realized the same*
*people were saying the same things about us. He'd say, "You're arrogant*
*and stuck up and you're dating my brother." And my response was, "It's*
*none of your business. Butt out." I'm not sure whether there was a*
*particular incident which turned that around. But in the second*
*semester of my sophomore year, I was in his junior-level Algebra class.*
*We were talking or something and realized both of us had a reputation*
*for being stuck up and standoffish. He because he was an athlete and a*
*pretty good student. Me because I was a good student and young, and*
*kind of an athlete, too. [EHS 68 AAF]*

*I had confrontation with a white woman teacher which – if not*
*racial, and I think it was – was sexist. About three weeks before the end*
*of the term, she told a white student and me we were both right on the*
*edge between a "B-plus" and an "A-minus." And how we performed the*
*remainder of the year would determine our grade. I noticed every time*
*he held his hand up in class after that, she called on him. She never*
*called on me when I held my hand up. She only called on me when I*
*didn't because I wasn't certain of the answer. At the end of the term, she*
*gave me a "B-plus" and I went out of my mind. I was furious. I marched*
*into her office and said, "Why did you give me a B-plus when you gave*

*the other student an A-minus?" She tried to talk me out of my anger.
"He knew the answers in class and you didn't." I pointed out she'd called
on him when he raised his hand and didn't call on me when I raised
mine. That I knew we'd gotten the same grade on the final. She finally
tried to intimidate me, asked why she should change my grade? I told
her, "Because I deserve it." She snatched the report card from my hand.
She changed the semester grade first, then changed the 9-week grade,
thrust it back and me and said, "You're just like your mother." And I
said, "Thank you." [smile] My mother had attended East and had many
of the same teachers I did. [EHS 68 AAF]*

*My classes at East were all accelerated. But some of the textbooks and
instruction at East were not as good as I thought they were at McKinstry
Junior. I was in an experimental program in math there, a School
Mathematics Study Group. We had algebra in 8th grade and geometry in
9th. Our books were designed to get us to come up with our own
theorems and proofs. And you would get extra credit for coming up with
a proof which was different from the book. As a sophomore in high
school, I was taking algebra III in a class with 11th graders. It was, "This
is the proof and that's it." It was weird to me and I didn't like it. In my
little "nerdlander" world, I thought it was dumbing down of the
curriculum. [EHS 68 AAF]*

*In 10th or 11th grade, our college prep English teacher said if you had
at least a 95 on the reading comp of the ITEDs, you didn't have to spend
the following nine weeks in class. You could do an individual poetry
project. There were three of us who qualified. I wanted to do it on black
poets. I had an amazingly difficult time getting her to allow me to do
that, because she said she didn't know anything about them. I suggested
that was a reason I should be allowed to do black poets and she finally
relented. My parents had books of black poetry at home and I went to
the library. You had to give a report to the class at the end of the nine
weeks. I started with Phyllis Wheatley and ended with Countee Cullen.
The class was amazed. I did "I, Too, Sing America" by Langston Hughes.*

*And people went "whoa." I talked about James Weldon Johnson's "The Creation" and others. The teacher later said to me, "I'm really glad you insisted on doing this, because everybody has learned a lot." That was the only real opportunity I had to learn anything about black literary culture at East. Because I was an "exceptional" student, I got to push boundaries others didn't. I realized then my experiences were different than many of my classmates, black or white. [EHS 68 AAF]*

*My dad died at the start of my senior year at Columbus and I was going to quit school. But I had a brother-in-law who quit school in the 8th grade and couldn't get ahead at John Deere because of that. He found out I was leaving school, came over and we had a big fight. He knocked me across the room and told me I'd better keep my ass in school. We were a little too proud to ask for help. But I went down someplace and signed up for social security, got a little bit of a survivor's benefit. I asked the owner of the duplex where we were living to lower the rent $5 a month, and we got cheese and powdered milk each month; that got me through school. Dad had managed to pay tuition at Columbus for my and me sister. After he died, Columbus didn't get paid for either. My sister graduated in 1966 and got a bill a few years later for her tuition. She paid that back. The Knights of Columbus or someone came along and paid my back tuition so I was able to graduate. They wouldn't tell me who. I ran in a gang in 8th and 9th. And I believe if I'd gone to East, I would have done a lot of . . . probably would have dropped out in 9th or 10th grade. Columbus gave me the structure I needed and the opportunity to have a great education. [COL 68 WM]*

*My American history teacher at West changed my whole outlook on what teachers were supposed to be. He was funny and handsome, and seemed to really care about us as students and made the class interesting. I always thought teaching was about checking off something to do. That class really was exciting. He instilled in me that American history could be fun, not boring and just something you wrote papers about. We had many, many group discussions. He taught so differently.*

*I found learning could be exciting and fun, which translated to my other classes. It led me to believe in lifelong learning. I went back to college in my 40s. American history is still really important to me. [WHS 68 WF]*

*Outside my parents, East football coach Howie Vernon was one of the major influences in my life. Vernon had a presence where he could walk into a room and look at you, not trying to scare you, and you'd look away. He could say, "I want you to run through that wall" and I'd run through the wall. I never lost a football game in high school. Howie Vernon was a dynamic personality. And I tried to take a lot of his characteristics and apply them to my life. Work hard and you win. That was something Howie Vernon taught me that stayed with me. [EHS 68 WM]*

*Most people thought East was black. I think part of it was because we were so strong in sports. Blacks dominated in sports so that was their reasoning. You'd say, "East High," and it was associated with sports. People thought it was dead in the middle of the black community and it wasn't. It was right on the cusp of the black community. There wasn't a ghetto. There were some nice neighborhoods around the school. Fourth Street with all the shops. Mama Nick's Pizzeria. East wasn't in some rundown black area whites were afraid to go into. However, if you lived on the West Side, you kind of thought that way. [EHS 68 WM]*

*When I was at East, I never thought once it was a disadvantage. Now I wouldn't have traded it. I think our teachers were good. They probably had to be a little tougher than most because we were a pretty rowdy crowd. [EHS 68 WM]*

*I always valued the multi-cultural experience that I received in the Waterloo school system and EHS. I often referred to it as the University of East High School. I have remained closer to EHS classmates through the years than college classmates. [EHS 68 WM]*

*I ran in a gang in the 8th and 9th grades, I believe if I'd gone to East, I would have done a lot of . . . probably would have dropped out. Columbus gave me the structure I needed. When parents enrolled their kids, they were giving permission for the nuns and the teachers and the principals to punish. Spank, slap your hands with a ruler. So, our classrooms were more controlled. And we had hall monitors. The biggest thing advantage at Columbus was the opportunity to have a great education. [COL 68 WM]*

*Attending West High wasn't an advantage, because you weren't exposed to a multiracial culture. We were white bread, lily white. That doesn't mean racist. It may be racist by definition because there was only one race in the school. I don't know the history of Waterloo. But the blacks couldn't buy a house on the West Side. [WHS 69 WM]*

*When the South did so-called integration, they took all the black students and put them into all the Caucasian schools. As a result, black teachers lost jobs. A lot of them came north to get employment, but they were not looked upon well. In a way, their education to me was inferior. I know a lot of blacks in the South and their writing skills are nothing like ours. If we wanted it or knew we needed it, we did receive a good education here. Because we had to compete with Caucasians. We weren't given an opportunity to do otherwise. Either you get in and get to the top or you don't. A lot of us blacks didn't go into teaching and a lot who came here from the South to get teaching positions left to go to John Deere. [EHS 69 AAF]*

My Master's degree was earned from Troy University (then Troy State) in the mid-1970s, less than 10 years after the University of Alabama had graduated it first black student. Most of my classmates in an education class were black teachers from south Alabama working on a degree for promotion or as a requirement to enter a doctoral program. The majority were graduates of traditional public HBCUs (historically black colleges and universities) in Alabama like Alabama A&M or Florida A&M, Alabama State, Stillman, and Fort Valley and Albany state universities in Georgia.

These people were sharp, contributed to the discussions, were generally congenial, but a couple had a chip on their shoulders. One of the white students raised the issue one night of the difference in the quality of education at an institution like Troy as opposed to a "black" school. The pushback from the black students was immediate, forceful but not defensive or confrontational.

Their argument was they had received better educations at their alma maters than many of their colleagues did at the top universities or white public schools. Their black professors were better than professors at those schools. They had to be. And they had been better prepared for their careers than white teachers in the primarily black schools in which they taught.

Those factors, they stressed, invalidate the perception black higher education was inferior and black graduates from black universities weren't as qualified. Point taken.

*If people knew Waterloo, they assumed I went to East High because I was black. When I told them I graduated from Columbus, the reaction was, "Oh, I didn't know blacks were Catholic." My maternal grandfather wasn't Catholic, but he wanted his kids to go to a Catholic school, even if they didn't want them. So, his kids were baptized Catholic. I don't think my dad became a Catholic until I was born. [COL 69 AAF]*

*The perception for some of the white kids was it was an advantage to be black in the Waterloo school system, because it was trying to do everything it could to make the black students all they could be. In some of the white kids' eyes, the district showed favoritism. Some black students thought they should have more rights than they did and were being discriminated against. But they were getting extra help at school. And if blacks were fighting, there would be no suspension, no penalty. But if white kids were caught fighting, they would be out of school for three days. There was a perception the blacks were receiving special treatment. [WHS 69 WM]*

*I fought with an E'dale person [Evansdale, a community the southeastern part of the Waterloo Community School District]. I didn't feel like being called a nigger that day. I asked him to leave me alone. It was a boy and he just decided it was going to be his day. So, I made his day for him. Every once in a while you saw a few blacks fighting. But not very often. Our black community in Waterloo was a very tight community until urban renewal came along. That and desegregation totally decimated the black community. [EHS 69 AAF]*

*I didn't really think about being disadvantaged when I was at West High. But when I was teaching and started to get a lot of African American kids, I realized it affects you a lot. I was in grad school when I first met Palestinians. How was I ever going to meet a Palestinian otherwise? Before then, when I would think about the Middle East, I thought of it in terms of Israel and the news media. But when I met actual Palestinians, I started to think about their points of view and a value systems and personal stories. It sort of changes you. But I didn't really think of Waterloo that way when I was a teenager. I think that way now. [WHS 69 WM]*

*When I was in high school, we had two cities and two school districts. The result was the West Side population lived in a bubble and only had the opportunity to interact with the rest of the population when and if they met on common ground, which was most likely in the downtown shopping district. [WHS 69 WF]*

*West High became more integrated halfway through my high school career. I was on the student council at West. We had an exchange my junior year with East High where our student council went over there and sat in on one of their meetings. We talked about what it was like being students at our schools. I learned East was a multi-cultural, multi-racial school that had some of the same problems we faced in the all-white school. Some of the same struggles. This black guy about my age said, "If you weren't here, I'd be sitting in the back." That statement stuck with me. I'd never thought about that until I heard him say it. That if it had been a class, he would have been sitting in the back. Walking through the halls, I found out the school wasn't 99% black. Most people thought East High School was 75% African American from the newspaper or television stories. That's what I thought before I went over there. And when you get over there and you see all these white kids walking up and down the halls, you go, "Wait a minute. Are these foreign exchange students or what?" I think it was 25% black. Going up and down the halls at East, I didn't feel any anger or resentment or anything visiting with the students. The student council visit was the beginning of my understanding there was a racial thing going on in the two high schools. [WHS 69 WM]*

*I felt advantaged, privileged for going to an all-white [West] school. Not having to integrate myself was one less thing I had to deal with. I knew the score up front. That wasn't the case with my kids. They all went on to college, too. Making the transition from high school to college was a lot easier for them than it was for me. There were two blacks at West High with me. West was multiracial when they attended. [WHS 69 WM]*

*Columbus was a very good school with very good teachers. I had a lot of black friends in the neighborhood who went to East High and I went to their parties. But I experienced a personal backlash when I went to a small private college in Minnesota. I got involved in black organizations with very few white contacts in the first couple of years. In my junior year, I thought to myself, "You want to go into business and most of the people out there are white. So, you're going to have to get out there and start getting involved with other things." So, in terms of race, I felt sort of a little disadvantaged going to Columbus – but not in terms of education. [COL 69 AAF]*

*This was in the day when East was the perennial champion and Columbus played them in football. East's football players were nine-foot-tall and ran like gazelles. I could play football, but I wasn't big and I wasn't fast. I remember one time Jerry Moses was running down the sideline headed for a touchdown. And I'm going to hit him so I can knock him out of bounds. I hit him as hard as I could. I couldn't get him out of bounds. I look up and he's scoring the touchdown. That was crazy business. Those guys were huge and fast and good. [COL 69 WM]*

There was some disadvantage to being at East, but it wasn't specific to black students. West High offered a better education, except for vocation. For college prep, West was better. *[EHS 69 WF]*

People didn't know about the famous tunnel At West High. They finally closed it up. Students were drinking and drugging and having sex and everything else there. And nobody ever talks about that tunnel. Nobody made any noise about it because it was the doctors' and lawyers' and judges' kids going to West High. *[EHS 69 AAF]*

The Waterloo school system was a very good environment to grow up in then. I think that's because of the integration. I was exposed to different cultures to a certain extent. Certainly working with folks of different ethnicity gave me a broader viewpoint. *[EHS 69 WM]*

Back then, there were six teachers of color in the Waterloo schools. SIX. *[Emphasized]* Out of all the schools. We accepted it as just being the way it is; we didn't know any different. When you think back and reflect on it, it's like, "Oh, my God." My kids and grandkids take education for granted. They take all the opportunities and the rights they have for granted. *[EHS 70 AAF]*

For an Eastsider, there's a hole in your mind about what happens on the other side of the river. When I was at East, I wondered what happened at West High. What it looked like. One of the rumors was West kids got all kinds of good stuff we didn't have. *[EHS 70 AAF]*

I played drums and so band was the most important high school experience for me. I was into all the bands, orchestra. I think of Waterloo as being a kind of somewhat a rough town, a rough element of people here. And the West Side was extremely stratified. You had the families which owned the smokestack companies. People riding high on top and a blue-collar base. Band was a subset of people, comfortable. Largely nice kids in band. *[WHS 70 WM]*

*I had a good education and I had good high school experiences at East, which is probably weird. It's just high school and every kid goes to it. I had an opportunity to grow up. The whole "how you gonna keep them down on the farm?" High school was, "Huh, I have a choice." That's the impact my high school experience had. [EHS 70 AAF]*

*I came out of Immanuel Lutheran pretty much ahead academically. So, I was in accelerated classes at East. Kind of a tight-knit group. And I finally did end up with a little group of friends. There was one black guy in the group of about 25-30. And we did most of our classes together. He was very intelligent, seen as exception to the rule by the group. Unusual for a black male to be in an accelerated class. But he was accepted. We were in some social setting, playing truth or dare. I was dared to kiss him. I guess that was a big thing. And I kissed him on the cheek. [EHS 70 WF]*

*Being at East gave me a more honest look at life in general. We don't live in a white-only society. I had a very positive learning experience in our integrated school. Never had a negative experience with a black person. It was my experience people who grew up in a predominantly white environment and are thrust into an environment where they're the minority had a rougher time adjusting than those of us who grew up in racially mixed environments. Being in an environment where I was a minority was an eye-opening experience. [EHS 70 WF]*

## The Perfect Storm Approaches Waterloo

Civil rights actions by the black community and its white supporters in 1966 and 1967 were generally peaceful and non-confrontational, but also resulted in little, if any, actions that led to substantive changes. Two black students intending to start a change process at East High would become the spark igniting a violent and widespread upsurge in activism in the school and community. (Figure 3)

*In 1968, Waterloo became a footnote to the national uprising, or rioting, depending on one's viewpoint, in what would become known as the "Long Hot Summer." Alongside the riots in black neighborhoods in Detroit and Watts, a riot erupted in Waterloo, shaking the complacency of the town, who believed that such a thing was impossible in small Midwestern cities and towns.[22]*

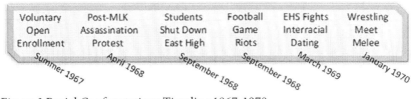

Figure 3 Racial Confrontations Timeline 1967-1970

## 1967 BOE "VOLUNTARY OPEN ENROLLMENT" DESEGREGATION STRATEGY

In the summer of 1967, the school board proposed "voluntary open enrollment" as a local solution to desegregation, allowing elementary students to attend any school with space for them.

That fall, the Waterloo Commission on Human Rights reported, "Although it appears that the climate for intergroup [integrated black and white] education has improved and there is a growing desire to grapple with the problem of segregation, the Waterloo school system does not seem to have a clearly enunciated policy relating to integration of its schools.[23]

In the summer of 1968, the success of the elementary plan prompted the BOE to extend open enrollment to the high schools on a limited basis where space was available. Forty black East High students would be enrolled at West High and 15 would be enrolled at Orange High. Fifteen students from those two schools would enroll at East. Junior high schools were ineligible for open enrollment due to space restrictions.[24]

According to Superintendent George Hohl, ". . . racial balance would be improved" because of the plan. The estimated fall enrollment at East was projected to be 1,750 students, about 19% (332 students) black. The 55 East students going to West and Orange equaled 16.5% of the 332 black students; that would reduce the black percentage at East almost 5% to 15.8%. Hohl projected the open enrollment plan would reduce the black enrollment at East to a 10% target in three years.[25]

Rev. Basil Foley, pastor of Payne AME Church on East Fourth Street in the North End, expressed "concern over the quality of education black children are receiving. . . . the black community has a new philosophy. We want to develop and upgrade where we are. We want schools that are good enough for our children."[26]

Hohl resigned in March 1970 to teach at Iowa State University.

In the fall of 1971, 21 black students registered at Hoover Junior High on the West Side under open enrollment. In 1963, 0.2% of the school's students were black. By 1970, it was 3.3%. In December 1977, several black Hoover parents approached the school administration to express concerns about discrimination and inequities although no issues had been raised about the Hoover or its administration in the previous six years. The unresolved concerns escalated to grievances in April 1978 and caused a three-day boycott of the junior high. [27]

By the spring of 1978, enrollment in the district had dropped from a peak of 19,873 students in 1967 to just over 15,200. Another 2,000 students were forecast to be lost by 1981.[28] While the numbers of blacks in the schools decreased as a result, many of the minority isolation schools hadn't improved in minority student ratios.

*Voluntary open enrollment in Waterloo turned out to be one-way with no white students travelling to black schools and fewer than 300 black children bused to white schools.*

*In effect [voluntary open enrollment] only permitted the more daring black parents to send their children to predominantly white schools in other attendance areas.[29]*

The school board was also dealing with an overcrowded Roosevelt Elementary when there were empty classrooms at Longfellow Elementary, less than three-quarters of a mile away on the most direct bus route. Parents objected "loudly" to the district's plan to redistribute the students by busing and the school administration capitulated, investing instead in temporary classrooms for Roosevelt.

Dr. David Cohen of the U.S. Commission on Civil Rights (USCCR) – widely considered a foremost national expert on civil rights and desegregation, and director of the USCCR's national race and education study and its report, "Racial Isolation in Public Schools" – met with the BOE's advisory Committee on Equal Opportunity Education in July. He told the committee busing was not only possible in Waterloo, but could be a solution to its segregation problem, wouldn't involve an unmanageable number of students or be too costly.

Cohen asserted the district shouldn't back down to protests over integration or busing.

*[The BOE should] implement plans with conviction and determination. . . . citizens who may "blow off hot air" at first will ultimately become confident that the school system is doing what is best for all the students. . . . desegregation [hasn't] worked when school boards "were dragged into it, kicking and screaming." Desegregation has been successful . . . when school boards have taken the attitude that "we're doing it because it's right, educationally." . . . opposition to busing is "ludicrous" . . . forty-three percent of all public school children ride buses to school every day. But . . . "a better education must be at the end of the ride" for both white and Negro students.[30]*

One of the committee's proposals discussed at the meeting was a lab school at Grant, where 99% of the students were black. That plan would come to fruition in 1970 in the Bridgeway Project.

*Because of its hearing in September 1967, the Waterloo Commission on Human Rights tied housing to school segregation.*

*If the past and present trend of white families to "flee" from the East Side of the city perseveres, the continued adherence by the [BOE] to the "neighborhood school attendance policy" can only result in increasing segregation in these Waterloo schools.[31]*

By the end of 1969, the commission had deemed open enrollment a failure.

*It is obvious the voluntary open enrollment plan has not reduced minority concentrations to the desired degree.*

*. . . the open enrollment program . . . is on a space available basis, and, to the best of our knowledge and information, is solely an involvement from east to west. While there have undoubtedly been some advantageous learning results for some of the children, we were struck by two other factors. First, that the responsibility of achieving a degree of integration has been placed upon the black community – a community that has not been responsible for the segregation which exists. Second, the lack of preparation of the school staffs in the receiving schools that might have prevented some of the estrangement, indignities and disrespect suffered by some of the open enrollment children.*

*It appears school integration cannot be obtained by voluntary participation of students and parents.[32]*

## JULY 1967 OJT PROTEST AND RIOTS

*Recently I returned from a while in the wilderness to find an American city in flames. I'd been out of touch with day-by-day news; ugly headlines focused on the savagery in Detroit. Promptly I reviewed the chronology of violent revolt in Newark and Nyack, in Harlem and Rochester and Waterloo, Iowa. . . . – Conservative radio host Paul Harvey.[33]*

*In 1967 when I was 15, I was sent to Washington, D.C., for three weeks during the summer. I was there when one of the riots occurred in Waterloo. I was sitting in my aunt's living room watching the 6 o'clock news and here comes Waterloo, looking like one of the places in the*

*South. People were in the streets and throwing things, and police were wearing riot gear. That was an eye-opening event. [WHS 70 WM]*

Black youths demonstrated for three days the second weekend of July to protest their parents' "acceptance" of segregated housing, education [and employment discrimination] in exchange for "good" jobs.[34]

"[Roving] bands of Negroes looted, firebombed and vandalized a number of businesses [on the 900-1200 blocks of East 4th adjacent to the Negro North End]. . . .[35]

They "overturned at least two cars and tossed several firebombs [that started blazes at the Nuebauer & Crowther Service Store, Hickey's Café and Standard Heating Equipment Company resulting in an estimated $5,000 worth of damages]. . . . Negro leaders said the uprising was not triggered by any single incident, but was caused by a 'lot of general things such as unemployment, housing and the rest of the problems that face the Negro.' . . . [The] state president of the N.A.A.C.P. [sic] called the city a 'tinderbox' of racial discord.'"[36]

According to Mayor Lloyd Turner, destruction was "mostly 'by young teenage people taking out their frustrations by damaging property'. . . . 'All it takes . . . is one spark' which was provided by a hard-core group of 12-14 Negroes, many of them with criminal records [the mayor said]."[37]

*As unlikely a place as Waterloo, a nice, small city of 75,000 in northeast Iowa's dairy area, was touched, too, by the madness. Waterloo's Negroes make up only 8% of the population, are well integrated into the schools, and enjoy an unemployment rate of a minimal 2.3% (well below the current national average of 4%). But trouble exploded anyway. A young Negro, in full view of a prowl car, deliberately knocked down an old white man who was sweeping the sidewalk in front of a tavern. His arrest touched off yet another 48 hours of rioting by Negro youths – to the perplexity of their elders. Said Albert Morehead, 68, a Mississippi-reared Negro who takes pride in the symbols of his success in the North – a neat frame house and around it flourishing patches of greens and flowers, "I can't see no call for it." . . . the most striking feature of Newark's riot . . . was that the young Negroes took it over. Some were seekers of kicks. Some, still in their teens were already infected with hate. And some were, in an extreme fashion, reflecting a yawning generation gap – the sort of thing that high school student Byron Washington, 16, was talking about when he said in Waterloo, Iowa: "The whites got to face it, man. This is a new generation. We aren't going to stand for the stuff our mas [sic] and fathers stood for."[38]*

"Representative H.R. Gross (Rep., IA) told the U.S. House the rioting in Waterloo – in his district –'reportedly because of an invasion of professional agitators from Detroit, Michigan. . . . [They] appear to be part of a national pattern.'" Republicans in the House were considering enactment of anti-riot legislation. Gross said "problems of a local nature should be 'left to the law enforcement of officials in Waterloo and in Iowa."[39]

*Time* magazine, *The New York Times* and the *Nashua (NH) Telegraph*[40] (Figure 4) carried stories about the riot.

Turner also cited the local OJT (On-the-Job) training program as a contributing cause. Part of the Iowa Manpower Development Council, it had been picketed recently for not keeping promises for jobs for young blacks.

The OJT project was established in the spring of 1967 at the Jesse Cosby Neighborhood Center in the North End. Its objective was to "help underemployed and unemployed persons obtain work and [OJT] in a semi-skilled or skilled area.[41] One report said – of 1,200 trained unemployed youth – only two were placed as bricklayers.[42]

Figure 4 Waterloo Riots Made the National News in 1967

Black leaders had worked out a plan with the mayor and the police to attempt to diffuse the riots that weekend, but a lack of communication between them resulted in the leaders not being recognized by the police and kept them from being effective.

Iowa Gov. Harold E. Hughes provided a guest editorial in the July 30 *Waterloo Daily Courier* in which he charged that, "Never has there been a time in our history when it was more essential for responsible citizens, both black and white, to keep cool heads."

*What is needed is convincing evidence that the white majority is sincere in its attention to give the Negro community equality of citizenship. On the other hand, what is needed is affirmation by the Negro community of their willingness to accept the responsibilities of equal citizenship and their rejection of the treasonable exhortations of the "Black Power" insurrectionists. . . . The criminal violence of the riots cannot be condoned or half-met for any reason. Neither can the shame of discrimination and ghetto living.*[43]

*Why the riots in 1967? Probably a new generation saw things differently. Some of the things some folks people had put up with weren't going to be acceptable anymore and rioting was the way to go. Some of the national black activists had something to do with that. And some people became copycats like other stuff that's negative. [WHS 60 AAM]*

The riots were also a topic of discussion in the *Waterloo Courier's* The Public Speaks letters. This one from July 28, 1967 was representative.

**Seek Equal Justice, Too.** *From the articles I have been reading, the Negroes are rioting because they want equal rights. Equal rights to acquire an education which is already available to those who want it regardless of race? Equal job opportunities which are earned according to everyone's education, talent, and hard work? And last but not least equal justice, too: the right to pay for their crimes of looting, destroying and killing?*

Rev. R. Joseph Parker, pastor of the AME Church, said the various factions in the Negro community needed to band together. "We've got to straighten out ourselves before we can straighten out the others. By tearing up the East side you're using the same tactics as The Man."[44]

## 1968 WATERLOO AFTER THE MLK ASSASSINATION

Roughly three weeks before Rev. Martin Luther King, Jr., was assassinated in Memphis, a Molotov cocktail was thrown into Municipal Judge William Parker's house in Highland. A "whisky bottle filled with a flammable liquid and a rag wick" set fire to the downstairs study in the front of the house around 10 p.m. He, his wife and baby were upstairs in their upstairs bedrooms, but no one was injured. The fire burned the curtains and the floor of the study in several places, and papers and books that were on top of the desk. In 1963, Parker was the first elected black municipal judge in the state of Iowa. "I don't have the slightest idea who did it . . . . I guess, though, after one's been on the bench for a few years, he can expect anything."[45]

The reaction in Waterloo to King's assassination was inconsistent with the climate of impatience, frustration, distrust and belief that

Figure 5 Iowans' Perceptions of Riots, August 1967

violence was necessary for change in the town. It was peaceful, respectful, restrained, non-violent. This contradicts several credible secondary sources that cited riots in Waterloo among the national incidents after King was killed.

NAACP Black Hawk County chapter president Dr. Warren Nash said the calm was "a combination of things. . . . the young people have at least listened to some of the things that have been said and they have gone along with the principle of non-violence. . . . the police have stayed 'invisible,' more or less . . . . If these attitudes persist, if we can continue with the same attitude, we can continue in peace and harmony."[46]

Praise for the community – including the youth – came from the mayor and the police chief, the school superintendent and the city's director of the commission on human rights.

The Waterloo Daily Courier editorial board agreed.

*. . . it is a demonstrated fact that the overwhelming majority of colored [sic] people in this area deplore these criminal activities ["by a few rock-throwing hoodlums"] as much as anyone else. Blaming the colored race for hoodlumism is as fantastic as blaming the white race for the crimes of white hoodlums. We should review for contrast some of the positive and constructive things which have [happened here] during the past week [following the assassination].*

*. . . hundreds and thousands of individuals – colored and white – living, working, mourning, praying and thinking together.*

*. . . memorial services. . . . at the Antioch Baptist Church [that] drew about a thousand people. Half of them were white.*

*. . . a Silent Vigil for the man who met a violent end in the pursuit of non-violence. About one-third of the people . . . were white.*

*. . . not only talking and praying. There was more than mouthing of glittering generalities. . . . final passage of the open housing ordinance by the Waterloo and Cedar Falls City Council. . . . the establishment of a Martin Luther King Memorial Scholarship Fund for Underprivileged young people.*

*. . . this community is making progress in civil rights; and it should continue to make progress to demonstrate that violence and counter-violence is no going to be accepted by the overwhelming majority of both races.*[47]

## Reflections from the Bridge

*All economic levels, all races and all classes should attend school together. . . . to have a democratic educational system. – Communication to the Waterloo Board of Education from the Iowa Civil Rights Commission, April 18, 1968*[48]

ERA 2 was a tumultuous one in which the demands from community factions and students for social integration and an end to school segregation became increasingly insistent. There was resistance initially, if not opposition, from other community groups, community leaders, the BOE, and school district and some school administrators.

After being battered by the perfect storm in 1968, things changed, as Kathryn Schumaker described in "The Politics of Youth: Civil Rights Reform in the Waterloo Public Schools."

*Inspired and empowered by the civil rights movement's successes in the mid-1960s, [black] Waterloo students [and their parents] asserted their own conceptions of racial equality and educational equity and, in the process, won concessions from the local school district. At the same time, the school board turned to school desegregation as a practical way to prove its commitment to racial equality in the schools. Shrinking enrollments turned school desegregation into a policy choice made when it became apparent that a realignment of school attendance zones would be necessary. White opposition to busing arose in Waterloo as the school board voted for a comprehensive desegregation plan, but opponents were ultimately not able to halt the implementation of the school board's plan.*[49]

That played out in the third ERAof *The Bridge Between.*

# Endnotes

[1] Waterloo's Unfinished Business. A report by the Waterloo Commission on Human Rights summarizing the testimony and making recommendations based on the testimony heard during hearing [sic] in Waterloo, Iowa, at the Clayton House, September 7, 1967. (November 13, 1967). Housing. Summary of Evidence, 6, 7.

2 During Vernon's seven years as head coach, the Trojans were state champions for three straight seasons from 1966-68 and had won 29 straight games through the 1968-69 season.

3 Common Patterns in an Uncommon Place: The Civil Rights Movement and Persistence of Racial Inequality in Waterloo, Iowa. An Honors Project for the Program of Africana Studies (2014). Shirey, T.E. Maine: Bowdoin College, 103.

4 The report didn't indicate if that data included the black East students' responses.

5 Survey of Black Students to School Board Tomorrow. (April 06, 1969). *Waterloo Daily Courier*, 13, 14.

6 High Society. Athletics and Academics Make News for Teens. East Queen Candidates. (October 06, 1967). *Waterloo Daily Courier*, 8.

7 High Society. Autumn Activities Fill Teens' Days. (October 13, 1967). *Waterloo Daily Courier*, 8.

8 It's Homecoming Time . . . At East High School . . . (October 11, 1968). *Waterloo Daily Courier*, 10.

9 1) Innovations at Annual Event. East High's Homecoming to Open with Breakfast. (October 01, 1969). *Waterloo Daily Courier*, 11. 2) East High Princesses Reign Over Game. (October 05, 1969). *Waterloo Daily Courier*, 38.

10 High Society. Homecoming Makes News (photo) (October 05, 1972). *Waterloo Daily Courier*, 17.

11 Climax Is Friday Night. West Homecoming Fete to Start with Powwow Event. (October 28, 1968). *Waterloo Daily Courier*, 8.

12 To Name Four Princesses. Full Week of Activities for West's Homecoming. (October 05, 1969). *Waterloo Daily Courier*, 16.

13 West High. (October 12, 1972). High Society. Homecoming Festivities Continue. *Waterloo Daily Courier*, 19.

14 Homecoming Candidates (photo). (October 04, 1968). *Waterloo Daily Courier*, 10.

15 Orange High Chooses Queen Crop (photo). (October 03, 1969). *Waterloo Daily Courier*, 10.

16 Candidates Named at Columbus (photo). (October 03, 1969). *Waterloo Daily Courier*, 10.

17 Former Hawkeye, East coach Murray Wier passes away at 89. (April 7, 2016). Sullivan, J. *Waterloo Daily Courier*. Retrieved from http://tinyurl.com/yaklew6x.

18 Walk Together Children. (May 22, 1971). Iowa Advisory Committee to the U.S. Commission on Civil Rights, p.8.

19 Roosevelt District Parents Win Battle Against Busing. 3 Mobile Classrooms Purchased. (August 7, 1967). *Waterloo Daily Courier*, Ten.

20 1) Arrest Five After West Center Beaten. (November 8, 1970), *Waterloo Daily Courier*, 13. 2) Injured Player Improved. (November 09, 1970). *Waterloo Daily Courier*, p.5.

[21] Probe Fight After Game, Three Held. East High Students Charge [sic] an Attack. (November 11, 1970). *Waterloo Daily Courier*, 8.

[22] 1960's-1970's: The Civil Rights Movement and Black Protest in Waterloo. Invisible City, Invisible Community, 5. Retrieved from https://sites.google.com/site/invcityinvcommunity/.

[23] Waterloo's Unfinished Business, 8.

[24] Open Enrollment Plan Extended to High Schools; 44 Negroes to West, Orange. (August 13, 1968). *Waterloo Daily Courier*, 8.

[25] Ibid.

[26] Ibid.

[27] Then and Now: Black Boycott in Waterloo. (2011). Anderson, R.B. Equity & Excellence in Education, 21:1-6, 149.

[28] Waterloo to Close 3 Public Schools. (March 08, 1978). *Des Moines Register,* 3.

[29] School Desegregation in Waterloo, Iowa. (August 1977). Kansas City, KS: A Staff Report of the United States Commission on Civil Rights, 7. Cited in *Walk Together Children,* 7.

[30] Propose Plans to Solve Segregation in Schools. Says Busing Possible in Waterloo. (July 28, 1967). *Waterloo Daily Courier*, 7.

[31] Waterloo's Unfinished Business, 7.

[32] Staff Report and recommendations of the Waterloo Commission on Human Rights. (December 4, 1969). Waterloo Commission on Human Rights, 9-10.

[33] Paul Harvey. Authority or Chaos. (July 29, 1967). *The Bluefield (WV) Daily Telegraph*, 8.

[34] Hearing. Waterloo Commission on Human Rights. (Sept. 7, 1967), 44.

[35] Seek New Steps to Avert Riots Following Night of Violence. Frustrated, Mayor Says of Negroes. (July 10, 1967). *Waterloo Daily Courier*, 1.

[36] Strife-Torn Waterloo in Uneasy Calm. (July 11, 1967). Lamberto, N. *Des Moines Register*, 1, 2.

[37] Seek New Steps to Avert Riots Following Night of Violence.

[38] RACES Sparks and Tinder. (July 21, 1967). *Time*, 90(3), 12-17.

[39] Iowa Cited in Riot Bill Plea. (July 13, 1967). *Des Moines Register*, 5.

[40] Many Residents of Waterloo, Iowa, Puzzled by Summer Riots. Older Negroes Blame Violence on Persons 19-25. (July 26, 1967). *Nashua Telegraph*, p. 25.

[41] Plan On-Job Training Project at Cosby Center for Unskilled. (January 24, 1967). *Waterloo Daily Courier*, 8.

[42] The 10th Worst City for African-Americans in the U.S. has a Story – This is How the Dream Derailed. (October 15, 2015). Bray, J. Medium. Retrieved from http://tinyurl.com/ycxf49lq.

[43] Guest Editorial. Hughes. No Immediate, Neat Solution for Tension. (July 30, 1967). *Waterloo Daily Courier*, Four.

[44] Riot (Continued). (July 10, 1967). *Waterloo Daily Courier*, 2.

[45] 1) City Judge's House Hit by Fire Bomb. William Parker's Study Damaged. (March 17, 1968). *Waterloo Daily Courier*, 2. 2) Throw Bomb into Home of Judge at Waterloo. (March 18, 1968). *The Des Moines Register*, 1.

[46] City is Peaceful. Peace (city). (April 8, 1968). *Waterloo Daily Courier*, 3.

[47] Editorials. Waterloo, Cedar Falls Stand for Civil Rights. (April 10, 1968). *Waterloo Daily Courier*, 3.

[48] Final Report and Recommendations to the Waterloo Board of Education, Waterloo, Iowa. (December 28, 1967) The Advisory Committee on Equal Educational Opportunity in the Waterloo Community Schools, I. The committee was established as a citizens' committee by the BOE to "advise and counsel the board . . . with reference to problems arising from concentration of Negro children and other children from culturally deprived backgrounds in certain schools. . . ."

[49] Schumaker, K.A. (Fall 2013). The Politics of Youth: Civil Rights Reform in the Waterloo Public Schools. State Historical Society of Iowa: The Annals of Iowa, 72(4), 356-357. Retrieved from http://ir.uiowa.edu/annals-of-iowa/vol72/iss4/4.

# *TBB* 8: ERA2 1968 – The Perfect Storm Batters Waterloo

*Negroes, Sweet and docile, Meek, humble, and kind: Beware the day*
*They change their minds! – Langston Hughes, "Warning"[1]*

*1968 was a "benchmark of unrest, tumult and change." – Experiences*
*and Prejudices: A Memoir Dealing with Both.[2]*

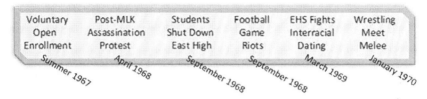

Figure 1 Events in the Fall 1968, Which Led to Changes in the Waterloo School
System
*Black students presented grievances to the East High administration at the start of*
*the 1968 school year, of which one of the most pressing was a demand for a black*
*history course in the curriculum. Concerned when the administration appeared to*
*be stonewalling the students' demand, students warned they should be taken*
*seriously. The events which followed forced the board of education to understand*
*the time had come for change in its segregated school system.*

The response of the black community to racial inequity and
injustice in Waterloo escalated in 1968 from civil-mannered marches
and endless, seemingly non-productive meetings with city officials to
confrontation and violence. Much of it centered at East High. (Figure
1)

*When their problems seemed to reach critical mass, black youth*
*demonstrated and even rioted in September 1968. Buildings along East*
*Fourth Street were torched and vandalized. The resulting flight of white*
*business owners on the east side is still felt economically today.[3]*

Correlation isn't causation, but some of the black students at East
who participated were children of activists who had lived through the
Rath Packing strike in 1947, and who remained actively involved in

other activities to bring about social change and racial equity in the town. Some students had marched and protested with their parents as children. In their minds, those experiences reinforced discussions with parents about the necessity to participate in bringing about change, and were influential in their high school and adult lives.

## 1968 East High Walk-Out: Antecedent to the Riot

Thursday, August 29, 1968, Terri Pearson and her sister, Kathy, presented East High principal Lawrence Garlock with a list of student grievances on behalf of the Black Student Union (BSU). Terri was an honor student and the girls' father was a community activist who was the first black union steward at Rath Packing Company.

The BSU wasn't a formal, approved school student group, but was in the formative stages. Addressing the grievances was suggested by the Pearsons as a way of reducing racial discrimination at East. Two of the most important and ultimately contentious were that no African American history course was being taught at East, and teachers and administrators were interfering in students' lives by discouraging interracial dating.[4]

There were 10 grievances.

*1. There should be black teachers as well as black counselors at East.* [Only one of 75 teachers were black and there were no black counselors.]

*2. Black students should be taught more about black race in American history classes.*

*3. White teachers and counselors should not be allowed to discourage a black student from attending the college of his choice.*

*4. Obvious prejudiced teachers should be dismissed from the faculty*

*5. All scholarship or achievement awards should be made known to all students, black or white, who are interested in competing for the award.*

*6. Disciplinary actions should be harmonious in situations involving either white or black students.*

*7. Black students should be permitted to establish the BSU as a regular club of East High School.*

*8. Black students at East High will henceforth be referred to as blacks, or Afro-Americans.*

*9. Teachers should not be permitted to dissolve any black group or club.*

*10. Teachers should not interfere with the personal lives of students.*

Garlock told the Pearsons some of the grievances had merit, but others needed review and further discussion by a faculty committee that would be appointed the following week during the first week of school.

Terri replied that "might not be soon enough." Concerned about the remark, the principal arranged to meet with her again the next day and sent copies of the petition to the administration office and the BOE.

The next day, at the second meeting also attended by assistant principal Don Hanson, Garlock gave Pearson a letter addressed to her and the BSU that summarized the procedure for review of the grievances.

And a caution.

*You did indicate this may be "too late" which means your group may be planning a school protest. This would be too bad because a disruption of school procedures might lead to suspension or expulsion of students. This would be unfortunate as grievances might be settled in a more reasonable fashion. /signed/ L.E. Garlock, Principal.*[5]

Monday, September 9, the first full week of school after the shortened Labor Day week, eight to 10 Negro students entered East at noon and went to Garlock's office to discuss teaching black history, but he wasn't at the school. Simultaneously, a fire alarm was set off on the main floor and the school was evacuated. When asked to return to class, some students, black and white, went to the student center instead.

Garlock suggested at the Board of Education (BOE) board meeting that night, "We may need to take steps to control the halls at East and support the teachers in the ordinary business of education" and have methods "to remove outsiders who come in and disrupt school."[6]

A board member who had received threats asked whether the students had been at East that morning "to inquire about black literature or did they come hoping something else would happen? And if they did come without intending to disrupt school, do they have a right to disturb students there?" An East teacher said, "We male teachers did not used to be afraid to step into a group of our students and demand discipline. We are becoming more reluctant. We fear attacks on members of our families and our properties."[7]

Reaffirming its discipline statement made after incidents the previous spring – that threats, abuse, harassment, insubordination and defiance of school rules and regulations wouldn't be tolerated – the board pledged, "If any such attempt is made to engage in such improper and disruptive tactics, the leaders and participants will be subject to appropriate legal and disciplinary action"[8] "to protect teachers and other school personnel from intimidation. . . ."[9]

The next day, Tuesday, a group of more than 100 "mostly non-students" entered East after classes had been dismissed and demanded a course in black history "be added immediately." Garlock told them the school's curriculum included black history, but no qualified teacher had been available to teach it.

On Wednesday, the 11th, a group of teachers agreed not to walk out of East if Garlock and Superintendent Dr. George Hohl would meet later that day with them and other faculty members. School was dismissed early for the meeting. A group of Negro students officially quit school same morning, according to an East High official.[10]

Because of the problems at East, the BOE closed the school for the final two days of the week.

On Thursday afternoon, September 12, the school board met with about 300 people, including East students and their parents, to review their group's grievances.[11]

The chairman of the protestors' group stated its agenda.

*We're trying to resolve this. We're tired of white people playing with us, and you'd better recognize it. . . . The present situation is something we are very concerned with. We don't come here on our knees. We come here as men. We feel we have legitimate complaints and we hope we can sit down as men and resolve the problem. . . . I don't trust any of you and you don't trust me. The BOE president responded, "We hope out of this meeting can come trust.*[12]

Several of the original 10 grievances presented by the Pearsons to Garlock had been rewritten (changes are in **bold**) and two had been added.[13]

The board provided the protestors with point-by-point responses; synopses of the board's responses are underlined.[14] [Author's notes are in brackets.]

1. *There should be black teachers as well as black counselors at East.*

Hohl said a number of recruiting trips to Negro colleges had been made. "We have made a considerable effort to obtain more black teachers, but we have had real difficulty. As you know, teachers of all kinds are in short supply. . . . We have tried, are trying, will continue to try. . . . For three solid years we have tried to obtain a black guidance counselor."[15]

[There wasn't a large pool of black teachers to begin with. Most prior to *Brown v. Board of Education* had been teaching in black schools in the South that were segregated by state laws. *Brown* didn't address how schools were to be integrated nor did it mention black-teacher retention. There was no guideline in the Civil Rights Act of 1964 nor in subsequent federal desegregation guidelines of 1966. In the 11 years after *Brown*, 38,000 black teachers and administrators in 21 southern and southern bordering states lost their jobs.]

2. [Rewritten.] ~~Black students~~ *Students should be taught more about black race in American history classes [later amended to include an immediate installation of a black history elective for credit].*

The school board president cited the lack of available material. The district's director of curriculum said units on Negro and other minority groups should be ready for distribution by the end of the week. [1965 East valedictorian] Charles Derden said he had reviewed the Waterloo school system's bibliography of material to be included in the social studies program [and found] "only one text was probably worth a dime. Only one with the balance needed [for a black history course.]"

3. *White teachers and counselors should not be allowed to discourage a black student from attending the college of his choice.*

Derden said he'd received "50 letters from colleges [but] I was told to go to the State College of Iowa [later UNI] because 'I could not compete' in those schools. I went to the University of Iowa because I didn't believe everything white man told me about myself. But if I hadn't believed any of it I would be in a better school today. Stop telling black students they are inferior because they're not." One of the few whites in the audience agreed "a white counselor can't be the one to determine a black student's profession." A parent noted two student protestors already been told they'd flunk out this year. "We're tired of this."

The board agreed to the next three requests – 4, 5 and 6 – "in principal [sic]," but asked for time to consider the wording of each.

4. [Rewritten.] ~~Obvious prejudiced teachers should be dismissed from the faculty.~~ *If there are teachers at East who do not feel they can treat or teach black students as equals to white students, they should resign or be dismissed from the Waterloo school system.*

5. *All scholarship or achievement awards should be made known to all students, black or white, who are interested in competing for the award.*

*6. Disciplinary actions should be harmonious in situations involving either white or black students.*

*7. Students should be permitted to establish the Black Student Union as a regular club of East High School.*

The board denied the request "based on present information." At a later meeting, the BOE explained this was an East school administration decision and it would support its decision.

*8. Black students at East High will henceforth be referred to as blacks or Afro-Americans.*

A white parent said, "If you use Negro, you should use Caucasian; if you use black, use white; if you use colored use grey and if you use nigger, use honky." The board agreed to the request, with board president Sydney Thomas noting, "Anything will improve the self-image for black people is legitimate," [but that] the use of "Negro" didn't mean it was derogatory. [The U.S. Census Bureau didn't replace the term "Negro," which had been used for more than a century, with "black" or "African American" until 2013.][16]

A Public Speaks letter to the *Waterloo Daily Courier* recounted an anecdote about a 10-year-old Afro-American boy who was asked by his teacher whether his preference was for being called "black" or "colored." He responded, "Teacher, I want to be called Terry."[17]

*9.* [**Moved from #10.**] *Teachers should not interfere with the personal lives of students.*

Many of the black students . . . said East High teachers had interfered with "interracial dating." One said "four teachers called the parents of the girls [last year] and told them [black boys were dating their daughter.]" Thomas agreed teachers don't "have a right to impose their feelings on others" and black-white dating "should be a matter of choice."

*10.* [**Moved from #9.**] *Teachers should not be permitted to dissolve any black group or club.*

[Jimmie] Porter [acting as chairman of the parents' delegation] reported "black kids standing together in the hall are told to move on, while for white kids it's okay." The BOE president commented "no distinction should be made between black, white or mixed groups, and a single teacher shouldn't have the right to disband clubs "but in certain cases, the school administration should."

11. [Added.] *The request to have a mass meeting concerning black history in East's auditorium should be acknowledged.*

Pearson explained that Principal Garlock had approved a request made on Monday to meet in the auditorium to go over the black literature proposed for use at East. Ten minutes before school was dismissed, it was announced over the public address system the meeting had been canceled. According to the board president, the meeting was canceled because the school board had decided Monday night it shouldn't be held because of "the atmosphere" and added "that decision might have been wrong."

12. [Added.] *Policemen at East should be removed.*

According to the board president, school board's intention was not "to have policemen at East High. We want to establish a rule of order so is not necessary."

A group of concerned citizens from the East Side and others in Waterloo, mostly white but with a few blacks, distributed a statement at the meeting demanding order be kept at the school.

*We, as a community, have a grievance with the blacks and whites in [the East High] area. We don't believe all of you have upheld your responsibility in creating the proper attitude . . . . We have tolerated many incidents. We have put up with many disturbances and we have accepted many of the reasons you give for these disturbances. But our patience is wearing thin.*[18]

This faction insisted the administration keep order, not only condoning "the use of police in cases where the administration considers their presence necessary, we demand it."

Municipal Judge William Parker noted near the end of the meeting, "We hear a lot about communication and the only way to have it is by confrontation. Our young people are telling us, we've waited too long."[19]

Jerry Solyst of the Black Hawk County Social Welfare Department added, "We in the white community had better understand we are in a grace period. We are in a state of moral bankruptcy and we don't even realize we are in debt. . . . It's not what we do, it's what we don't do that matters."[20]

The same day as the BOE-parent's meeting, "Police Chief Robert Wright, backed up by [Mayor Turner] . . . decided to throw away the gloves in combating agitators and young demonstrators who were involved in [the] disturbances" that resulted in the closing of East.

*The police department has attempted to avoid violence by appeasement and softness in dealing with explosive situations. We have been criticized for this and for lack of action. Now we are going to deal head-on with the problem that faces our community with strict enforcement and by taking strong action for which we have full support of our city administration. . . . Our community cannot tolerate a continuation of the intimidation by threats of personal harm and threats of violence upon our teachers or anyone else by outlaws.[21]*

It was a policy the police would follow during the riots that weekend.

Wright named several of the people who had confronted teachers after school on Tuesday, each of whom had what were "extensive criminal records" and were reported in the *Waterloo Daily Courier*. He withdrew one of the names the following day stating the individual had been misidentified as one of the group.

On Friday, Black, Inc. – a newly incorporated black coalition of black students, former students and parents – rejected the charges the students' conduct had been improper and the result of a "hoodlum" element.

*The original disturbance was not due to a few days of intimidating teachers but to years and years of the school system's and teachers [sic] intimidating the future lives of black students, beginning in kindergarten. . . . We have adopted the same slogan other agencies have adopted [ – ]"we're not going tolerate any violence either, in any form. We're dealing with our problems head on, too". . . At the same time, [we] deplore the insidious behavior of the Waterloo Police Department in dealing with our "hoodlums."²²*

As a footnote, East High "did not choose to select a good citizen," black or white, for the Daughters of the 1968 American Revolution Good Citizen Award at the end of the year.²³

*My fellow white students fought the whole concept of teaching black history in the Waterloo schools. I can remember kids asking, "Why don't they teach Smith history or the Jones history?" [WHS 69 WM]*

*There was a reason the blacks walked out at East. I sensed a militancy. They were angry with the people who had the power to change things. They didn't target other students. The target was the administration or teachers. Some teachers were nervous about the tension. They were sometimes intimidated by black students. Except my biology teacher, who was black. Every other teacher was white. [EHS 70 WF]*

*A week or two before the riots in 1968, I'd skipped school with my boyfriend; I was 15 at the time. He was a bad influence on me. I married him. [laughs] When we came back to East, we knew something was wrong. Most of the black kids were outside. I was really scared. My boyfriend said, "We're not going back today. I'm taking you home." I don't know how long the school was shut down. Probably not more than a couple or three days. Then there were the fires. It was a scary time. [EHS 70 WF]*

## Riot at the Football Game and into the North End

The BOE closed East on Thursday and Friday, September 12ᵗʰ and 13ᵗʰ, and almost canceled the home-opener football game on Friday night. The visiting team was traveling from Chicago, a distance that was a consideration in the decision. There was discussion among East and district administrators, and the mayor's office about whether the decision would be an overreaction, given the meetings that had been held with protestors the end of the week.

Ultimately, the board allowed the game to be played with a significant police presence from both the city and county.

*I was in college at the time. My dad was feeding me information about the unrest in the North End. I didn't understand it. There weren't any problems in Waterloo race-wise until then. I knew those guys and the guys I knew weren't violent. You heard some blacks carried knives, but I never saw a knife when I was at East. The early stories about the 1968 riot was some kid was causing trouble. Then things really got serious with the burning of the buildings after the football game. [EHS 65 WM]*

*I used to hang out at Pinky's Bar on East 4ᵗʰ Street, owned by the Van Erems. When the riot occurred, Pinky was in the window. Most of the places on East 4ᵗʰ there were damaged or burned down, but Pinky's wasn't. [COL 66 WM]*

*I thought 1968 had been coming for a long time. Things were coming to a head. I didn't believe it when the black rioters burned down most of East 4ᵗʰ Street by the railroad. That's where I grew up. We went to the Webbeking's Bakery twice a week. We went to the A&W. So, it was pretty weird to me. [OHS 67 WF]*

Friday night, September 13 – the "worst night of racial-based disturbances in [Waterloo's] history"²⁴ – occurred in three stages.

The first two occurred at the football game at Sloane Wallace Stadium and the third played out with rioting in the North End the following 72 hours.

East was 19-0 going into the 1968 football season and was the mythical state champion the previous two seasons. Its opponent was St. Joseph's Academy of Westchester, IL, which was playing its first varsity game ever. Two minutes before the end of the first half, leading

46-6, East replaced its starting players with reserves, who played the entire second half in the 65-20 win, the 20th straight for the Trojans.

The first outbreak began when police officers providing normal security at the game arrested a 17-year-old "Negro" who was wanted on a warrant for malicious injury to a building. His friends objected, and officers moved him outside the stadium fence and closed the gates. Several people climbed the fence, argued with the arresting officers and a fight broke out between the two. ". . . police tussled with other members of the crowd. Some of the combatants were hit with police billyclubs while attempting to block entry [of the person in custody] into a police car."[25]

The second stage occurred as many of the roughly 4,000 fans started leaving the game just before halftime. A white girl leaving the stadium with about a dozen other white girls "stumbled over a foot of a colored girl." Whether it was an accident or she was tripped, words were exchanged and a fight began.

One of the white girls was slugged in the head by a black girl and shoved against the fence surrounding the stadium. The white girl fell to the ground with her hands over her face and head. The Negro girl continued to slap and hit her, knocking her glasses to the ground.[26]

Some of the white girls, and Negro girls and boys tried stopping the fights, but others were urging them on. There were no white boys present, according to the *Waterloo Daily Courier* stories.

*Police intervened, but the blacks in the crowd pushed and shoved them against a car. Reinforcements arrived and several of the mob were sprayed in the face with Mace.*

*[A] policeman fired a blank cartridge into the air. . . . Several persons in the crowd, again mostly girls, began screaming curses and taunting policemen. The Negro boys joined in and more scuffles followed. More Mace was sprayed. Billyclubs were used in a few instances. Two Negro girls were carried unconscious from the stadium, the victims of clubs according to Negro witnesses. [The incident last roughly 20 minutes, but] scoffs, dares and even threats toward police continued. Police from*

*throughout the county, from other counties, auxiliary police and state patrol arrived. Isolated fights between white and Negro boys [occurred]. . . . the stands emptied quickly, a full two minutes before the game ended. The crowd came through the gate, some shocked, some embarrassed, some afraid and a few, mostly youths, angry with the police."[27]*

One Negro girl was hospitalized[28] and 11 people were arrested. All were released after being booked at the police station.[29]

*My sister and a friend were beaten during the riot at Sloane Wallace. They were headed back to their car and got caught. Ironically, one of my sister's assailants was a black girl who had a locker next to hers at East. They didn't always get along, but I don't know if the other girl just availed herself of the situation. The people who broke up the attack on my sister and her friend were a group of black men. Police weren't charging anyone. It was a riot, a little too chaotic. And it was the assailants' words against the victims' words. [EHS 70 WF]*

*The opponent was supposed to be some high-powered boys' school out of Chicago, supposed to be a great showdown. At half time, we were beating these guys so bad. It was 65 to 20. I think it got boring. There was a little scuffle in the crowd and it started to spread. Some guy would see it and say, "I'm going to get down there and start swinging." Sloane Wallace field was in a neighborhood of homes; there wasn't a parking lot everybody went to. Some of the parking was four or five or six blocks away [on the residential streets]. We were taught to walk together in a group. People in the South End Zone went one way and the people in the North End Zone went the other way. There were a lot of skirmishes. [EHS 71 WM]*

*I was in the 9th grade, so of course I couldn't drive. My dad took my best friend and me to the game, and picked us up when the fighting broke out. We didn't take my friend home; she stayed overnight. Our house was at the dead-end of Franklin on Mobile [south side of the North End.] So, we were close to the rioting. My dad said, "If I tell you to*

258

*move in the middle of the night, don't ask questions. We're moving. Just don't ask any questions." And he stayed up with a shotgun to make sure nothing happened. [EHS 72 WF]*

*I was at the football game with some of my girlfriends from Logan Junior. Trouble had been brewing all summer long and my parents told me where I was immediately to go if anything happened. It all erupted into gunshots and it was just a free-for-all out on the field. My older brother's girlfriend got knifed and had to go to the hospital. She was in the hospital for a couple of days and nights. [CEN 73 WF]*

The disturbance escalated into a rampage that continued down West 4th Street, across the bridge to East 4th Street and into the North End where it became a full-scale riot.(Figure 2)

*When I was a sophomore at East, there was so much pent-up frustration and anger in all the black kids my age. Friday night was the opportunity to tear some shit up, so that's what we did. We would ride to Sloane Wallace Stadium for football games. Many of us black students would walk back to the East Side from Sloane Wallace after a game. We did that on purpose. We knew we'd have to fight our way back. The people came out of their houses, and threw bricks and tomatoes because we were blacks walking through a white neighborhood. And we had to fight. We wanted to fight back to the East Side. It felt like retaliation. [EHS 69 AAM]*

*I was playing football at a West High away game that night. Our house was on West 5th [three blocks south of the stadium]. In 1968, race riots were a common thing. A lot of the East Side folks walked to the games at Sloane Wallace and, when the game was over, they'd bust up windows on West 4th and 5th. The windows at the bakery near our house and the phone booth outside of it got busted up that night. My mom was scared there by herself. We talked afterward more about self-defense than anything racial. [WHS 69 WM]*

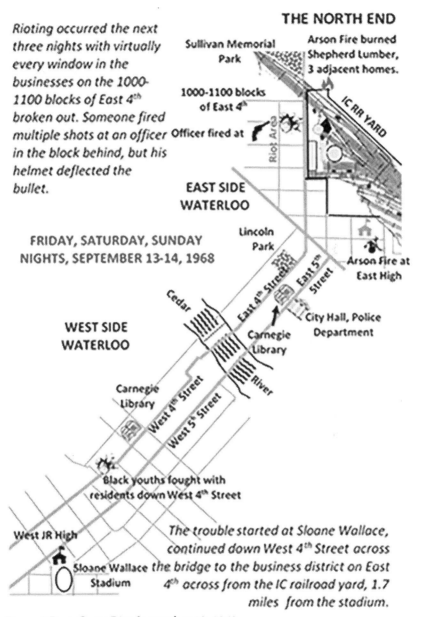

THE NORTH END

Rioting occurred the next three nights with virtually every window in the businesses on the 1000-1100 blocks of East 4ᵗʰ broken out. Someone fired multiple shots at an officer in the block behind, but his helmet deflected the bullet.

Sullivan Memorial Park

Arson Fire burned Shepherd Lumber, 3 adjacent homes.

1000-1100 blocks of East 4ᵗʰ

Officer fired at

Riot Area

IC RR YARD

EAST SIDE WATERLOO

FRIDAY, SATURDAY, SUNDAY NIGHTS, SEPTEMBER 13-14, 1968

Lincoln Park

Arson Fire at East High

East 4ᵗʰ Street
East 5ᵗʰ Street
Cedar

WEST SIDE WATERLOO

City Hall, Police Department

Carnegie Library

Carnegie Library

West 4ᵗʰ Street
West 5ᵗʰ Street
River

Black youths fought with residents down West 4ᵗʰ Street

West JR High

Sloane Wallace Stadium

The trouble started at Sloane Wallace, continued down West 4ᵗʰ Street across the bridge to the business district on East 4ᵗʰ across from the IC railroad yard, 1.7 miles from the stadium.

Figure 2 Post-Game Riot September 13, 1968

260

The Friday night riot was confined to the 1000-1100 blocks of East 4th Street, although skirmishes between police and the rioters occurred in the surrounding neighborhoods to the east and north of the IC railroad tracks. (Figure 4)

The windows were broken out of virtually every store.

Waterloo Daily Courier, Thursday, September 19, 1968, Page 7, upper right-hand corner of right-hand page.

Figure 3 Shepherd Lumber Company Ad Four Days After It Was Burned by Arson During the Riot

Shepherd Lumber Company on the north end of the IC property was destroyed by an arson fire that could be seen for miles. (Figure 3) The fire spread to three houses in the block, all of which were destroyed. The uninsured black homeowners lost everything they had.

*It wasn't the local black people who were the trouble during the riot. It was the imports from Chicago and Kansas City which were doing all the damage and burned down Shepherd Lumber. [EHS 64 WM]*

*I've heard it was the police who put the Molotov cocktail in the lumber yard to start things. The police have always been looked upon the black community in Waterloo as being very racist. I thought of them of as racists because of incidents and their sense of superiority over the black people. There were some nice policemen, of course, who were on the up-and-up. A lot of them weren't. My father told me about the cocktail. And he was pretty hooked into the community. [COL 69 AAF]*

*In the 68 riot, [name withheld] burned down the lumber yard. He's the one who set it on fire. It wasn't the cops. I think he got 10 years for that. But there were a bunch of us involved in tearing it up. And they brought in the National Guard and they came through East 4th Street with tanks,*

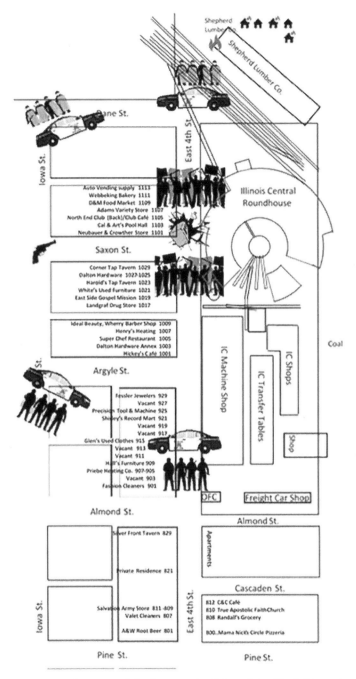

Figure 4 The Area of the Riot on the Edge of the Black Triangle

*the whole nine yards. They had us in Newsweek, Waterloo, IA. [EHS 69
AAM]* ["Name Withheld" was one of the people with criminal records
named by Chief Wright as participants in the confrontation with
teachers at East on September 10.]

*I was there during the riot to try and keep my business's four big front
windows from being busted out. I had a double 10-gauge shotgun and
had a bandolier on [a broad belt worn over the shoulder with a few
small loops for holding extra shotgun cartridges]. We didn't fire it. We
didn't know if it would fire. We took he gun out years later and it fired.
Blew a huge 10-gauge hole in something and knocked me on my ass.
And I had a knife, a big machete. We lost one window. A guy had a cast
on his arm, got between me and my partner. He hit the window with the
cast and out it went. Some of the mouthy locals involved were hollering,
"That's what you whiteys get." They had a whole bunch of police down
there and they were going to run the mob out. Dr. [Warren] Nash [head
of the Waterloo NAACP] was there and said he had them under control.
But he didn't, because they started looting and throwing things. Then
"boom," the lumber yard went up in flames. The police ran the
demonstrators up East 4th Street across the railroad tracks toward
Newell with a few old police cars. After the riot, we had a hard time
getting anyone to come to the store. They wanted us to deliver, because
they wouldn't send their wives to the North End. Even loyal customers.
Only a few were gutty and would come down during the day. But after
dark, we had to close because there was no business. And we moved the
business the next year. [EHS 64 WM]*

The rioters burned East 4th Street businesses. The grocery store, our
record shop, Webbeking bakery, the pool hall, Shepherd Lumber, every
place we had. It was anger and not thinking things through. [COL 64
AAM]

*Somebody told me there were a couple of carload of black militants
from Detroit or Cleveland who'd come to Waterloo to start more stuff. A*

*lot of the blacks in Waterloo had enough of them after a couple of days and told them to go home. [COL 68 WM]*

*There was a guy who came into Sullivan Park. He was going from city to city giving these revolutionary H. Rap Brown speeches and inciting us to riot. And they angered us and we wanted to do something about retaliating. We'd become socially conscious, reading Frantz Fanon's "Black Skin, White Masks"[1] and believing in black nationalism. We'd joined the Black Panther party. Three of us were laying in Sullivan Park talking about shooting a policeman. Which will tell you how angry and misguided we were at that young age. Let me make it straight – I thank God it didn't happen. Somebody that night said, "No, we better not do this." And cooler heads prevailed. [EHS 69 AAM]*

Arsonists threw an incendiary device into a ground-floor typing classroom at East High, but the fire department extinguished the blaze before it spread out of the room.

Preliminary estimates of vandalism damage and the fires from the riot was set at $100,000, according to The Waterloo Daily Courier.

Black Hawk County sheriff's deputies and 25 Iowa Highway Patrol officers were dispatched to assist the Waterloo police.

Seven policemen were injured; three were hospitalized and one was taken off duty for recuperation at home.

A police sergeant suffered a hairline skull fracture when a bullet ricocheted off his helmet when someone in a group of about 150 people fired five shots at the police as he was running away. The first one hit the sergeant. He fell to the ground and police reported some of the group tried to kick him while he was down.

The gunman escaped as the crowd broke and ran, which prevented police from returning fire.[30]

Another sergeant was hospitalized after being struck in the chest by a piece of concrete thrown by one of the black rioters.[31] Only two people were arrested, a 15-year-old for delinquency by assaulting an

264

officer and a 17-year-old for carrying a concealed weapon. Both were
released after being booked at the police station.[32]

*My dad was a police doctor, a reserve cop, and was working on the
injured when one of the police officers was brought in who was really
hurt bad. My dad worked on him. And then they brought in a middle-
aged black man and my dad just stepped back. It was an impulse. When
he was told this guy had been trying to protect his home from the rioters
who beat him up, that made a difference and he treated the guy. [WHS
66 WM]*

The mayor imposed a city-wide curfew from 8 p.m. to 6 a.m. for
people 21 and younger, and all liquor stores in Black Hawk County
were closed.

The Iowa National Guard was also sent in by the governor for the
first time since the Rath Packing strike 20 years earlier. But the rioting
was ebbing by Saturday and Sunday nights. An estimated 300-400
guard troops patrolled the North End for several weeks after with
rifles, sheathed bayonets and smoke grenades in jeeps and 2½-ton
trucks.[33]

*That night, sitting on the front porch drinking a Coke and smoking a
Tiparillo, I looked toward the railroad bridge down Mobile Street and
could see the National Guardsmen with their rifles silhouetted in the
moonlight walking down the tracks. [COL 68 WM]*

High unemployment in young black men in Waterloo was one of
the major reasons cited for the discontent behind the riot.

In 1967, unemployment in Waterloo was 3.2%; the national average
was 4%. Unemployment remained relatively consistent and stable in
1968, with a slow rebound in the local economy. Job openings were
increasing in all areas but manufacturing. Weekly earnings in the
metro Waterloo area increased 4.2% in 1968, but the cost-of-living
index rose 4.8%. "Racial barriers [were] falling [in 1968] to a point
where employers are requesting non-white applicants [from the local
Iowa State Employment Office]. . . . The ideal situation would be for

minority group unemployment to decline to a level with white unemployment. . . ."[34]

In the summer of 1968, 2,444 youths registered for summer jobs, but only 12% were placed, 50% in the "needy or deprived youth" category.[35]

## THE RIOT FROM GROUND ZERO

*One of the jobs I had when in college was night desk clerk at the Holiday Inn [on top of the hill on the West Side five blocks from the Cedar River]. We had 11 floors facing the river and there were a lot of calls from guests that night wondering about what was going on. They could see the lumber yard burning [two miles away] from their rooms. There was a mobile command post set up in our parking lot, with six or seven highway patrol cars, Waterloo police and sheriffs. The football team from Chicago that East played was staying there. One of their star players got a concussion at the end and was taken away by ambulance. The coach talking to people in the lobby said, "We play a lot of tough competition in the Chicago area, but these guys are a bunch of animals." [EHS 66 WM]*

*The blacks burning down their town didn't make any sense to me. I could see where the Southern black was discriminated against. But I never felt the Northern black was discriminated against much. They could have made as much out of their lives as any poor white person. If there were black people in town who didn't have a good a job, it's not because the opportunity wasn't there. [Jobs] were there at Rath's and John Deere. I don't know what kind of position would have been available for them, but there were plenty of white people working in those same jobs. [EHS 66 WF]*

*During the 1968 riot, I was sitting on my motorcycle on East 4th street at Whitey's Drive-in, on the street along the curb. There were hundreds of people in the street, pushing and shoving, headed toward downtown. Suddenly, I was surrounded by black people. And I realized I'd screwed up. Two of my black friends came out of the crowd. They pushed me and*

266

*my bike around behind Whitey's, and told me to get out of there. [COL 67 WM]*

*The summer of '68, my black friend, Frank, came over when the riots were going on. At the time, it was just me and my sister living together on the corner of Mobile Street and Independence Avenue. He wanted me to go to his grandmother's house in the North End. Frank's folks left when he was in the 7th or 8th grade, were in Watts in Los Angeles; they didn't want him living there. There was a railroad bridge down Mobile Street from where we lived. There was a barricade, a bunch of black guys, with rocks and sticks and I think there was a couple of rifles. I was sitting in the passenger seat and we got stopped. Frank got out to talk to them. I kept my mouth shut and sure wasn't going to get out of the car. They opened the barricade and let us through. That was kind of weird. [COL 68 WM]*

*In 1968 when the National Guard was in town, there was a 10 p.m. curfew. One night a girlfriend came over to my house and I had to get her back home before 10. We're driving down Jefferson Street and the radiator on the car blows up. [laughs] "Oh, God." So, here we are just going crazy. The car's right in the middle of the street. The National Guard comes along in a Jeep and pushes us up into a parking lot. We walked about four blocks to a gas station to call my dad. Someone at the station asked if we'd tried to start it. "Well, no." They suggested we go back and try and start it and, if it did, drive back to the station. We walked back and it started, so we drove it to the station. My dad came and we took my friend home. I don't remember if we got home before the curfew or not. [WHS 69 WF]*

*I was 13-14 when all hell was breaking loose in Waterloo with demonstrations, burning things. My dad and a couple of his buddies were in redneck heaven and hassled the demonstrators. I told him I didn't think was very appropriate. Not sure it did any good. I've always been kind of for the underdog, have empathy for other groups. And doing the right thing. [COL 69 WM]*

I associated the things were happening in school and Waterloo in my junior year [1967-68], and then worse again in my senior year with what was happening in the country at the time. The shooting of Martin Luther King really got the ball rolling. And the first football game in the fall of 1968. There were rumors all around there was going to be trouble. And there were all kinds of police cars around Sloane Wallace Stadium. The game went on with no incident and then, after the game, people started swarming on the field and there was commotion and confusion. And a lot of traffic. Traffic was jammed. We sat on the band bus with cars around us and couldn't move for a long time. The air had been let out of the tires on the police cars so they couldn't get back over to the East Side. That was the night when Molotov cocktails were thrown into East High, into the secretarial education wing where typing was taught. We missed school for a couple of days after that. I heard outside agitators had come from Milwaukee or Madison, somewhere in Wisconsin, who were there at the game. [EHS 69 WF]

I was a junior when the riots occurred. We went to a sports assembly in the auditorium. Every time a black athlete got up, everyone would applaud. When a white athlete was recognized, there was no applause. The principal said, "If you can't applaud for everybody, don't applaud at all. And if you can't abide by that, leave." Most of the auditorium got up and left. [EHS 70 WF]

I lived up near McKinstry and we could see the flames from East 4$^{th}$ Street [a half-mile away]. The sky was lit up. A friend and I drove down to see what was going on, but the police stopped us at Walnut and 4$^{th}$ and said we couldn't drive any farther. We had to sprint to Mama Nick's where I worked. It was open, and was feeding the police and the National Guard. That's all they were serving. We were put to work and I remember the police comparing the nicks on their billy clubs. "And this is where I got this one tonight. . . ." [EHS 68 WM]

Our house was at the dead-end of Franklin on Mobile at the south edge of the North End. So, we were close to the rioting. Then the

*National Guard came in and patrolled, and then it was like, "OK," we knew we were going to be protected and nothing's going to happen. My folks never ever thought about moving. In fact, my dad died in 1994 and we had to pry my mom out of the house a year later. She grew up there. We were never fearful of where we lived. Looking back, that wasn't the normal experience growing up in Waterloo. Other people may have experienced that. But I never felt that, "Gee, someone's out to get me." Maybe it was naivete. [EHS 72 WF]*

*During the uprising in 1968, I was in junior high and most kids were afraid. I call it an uprising. It was a riot. I had a lot of black friends. They told me, "You head for home. We'll cover you." Because I had grown up with them. And I walked home from Logan to Donald Street [about six blocks] without a problem. The same thing happened one day at East. There was fighting going on between blacks and whites. Black friends again told me to head out and they'd cover for me. [EHS 73 WF]*

## REPERCUSSIONS: NIGHTTIME FOOTBALL GAMES BANNED

*The East and West high football game was THE rivalry game each year. But so much stuff went on when the football games were played at night they moved the games to the daytime. East was singled out. And we still beat the snot out of everybody. I went to all the games and never had an issue. I understood why it was done. It wasn't as much fun in the middle of the afternoon. One year they tried to get representatives from East and West to meet on the bridge, and come up with some way to calm things down. Given the title of your book, that's interesting. At least an effort was there. [EHS 70 WF]*

Following the riots, the Waterloo school board agreed to move the rest of East's home football games to 4 p.m. at the request of Mayor Turner and the city council. An exception was made for its final two games with Big Four cross-town rivals Columbus and West [Cedar Falls was the fourth member]. Those were moved to Saturdays at 1:30 p.m. on the first two weekends in November.

Touted by the *Waterloo Daily Courier* as the "Biggest East-West Game Ever" in the football rivalry that began in 1909, East was unbeaten at 8-0 and West was 7-1. Out of the 55 games played [the teams didn't play five of the years from 1920-1930], each had won 25 and there had been five ties. The Wahawks hadn't beaten the Trojans since 1962.

At stake[36] –

1. The mythical Iowa state championship. [West was ranked No. 5 in the state.]
2. The Big Eight Conference Championship [East. West, Cedar Falls, Ames, Fort Dodge, Marshalltown, Mason City and Newton].
3. The Black Hawk County Big Four championship.
4. A 27-game East unbeaten run.
5. An unprecedented third straight undefeated season for the Trojans.
6. A record for consecutive victories in the East-West series. [The previous record was five straight by East from 1943-47; West's best consecutive record was three straight from 1960-62].

Trailing 28-13 with 3:05 left in the game, West scored two touch downs, the last coming with 56 seconds remaining in the game. The Wahawks made an onside kick, but East recovered it and ran out the clock. West "gained as much respect as is possible to earn in a losing cause" in a game before 6,500 fans that "certainly will go down as one of the most fiercely contested" between the two schools.[37]

## *Assessments in the Aftermath of the Riots*

*This is a second- or third-hand story about the 1968 riot, but one of the guys I went to church with was in a frat at Iowa State and had come back for the East football game. The frat had a fire truck they brought to Waterloo. It made a pass up and down East 4ᵗʰ Street. And some racial epithets were thrown from the truck. I don't think he and his frat brothers were any more racist than anybody else. Depending on what circle you were in, you put on a different suit of clothes. You might tell some racially tinged jokes in one circle of friends and in another circle, you'd bemoan Jim Crow laws. To a certain sense, you had to that do in high school at the time to survive. [EHS 67 WM]*

*My sister got beaten up badly the night of the riots. I was talking with her the other night [2016] about it. My family never blamed the black community. It was just part of an unfortunate social situation. My parents never thought ill of anybody. [EHS 70 WF]*

Calls for investigations into the riots came from many quarters. The BOE and a grand jury formally investigated the riots at the end of 1968, and additional studies were conducted in the late 60s and early 70s by the state Department of Public instruction and the U.S. Commission on Civil Rights as the school board grappled with ways to find a strategy for satisfying local, state and federal pressure for integration.

Twenty-two United Methodist ministers called for "a concerted effort to discover the deeper root causes leading to the disorders." The group commended East administrators, students and parents, and the BOE for "the positive actions they have taken. . . ." and Catholic Charities for its establishment of housing for low-income people.

*But we dare not assume because order is established, the problems are solved. Rather we call upon the entire community, its government and its agencies, to recognize our involvement in and responsibility for the crisis that controls us and to respond with sensitivity and commitment to the needs of persons around us, toward the end we may become a community in which all citizens may find equal opportunity for fulfillment and growth.*[38]

## GRAND JURY REPORT, FEBRUARY 1969

A special Black Hawk County grand jury was convened two weeks after the riot to "investigate the disturbance . . . and to further investigate the problems of minority group and other disadvantaged persons in Black Hawk County."[39] Its report was issued five months later.

No indictments were returned; the seven-member jury ruled there wasn't sufficient evidence on which to base indictments for the vandalism and arson that occurred during the riots. It also found no evidence of participation by outside agitators or that they would be participants in future disturbances.

It did say in its lengthy report the community "must act now" to solve the problems that led to the disturbances.

The key findings of the grand jury were:

- *Stated Waterloo's de facto segregation in the schools is "a clear violation of the law. . . . is downgrading to individuals in our community" and plays "into the hands of extremists and others who preach revolution and hatred."*
- *Noted "some White [sic] citizens" are afraid their children would be adversely affected under "true integration" [but it recommended] " . . . immediate integration at the elementary school level, where discrimination and prejudices . . . are practically non-existent and the minority or disadvantaged child is more readily accepted . . . even if it means dividing the city of Waterloo down the middle of 4$^{th}$ Street, rather than using the barrier of the river, or completing redistricting all of our communities within the county. . . ." It commended the school district for the open enrollment program and black history course.*
- *Called realtors to adopt an "equal opportunity" statement in their housing ads and that Negroes be encouraged to "obtain housing in areas other than the ghetto."*
- *Called for additional recreational programs which would encourage "disadvantaged individuals" to participate with other community residents.*

- *Recommended the director of the Waterloo Human Rights Commission be "closer to the office of the mayor."*
- *Acknowledged the friction between police and minorities had been a double standard for many years. It said some law officers "cannot act without prejudice" [and there needs to be] "more properly qualified law officers . . . supported morally and financially by the community" and [called for] the uniform enforcement of laws.*[40]

The grand jury also recommended another jury be impaneled in six months to see it its recommendations were followed or, if not, why. There's no record that it was.

On the same day the grand jury report was issued, the police department and the Waterloo Human Rights Commission announced a project to open communications between law enforcement officers and the black community. It would feature two groups of five officers and five Negro citizens, including a woman and a high school student. The groups would participate in eight weeks of "sensitivity" sessions led by a moderator from a local psychiatric clinic. The *Courier* story about the program abutted the four-column second part of the grand jury report continued from two pages before.[41]

There's no record of any progress in or final assessment of the program.

Three days later, on February 05, East High principal Lawrence Garlock asked to be re-assigned. "(Due to the] difficulties experienced last September at East. . . such a reassignment would be in the best interests of East High School.[42] In late April of 1969, he was appointed director of a new pupil accounting program starting July 01.[43]

## CITIZENS COMMITTEE REPORT, FEBRUARY 09, 1969

*No Waterloo citizen was untouched by the tension which followed the disturbances at [East High] early in September, 1968. . . . When did the trouble at East begin? Not in 1968 – not in 1960 – perhaps not even in 1950. . . . resentment toward East High School has built up through the*

*years in the black community as a result of injustices that existed. These*
*past wrongs, in the minds of many black youths, appear to justify their*
*rebellions today.*[44]

The 10-member special citizens committee comprised of blacks and whites representing a cross-section of Waterloo was appointed by the Waterloo Chamber of Commerce in September 1968 to investigate the "underlying causes" of the racial unrest. It spent 1,000 man-hours hearing and reviewing testimony from more than 50 people.

A major contention in its report, also released in February 1969, was "maintaining discipline [necessary for an orderly society] starts with parents and extends to the schools, law enforcement authorities and the courts." It reiterated conventional wisdom that schools with "weak administration and a mixed student body in a racially tense situation have serious disturbances," without concluding either is a cause. The committee recommended the BOE and superintendent evaluate school administrations "and strengthen leadership as necessary" by the fall of 1969.

In a major departure from the grand jury's findings, the committee concluded outside influences "have affected and invited racial tension in Waterloo. . . . [but we] also believe Waterloo was and would have been a racially tense city without inside influences."[45]

## STATE DEPARTMENT OF PUBLIC INSTRUCTION REPORT, FEBRUARY 1969

The State Department of Public Instruction (DPI) special committee created to investigate the disturbances at East reported "potentially dangerous divisions [remain] among the student body may erupt at any time."

*The black students are split into two major camps, the black militants and the black students working for cooperation and common solutions . . . The militants do not seem to be a cohesive group. As a counterpart, the white student population has members who have deep seated resentment of the black race in general. . . . some white students called for*

*segregation with answers such as, "If they don't like it here they can go*
*somewhere else"... [and] more "insidious" answers such as "I'm not*
*prejudiced but I do feel they would be better off in their own school."[46]*

The committee noted most students, black and white, indicated a
willingness to cooperate in the interests of the school. But "many
students made it quite clear they felt their parents and other adults
were so set in their beliefs that nothing constructive could come from
involving them."[47]

"Basic community racial problems" were cited as the "root causes"
for the events, noting that didn't mitigate the need for some policy
changes at East High. "The events which led to the closing of East High
School appear to have their beginning in the basic problems of racial
discrimination in housing, employment, representation on public
policy making bodies and the isolation of the East and West side."[48]

It also stated, "It appears the BOE is not communicating with the
patrons of the school district, especially on the East side."[49]

Among its 138 recommendations, the DPI committee
recommended the school and community look beyond the "immediate
problem" and attack "the many problems of race on a broad front."

*The fundamental problem for the community is to develop an*
*attitude that we can solve our racial problems.... the question is this:*
*'Does Waterloo want to bring it about. [sic][50]*

Nine changes made at East between September and November were
acknowledged by the DPI, including the offering of a black history
course.[51] Enrollment in the course doubled in the second semester.[52]

The DPI committee also disagreed with the grand jury finding
about outside interference, concluding "persons not enrolled at the
school had a significant role in its closing [but] black students had
some cause for complaint that would have come to the fore eventually,
with or without . . . outside assistance."[53]

The report was based on a series of hearings with a variety of people, including East students, in Waterloo in November and December 1968.

A week after all the reports had been released, superintendent Hohl noted at least 13 organizations, in addition to the previous three, had surveyed and investigated the Waterloo schools during the previous two years.

They included the National Council of Christian Churches, the UNI committee for responsible minority education, the Waterloo Human Rights and the Iowa Civil Rights commissions, the U.S. Office of Education, the U.S. Office of Economic Opportunity, the Waterloo Citizens' Committee, two school board advisory committees and the North Central Association of College & Schools.

*I don't know that this is any distinction, but I doubt any public school system, at least in the Midwest, has been as well analyzed.*[54]

## Fall 1968: Black History Course Offered at East High

The study guide for the Black History and Culture course stated it "should provide the black student with a stronger sense of identity and pride in his heritage. For all students the course should lead to a fuller appreciation of and respect for the black man."[55]

It had eight goals.

1. To make students aware of the vast, positive involvement of blacks throughout history
2. and of black cultural history.
3. Give opportunity for student involvement and participation in the class.
4. Foster self-respect and self-understanding in black students
5. and to acquire a new identity and image.
6. To promote mutual respect between blacks and whites.
7. To secure accurate and full information for rational and constructive thinking and action.

276

8. To instill a sense of responsibility for individual behavior and actions.

"The course has had quite an impact on those white students enrolled. . . . [Achieving] the final purpose can be determined only by the future [hopefully by students enabled] to develop clearer values and positive attitudes of the roles that make for responsible citizenship."[56]

## March 1969: Interracial Dating Interference by Teacher

The ninth of the 12 grievances presented by black East High students and parents in September 1968 was, "Teachers should not interfere with the personal lives of students." BOE president Dr. Sydney Thomas agreed at a board meeting with the protestors at the time teachers don't "have a right to impose their feelings on others" and black-white dating "should be a matter of individual choice."[57]

On Monday, March 04, 1969, roughly 200 black and white students staged a "mostly orderly" sit-in at the East High student center just before noon protesting the alleged interference in an interracial dating situation and calling for the dismissal Edna Lenicek, a counselor and Director of Activities at East. (Figure 5) They charged she had notified the mother of a white girl that she was dating a black youth in violation of the agreement high school staff wouldn't interfere in student lives.

Lenicek was named by several East graduates with whom I talked as having a reputation of notifying parents about interracial couples from as early as the early 1960s.

*If a white girl was thought to be dating a white guy, she would be called into the counselor's office, the dean of girls, Edna Lenicek. I was confronted one time about supposedly dating a white girl. She was a friend. Were we seeing each other? Yes, but as a friend. I was confronted by one of the coaches. He said, "If you are doing that, when it comes time to go to college we're not going to recommend you." I was a little dude in high school, about 145 [laughs], but I told him point blankly, "You're not going to tell me what I can or can't do. I'll date or talk to or see whoever I want to. I don't really care what you do." The stop-biracial-dating attitude had to have been circulating among the administrators. [EHS 61 AAM]*

Figure 5 Black Students Protest Interracial Dating Interference at East High
Copyright © 1969 David Weldon. Used with permission.

Three hours after the sit-in had begun, about 150 black and several white students left school, and were suspended indefinitely. They met at the Midtown Center to discuss the protest and asked media to leave.[58]

About 25 protestors showed up at the basketball game in the school's gym that evening with signs such as "Student Power" and "We Don't Need Love Guides."[59] A mimeographed flyer was also distributed explaining who they wanted to have fired and why during the "orderly demonstration."

Tuesday morning, the suspended students released a statement that school administrators "would rather put us out of school rather than pay attention to why we were there" and Garlock had told "black athletes" they wouldn't be allowed to play in the Monday night basketball game if they participated in the protest."[60] The Trojans were ranked No. 2 in the state going into the opening round of the state AA district basketball tournament.[61]

The school board held a special meeting at a Waterloo restaurant that morning over the protest, but issued no statement. Garlock said the school administration was investigating the complaint and the case "is not something to be tried in the newspapers." He said students had been warned at the sit-in they would be suspended if they didn't return to class. One board member categorized the protest as based on "rumor and innuendo."[62]

At noon on Wednesday, Hohl reported a thorough investigation conducted by the district's head counselor, Glenda Mabrey, "clearly shows Miss Edna Lenicek did not in any way interfere with the students' personal affairs by giving information or advice on the matter of dating."[63]

He reported the girl's mother had requested Lenicek visit her home "to discuss another matter unrelated to the matter of unrelated to the matter of interracial dating." The full report of the investigation wasn't released to "protect the personal feelings of the two students and their parents."[64]

". . . the agreement reached with black students last September [that] 'teachers should not interfere with the personal lives of the students in matters not related to school'" hadn't been violated, Hohl said.[65]

He commended the students for "avoiding an unruly demonstration," but cited their actions as "in violation of the rules and disruptive to the entire student body and faculty."[66]

A Waterloo Daily Courier editorial concurred.

*By their precipitate action, based on misinformation and hearsay, the students ignored the rights of hundreds of East High students and teachers and particularly Miss Lenicek.*

*Incidentally, none of the so-called "demands" by students in this case has been to the school administration. Student "demands," when accompanied by disruptive tactics infringing on the rights of others, provide no basis for constructive involvement of those students in the school program.*

*Legitimate, constructive requests and suggestions of students have
been, and will continue to be, treated with respect, but standards of
conduct must not be diminished or ignored in the schools.* [67]

Parents and students were required to attend a Wednesday night
meeting in the school auditorium to arrange for reinstatement of those
suspended. Eighty to 90 admit slips were picked up and the students
were allowed to return to classes. Others weren't allowed to return
until parents had made proper arrangements with the school for them
to do so.[68]

Spokesmen for the blacks had presented "demands" at the
Wednesday night meeting, including that no black students would be
put on probation and that suspensions be erased from the students'
records. Two others were that Lenicek not be on the East faculty the
following school year and Garlock apologize to the basketball players
for his "threats." The players returned to class and played against Big
Four opponent Cedar Falls, losing for the first time in three games to
their rival, 56-51.

*Four black parents took the opportunity to "rap" the district's
administration for not discussing the complaint with the students,
asking, "What happened to the East High grievance committee? Who
could these students go to for satisfaction?"*

*The city of Waterloo passes fair housing ordinances, yet black people
are not allowed "actual mobility." The school board passes resolutions to
guarantee students certain rights. However, no support is given to the
students when their rights are violated. . . .*

*You ask black people to go through legal channels and then show us
that as far as we are concerned, there are no legal channels. . . . how
many more rules can black people ask and fight for, only to have them
ignored. [sic]*

*Some folks fail to realize the things are important to black citizens. It
should have been a clear indication to the East High school*

*administration that, if 150 black and white students were complaining, there was good reason for them to be heard and not threatened.*[69]

Letters to The Public Speaks in the *Waterloo Daily Courier* backed Lenicek and challenged East's "black militants."

*With all the unrest going on at East High. . . this year, I think it is very unfair and poor tasted to bring an important and very wonderful teacher into the picture. She has done more for the Negro students at East than any teacher I know of [as an East graduate]. . . I, and a lot of others, are concerned about the problems that have risen. Also, I think most of the students bring it on themselves. If they would stop and think before they act, it might help.*

*[They] demand a black history class; now why don't they get in there and find out all about it instead of seeing what else they can stir up or demand? [The 150 student protestors] said it wasn't anybody else's business when the black boy and the white girl dated, then why didn't they let these two kids settle with their parents? It wasn't really [their] business was it? I would say if anybody is prejudiced, these black kids are doing so against Miss Lenicek. Maybe she doesn't give in to every whimper.*[70]

The Waterloo Human Rights Commission also investigated the complaint and informed the BOE the discrimination complaint against Lenicek "had no foundation in fact and was 'based on hearsay.'"[71]

## Fall 1969: Black Students Bused to NU High[72]

In 1968, the WCSD board and Northern University High School were in negotiations to enroll black Waterloo students in the small, private high school run by the University of Northern Iowa (UNI) in Cedar Falls.[73] UNI Dean of Instruction William Lang asked the school board to designate it as an "attendance center" for the Waterloo school district, with 15 students enrolled in the first year with the hope of 100 in future years. Having black students at Price would "help better prepare teacher education students to teach in racially mixed schools."

The selection process for students was designed to create a group "broadly representative, socially, economically and educationally of the black [Waterloo] community. . . . [Students] interested in continuing their education at the laboratory school through 12th grade and those with parents which we felt were interested in taking part in school activities."

When BOE member Mrs. Norma Rehder questioned why the board should pay for a benefit UNI, Betty Furgerson, a black member of the selection committee from Waterloo, countered.

*The question is not so much what the Waterloo kids would gain but what they would bring. . . white students at UNI would benefit along with the student teachers, many of which come from all-white towns. This is the first time anyone has ever come to the black community and said, "You can do something for us." The rest of the time we have to go and beg for what is rightfully ours anyway. If you can't understand the psychological implications of that, I can't explain it.*

Spending funds to send black students to the lab school when they weren't taking advantage of the open enrollment in Waterloo was questioned.

Former Black Hawk County Department of Social Welfare director, Ruth Anderson, said it wouldn't be difficult to explain if the kids were asked "why they didn't want to go to West or Orange. I suggest you let sleeping dogs lie."

A 1968 Northern University grad denounced the school in a letter to the *Waterloo Daily Courier*'s editorial section, "The Public Speaks." His response was based on knowing "how most of the students felt about this through many discussions" and "discussions with "many diversified people." His two major points: first, it will "gain nothing" in terms of creating better black and white relationships. Second, local families on the waiting list for admission will "be pushed further down the waiting list."

*Throwing blacks and whites together for eight hours per day will not fulfill the job [of getting people to become more "friendly"] and more problems will arrive to solve. . . . Is it right to deprive children across the street from attending Price Lab School while blacks are brought into the community? This makes the school less available to less [sic] students and forces those that have waited to lose all hope. Curt Lindaman, Student; UNI [Address withheld]*[74]

The district accepted the plan, agreed to pay the tuition and UNI paid the transportation costs for the district's buses. For the 1969 school year, the district was allowed 33 spaces in kindergarten through sixth grade, and nine spaces in seventh and eighth grades. Siblings of students already in the program would have priority, but the remaining elementary school spaces were allocated to students from Grant Elementary.[75]

## October 1969: BOE Commits to Ending "Minority Concentration"

The Waterloo BOE put its stake in the ground when it proposed a policy statement on October 14, 1969, committing to "the elimination of the heavy concentrations of minority group and disadvantaged children from the schools, and to develop plans to achieve this end."

The proposed policy would support the one adopted in February 1967 that committed the school district to providing "equality of [educational] opportunity [which] requires that educational programs and resources must be defined and utilized to help every child overcome any handicaps, cultural, economic, physical, emotional or mental."[76]

The statement noted the Open Enrollment program and Grant School Bridgeway project were among "many programs" that had already been initiated to "equalize the opportunity for minority and disadvantaged children." Another was the enrollment and busing of Negro students to the Price Lab School at UNI.

The chairman of the board deferred discussion on the proposed policy until a meeting two weeks later.

On 28 October, the BOE unanimously approved the statement after a discussion with an overflow crowd present. Endorsements had been received from the Committee on Equal Educational Opportunity and the Waterloo Education Association [WEA].

A white resident inquired how far the board intended to "go with this? Elimination of de facto segregation would require students to be bused both ways, not only from disadvantaged neighborhoods." A board member noted the policy only said heavy minority concentrations would be eliminated, but doesn't say how. That would require the "resources of the entire community" in implementation.[77]

A black parent asked, "How far will people in Waterloo carry this now before they start playing games again? Let's get mad at each other once and for all and get this solved."[78]

## January 1970: Wrestling Meet Mêlée[79]

A "disturbance," "brawl," "fracas" or "melee" racial disturbance "erupted" at the 39th annual East-West wrestling meet at East High on Saturday, January 17, which was canceled after the disruption two matches short of being complete.

*The unruly situation appeared to develop when two black spectators ducked under the restraining ropes and walked behind the West High bench. . . . As West Coach Bob Siddens approached the two, one stepped forward and shoved him. Almost spontaneously a large portion of the fans on the East side of the gym poured onto the floor and the [roughly 20-minute] melee started.*

*Siddens, who was hit in the head with a chair and kicked in the stomach during the fracas said: "All I did was walk over and tell those kids to get away from the ropes. I feel terrible about the whole thing. There are a lot of nice people over here [at East High] and the whole thing makes me feel real bad."*

284

*[The meet was] until this time considered to be the premier high
school wresting meeting the state. . . .* [80]

## The view from the bleachers was a little different.

*My date and I were sitting in the stands. A lot of the East fans had
wooden canes with the shepherd's hook on it and they were beating them
on the stands between matches in a rhythm thing. The West wrestlers
started to win the match. For some reason, somebody came out of the
stands and started to attack one of the West wrestlers. And all hell broke
loose. Everybody was on the gym floor. I was trying to get the heck out of
there with my date. We went to the front door of the gym and saw a
whole bunch of black young people on the steps outside. So, we were
trapped. Three or four rows ahead of me was a white classmate from
West who had been stabbed in the back. It was the first time I'd really,
really been scared. I thought, "Oh, my God. This is going to end up bad."
The police finally arrived, we got out of there, got in the car and drove
home. Afterward all the East-West sporting activities were held
Saturday afternoons -- football games and wrestling matches and so
forth -- at least for a while until things cooled down. [WHS 69 WM]*

*We knew there was tension at East and were aware of the
discrimination. We weren't surprised the riot took place. I was at the
wrestling meet with a couple of my friends. It was at West [it was at
East] and the stands on the other side were pretty much all East High
kids. We were sitting up high. Both team benches were across from us in
front of the East High fans. Our coach, Bob Siddens, was standing on the
right end of the West team bench near the end of the gym watching the
match in progress. A young, tall black guy, probably a few years out of
school, entered the gym from the hallway. Instead of turning and going
up into the stands, he walked out toward the mat in the middle of the
gym. I don't know if he thought he was going to cross the floor or what.
Siddens tried to guide him away. The guy reacted – he refused to follow
Siddens' directions and hit the coach on the head with a chair. It was*

*flash point in a tinderbox for things to get out of hand as quickly as it did that turned into an altercation in just an instant. It escalated so fast. My perception was all the black people came out of the stands and onto the floor. The comical memory which stayed with me is when one our [West] wrestlers who wrestled at 170 pounds – a good size for a wrestler, the toughest kid in school, a muscle-bound guy, who was in street clothes because he was out with an injury – stood up and turned around like he's going to stop the people from coming out of the stands just by holding up his hands. He parted the sea. They went around him. No one took him on. There were a dozen or so black girls who formed a circle on the middle of the mat and danced around like we used to think of Indians doing a war dance. We were kind of petrified and scared. I wondered how we were going to get out of there safely. It was our gym, but there were a lot of black kids there. And our perception was they just want to beat us up. [WHS 70 WM]*

A community group convened the following week to review the incident, including East High officials; Black Hawk County Attorney Dave Dutton, who had been involved with prosecutions in the 1968 riot; Waterloo Mayor Lloyd Turner; Waterloo Human Rights Commission executive director and former East state champion wrestler Pete Middleton; and five officers from the Waterloo police department and Black Hawk County sheriff's offices. The group's statement about what occurred only inside the gym made it clear the "disturbance in the gymnasium was not a racial incident."[81]

The group noted that the two black men who ducked under the restraining rope that led to the "brief" confrontation were a "pair of fans (not associated with either school) . . ."[82] And it added this caveat:

*. . . this is not to deny some participants may have been motivated by racial feelings, even as some may have been motivated by school partisanship.*

286

*There were no hostile interracial confrontations between spectators or between spectators and authorities which triggered the fracas or caused it to continue in the gym.*

*The students and faculty of the Waterloo school system are to be commended for their efforts to prevent this disruption, and it is our firm belief this single event will not undo the progress which East High School students and faculty have made toward improving their school spirit and image.*

*The absence of over reaction by authorities, and the combined efforts of black and white citizens to bring the situation under control. . . and the willingness of the total community to see this event as foolish actions of a few rather than the concerted efforts of any class or group are hopeful signs of racial understanding in our community.*[83]

The events that occurred outside the gym after the match were also investigated, including possible charges from alleged assault on spectators leaving the building.

Five of the defendants involved in the disturbance were permanently banned from attending any school activities – an 18-year-old, two 19-year-olds and two 20-year olds. The court affirmed "the authority of any school official, including coaches, to keep spectators out of the areas reserved for athletes in such contests." A defense witness had suggested Coach Siddens "had no business" confronting a spectator while a deputy was on hand. Charges against two others were dismissed.[84]

Because of the disturbance at the meet, the city of Waterloo asked the Iowa High School Athletic Association to withdraw West High's sponsorship of the Class AAA district wrestling tournament from McElroy Auditorium on February 27-28. The association transferred the event to Charles City.

*The Waterloo Daily Courier* took exception with the city's decision in a two-column editorial in the upper left-hand corner of the front page rather than on the editorial page.

*The Waterloo request was an over-reaction. . . . The events . . . did not justify the removal of the . . . tournament from this county. . . .*

*No students of either school have been identified as being instigators and the disturbance was quickly quelled through the cool-headed cooperation of both school personnel and spectators of all races.*

*An incident at a Cedar Falls High basketball game [in a different school district] earlier this winter in which students, as well as non-students, participated, was handled in accord with common sense. Those deemed to be responsible were punished and there was no suggestion the entire athletic program be disrupted.*

*. . . around 9,000 fans watched a hotly contested East-West football game at Sloane Wallace Stadium last fall [1969] without incident and last Friday night's East-West basketball game was conducted before about 1,800 at West in a highly competitive, but sane atmosphere. . . . It seems ridiculous the great strides made over the past 16 months [since the 1968 riot following the East football game] . . . have been jeopardized because of the action of a few and one hasty over-reaction. We hope Waterloo in the future will keep any such incident in perspective and not react as if it were a crisis.*[85]

## Reflections from the Bridge

In weather, high pressure means good weather. In the Waterloo environment, the pressure on parties from both sides of the integration and segregation issues had the opposite effect, facilitating conditions that resulted in the most violent week in the town's history in September 1968.

ERA 2 was a tumultuous one in which the demands from community factions and students for social integration and an end to school segregation became increasingly insistent. There was initial resistance if not opposition from other community groups, community leaders, the BOE, and school district and some school administrators.

*Inspired and empowered by the civil rights movement's successes in the mid-1960s, [black] Waterloo students [and their parents] asserted their own conceptions of racial equality and educational equity and, in the process, won concessions from the local school district. At the same time, the school board turned to school desegregation as a practical way to prove its commitment to racial equality in the schools. Shrinking enrollments turned school desegregation into a policy choice made when it became apparent a realignment of school attendance zones would be necessary. White opposition to busing arose in Waterloo as the school board voted for a comprehensive desegregation plan, but opponents were ultimately not able to halt the implementation of the school board's plan.[86]*

That played out in the third ERAof *The Bridge Between*, the school years from the fall of 1971 to graduation in June 1973.

# Endnotes

[1] Langston Hughes' poem, Roland Hayes Beating," referred to commonly as "Warning," was about the African-American singer regarded as the first performer of his race to gain international fame. He and his family were shopping in a whites-only section of a shoe store in Rome, Ga. In July 1942, they were put out of the store. Hayes defended his family, and police beat him in front of their daughter and arrested his wife. A week later, Georgia Gov. Eugene Talmadge warned other Black people who didn't heed the Jim Crow laws of the south could either leave the state or suffer more of the same. Roland Hayes. Little Known Black History Fact. Chandler, D.L. BlAckAmericaWeb. Retrieved from https://blackamericaweb.com/2017/01/18/little-known-black-history-fact-roland-hayes/. Roland Hayes: The Inspiration Behind Langston Hughes Poem "Roland Hayes Beaten." (November 25, 2015). Jones, J. Black Then. Discovering Our History. Retrieved from https://blackthen.com/roland-hayes-the-inspiration-behind-langston-hughes-poem-roland-hayes-beaten/.

[2] Experiences and Prejudices: A memoir dealing with both; endeavoring to understand. (December 2009). Bowie, T.F. Bloomington, IN: Xlibris, 96.

[3] Waterloo race relations still an issue 40 years after city report. (September 09, 2007). Steffen, A. *Waterloo Daily Courier*. Retrieved from http://tinyurl.com/ycr9j3kt.

[4] Narrative of the East High School Problem in Waterloo, Iowa (November 7, 1968). RG 073 Education/Public Instruction, Education Equity Section, Waterloo School Reports, 1968-1973. Box 17. Des Moines, IA: State Historical Library & Archives, State Historical Society of Iowa, 1-2.

[5] Narrative of the East High School Problem in Waterloo, Iowa, 2-3.

[6] Board Pledges Discipline at East After Disorders: False Alarm Empties School During Negro Protest. (September 10, 1968). *Waterloo Daily Courier*, 3.

[7] Ibid.

[8] Protestors at East: Again, Seek Class in Negro History. (September 11, 1968). *Waterloo Daily Courier*, 6.

[9] Board Pledges Discipline at East After Disorders.

[10] East High Classes Let Out Early. Teachers Want Faculty Meeting. (September 11, 1968). *Waterloo Daily Courier*, 1, 2.

[11] School Board Studies Negro Grievances. (September 13, 1968). *Waterloo Daily Courier*, 1, 3.

[12] Ibid.

[13] Ibid.

[14] Ibid.

[15] To Answer Grievances at East. Continued from Page 1. (September 13, 1968.) *Waterloo Daily Courier*, 3.

[16] The term Negro began to decline after black activist Stokely Carmichael's seminal book, *Black Power: The Politics of Liberation in America,* in which he argued "the term implied black inferiority." Black was the preference among the majority of blacks by 1974. The Associated Press and *The New York Times* abandoned Negro in the 1970s, and the U.S. Supreme Court had "largely stopped using Negro" by the mid-1980s. When Did the Word Negro Become Taboo? (January 11, 2010). Palmer, B. Slate: answers to your questions about the news. Retrieved from http://tinyurl.com/cswpgqc. The suggestion to replace "black" with "African American" was initiated by civil rights activist C. Delores Tucker who made a "highly passionate argument" for the term during a strategy session with presidential candidate Rev. Jesse Jackson, the National Rainbow Coalition, the Operation PUSH (People United to Serve Humanity) board and other high-ranking campaign supporters in Chicago in December 1988. Her reason was "Nobody lives in Blackland!" Afterward, Jackson encouraged "Black Americans to drop 'black' and replace it with 'African'. . . .Black does not describe out situation. We are of African-American heritage." SOURCES: 1. Don't Call Me African-American. (May 09, 2012). Easter, E. Urban Intellectuals: Positive Black Stories and Images. Stolen Moments:

Urban News Service. Retrieved from https://urbanintellectuals.com/2015/10/20/do-you-know-the-day-black-people-became-african-american/. 2. Don't Call Me African-American. (May 09, 2012). Regions: New African Magazine. Retrieved from http://newafricanmagazine.com/dont-call-me-african-american/.

[17] The Public Speaks. 'Terry' Wants to Be Called by Name. (September 30, 1968). Wilken, W. *Waterloo Daily Courier*, 4.

[18] East High May Reopen Tuesday, Walkouts to Go on Probation. (September 15, 1968), *Waterloo Daily Courier*, 15

[19] School Board Studies Negro Grievances, 1.

[20] Ibid.

[21] Tougher Action in Disorders Pledged. Link Criminals to East Trouble. (September 12, 1968). *Waterloo Daily Courier*, 1, 2.

[22] Blacks Defend East High Activities. Denies Students' Conduct Improper. (September 13, 1968.) *Waterloo Daily Courier*, 5.

[23] Waterloo DAR Chapter Names Five Area Students as Good Citizens. (December 3, 1968). *Waterloo Daily Courier*, Ten. Retrieved from www.newspaperarchive.com.

[24] 13 Arrests Friday Night. Gunfire and Arson Mark Race Fights. (September 15, 1968). *Waterloo Daily Courier*, 15.

[25] Night of Violence Starts at Stadium. Fights Erupt During East High Opener. (Sunday, September 15, 1968). Waterloo Sunday Courier, 10.

[26] Ibid.

[27] Ibid.

[28] Seven Policemen Injured, 13 Arrests Friday Night. (September 15, 1968). *Waterloo Daily Courier*, 15.

[29] Violence (continued). (September 15, 1968). *Waterloo Daily Courier*, 16.

[30] Seven Policemen Injured.

[31] Violence (continued).

[32] Ibid.

[33] Guardsmen Control Waterloo. City Calm After Night of Strife, Curfew Imposed. (September 15, 1968). *Waterloo Daily Courier*, 1.

[34] 1) Only Manufacturing Lags. (March 23, 1969). *Waterloo Daily Courier*, 18. 2) Metro Rate of Jobless Still Low. Under U.S. Average Throughout the Year. (January 14, 1968). *Waterloo Daily Courier,* 64. 3) Job Opportunities Here. Building, Retailing Promising Fields. (February 10, 1969). *Waterloo Daily Courier*, Three.

[35] 12 Percent of Teens Found Jobs. (September 15, 1968). *Waterloo Daily Courier*, 10.

[36] Biggest East-West Game Ever. Loop, Big 4, No. 1 Rating All on the Line. (November 8, 1968). *Waterloo Daily Courier*, 17, 19.

[37] East Maintains Streak – Barely. No. 5 West Bows 28-27. (November 10, 1968. (*Waterloo Daily Courier*, 43, 44.

[38] Resolution on Disorders. Methodist Ministers Call for Study of Root Causes. (September 20, 1968). *Waterloo Daily Courier*, 24.

[39] Reports on Racial Orders. Grand Jury Blames Bias in the Community. (February 02, 1969). *Waterloo Daily Courier*, 13, 14.

[40] Reports on Racial Orders. Grand Jury Blames Bias in the Community, 13, 15.

[41] "Sensitivity" Experiment. Project Designed to Aid Police-Blacks Relations. (February 2, 1969). *Waterloo Daily Courier*, 15.

[42] Principal at East. Asks Board to Reassign in District. Transfer Asked for "Best Interest." (February 05, 1969). *Waterloo Daily Courier*, 3.

[43] Pupil Accounting Post. Garlock Assigned to New Program. (April 29, 1969) *Waterloo Daily Courier*, 5.

[44] Text of Report by Citizens Committee on Racial Tensions (Story on Page 13). Retrieved from https://newspaperarchive.com/waterloo-daily-courier-feb-09-1969-p-8/.

[45] Citizens Committee Advises New Thinking on Race Idea. Advocates Planned Method of Mixed Schools, Housing. (February 09, 1969). *Waterloo Daily Courier*, 13.

[46] Eruptive Potential at East High Told. State Report Finds Polarization. (February 16, 1969). *Waterloo Daily Courier*, 13.

[47] Citizens Committee Advises New Thinking on Race Idea.

[48] State School Department Reports on East High Disorders. Blames Citywide Problems. Isolation Termed Basic Root Cause. (February 12, 1969). *Waterloo Daily Courier*, 1.

[49] Eruptive Potential at East High Told. State Report Finds Polarization. (February 16, 1969). *Waterloo Daily Courier*, 13, 15. (Jump headline "EAST" was incorrectly inserted as "REMAP.")

[50] CAC Head Asks Goals. End Race Studies and Act: Snyder. (February 13, 1969). *Waterloo Daily Courier*, 3.

[51] State School Department Reports on East High Disorders.

[52] School Building Program Launched. $7.8 Million Authorized for Projects. January 19, 1969). *Waterloo Daily Courier*, 35.

[53] Eruptive Potential at East High Told. State Report Finds Polarization.

[54] Ames [Superintendent] Thanks Board. Sees East Report as Aid to Others. (February 13, 1969). *Waterloo Daily Courier*, 5.

[55] Black History Students: Argue Agreeably? (November 01, 1968). De Bonis, L. Teen Page Correspondent. *Waterloo Daily Courier*, 10. ["L. De Bonis" is my sister, Lucy, who graduated from East in 1969].

[56] Ibid.

[57] School Board Studies Negro Grievances.

[58] Suspended East Students Say Demands Are Ignored. Ask Teacher Be Fired in Dating Row. (March 04, 1969). *Waterloo Daily Courier*, 6.

[59] Ibid.

[60] Ibid.

[61] Defense Shines in 56-51 CF Win. Third Time Fatal for Trojans. (March 04, 1969). *Waterloo Daily Courier*, 13.

[62] Suspended East Students Say Demands Are Ignored.

[63] School Officials Deny Charges Dating at East Interfered With. Parents and Officials in Conference. (March 05, 1969). *Waterloo Daily Courier*, 5.

[64] Ibid.

[65] Ibid.

[66] Ibid.

[67] Ibid.

[68] School Officials, Blacks Meet Again. Black Student Spokesmen in Demands. (March 06, 1969). *Waterloo Daily Courier*, 5.

[69] School Officials Deny Charges Dating at East Interfered With.

[70] The Public Speaks. Suggests East Students Think Before Acting. (March 06, 1969). *Waterloo Daily Courier*, 4.

[71] Private Industry recruiting Blacks. (April 04, 1969). *Waterloo Daily Courier*, 03.

[72] School Board Tells Policy. Open Enrollment Plans Attacked. (August 27, 1968). *Waterloo Daily Courier*, 3.

[73] Northern University High School was officially designated at UNI as the Price Laboratory School. Founded in 1954, it closed in 2012.

[74] Hits Plan to Admit Blacks to Price Lab School. (July 19, 1968). *Waterloo Daily Courier*, 4.

[75] Additional Waterloo Black Students to be Enrolled in Price Lab School. (June 24, 1969). *Waterloo Daily Courier*, 6.

[76] School Board Policy to Call for End to Minority "Concentration." Statement Asks Equal Opportunity. (October 14, 1969). Waterloo Daily Courier, 8.

[77] School Board Pledges End to De facto Segregation. But Busing Program May Stay on Voluntary Basis. (October 28, 1969). *Waterloo Daily Courier*, 6.

[78] Ibid.

[79] Assault Charges in Mat Melee Planned. Seven Arrests Expected in the Incident. (January 22, 1970). *Waterloo Daily Courier*, Six.

[80] West Halts East 25-12. Disturbance Halts Meet after 10 Bouts. (January 18, 1970). *Waterloo Daily Courier*, 39.

[81] Assault Charges in Mat Melee Planned.

[82] An Editorial. Wrestling Meet Removal Was an Over-Reaction. (January 22, 1970). *Waterloo Daily Courier*, 1.

[83] Assault Charges in Mat Melee Planned.

[84] Judge Explains Ban on Errant Mat Fans. (February 01, 1970). *Waterloo Daily Courier*, Fifteen.

[85] An Editorial. Wrestling Meet Removal Was an Over-Reaction. (January 22, 1970). Waterloo Daily Courier, 1.

[86] Schumaker, K.A. (Fall 2013). The Politics of Youth: Civil Rights Reform in the Waterloo Public Schools. State Historical Society of Iowa: The Annals of Iowa, 72(4), 356-357. Retrieved from http://ir.uiowa.edu/annals-of-iowa/vol72/iss4/4.

# *TBB* 9: ERA3 Fall 1971–Spring 73 – Post-Storm Surge

*There were cliques in high school. You had the jocks and the intelligents at the top. And then you had a subclass of "all-right kids" who weren't the cream of the crop or the popular ones. There were the mediocre students, then the "C" and "D" students. And the band and "A" choir. [EHS 71 WM]*

*Our generation was more about hippies, peace, drugs and sniffing Pam than civil rights. We had a classmate who died sniffing Pam. [EHS 73 WF]*

School desegregation became a priority for the Waterloo Board of Education (BOE) at the end of *TBB* ERA2 after four years of turbulence, violence and resistance to outside pressure from from 1966-1970 to integrate its schools.

Kathryn Schumaker, a civil rights professor at the University of Oklahoma Institute for the American Constitutional Heritage, explained the process in her 2013 article, "The Politics of Youth: Civil Rights Reform in the Waterloo Public Schools."

*In the end, it took open enrollment, along with the busing and civil rights laws, to further integrate the public schools in other sections of Waterloo beyond the East Side Triangle that African Americans were restricted to live in.*[1]

The Bridgeway Project was launched in the late 1960s to decrease the enrollment of minorities in East Side schools.

In the summer of 1971, a BOE member told the Iowa committee of the U.S. Commission on Civil Rights (USCCR), "The school system has no plan for desegregating its schools, nor is it trying to develop one."[2] The USCCR committee had recommended a commitment to desegregation should be first priority for the district.

In October, the board adopted a breakthrough student-involvement plan with the goal of "student representation in all matters to them [including decision-making processes.]" It also provided for a process to challenge a principal's decision by having a representative meet with the BOE's parent advisory committee, the school superintendent and the board president to attempt to resolve the issues.[3]

Opening Central High and closing Orange High in the fall of 1972 was a key element of the district's desegregation strategy.

In addition, the district was beginning to feel the effects of declining enrollment on its budget, which would affect both schools and desegregation plans associated with them.

Iowa public school enrollment in the fall of 1972 dropped 1.4% from the previous year, the third consecutive year of decline since the Baby Boomer enrollments peaked in 1969. Enrollment in the Waterloo public schools dropped by 2.9% from 1971-72, double the state rate, and were projected to drop the same amount for the following school year.

Catholic schools in Black Hawk County experienced a six percent decrease in enrollment. Columbus High was down by 10.1 percent.

## High School by the Numbers

Principals at East and West continued to change in ERA3. (Figure 1) Howie Vernon – whose teams had the longest football winning streak in Iowa with 57 consecutive wins and were state champions from 1966-1968 – left to become the offensive coordinator at the University of Iowa. Alan Krebs, who had been vice principal since 1969, was named as his replacement. Harold Burshtan accepted a position as principle at an Illinois high school when his WCSD contract expired in July 1972. The new principal, Jerry Fain, was a native of Nevada, Iowa, and a graduate of the University of Northern Iowa (UNI). He had been principal, assistant principal and coach in the McHenry, Illinois, school system for the previous nine years.

Dick Miles, who was principal at Orange High School since 1959 moved to the new Central High School in the fall of 1972 when Orange was closed.

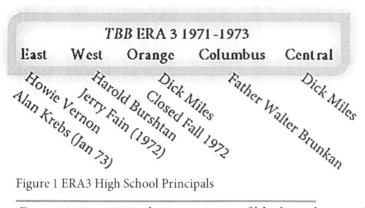

Figure 1 ERA3 High School Principals

From 1963 to 1970, the percentage of black students at East increased 38.7%; the number of East students increased only 1.7%. (Table 1) to 1970, enrollment at West increased 21.1%. Total WCSD high school enrollment went up 12% in the same period. The population of Waterloo went up by 14.4% from 1963-1970; the black population went up 36.6%.[4]

| Table 1 Percentage of Blacks in High Schools, 1963 & 1967 | | | | |
|---|---|---|---|---|
| | 1963 | 1967 | 1970 | 1973 |
| Waterloo | 6.7%** | | 8.7% | |
| East | 15.0% | 20.8% | 23.8% | 20% |
| West | 0.0% | 0.5% | 1.4% | 7.3% |
| Orange | *** | 0.0% | 0.0% | Closed |
| Central | Opened 1972 | | | 14.3% |
| Columbus* | 0.0% | 0.0% | 5.0% | N/A |
| * Estimates only. ** From the U.S. Census Decennial Census, The Bureau didn't start issuing updates between each census until 1990. ***Joined the WCSD in 1964. N/A not available. | | | | |

Three elementary schools closed during ERA2 1967-1970 and three were opened. (Figure 2) Schools that had never black students were part of the district's adjustment to declining and shifting population patterns and to meet the state and federal guidelines for minority isolation schools.

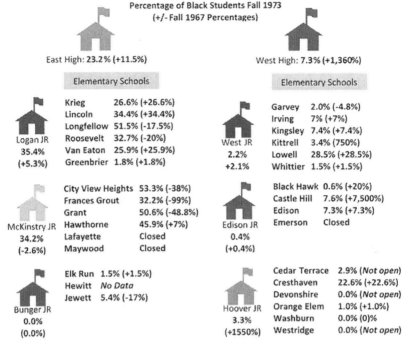

**Percentage of Black Students Fall 1973**
**(+/- Fall 1967 Percentages)**

East High: 23.2% (+11.5%)                    West High: 7.3% (+1,360%)

Elementary Schools                           Elementary Schools

Logan JR 35.4% (+5.3%)
Krieg       26.6% (+26.6%)
Lincoln     34.4% (+34.4%)
Longfellow  51.5% (-17.5%)
Roosevelt   32.7% (-20%)
Van Eaton   25.9% (+25.9%)
Greenbrier  1.8% (+1.8%)

West JR 2.2% +2.1%
Garvey    2.0% (-4.8%)
Irving    7% (+7%)
Kingsley  7.4% (+7.4%)
Kittrell  3.4% (750%)
Lowell    28.5% (+28.5%)
Whittier  1.5% (+1.5%)

McKinstry JR 34.2% (-2.6%)
City View Heights  53.3% (-38%)
Frances Grout      32.2% (-99%)
Grant              50.6% (-48.8%)
Hawthorne          45.9% (+7%)
Lafayette          Closed
Maywood            Closed

Edison JR 0.4% (+0.4%)
Black Hawk 0.6% (+20%)
Castle Hill 7.6% (+7,500%)
Edison     7.3% (+7.3%)
Emerson    Closed

Bunger JR 0.0% (0.0%)
Elk Run 1.5% (+1.5%)
Hewitt  *No Data*
Jewett  5.4% (-17%)

Hoover JR 3.3% (+1550%)
Cedar Terrace  2.9% (*Not open*)
Cresthaven     22.6% (+22.6%)
Devonshire     0.0% (*Not open*)
Orange Elem    1.0% (+1.0%)
Washburn       0.0% (0)%
Westridge      0.0% (*Not open*)

Figure 2 WCSD Black Enrollment Profiles, 1973 School Year

The data suggest two things: black residents were not able to easily buy homes on the West Side and that there was a white migration from the East to the West Side during that period.

## High School's a Brand New Game

*When I got to East after McKinstry, a lot of the kids from Logan knew some of my friends. We assimilated and I gained a lot of Logan friends. Mostly black kids. The white kids at East were a little uncomfortable about that. They were wondering why this white kid was hanging out with the blacks all the time. In gym class I got the look, "What makes you special?" Among athletes, it didn't matter color you were. You were in the "in crowd" anyway and everybody hung out together. There were many white students I went through Hawthorne and City View with who were good friends with the black kids. [EHS 73 WM]*

## Racial Relationships

A column by *Waterloo Courier Teen Page* East High correspondent Carol Dyball in December 1972 noted students found hate and prejudice "spiteful" and would "replace any hate with love" in the hearts and minds of people.

*"I'd change the colors of every person in the world." [Junior Carla Hutchins.] The world would be rather dull with everyone the same, but there couldn't be any complaints about color."*[5]

High school students in Waterloo were less isolated from and less immune to the conflict among the community, city administration and school district directed by the school board in ERA3 than those in previous decades.

*Confrontation was pretty much the way we lived every day at East. I was raised to NEVER [emphasized] use the "n" word, to treat people respectfully, and to expect to be treated fairly in return. At East, it always felt like there was no end to apologizing for being white, for things I had not done. [EHS 71 WM]*

*I had a confrontation with two black girls when I was at East. One of them came to me at our 30th or 35th reunion and apologized. She said, "I wanted to be your friend in school. But [name withheld] wouldn't let me." She told the girl we'd been friends since kindergarten. The girl said, "I don't care. I don't like her. You can't be friends with her." The woman telling me this had gone along and those two girls pounded my head in the ice on the sidewalk one day. The girl who apologized – we're sisters to this day. [EHS 73 WF]*

*The teachers we had the 1970s were very different than the teachers who were there in the 1960s. Some teachers were afraid of the blacks. Some stood up to them. I remember there was a fight one day. One of the teachers got right in between them. He lost his watch. But at least he broke it up. Not all the teachers would have done that. [EHS 73 WF]*

*We had the flood one year, and a bunch of my black friends and I walked downtown from City View one morning to help with the sand bagging and get free sandwiches. Later that afternoon, my friends, a bunch of other kids and I were on a truck going to deliver sandbags. I was the only white kid on the truck. [laughs] As I got on, a couple of black kids didn't like it. I told my friends it was OK, I'd see them later. And I started walking home, which is quite a walk from downtown to City View. My friends caught up with me about 10 minutes later and we all walked home together. [EHS 73 WM]*

*Sometimes some of the other black girls were very aggressive in their behavior. And because my skin color was whiter than white, I don't know if they expected me to be act more white. They'd push back sometimes, and I'd back down and tell them, "Don't worry about it." [EHS 74 WF]*

*Blacks were being bused to West, but I didn't really become friends with any of them. Some of the black guys would acknowledge you and talk to you in the hallway. "Hi. How are you doing?" Not mean things. Flirting. The black girls were kind of mean and I always thought it was because the black guys talked to us. I remember a black girl telling me she was going to kick my ass out of the window. She didn't say why. [WHS 74 WF]*

*Columbus taught you everybody was the same, everybody was equal. It was a little more of an enlightened approach back then. I would hear that at school and something else at home. Particularly from my dad. Because he had a different opinion about things. [COL 75 WM]*

*Most of my friends in City View were black. We played outdoors all the time growing up. As I got older, one of the main things we did was play a lot of football. Occasionally I'd invite some of my white friends who didn't live in City View to come play. And sometimes they would. But I didn't go out of my way to invite them. I hung in two different worlds in high school. I really wasn't an athlete. But my friends taught me football and I got into the sandlot version. It was a fun experience. I was basically an artist to another group of people. The white kids I hung with weren't the athletic types. Inviting them to play football would be really odd. [EHS 73 WM]*

*I don't remember a whole lot of racial strife between people at school. I saw a couple of black-white fights. The ones I remember fighting were whites, the punks and the bad guys. They loved to fight. Didn't matter who. I had blinders on in high school, didn't pay too much attention to things that may have gone on. I didn't dislike school all that much. I went in, did my work and was ready to go by the time the bell rang. When it rang, I was out of there. [EHS 73 WM]*

An argument in the East High library in February 1973 resulted in a white student being stabbed and a black student being arrested for carrying a concealed weapon.

Both students had permission to use a friend's car, which caused the argument. After a chair and a book had been thrown, the assailant took out his switchblade knife, he said, to protect himself because of a broken hand he was afraid to use in a fight. The victim was stabbed in the abdomen, but wasn't injured seriously. The assailant received a five-year suspended sentence and probation.[6]

A report by the Iowa Department of Public Instruction (DPI) noted that the stabbing of a white student by a black student three years earlier would have been seen as a racial incident, resulting in unrest or violence in the school and Waterloo.

*The way the incident was handled says a great deal about the student, the police, the administration and the parents involved. What it says about Waterloo is that the situation was handled in a spirit of mutual understanding and cooperation. [The community] accurately perceived [it] as an altercation between two students.[7]*

# Racial Bias in High School

The perceived academic biases experienced by students in ERA1 and ERA2 were less of an issue for *TBB* contributors who graduated in ERA3. (Table 2)

*The black students may have been disadvantaged in terms of not having black history taught at East. But they weren't disadvantaged in terms of an education. I thought we had some really outstanding teachers, good educators, professionals back then. Some really educated people. And for the students who were really there to get an education, it was available for them. Some people would just want to raise hell to be raising hell, using the black-white issue. Or maybe they didn't have a black counselor or administrator for a role model. Granted there weren't black administrators and black teachers [at the other high schools or towns around Waterloo. [Table 1] But they didn't hire inferior white educators. Teachers didn't teach the white people one way and the black people another way. Teachers simply taught and you had the choice to get the education or not. If you chose not to, you were left out, not because of the quality of the teacher. That was just making an excuse. Both blacks and whites got a good education. Down the road, the district was able to hire blacks and brought the percentage up. [EHS 71 WM]*

| FACULTY PROFILE | East High School | | | |
|---|---|---|---|---|
| | Female | | Male | |
| | Black | White | Black | White |
| ERA 1 1963 | | 18 | | 34 |
| 1964 | | 25 | | 39 |
| 1965 | | 24 | 1 | 41 |
| 1966 | | 28 | 1 | 41 |
| ERA 2 1967 | | 29 | 1 | 53 |

Table 2 Black & White Faculty at East & West High Schools, 1963-1973

| | | | | |
|---|---|---|---|---|
| 1968 | | 33 | 1 | 53 |
| 1969 | 2 | 14 | 1 | 42 |
| 1970 | 4 | 28 | 1 | 42 |
| ERA 3 1971 | 5 | 34 | 2 | 47 |
| 1972 | 4 | 29 | 1 | 49 |
| 1973 | 6 | 20 | 2 | 22 |

| FACULTY PROFILE | West High School | | | |
|---|---|---|---|---|
| | Female | | Male | |
| | Black | White | Black | White |
| ERA 1 1963 | 1 | 23 | | 33 |
| 1964 | 1 | 27 | 1 | 37 |
| 1965 | | 35 | 1 | 45 |
| 1966 | | 35 | | 48 |
| ERA 2 1967 | 1 | 36 | | 60 |
| 1968 | 1 | 38 | | 61 |
| 1969 | | 39 | | 66 |
| 1970 | 1 | 45 | | 72 |
| ERA 3 1971 | 1 | 55 | | 99 |
| 1972 | 1 | 42 | | 66 |
| 1973 | 6 | 38 | | 57 |

When Walter Cunningham[8] was principal at East, some of the blacks would whine about this and whine about that. And he'd tell them, "Don't talk about her that way, she's a great teacher. You're pulling the race card." He didn't pull it. [EHS 71 WM]

I got an "A" in the black history class and the black students were struggling to get a "C" or a "D." I felt bad, but I was doing the work. I wanted to learn and get good grades. I didn't know if I was being given those grades because I was the only white student and they wanted the program to be successful. I was too shy to ask. [EHS 71 WM]

*There weren't a lot of black kids in my classes and the ones who were there didn't seem to want to work hard. I couldn't figure that out and wondered, "Why are you here?" There was one black guy in history class who would stand up in the middle of the class while the teacher was talking, tuck his shirt in, pull his pants up and sit down. And I thought, "What's with this guy?" And nobody said anything. He later ran for mayor but didn't win. [EHS 71 WM]*

## Racial Division in High School

*One of the things that came out of all the trouble [in 1968] was the first black history class. It was an elective and I took it because I wanted to find out what blacks thought. I was the only white kid in the class. I was a little defensive because I was constantly asked to explain why white people did this or did that. I didn't learn much, because I was busy answering questions. I didn't realize it at the time, but I was experiencing what they did every day. [EHS 71 WM]*

By the 1970s, contributors' comments about racial divisions shifted from the school environment to what was happening in and the influences of racial relations in the external social environment, both local and national.

Proposed desegregation programs in Waterloo put pressure on both black and white students, which gave them a common "enemy" – the school board and administration – and reduced tensions among them. There's also a heightened sense of sensitivity to the black experience by white students in the ERA3 comments. This doesn't infer the *TBB* contributors in ERA1 and ERA2 weren't sensitive. The relative importance of the experiences, perceptions and insights of those in each ERAwere inherently different, since their educational pathways and school environments were different.

*Race riots were breaking out all over the U.S. when I was in high school. I was angry. I thought it was about time. The downtown section on the East Side next to the IC was gradually becoming more and more run down. Part of that had to do with the businesses and part had to do with black people . . . businesses were run by white people. The bakery, A&W root beer. That area was a bit mixed, but most of it was black. [COL 69 AAF]*

*We didn't talk about the East Side situations at Columbus. We did in my neighborhood [on the East Side]. I was involved in some of that, too. We had youth group in the old Elks Club near East High. I marched a couple of times. When they had the riots, my dad told us to stay inside. He said, "If you go outside and get in trouble and are jailed, I'm going to leave you there." [laughs] [COL 69 AAF]*

*We were in the [East] band room one day and there was noise outside. We all looked and there were black kids marching around. We started joking around about it. We didn't understand what the problem was. Turned out it was racial issues. Three years after the King assassination. They felt they weren't equal. [EHS 71 WM]*

*There were a lot of riots in the nation when I was in school. And a lot of issues, predominantly in the South, which weren't going on in the North. We saw stuff on TV and I thought, "Man, we've got that kind of problems in our society? I just thank God I'm not in that environment. That I'm here where I am [in Waterloo], can live a peaceful life. Or I can go where I want to go." I didn't grow up in the environment of water fountains for blacks and whites. I was fortunate God put me in a place I could grow. [EHS 73 AAM]*

*My brother was at a basketball game one time talking with a good black friend of his. Other blacks came up, hit his friend on the shoulder and, "Come on, let's go, Tom." That wasn't his name. It was a reference to him being an Uncle Tom. Right after Martin Luther King died in 1968, the blacks at East High organized a tribute to Dr. King at a school assembly. But they didn't tell anybody about it, which was the strange thing. Maybe it was out of fear. That they wouldn't be allowed to do it. There was a lot of tension at the time. At the rally, people just got up and started talking about Martin Luther King and what a great man he was.*

*My brother was interviewed on the radio and the first question was, "How did you feel about the blacks doing that?" My brother and our family felt that was an unfair way for the media to start the interview. But I've learned the media can manipulate the news to get the story they want. [EHS 73 WF]*

*I had black friend in high school and we're friends on Facebook today. Back then friendships were more confined to school activities. I don't know if it was human instinct. But there were no blacks on swim and tennis teams all three years I competed. During those teen years, there's so much going on as we develop into adults we couldn't just relax like we do in adult life. You're more free as an adult to be who you are. [EHS 73 WF]*

## RACIAL BIAS IN THE CLASSROOM

*I was in a lot of the college prep classes. It was pretty white in most of them, not that there weren't black kids. There were. And they were smart and should have been the classes. I don't know if the classes were white because that's what the blacks chose or that's what was chosen for them. I have no idea. There was talk black students were counseled differently. [EHS 74 WF]*

*When I was in college, I learned about something in black history a black person had done. I don't remember exactly what, but it was significant. And I thought, "I didn't know that. Why wasn't I taught that in high school? That should have been in my history book. It should have been in history, not just black history." I started questioning whether I learned history or white history. If whatever it was had been achieved by a white man, I would have been taught all about it. And it shouldn't be that way. There shouldn't be a black history class. It should be history. I didn't have a recognition of how much of history was missing because we didn't include black history. [EHS 74 WF]*

## BIRACIAL DATING

*The first time I saw biracial couples was when we moved to Cedar Rapids in the early 90s. I never saw so many biracial couples in my life. That was weird. With Waterloo having such a high population of black people, you would have thought here would have been more there. [EHS 73 WF]*

*You had biracial couples in high school. It happened. When you mix black and white, you don't care about color. You care about character. If you don't bring race into the issue, but look at the person's character from the inside where there is no color, that's how people fell in love with someone with different skin. [EHS 73 AAM]*

Biracial dating was less of an issue for students in ERA3. The battle against the administration's program to curb interracial dating at East in the late 1960s had essentially declined, and the local and national social stigma for biracial couples was weakening.

*There was one black guy, a very nice guy, who wanted to take me out on a date. I told him he was a nice person, but I didn't think it would work, because of my parents. They weren't prejudiced, but they didn't let me go out on dates anyhow. [EHS 70 WF]*

*You couldn't have a black date a white girl when I was in school. That was taboo. But it was almost as much of a taboo for a white guy from the West Side to date a white girl from the East Side. For a white girl from the East Side to date a white guy from the West Side, it was like moving up. A girl from the West Side dating a guy from the East Side wasn't hip. For the black guys, they thought it would be great to date white girls. The white guys didn't particularly like it, but there wasn't a lot they could do about it. For black girls. You didn't even think about dating a white guy. Not even close. If there was biracial dating, it wasn't public. Dating was on the sly. It wasn't where a black guy would walk into a dance with a white girl. Maybe after the dance they did get together down by the sand pits. [EHS 71 WM]*

There was a biracial couple who dated a long time. We thought they were good together. He had a white mom and a black dad, so he was biracial himself. I knew him from class. He was a very bright, articulate young man, so he was accepted anywhere, which helped him out. But they were considered a biracial couple. I know the two moms had a little trouble with it. But not our classmates. [EHS WF 71]

I remember biracial couples who wanted to date. But one or the other of them would get the heat. There were black boys I knew who were interested in white girls and the black girls would get upset. Or the white boys would get upset. To my knowledge, there were never real couples out for anybody to see. In my neighborhood, a Protestant dating a Catholic was worse. [EHS 72 WF]

Biracial dating caused a little bit of a stir. Some of the black girls didn't like the idea the black guys were going with the white girls. I had to deal with that one time. I was dating a black guy and he started dating a white girl. She was supposedly my friend, we were on the cheerleading squad together. I was jealous he was dating a white girl who was supposedly my friend. You never saw black females with white males. Because of the way, we were raised, I think with fathers and brothers. Even to this day I wouldn't think about dating outside my race, because I was raised to think like that. I went to lunch one day at East with one of the white football players. When I was in Catholic school, all I liked were white guys, because that's all I knew. [EHS 73 AAF]

In my senior year, I noticed there were more white girls kind of "cozying up to" – falling head over heels for – black guys than the two previous years I was there. Some were cheerleaders who started hanging out with some of my black friends. These were good guys. It shouldn't have mattered what color they were. [EHS 73 WM]

There was some reaction from both sides at East who thought interracial dating was wrong. One black guy said one time, "I don't *know why the black guys want to date a white woman. There's plenty of black women around. Keep it in your own race." [EHS 73 WF]*

*When I was in junior high, I liked a black boy and there was a black girl who didn't like that I did. And wanted to fight me outside behind the school. We met and shoved each other around a little bit. I felt at the time it was more of an, "If I don't stand up to this, it's going to be a problem." After that, we were good friends because she found I couldn't be pushed around. My parents eventually found out about my black boyfriend. They found out everything. They really liked him. But I think the concept [of interracial dating] was so new, they weren't ready. I had an older sister and she had a similar situation. [EHS 73 WF]*

*Don't fool yourself. There were biracial couples at West High, undercover. One of the black football players, all he had was white girlfriends. But it was all undercover. But at East High it was straight out. I tried to have me a white girlfriend and my mama said if I had a white girlfriend, "She better never come up into my house." [laughs] [EHS 74 AAM]*

*Interracial dating was new. In a way, it was a good thing and a bad thing. Just like integration was a good thing. When we were segregated, we knew we had to take care of our own. And then when we got desegregated, it was like, "Man, I've got white girlfriends and white friends. And I'm acceptable. We're cool now." The bad part of it was not every white person felt that way. There was still prejudice on both sides. You seldom came across any black women messing with a white dude. Now they do. Back then, that was a needle in a haystack. But you saw the white girls with black guys. But the black man heard about it. Black girls gave the black guys a lot of grief. "You going with that white girl, you traitor!" They were called "Uncle Tom." The white girl came to the black neighborhood. The black guy didn't go to the white neighborhood. The perception was she can't get no good loving from the white dude and the black dudes can take care of it. [EHS 74 AAM]*

Several of white East High female graduates were involved in interracial relations and marriages after graduation. The wasn't true for the either black or white contributors from the other four high schools.

## The High School Experience

*I didn't do any cruising on the strip. My dad had his thumb on me. We reported in. When East went to Sioux City to play football and we took a charter bus. And the bus was going to get back to East later than we planned. I was so happy we stopped in Fort Dodge so I could call and say we'd be late. [EHS 72 WF]*

Central High school opened in the fall of 1972 with students from West, East, Columbus and Orange High, which was closed. In early February 1973, about 100 Central students participated in a sit-in requesting a policy change that required them to stay on campus during the noon lunch hour, which was typically less than one-half hour.[9]

Open lunch had been the BOE policy until 1964 when it was changed and students were prohibited from leaving the school grounds during lunch. The reason given by the school district was that it was liable by law for the safety of all students during school hours, which included the noon hour.

The issue wasn't as important as student desegregation protests in previous years, but it was the first student activism since in the high schools since and the first for the new high school.

The protestors returned to class after 10 were selected to meet with East and West high representatives about approaching the school board to change the rule.

A motion to open school lunches at the BOE meeting on February 27 failed for lack of a second. The reason given was that existing school policy prohibited students from using cars during school hours, which they would during the lunch hour, a school hour. The Central High student body president argued ". . . a person is supposed to be responsible [when licensed] . . . Let us prove that responsibility." When the motion failed, the students walked out.[10]

In support of the measure, the East High student body president reported 80% of students, parents and faculty favored a trial suspension of the no-car rule, as did Waterloo restaurant owners who'd been surveyed.

A trial suspension of open lunch received board approval on March 12 for high schools that wished to participate. West High students said they didn't.

The open lunch hour went into effect at Central two days later.[11]

The trial suspension was to be reviewed by the BOE at the end of the year. Superintendent George Diestelmeier told students they would be "expected to return to class on time, obey traffic laws and etiquette rules" when off campus.[12]

No source was located that indicated whether or when open lunch became permanent.

*My first year at Central was the first year for all the students and my senior year. I was kind of in my own world that year. I was only at school half-time because I was through with all my classes and was basically doing extracurricular activities. I don't remember any racial tension or know there were that many black students. The only tension was we weren't united as a school. [CEN 73 WF]*

## EAST HIGH WAS A TOUGH SCHOOL

The traditional perception about East High was its "toughness" was due to black students who were more likely to cause trouble than the white students.

*When Howie Vernon was principal [at East], he had things in control. People would be pretty much respectful. After he was gone, I went into school after graduation one time and there was this black girl yanking on the tie of a black teacher, choking the crap out of him. He had his hands out, straight out, and wouldn't touch her. She was choking him like mad and her mother was beating on her, telling her,*

*"Let him go!" There was no respect. It was totally out of control. [EHS 71 WM]*

*East was a tough experience, but it made you a tough person. There was a lot of togetherness. It's like a brother and sister. You can fight among each other, but nobody else better call my sister or brother names. We were that close. It was a very strong school and very competitive. It was probably one of the times East experienced some of its best success in athletics and had some best athletes that ever went through there. I was very fortunate to be a part of it at that time. [EHS 71 WM]*

*It was tough, but the toughness was more because of the unique make-up of East and the turbulent times we were living in – Vietnam, Kennedy assassinations, MLK assassination, cultural revolution. It all seemed to percolate under the surface of the obvious racial tension. [EHS 71 WM]*

*There was probably at least one fight every week if not a couple of times a week. The best fights to see were two black women. I told my husband that and he wouldn't believe me. At one of my class reunions, he asked some of the black gals at the table if what I'd said was true. They told him there was nothing better. "Yeah, we don't hold anything back." Back in those days it was fight 'til the end. The black women were hot-headed. They fought more than the boys did. [EHS 73 WF]*

*The years I was at East, there was a boy shot at school, down in the basement near the shop. [No record of this incident was located]. There would be ruckuses where eggs would be thrown up and down the stairwells. And there was a stabbing my sophomore year. People not from Waterloo always thought East was a rough school. Mostly black. But I blame media bias. They were always reporting about the East Side and everything going on there. [EHS 73 WF]*

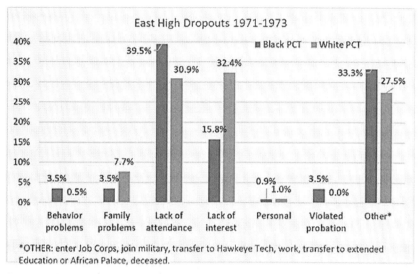

Figure 3 East High Dropouts by Race, 1971-1973
The two major causes of dropouts at East from 1971-73 were reported as lack of attendance or lack of interest. One third of black and almost 30% of white dropouts left school for a substitute form of education, personal development or financial support; deceased students also counted into the dropout rate.

Offenses that resulted in suspensions at East High from 1971-1973 included assault, behavior, cursing, fighting, fireworks, improper dress, insubordination, larceny, pot, smoking, threats and truancy. (Figure 2) Of the 474 suspensions in the 1971-73 school year, 60.8% were white students. The following year, there were as third as many suspensions; 68.5% were white students.

Dropout rates were also perceived to be an artifact of East High's black student population and its toughness, although data also challenge this perception. Roughly one-third of both black and white students dropped by East in 1971-73 were for lack of attendance or interest. Roughly one-third of both were reported as having dropped out for a substitute form of education, like African Palace[13], personal development or financial support.

## ATHLETES WERE ELITES

*I didn't play football or wrestle and West was always perennial champions. Swimming was a way to get attention from the girls and respect from the other guys. What I learned about the work ethic and competition was important to my life. That's taught better in high school athletics than it is in the classroom. I wish academics were as important in high school as athletics. There were no blacks on other swim teams. The wisdom was blacks don't swim and whites can't jump. [WHS 74 WM]*

The favorite part of high school for many was sports. Countless research studies discuss the life-long benefits of high school sports – improved academics, competitiveness, leadership, motivation, social skills, lifelong fitness, teamwork, et al.

For many who contributed to the *TBB* story, the benefit of sports was the camaraderie, the sense of belonging, the bonding, the sweat, the adrenalin rush, the euphoria of success, "the agony of defeat," the attention and adulation.

Sports is a stronger theme in ERA3 as desegregation broke up the long-standing championship junior high and high school teams.

*As an athlete, it was all about team. Working, playing together, everyone achieves more. We were looking to win, working together and solving that goal. Black and white didn't come into it. Sports really helped a lot. When you put the uniform on, you didn't see color. You just saw Orange and Black [East High's school colors]. [EHS 73 AAM]*

Relationships among athletes extended beyond the school's social environment.

*If you were an athlete, black teammates at East became friends and you got to know them a little better. You had to work to together as a team. One time we got some guys together to shoot some baskets at Grant School. It was night and some other black guys came up and started playing basketball, non-athletic kinds of guys. My black friends said it was probably time to pack it in and move on. They were basically saying, "We got your back, but let's not have a problem here with these guys." [EHS 71 WM]*

## ADVANTAGE/DISADVANTAGE FOR HAVING ATTENDED A HIGH SCHOOL

*Attending East gave me a leg up on others who led a less diverse high school life, because I was forced at a much younger age to deal with the feelings of other people. And to try to understand their perspective and attitudes towards myself, and the world we all live in. [EHS 71 WM]*

*To this day, I feel graduating from East is something to be proud of. I've embraced people of other races throughout my life, welcomed them into my home, and developed long-lasting friendships with them. [EHS 71 WM]*

*My 10th-grade geometry teacher had an impact on my life. Math was easy for me, but there were all different levels in the class and many didn't grasp it. But he reached every one of us. I remember him working with kids who had no idea what an angle was and saying to us who were able to do it, "All right, you go ahead and do it" while he worked with them, accommodating everybody. That was unheard of then. And he did it in a way that wasn't, "Those kids don't know anything. Let them GO [emphasized]." Did it in a way that everybody liked him. He probably wouldn't be teaching today, because he had a bottle in his drawer. [EHS 72 WF]*

*I was at East when Walt Cunningham was assistant principal and he was the disciplinarian. He didn't let anybody get out of line. I got dragged in there once for something I hadn't done. Something had been stolen out of the locker room during PE. I was in the academic vice principal's office when it happened. But got hauled in because I wasn't in PE. Mr. Cunningham chewed me up one side and down the other. And I'm like, "I didn't do it." Then the academic VP came in and verified my story. Walt ran a tight ship and nobody crossed the line. And he knew*

*how to talk to everybody. East High was pretty mild when I was there.*
*[EHS 72 WF]*

---

*I feel advantaged for having gone to a racially mixed school. When I*
*look at the experience of being around somebody that was different than*
*I was, I learned to get along with everybody. To treat people as equals.*
*Because we are all the same. I don't think my education suffered. I got*
*what I needed to get. I wouldn't have traded going to East for anything.*
*[72 EHS WF]*

---

*We had a cohesive environment at East High, black and white. We*
*played sports together, worked together. There weren't fights or issues.*
*We were all one. We were so busy trying to get an education and*
*survive. Our mindset was achievement and getting out of 'Loo and*
*getting on with our lives. Making the best of a situation. You got a*
*chance to network, collaborate, work with, cry with different races of*
*people. That's important. If you grow up in a setting of just your people,*
*your persuasion, your color. You don't get to know personally what it's*
*like to be with a person of a different race. You don't learn we have the*
*same things in common – the American dream. Marriage, education, a*
*good life. [EHS 73 AAM]*

---

*East High School was so big, the guy I sat next to at graduation – over*
*500 people – I'd never seen or met him my entire time at East. [EHS 73*
*WF]*

---

*I was advantaged for having gone to an integrated school because I*
*learned to live with people. And I'm not prejudiced against people. I*
*think people who went to all-white high schools are at a disadvantage to*
*a certain extent. They're not equipped to handle real life. When the*
*things to start happening in a small town where they may live, their*
*reaction is, "We don't want that happening in our town." They go to*
*these bigger towns and are overwhelmed. [EHS 73 WF]*

---

*Lack of diversity in school was a disadvantage. We lived on the West*
*Side and I spent most of my time at school. Nobody at Orange talked*

*about blacks. West Siders didn't know blacks or have black friends and they used racial slurs all the time. I was very offended by that. [CEN 73 WF]*

---

*Some of my friends lived in City View [on the East Side of the North End] and had to go to West High eight miles away rather than East, three miles away. I never wanted to go to West. I wanted to be at East High. East High had a lot pride. There wasn't anything that could compare to it. It put me in the position to have experiences which allowed me to become unbiased in judging people, on any side of this side community over any of the bridges. I learned to judge a person by the content of their character. [EHS 73 AAM]*

---

*When you walked into a bathroom wearing the East orange & black colors at other high schools which didn't have black students, especially outside of Waterloo, people thought there were riots in school every day and they asked about the killings in the hallways. "What's it like and are you scared?" At some of the schools, the perception was, "Oh, my god, you're from East Waterloo" and they'd go schizoid, almost cleared a path when you walked in. Which was convenient, because nobody messed with you. [EHS 74 WF]*

---

*Father Walter Brunkan had an influence on me at Columbus and in my adult life. He helped found Columbus, was vice principal then principal in 1968 for 20 some years. Plain spoken. An inspiration. Even faculty members were in awe of him. He was a normal guy. To the point, a good administrator. He had a vision for the school. He instilled values about working hard, caring for people. [COL 75 WM]*

## Search for an Acceptable Integration Strategy

*In my social foundations of education class in college, I did analysis of the Waterloo school district for an assignment. Analysis of the population, the diversity, money spent in the different schools, teachers' education, the economics and who lived where. One of the things which surprised even me was only 19% of the students were black in 1970. But everyone had the perception East was all black. That was about the time the federal government said the schools had to be integrated. And the school board said, "You can keep your federal money, we're going to do this our way." The district lines hadn't changed. There wasn't open enrollment. And that's how they ended up with such screwy borders for the different schools, [EHS 68 WF]*

The Civil Rights Act of 1964 mandated desegregation. However, it wasn't until 1974 that the school system developed a meaningful integration plan for its schools. (Figure 3)

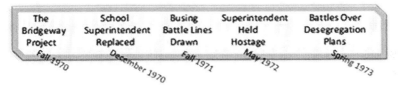

Figure 4 Five Major Events in ERA3 that Affected the Community & The Schools

*There were five major events in ERA3 that were an extension of the activism of the black community, the black students and their parents, plus an increasing number of white supporters that changed the direction of segregation in the Waterloo schools in both the near term and the future.*

In the 1954 case *Brown v. the Board of Education*, the U.S. Supreme Court ruled racially separated schools were "inherently unequal" and outlawed school segregation. A decade later, the Waterloo school district started using student transfers, a magnet program, building closings and attendance boundary changes to reduce the concentration of African Americans in certain schools.

Those efforts failed, primarily due to community conflicts and lack of support.

But in 1970, the continued pressure on the Waterloo school district from the black community and the local human rights commission, the Kansas City USCCR office and the Iowa DPI, East and West Side parents, and the philosophically polarized Citizen's Committee of the East Side and the Neighborhood Schools Association (NSA) forced the

Waterloo Board of Education (BOE) to create, evaluate, implement and test a variety of solutions.

The students were caught in the sea change of that they were generally unaware.

The community and the BOE were extremely busy during *TBB ERA*3 proposing, testing and implementing several solutions to the segregation in the Waterloo schools. This resulted in shifting school boundaries, dismantling the long-time neighborhood schools structure preferred by both black and white parents, segregation notwithstanding, and the necessity for busing, the most inflammatory civil rights issue in Waterloo and nationally.

## 1970 THE BRIDGEWAY PROJECT

*The Bridgeway project was a difficult time for all of us in grade school. Putting black children in predominantly white schools and vice versa. We were forced to segregate with not a lot of help from the adults. Many schools would close for days due to black and white tensions, but I believe we finally started making progress. Today, having a rainbow of grandchildren, I'm pleased to see things changed. [WHS 77 WF]*

Grant Elementary in the heart of the North End was 99.9% black. In 1970, it was designated as an integrated magnet school for educational innovation with an objective of a half-white, half-minority student balance, a moved described by a school board member as a "voluntary way to school desegregation."[14] The experiment was called the Bridgeway Project.

An experienced principal was assigned with a $120,000 budget to make physical alterations to provide open classrooms and learning centers to accommodate traditional and team teaching in ungraded classes. He was also given authority to recruit staff from the entire district.

BOE member Charles Dalton said, "[Bridgeway] will improve and expand educational opportunity for our young people. The students and Waterloo community will benefit [students] in education, human relations and understanding." Dr. Robert Harvey, the only black BOE member, called Bridgeway "the first step in a long-range program . . . toward equalizing and providing quality education for the total school population. . . . The culturally deprived and disadvantaged child will no longer be denied in any school because of race." He added the response by the community to this "new departure in educational endeavor can be heart-warming."[15]

Two black and two white parents who pre-registered their children for the Bridgeway Project cited interaction with children of the other race, and expansion of their students' social cultural and experiences as major participation incentives.[16]

In the first year, 76 white students enrolled in Grant and 68 black students transferred from Grant to white-majority schools.[17] The white students came from 15 different elementary schools and the parents of the black students placed their kids in five different district schools.[18]

In 1977, a staff report of the USCCR Midwestern Regional Office observed, "The qualities of Grant School – desegregation among them – are evidently attractive to white parents: the school board president, who was a leader of the antibusing Neighborhood School Association (NSA), sends his child to [the] school."[19]

## 1970 REPLACING THE SCHOOL SUPERINTENDENT

*GOOD LUCK to George Diestelmeier who Tuesday was named superintendent of the Waterloo schools. – Waterloo Daily Courier Editorial the day after his appointment four days before Christmas 1970.*[20]

Dr. Gene Lubera became the Waterloo school superintendent in October of the 1970 school year. A year later the communication gap between him, and the school board and community had widened to the point that the school board refused to renew his one-year contract. The superintendent and the board had several areas of disagreement during the year, and board members often made statements at board meetings about them.

In a Sertoma Club speech on September 16, 1971, Lubera said a KWWL television report about busing and cluster schools misrepresented his statement about the issue.

*I'm going to see that the press doesn't get more than "Mickey Mouse" news out of [the school administration], he told the members with media present. I'm going to protect myself and I'm going to tell my people we're going to protect ourselves. . . . We need laws to muzzle the press like we need laws to muzzle machine guns.*[21]

Dalton and other BOE members responded immediately, asserting commitment to the board's policy of informing the community through the press. "The press can be assured they will get complete information. Personnel of the school district will continue to cooperate as in the past in order to inform the public."[22]

Bill Severin, the *Courier*'s respected front page "The Iron Duke" columnist, took his gloves off when he wrote the following day that Lubera "seems to be suffering under the illusion the plans he has for administration of the schools is none of the public's business. . . . [His] tantrum Thursday was apparently prompted by anger at a report by the electronic media. But one thing is certain. On balance, he can't complain about the treatment he has received from the press during his relatively brief period of service in Waterloo."[23]

On Monday, September 20, a short three-paragraph article appeared in the *Courier* reporting Lubera's contract for the 1971-72 school year was "still" under discussion by the BOE. Ironically, the story was on the Obituary page.[24]

His resignation – which was requested by the board – was accepted by the BOE at its meeting that night, effective by December 31.[25]

In his letter, Lubera said he was resigning "against my better judgment."

*I cannot help but wonder if the Board of Education should not share the responsibility with me for any so-called breakdown in confidence and support. At no time during this brief administration was the board supportive in their remarks and feelings.*[26]

A *Courier* editorial reacted to the resignation two days later and provided a profile for the next head of the school system.

*Lubera's remarks about 'muzzling the press' . . . cannot be credited for his dismissal. Those intemperate remarks were only symptomatic of a deeper communication problem that had existed for some time. . . . [He] unfortunately failed to inspire the kind of confidence from others that his job requires, and he was asked to resign.*

*The Board must select a trained, intelligent administrator who has demonstrated the ability to work with people – and in our view, the mad doesn't necessarily need a Ph.D. to fill this bill. The important thing is his proven capability to perform a tough job.*[27]

The editorial was perceived by many in the town as a not-so-subtle endorsement of Diestelmeier, Lubera's deputy superintendent who also had been assistant superintendent for eight years Lubera's under predecessor, Dr. George Hohl. He'd been overlooked by the board to succeed Hohl, ostensibly because he lacked a Ph.D.

Diestelmeier sent a letter to each board member on September 29 requesting to be considered formally this time. "[Dr. Lubera's resignation] creates a situation that makes it essential that my position . . . be clarified in order to answer questions that are being asked in our community. Therefore, I am submitting this formal request to be considered as a candidate for superintendent of this district."[28]

He said he had discussed his application with Lubera and it wouldn't "hamper our relationship or the operation of the schools." [29]

On October 15, "The Iron Duke" column led with a short paragraph that reported three service clubs had taken straw votes and all showed "strong support" for the deputy superintendent.[30] He also received an endorsement from the junior high principals.

With no decision made by the BOE in mid-October, the Courier ran a two-column, almost half-page lead editorial on October 20 headlined, "Diestelmeier Merits Post of School Superintendent" that nudged the BOE to "get on with it" and name Diestelmeier as superintendent.

*[Beyond his wide support among community groups]. . . . there's ample evidence that [he] would be a capable superintendent. He's recognized as an able administrator, and has held both teaching and administrative posts since joining the school system in 1948. Over the years, [he's] had a hand in planning new school buildings, overseeing special services, setting up budgets and in coordinating the day-to-day operations of the schools . . . . he knows the community well . . . . [was] administrative assistant to Supt. Jack Logan . . . . assistant superintendent during the 8-year term of Dr. George Hohl. . . [and] deputy superintendent to Dr. Gene Lubera . . . . no "outsider" could match Diestelmeier's ready understanding of Waterloo problem. One hitch in the minds of some school board members seems to be that [he] lacks a doctoral degree. . . . [which has not been set by the BOE as one of its requirements. . . . Diestelmeier meets all the criteria set by the board. . . . is a "known quantity" in the community. He has performed capably for a number of years as an administrator in the Waterloo system. He deserves a chance at the superintendent's job.*[31]

On December 21, Dalton announced Diestelmeier had been selected over four other candidates and would be the new superintendent effective January 1.

Accepting, Diestelmeier said, "Combining our talent [on the administrative staff] with the resources of the community we, as a team, will find solutions to local educational concerns that will benefit our pupils."[32]

The next day a Courier editorial noted the challenges he was taking on.

*(He] has his work cut out for him. The district is now in the throes of deciding how to re-align attendance boundaries to accommodate the new Central High School. And one of the options is the controversial*

*"cluster" plan which would involve considerable busing. . . . Diestelmeier takes the job at a time when some tough decisions must be made. He'll need the support of the community.*[33]

Little did the *Courier* editorial board know how prophetic its appeal was.

In May 1971, a Waterloo BOE member made this statement in a closed meeting with the Iowa State Committee of the U.S. Commission on Civil Rights.

*The intent of the school administration and the school board is to proceed very gradually and with great caution. The Waterloo school district will probably do only a little more than it is forced to do to achieve desegregation of its schools. The school system has no plan for desegregating its schools, nor is it trying to develop one. Now this system buses something less than 300 children to white schools in what is called "voluntary open enrollment:" the children only go to schools where there is available space—and only those who volunteer to participate.*[34]

It's an accurate summation of the school board's position on desegregation. There's credible anecdotal information the school board at one point in time, responding to external pressure to desegregate, stated it would forego state and federal money to be able to run the school district as it saw fit without outside direction.

Desegregation would be Diestelmeier's constant and most challenging responsibility during his tenure.

## 1971 BUSING BATTLE LINES DRAWN

*I drove a school bus for eight years. It wasn't open enrollment – it was busing. Some of the grade school kids were on the bus more than a half an hour in the morning and again in the afternoon. [EHS 66 WF]*

*When one drives by Grant School, you see all blacks and all whites grouped together. Has [busing] done anything when one [sees this?] – NSA President Robert Clark*[35]

Both the Citizen's Committee of East Waterloo and the NSA would be key players in school activism in ERA3 of *The Bridge Between*.

The NSA was formed on September 21, 1971, as a group opposed to busing for desegregation. Its self-described "sole purpose is to strive to preserve the traditional neighborhood school concept. . . ."[36] The organization's four positions were:[37]

1. Favoring integration on a voluntary basis.
2. Favoring neighborhood school concepts.
3. Opposing a city-wide program of involuntary student assignment.
4. Opposing a city-wide program of involuntary student movement.

Clark criticized a local TV newscast that inferred the NSA leaders were a "racist" group. Stating blacks had been invited to join the group, he said, "I'm one of the leaders. I'm not a racist and I don't like it. These meetings are open to everyone, anybody is welcome."[38]

In two months, the group had 2,700 members. Two weeks after the Iowa DPI consultant team working with the Waterloo school board on integration strategies issued a report in November calling for mandatory busing, the NSA had 5,420 paid members.[39]

*I fought against [busing] because I thought it was wrong. That the school board would rather take kids all over town in buses because in these poor areas they're talking about – the East Side – they couldn't hire as good a teacher as they could on the West Side or Columbus and Cedar Falls. And I thought, "Why can't we have those West Side teachers on the East Side?" I don't believe busing has achieved its purpose. I think it's been a huge expense. But the government said if we didn't do it we would lose tax money. So, we had to do it. I don't believe it would have been more expensive to hire some better teachers on the East Side. I don't believe busing has been cheaper than what would happen losing federal money. [EHS 66 WF]*

*When busing started, a lot of East Side kids went to the West Side for integration, but they never bused any West Side kids over to the East Side. So, West kept getting bigger and bigger. Right now [2016] on a good day, East High is 950 kids and West is 1600 kids. The disparity is really noticeable. And that's grades nine through 12. The closeness we had when I was in school has been a victim of change. The transient moving from school to school took away a lot of the fierce loyalty. Students can transfer voluntarily. A lot of kids transfer here and there. When we went to Logan, everyone went to East High School. You went to McKinstry, everybody went East High School. Today, for example, if the test scores at Logan Junior, which is now Carver Middle School, are lower, a kid living right on Logan Avenue can transfer to any other school which is a high achievement school. In the old days, it was "tough crap," you go to school where you live. [EHS 71 WM]*

*My most impactful high experience was in my senior year. I took one class in advanced electronics at West High which wasn't offered at East and was bused over to West High. There were other eight to 10 other East students bused over for the class, which was basic electronics, one of whom was black. The instructor set me up with my own advanced program beyond the basic level. [EHS 71 WM]*

*We didn't mess around too much on the West Side, man. They didn't want us there no way. That's what we hated. We're being bused to school at West High and these white people don't even want us over here. I lived right next to Highland, which at that time was where the rich white people lived on the East Side. I had white friends, but they didn't want to talk about the school system. My black friends and I talked about it like, "What are we doing over there at West?" We didn't like it. The white people are prejudiced. We should be going to East. They brought whites from the West to East High. And boy, they hated that. [laughs] And the way they made us feel at West High, that's how we made them feel at East High. We'd go to East football games at Sloane Wallace and walk home to the East Side. There used to be so many police out there following us. And we would ask, "Why doesn't West ever come over to the East Side to play?" But those white parents weren't going to come over to the East Side. [long laugh] [EHS 74 AAM] [There wasn't a serviceable stadium on the East side.]*

*As an 18-year-old in the early 70s, why would someone from West want to go to East High? [WHS 74 WM]*

When Diestelmeier retired in 1982, Betty Jean Furgerson, a member of the school board and director of the Waterloo Human Rights Commission, cited that an early busing experiment had included busing white students from some prominent West Side families to Grant School on the East Side, which had a student population more than 90% black.

*George knew the politics of the town and what needed to be done. So later when we began to deal with busing all over town there were some prominent people who already had been through it. . . . He had a real good feeling for his community and it showed when be steered it through some of the early problems [with integration in the 1970s]. . . . If this had not been George's home community I am not sure be would have survived as long as he did with the tough decisions that had to be made.[40]*

## 1972 PARENTS PROTEST USE OF *LITTLE BROWN KOKO AND THE PREACHER'S WATERMELON* TEXT

*One of the largest peaceful demonstrations in the civil rights period in Waterloo[41] [occurred Wednesday, May 24, 1972, when a group of about 30 black parents and Coalition for the Black Community members marched] into the startled [Alice Margaret Hayes', 67] classroom [at West Junior High School in Waterloo, IA and announced they wouldn't leave] until she was fired[42] [for using] material in class which was offensive to everyone. . . ."[43]*

The "material" used by Mrs. Hayes was the book *Little Brown Koko and the Preacher's Watermelon*.[44] She'd "been reading the story . . . to her speech and drama class [for the previous 10 years as part of the class unit on "dialect"][45]. "When black students began busing to the school three years ago, Mrs. Hayes was always careful to ask if any objected, recognizing the stereotype the title implies. This year members of Waterloo's black community were riled by the story, and expressed their feelings two weeks ago [with the classroom protest]. . . ."[46]

One paragraph from the book termed typical of the rest of it by the group says, *"Just then a great, big idea popped into Little Brown Koko's black wooly head. What do you think he did? Why, he took a knife out of his pocket – the one grandpap had given him for Christmas and it would really and truly cut things too."*[47]

The group spend the entire day in the classroom, and promised to return the next day and "fill the school." They told Principal Joseph Boyle his name should be added to the list to be fired. Doyle explained the matter had been brought to his attention the previous week, it was being investigated, and he and the district's school-community relations coordinator had already met with a group of concerned parents.

Several black students had presented him with a petition that stated the material was offensive, recommended actions and stated they would take whatever action was needed if they weren't. He also told the parents he wouldn't recommend firing Mrs. Hayes with her 30 years of service based on one piece of material she used. Only her firing was acceptable to the group.[48]

The parents' response was unbending.

*It's too late for an apology on something like this. We understand she's been using this for 10 years. We question how much more material like this is being used in Waterloo schools. We have taken over the class so she can't teach the kids any longer and will continue to come to the school until she is fired. It ought to be clear that we're going to stay here.* . . ."[49]

Superintendent Diestelmeier delivered a letter to Doyle recommending Hayes be suspended from her teaching duties for the rest of the year.[50]

The Waterloo school board, composed of six whites and one black member, however, voted 6 to 2 to reinstate Hayes. Saying she was "acting in the interest of all concerned,"[51] she chose not to return. The last day of classes was June 01, five school days after the occupation.

On May 25, the day after the parents took over Hayes' classroom, white West Junior students massed in the hallway front of Doyle's office for about 10 minutes at the start of school chanting, "We want Mrs. Hayes." They and several black students went to the auditorium where Doyle said he would talk to them.

A black student asked white students if they even "knew the facts. I don't think you really know what happened."[52]

After 20 minutes of more chanting for Hayes during which Doyle wasn't given a chance to be heard, he dismissed school at 10:15 a.m.

*Jet* magazine[1] said the *Waterloo Daily Courier* story reported "the students merely chanted, 'We want Mrs. Hayes,' during the protest."[53] The article disputed that account.

"Black students and parents charged that the white students 'put on a white power rally' [in the auditorium] during which they shouted, 'Down with niggers! Up with Mrs. Hayes.'"[54]

Diestelmeier and community-school relations coordinator Ray Richardson went to the junior high school that morning, and some 100 white students met with Richardson at the school administration building shortly before noon.

---

[1] Jet was founded in 1951 by John H. Johnson of the Johnson Publishing Company in Chicago and is an American weekly marketed to African-American readers.

## 1972 Occupation of the School Superintendent's Office[55]

While the protest was occurring at West Junior, a group of an estimated 150 black adults and children gathered at Sullivan Park on East 4th Street kitty corner from the IC railroad for a "strategy meeting." At 3 p.m., they began marching around the school administration building, which was about two miles away on the West Side.

*Our first apartment when I was married after high school was right across the street from the school district office. I will never forget the heartache and the scariness when there was a riot circling the building because they were upset Mrs. Hayes told the "Little Black Sambo" story she always did. It was a speech class. She told stories in class. She was very dramatic. Somebody decided to be racial and she should be fired. I was very scared and was like, "What on earth?" I was so hurt because I loved Mrs. Hayes. I had her from 7th grade and was in all her classes. She impacted my life and loved her to no end. And she went to my church. I remember going to Sambo's Restaurant in Waterloo. And nobody thought anything about it. We ate pancakes and stuff. [WHS 70 WF]*

The protestors entered the building and took over the superintendent's office. (Figure 4) When Diestelmeier tried to leave, he was told "he would have to walk on, or over, the people there to do it."[56] And his office would remain occupied until their demands had been answered. These included a special board meeting to fire Hayes and Doyle, closing West Junior High for the final few days of the school year and immediately beginning in-service training for school personnel.

Figure 5 Superintendent George Diestelmeier

*Because of the recent events at West Junior High School; and because of all the humiliating incidents our children have been subjected to in the Waterloo School System; because of the insensitivity of the superintendent and the majority of the school board to our needs at the other schools; because of your treatment of the 10 points presented by Dr. Robert Harvey; we come as concerned citizens to make [these] demands: . . . .* [57]

At 6:10 p.m., the assistant county attorney spoke to the protestors with a bullhorn.

*We ask that you allow [Diestelmeier] to go to the public meeting. We come in peace. We ask that you leave peaceably. If you don't we will use the laws of Iowa to remove you." A note was held up to the window stating that the people inside couldn't hear what he was saying.* [58]

At 7:11 p.m., with the sit-in unresolved, officers broke into the office and escorted Diestelmeier out "pale and visibly shaken." He first asked authorities to talk to school board members and administrators who were meeting to decide whether schools would be open on Friday. [59]

His second request was to be allowed to re-enter the building to talk to the sit-in group still in the office. He argued the protestors "merely 'wanted to make their point'" in the Hayes controversy. He was persuaded not to do so and was driven home by a police detective. [60]

The school board went into an emergency meeting while about 150 blacks sat in the reception area and said they wouldn't leave, but wouldn't resist arrest. The assistant police chief promised no mace, night sticks or handcuffs would be used if the protestors submitted to arrest peaceably. One woman responded the building was a public place. "It's our building. We don't have to leave."

County Attorney David Dutton arrived at 7:30 p.m., emerged from the emergency school board meeting at 8 p.m. and talked to the group. He told them he was asking for an injunction against the sit-in and warned the group about the "new Iowa criminal trespass law which

[made] occupying a public building when asked to leave an indictable misdemeanor."

Noting both sides were convinced of the "justness of their [situations]," Dutton said, "We have to keep order. Our job is not to engage in any rough tactics. We want to treat you as citizens who deserve respect."

He returned at 9:55 p.m. with the injunction, but waited about five minutes before reading it until the Joe Frazier-Ron Stander heavyweight fight the protestors and others were watching ended.

Dutton told them any person who violated the injunction would face a six-month jail term and some were already guilty of criminal trespass due to the damage. Those remaining had a choice of being booked at the school administration building and being contacted later by authorities or being booked at the police station at city.

Some of the protestors left, but about 65 chose to be arrested and taken to the police station. Two dozen helmeted officers entered the lobby and arrested the protestors without incident. They were booked, photographed and released on their own recognizance. One report said 63 were led out of the school administration building, but only 32 were booked.[61]

During the occupation of the superintendent's office, the "group of blacks played soul music on the piano, munched potato chips and watched another fight on television. . . ." Phone lines were torn out, including the phone in the superintendent's office, receivers from phones in the reception area and the school board room were removed, a pay phone was tied up and not even newsmen could call out of the building.[62]

The next day, Friday, none of the black students at West Junior were in school. About 100 white students walked out and called to others to join them from the other side of the 5th Street, across from the school.

Innocent pleas were filed on June 30 by all 23 adult defendants charged with criminal trespass in the occupation of the school superintendent's office.

## The Public Speaks

*[May 28] Can vigilantes dictate to our school system? The apparent answer to this question is yes. . . . Is it democratic when a group of 30 can come into a public classroom and threaten not to leave unless a teacher, who has been teaching for 30 years, is immediately suspended? The answer to this is obviously no. However, the morning of May 24 it happened at West Junior High. . . . why go through proper channels by taking your complaints to the principal or superintendent. . . . when you can take your vigilante committee and barge directly into a classroom and threaten the school administration and know you can get away with it? Undoubtedly some of you will immediately say I am prejudiced. However, are you saying this because you really believe I am, or because you're afraid of the simple truth? Van G. Miller*

*[May 28] After seeing the action that took place at West Junior High over a simple little story, I think it's time the majority spoke up. . . . what right do 45 students have to disrupt the schedule of 1,200 students? This "Civil Rights" bandwagon has been ridden too far, and unnecessarily. . . . It seems this certain group of people holler, burn, demonstrate, and protest against segregation, but they do, in fact, segregate themselves. For instance, there is a club here in Waterloo that was set up by and for black women. . . . a group of black businessmen [set] up their own little organization. . . . [there's the] "Miss Black Waterloo" contest. . . . the big, fancy explanation . . . [is] "helping them better understand their ethnic background," but let a white person try this and his accused of being a segregationist, a racist. I can't even imagine the hollering that would go on if there were a "Miss White Waterloo" contest. All I can say . . . is these people are the best campaigners George Wallace ever had. [Name Withheld]*

*[May 30] When I was a child, one of my favorite stories was "Little Black Sambo." I thought he was really a clever little boy for outsmarting the tigers the way he did. Children see things so much differently than we do as adults. Why can't we all love on another as people should? Oh, how wonderful that would be. But, no, that's not nearly as exciting as our fighting. Our poor beautiful innocent children. Forgive us all! Too bad we don't have some of the children's brains. Maybe then we would have a lovely country to live in. My skin is white, but my heart is all colors, and very sad. [Name Withheld]*

*[June 7] Back in 1924, the witty H.L. Mencken of the Baltimore Sun reported the events surrounding the dismissal of John Scopes, a high school biology teacher. . . . [who exposed students] to Charles Darwin's "Origin of the Species" describing evolution. Scopes was dismissed because his subject matter was regarded as derogatory to human beings. . . . If Mencken were alive to report parallel events in the Waterloo school system, he would need to make a few revisions in his . . . reports . . . [about] an English and speech teacher who "honestly exposed her classes to Blanche Hunt's 'Little Brown Koko and the Preacher's Watermelon,' a children's short story illustrating an author's abundant and repetitive used of adjectives. . . . two school board members do not wish this kind of intellectual pursuit. . . . [and would perhaps] be content if our children merely learned by rote selections from Bunyan's "A Pilgrim's Progress" or "Bay Psalm Book" and nothing else. Scott Hughes*

*[June 7] My daughter was suspended for walking out [during the protest at West Junior]. I feel the schools are using our children. This is a protest against prejudice in any form. The school's personnel is [sic] guilty of pitting children against each other. When you administer any form of discipline, it is the child you must look at, not his or her color or economic status. . . . I have five children who have gone through the schools of Waterloo. Four daughters have graduated from high school. The one I have in school now will be the fifth. As a mother, I will say they learned the three R's well, but they learned very little about the*

persecution of minority groups. They will live well in the middle-class society, but they will not understand the heartaches of minorities. . . . [which isn't] entirely the schools' fault. I must also take part of the blame because I also believed only in the material things of life and not the human aspects. . . . We can all learn a valuable lesson from this protest. I never once heard the word "love" mentioned from either side. Is that word so hard to say and practice? Accept people for what they are, not for what their color or status in the community is. Leulla Morelock

[June 8] After all the demands for black literature in the schools, why all the protest about the story of "Little Brown Koko and the Preacher's Watermelon?" That's black literature. Regarding Koko's thick, wooly hair, that shouldn't be so degrading what with all the Afro hairdo's [sic] so prominent today. About cutting up the watermelon with a sharp knife, we always use a sharp knife to cut our watermelons/ Is there another or a better way? I'd like to know it. So, what's the gripe? [Name Withheld]

[June 14] A hundred years ago Mrs. O'Leary's cow kicked over a lantern that started a conflagration which destroyed most of Chicago. Recently a story was read in a school that gave rise to a chain reaction of a different nature, that has engulfed the entire city of Waterloo and has endangered peaceful relations. . . . The story itself was just the match that lit the pile of grievances which have building up for a long time . . . . The pity . . . is white people see nothing wrong with the presentation of the story or anything offensive about it, and do not understand why the blacks should be so worked up. [They're] content with the stereotype presented, while the distortion is painful to the blacks. There are some whites . . . who do understand . . . . [and] stoically endure the taunts and ostracism [and being called] "nigger lovers" . . . . Outward conditions are not going to change until the inner heats a purged. The branches of inequality will fall off only when the roots of insensitivity are removed. Grace B. Potter

In March 2016, several participants of the 1972 sit-in protest met in Diestelmeier's old office in the school administration building to share their recollections as part of a Black History Month story in the *Waterloo-Cedar Falls Courier*, "Remember Waterloo schools sit-in."

The headline on the front page of the *Courier* said, "Diestelmeier Held Hostage."

That wasn't true according to the reunion members.

*He could have walked out – but not without walking on top of them as they lay in his office. Diestelmeier wasn't going to do that. He knew the protesters and they knew him. They respected each other. "George just sat there. We talked just like we're talking now," said [Harris] Cease [publisher of the Waterloo Defender black newspaper]. There was no reason to be upset. . . . There was no fear in him."[63]*

Bev Smith, WCSD's associate superintendent for human resources and equity, was one of the protestors in the hallway outside Diestelmeier's office. A 1970 East High School graduate, she was a student at Cornell College in Mount Vernon at the time.

*[The reunion] just kind of blew me away. It flooded back to me, the power of that time. I got to be a part of that. That was a part of history. At the time it didn't hit me like it does now. It was overwhelming just as I started looking at where we were then and where we are now. It's just amazing. [She told the group] you're heroes and heroines. [But] we're still nowhere near where we need to be. And we have so much left to do."[64]*

Smith is responsible for recruiting and retaining minority teacher talent in the system.

The sit-in was another tentative step in the school system's integration.

*Painfully, grudgingly, things began to change. The Waterloo School District may have been tardy to class on desegregation, but it was a quick study. Unlike many cities across the country, Waterloo adopted a school desegregation plan without a court order a few years later.[65]*

The *Courier* editorial board offered its state-of-the-community perspective.

*Neither the Waterloo Schools nor the city of Waterloo as a whole has become a utopia of racial inclusion. But it is important to note how far we have progressed from the days of the sit-in. Those involved are the ones who saw our community through trying times, and we are the better for it. . . . The 1972 sit-in was resolved and resulted in tangible change because key people treated each other with respect and saw each other not as colors, but as neighbors, friends, co-workers and parents who could reason together and resolve differences, especially when young people are at stake. Let us carry forward their example, in thought, word and deed, to future generations.* [66]

## 1972 PICKETING OF LOGAN PLAZA STORES

The protest group that had occupied Diestelmeier's office "continued picketing despite a temporary injunction that was issued against them" and expanded their protest into a boycott of Waterloo businesses, focusing on the Logan Plaza Shopping Center on Logan Avenue and East Hanover Street.

On June 21, the first person to be sentenced in connection with picketing at the plaza was given a 12-day jail term in the county jail after having been found guilty in a trial by judge. The person had five prior assault and battery charges extending back to 1964. [67]

A list of demands was presented to the four Logan Plaza merchants:

- a hiring quota system for blacks based on the amount of black business at each store.
- 80% of employees at all levels be from the blacks or low-income whites from the East Side.
- promotion of qualified blacks when openings are available.
- prices comparable to other Waterloo stores.
- a change in personnel attitudes toward food stamp and black patrons.[68]

Another was the plaza merchants "immediately stop discrimination" against the *Waterloo Defender*," the local black newspaper, in buying advertising and sign a contract that job openings for minorities would be advertised through the paper. The publisher and five directors listed on the paper's articles of incorporation were leaders of picketers at the Logan Plaza. [69]

The picketers took a one-and-a-half-day break after the demands were submitted, but resumed when the merchants wouldn't meet all of them. [70]

After three weeks, the boycott had "caused a [70-80 percent] loss of business to [the four stores]. . . ." The manager of the Ben Franklin Store filed a complaint with Waterloo police on May 28 charging customers were bothered by black pickets urging shoppers to boycott the stores.

Tension surrounding the boycott was heightened by individual acts of violence at the picket lines. Two black girls were hospitalized with leg and back injuries after apparently being struck allegedly by a car deliberately driven into the picket line by a 52-year-old white woman. No charges were filed against the driver, who said the girls were pushed in front of her car.

Noticeably absent from the picket lines were members of the local [NAACP] chapter and many of the towns black ministers. J. Russell Lowe, Waterloo's NAACP president, implied he had not involved the group because he "had not been requested to meet with the folks who are boycotting." Lowe added his policy towards the boycott was, "If I do not join you, I will not hurt what you are trying to do."

*Jet* magazine's story covered the long-range effects of the boycott from a white perspective.

*"This type of thing generates the kind of publicity which makes families and businesses afraid to locate here," said Robert Buckmaster, former mayor of Waterloo. [A community leader throughout his adult life, Buckmaster was mayor for nine months in 1947, appointed when the elected mayor died.] He said he and other whites have worked with*

*"responsible Black [sic] leaders" to bring about viable interracial relationships in Waterloo. "But now, [the boycotters have] yanked the rug out from under me," Buckmaster said. "I've lost credibility in the white community. Now, the whites are coming to me and saying, 'See . . . [sic] I told you that you couldn't trust them.'"[71]*

The picketing at Logan Plaza ended July 01 after almost six weeks following a meeting between the pickets and representatives of the four stores at which a proposed agreement was reached. It was approved by the black community at a 1 p.m. meeting. The official announcement said, ". . . a working agreement was reached relative to the demands which were presented to the store managers [on] May 26." One of the protest leaders advised that, while the Logan Plaza picketing was over, "some type of future action might be taken against other businesses in the city."[72]

During the six weeks of picketing, the school board adopted policies "closely congruent with black demands while the [Logan Plaza] shopping center stores agreed to hire more blacks. 'When we look at the cost of the demands,' [Waterloo Human Rights Director Willie] Mosley said, 'we got a negative response. We polarized the community more than it has been polarized before.'"[73]

A change of venue was ordered on July 6 for the trial of one of the picketers on assault and battery for allegedly kicking a Logan Plaza customer crossing the picket line [on June 5].[74] As a result, the Black Hawk county attorney asked the judge the following day to also transfer all 33 remaining cases to the Cedar Rapids, Iowa, municipal court. The judge said he didn't know if the defendants in those cases wanted changes of venue or whether any would be given.[75]

## The Public Speaks

*[June 14] I was employed at Logan Plaza . . . until lay-off recently due to picketing there. It's pretty bad when blacks destroy the jobs of those willing to work. . . . My employer is in trouble. He's lost a lot of business from the harassment of customers. . . . Even after all the picketing is over*

*I probably will not be called back because of all the business that has permanently been destroyed. It wouldn't be so bad if only the police would stop the blacks from harassing the people, black and white, who wish to use the stores. . . . It seems when an incident occurs the police have their backs turned. Then they rush over to escort the shopper away. [Name Withheld]*

*[June 21] If there are any sane, rational and fair-minded leaders in the black and white communities in the present Waterloo school crisis, it is time that they rise to the occasion. . . . the taxpayers of this community, all the students and personnel associated with the Waterloo school system deserve far better. It should not be forgotten that everyone has the right to be heard, but no one has the right to demand to be obeyed. . . . Also, white people should have some civil rights in regard to fair hiring practices and placement of personnel. [The current demands by blacks are simply] reverse racism directed against those white people who have a right to expect fair hiring and replacement practices. Justice, not overreaction or appeasement, is what is needed and respected. So, let's stop picketing innocent store operators, and stop the sit-ins, the walk-ins, the stand-ins, the walk-outs, the destruction of property and the absurd demands. . . . [and] get down to some serious, common sense, rational discussions. . . . It is long overdue. [Name Withheld]*

*[June 21] . . . the black people have gone too far this time with the picketing at Logan Plaza. Why are they trying to ruin all the business places on the East Side? . . . It won't be there long and there won't be anything left on the east side. Then they will start complaining that they need more new buildings put up for them. I've been shopping at the Logan Plaza for years, and I don't want any black or white telling me not to shop there. I call that plain dictatorship. The pickets have called me some pretty raw names, but like the saying goes, "Sticks and stones. . . ." I say grow up and stop acting like a bunch of kids. [Name Withheld]*

*[June 21] As a concerned resident of Waterloo, I've had it with this Logan Plaza incident. . . . [which] is hurting both the blacks and whites*

*of this community. I have read the 14 demands and all I can say is these people are unreasonable. You can't fire a white principal and replace him with a black [one]. If a vacancy occurred and a black is qualified for the job, then put him in that position. But I don't agree with kicking someone out just because his skin happens to be white . . . . [Blacks complain] their kids aren't getting the same education as the whites. I disagree. . . . If a child is black, yellow or red, he can learn something just as long as he has the will to learn. . . . What our city needs more than bridges across the river are bridges between blacks and whites. . . . [Name Withheld]*

*[June 23] Well, Lincoln freed the slaves. Now let's get a new mayor to free the white people in Waterloo. Other towns around are laughing at us. [Name Withheld]*

*[July 7] From the outset of . . . the West Jr. sit-in, to the take-over of the School Administration Building and the month-long picketing, I have been one of the most outraged citizens of Waterloo. Being involved in a minor incident at Logan Plaza did not help matters any. As usual, most people are heaping the lion's share of the blame upon the blacks, which seems only logical since it was they who were doing most of the protesting. . . . [Why is little or nothing said about] the whites who picketed and demonstrated at the school and Plaza along with the blacks [are as much, if not more, to blame than the blacks]? The peaceniks, disenchanted college students, etc., always seem to find a black cause upon which to attach themselves. Yet, when the man on the street sees things like Logan Plaza he cries that the blacks are taking over America. Blacks, when are you going to wake up and see that you are only being used by people who are trying to further their own causes? . . . . [sic] It is my opinion that the best thing that can come out of this is for the community to realize that some whites and not all blacks went along with these demonstrations. [Name Withheld]*

## 1972 CENTRAL HIGH SCHOOL OPENS IN THE FALL

Waterloo voters were asked in the fall of 1968 to approve a $5.8 million bond issue that would include a new high school for 1,500 students. It would serve all sections of the city to ease serious overcrowding in the three existing public high schools – East, Orange and West – and handle projected future high school enrollment increases. (Figure 6)

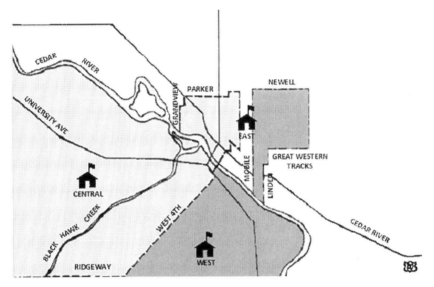

Figure 6 School Boundary Map for Central High School Opening in 1972

There were 14,000 students in the district in 1960. Enrollment for the fall 1968 school year would be 20,000 with a projected increase to over 21,000 by 1972.[76]

The bond issued was passed.

*In Westbourne Terrace addition North of Platt's Nursery. Excellent school situation. Brand new high school within ½ mile in fall 1972.[77] Real Estate Listing, fall 1969.*

In the time when a majority of classified real estate listings in the *Courier* prominently identified the school for the residence, realtors were already pushing the proximity of the new high school to listings two years in advance.

Central High School opened at Huntington and Hackett Roads on the West Side in 1972 at an estimated cost of $4 million. The two major advantages were "good" access and it's "a great distance" from the city's three current high schools, according to Superintendent Hohl.[78]

When it opened, Orange High School closed. Orange had a long and rich history, graduating its first class of nine students in 1918. The last class to graduate from Orange High in 1972 had 110 students.[79]

*I never felt the Waterloo schools did anything for the black students and families. Their solution was to build Central. It didn't take a genius to figure it out. Why are they building Central? So, the whites don't have to go to school with the blacks. [EHS 66 WF]*

*The district started busing when it started self-desegregating the schools. A lot of East Side kids went to West, but not many bused from West to East. Then the school board built Central High School as kind of an appeasement. Some of the East- and West-Side kids went to Central. The concept of the neighborhood school was lost. I taught at Central and that was really a tough school, because it was the melting pot. There was really no school loyalty. [EHS 71 WM]*

*I left McKinstry Junior High and went to East in the fall of 1971. There wasn't open enrollment. It was busing. And we got upset. Because McKinstry was 5-1 football and Logan was 4-0 that year. Logan and McKinstry were getting ready to join together at East. We would have probably won the state championships in football and basketball and wrestling and everything else. Busing broke that up. And we felt like the white man did this on purpose to split us up. That's when they started sending blacks to West High. And came up with Central School. [laughs] I really don't even understand. Why are they having a central school? Because there's always been an East and a West high. I don't know whether it was a money thing or what. We used to call Central a penitentiary back in the day because the windows were so high up, you couldn't get out. And then they closed it after 10 years. [EHS 74 AAM]*

*Central High was going to open our senior year and people started talking about "maybe I will go" there. For some of them it was closer. Some of them just thought it might be nice to go to a new school and many went with friends who were going. Some we like, "I'm just don't want to want to be at East anymore." [EHS 73 WF]*

*I went to Orange Junior my 9th-grade year. I didn't want to be there because my friends were at Logan. It was a different environment and it was a little difficult for me at the beginning to break in. It was a small school and the other students had all gone to school together since kindergarten. Orange High School closed at the end of my junior year when Central opened to help Waterloo integrate its schools. That's where I ended up. [CEN 73 WF]*

*A group of students was taken from East and West and from Orange, and sent to Central. Nobody wanted to do it. Everybody in class was very unhappy because everybody wanted to finish high school at the schools they'd been attending. The student council was trying to merge everyone into Central. Trying to integrate teams. Because players had competed against each other in their previous schools. But it was the school district's way of trying to improve integration which had to be done and it was probably the best year to do it. [CEN 73 WF]*

*I had my choice, to go to West or Central. And there was no way I was going to go to West. [CEN 73 WF]*

## 1973 BATTLES OVER DESEGREGATION PLAN

In 1972-73, the board of education conceded the voluntary transfer program hadn't desegregated the district's schools and more aggressive integration action was needed. It instructed the school administration to prepare and submit a plan to reduce school "minority isolation," the latest bureaucratic buzzword in desegregation.

Federal guidelines at the time classified a school with "minority isolation" as one with more than 50% minority enrollment. According to Iowa guidelines, however, any school in the Waterloo district with more than a 34% population qualified as minority-isolated.[80]

In 1972, the Iowa State Board of Education issued non-discrimination guidelines designed to help school districts end racial isolation and imbalance in many of Iowa's urban communities.

Any building with a minority population more than 20% over the district's overall minority population would be deemed "out of compliance." That school district's board of directors would then be required to act to reduce the minority percentage or defend the imbalance as nondiscriminatory [e.g., a planned "magnet school" or "50-50" school].

Eight Waterloo school district buildings were out of compliance in the 1972-73 school year, according to the State Department of Public Instruction (DPI). This added additional pressure on the district's integration planning.

On March 13, the superintendent presented four desegregation proposals to the BOE, two of which were rejected. It directed the administration to continue to develop the two others generically labeled "A" and "B." (Figure 7)[81]

Plan A used current high school boundaries for elementary schools, which would potentially reduce minority students below 33% in minority isolation schools. Students from schools with high minority populations would be blended with or reassigned to non-minority schools to meet the state guidelines.

The upper left quadrant in Figure 3 is shows the high school boundaries and the lower left depicts how schools with minority isolation would be grouped within those zones.

Referred to as a "cluster plan," Plan B was projected to result in minority isolation reduction between 13-15% by grouping with limited areas. The upper right quadrant in Figure 3 shows the elementary schools' zones. All the minority isolation schools were on the East Side.

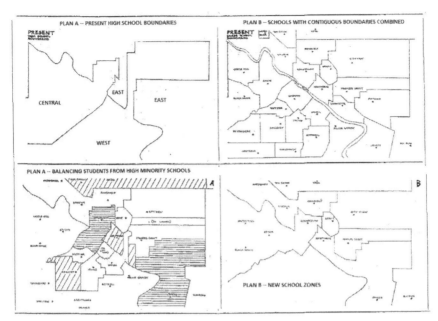

Figure 7 Options for Desegregation Plans "A" and "B"
*After months of submitting desegregation proposals which were sent back by the BOE for revisions or rejected out-of-hand by parents, the school board was presented with the "final two best options."*

The lower right-hand quadrant shows groupings for contiguous schools that would reduce minority isolation.

Both plans included the closing of three elementary schools – Lafayette and Maywood in the southeast area of the East Side, and Emerson on the West Side. The school closings were recommended to "economically operate the district." The age and capacities of the three schools, and enrollments and projected enrollments were the major criteria.[82] Parents picketed the schools to protest their closings.

In both plans, transportation would be needed for some students. The term "busing" wasn't used.

There was an urgency to approve a desegregation plan needed by early April so it could be included in application for federal Title VII funds to help implement it.

Following the presentation of the two plans to the BOE and the public in attendance, the NSA asked the board to drop any desegregation plans and "stop trying to solve social problems."

*NSA organizer Harold Getty, elected as its president, said the group objects "to state and federal bureaucracy dictating in a most undemocratic way the affairs of our schools."*

*The NSA urged the board to appeal to the community and its leaders "to do everything possible to prevent discrimination against any person regardless of race, creed, color sex or national origin. Integrate on a voluntary basis; assure the possibilities of open housing in a voluntary way; and maintain law and order and swift prosecution of violators and lawbreakers."[83]*

A special meeting for the BOE to consider the two plans was set for April 05 in the auditorium of West High to accommodate the expected turnout.

The week before, school administrators held four community meetings on both sides of the river to explain and answer questions about the plans. Attendance ranged from 125-500 and were generally contentious, if not confrontational.

Opposition to the plans was organized. Some opposed to busing component of the plans, but accepted the school closings could be a budget issue. Most believed either plan was only designed to satisfy integration guidelines.

Three people who spoke at several of the meetings in favor of the school closings and desegregation received little support from the board or the audiences.

Major parent concerns were hazards students would encounter on longer bus routes that would have to cross busy highways and the breaking up of neighborhood schools. Both were the same as those of parents in communities throughout the U.S. dealing with mandated or voluntary desegregation.

Several people commented at the local meetings the BOE "should either begin representing us or we should elect people . . . who will. . . ." One person suggested parents' rights "to have our kids go to school where we want [is being violated by the need to reduce minority isolation] . . . Take the message to Uncle Sam and tell him how we feel."

A parent who was also a part-time employee of the district's hot lunch program said the program wasn't needed, which would save the district money, and quit her job at the meeting.[84]

The NSA maintained an anti-desegregation presence throughout. Getty said the district should forego applying for federal Title VII funds that would be used "for purposes contrary to the intent of Congress and we intend to do everything possible to block the granting of the funds or their expenditure for the purposes we deem illegal. . . ."[85]

The BOE voted 4-3 at the meeting to approve Plan A, creating elementary school boundary changes within high school boundaries to prevent re-segregation and closing the three elementary schools for the fall 1973 school year. The motion also directed the school administration to include the approved plan in the district's federal Title VII funding application that month.

The 3-3 tie was broken by board president James Sage. It would cost him his seat on the board.

About half of the estimated 600 people attending the special meeting walked out after the vote with shouts of "Freedom, Freedom" and "Let's take it to a vote of the people." Many were members of the NSA, which immediately drew its line in the sand over the plan.

The morning after the vote, NSA president Getty said he was in shock, but indicated the group would take actions to block the plan's implementation and intimated the school board membership would also be evaluated. "[The board] went against the wishes of the majority. . . . I've heard comments on boycotting the schools. . . . small communities within a 30 to 40-mile radius of Waterloo had better dust off their building permits because I think their population will increase rapidly."[86]

The plan was supported by the Waterloo Education Association (WEA), the Black Hawk County chapter of the NAACP, SHARE, the Title VII advisory committee and the League of Women Voters.

The NSA had requested two injunctions from the courts in Waterloo to bar the board from receiving details of the plans at the special meeting and from implementing the plan until all administrative appeals were completed. Different judges denied both.

On June 29, the NSA lost its third attempt to defeat the approved plan when Black Hawk-Buchanan Joint County School Superintendent upheld the right of the board to implement it.

Following the setbacks, the group stated at the end of June its next four steps to block the desegregation plan would be:

1. to file an appeal with the DPI, the final step in the administrative appeal process;
2. to file an appeal with the Iowa Supreme Court to reverse the decision by a local court not to block the board from implementing its plan;
3. to use all of its economic resources to defeat board president James Sage and member Rev. Kenneth Gamb, whose terms were expiring; and
4. to file discrimination charges against the BOE because not all district schools were included in the plan.[87]

On July 17, two weeks before the filing deadline for the September 11 school board election, the NSA announced its major priority was ousting Sage. It also said it would only endorse two candidates for the three open seats, but not until after the August 2 filing deadline. It asked the others to drop out of the race when it did.

The next day, Gamb notified Sage he was returning to graduate theology school that would result in his moving of the district. He indicated he would resign from the board on September 01, 10 days before the election, with four months left in his term.[88] Gamb actually resigned on August 24, a little more than two weeks before the vote.[89] His seat was unfilled until the 1974 election, at which time the board again had a full seven members.

As promised, the NSA filed an appeal with the Iowa DPI to block the board's plan. Getty admitted, "We have just about exhausted our legal means of challenging the plan. We have been to district court, the county superintendent and now the [state DPI]. So far, I don't think we have seen any justice. If the DPI rules also in favor of the school district's plan, we will appeal to the Supreme Court of Iowa."[90]

**NSA Endorses**

# REHDER • MᶜKERNAN • MIXDORF

Dear Members and Concerned Citizens:

This is the time when we and all of the people of our fair city have the opportunity to exercise our privileges and our rights by electing in an orderly and democratic fashion our representatives to serve on the Board of Education.

Inasmuch as the decisions of our School Board are of primary importance to all of us, we cannot urge you enough to assist in the election of Mrs. Rehder, Mrs. McKernan, and Mr. Mixdorf to represent you responsibly and sensibly.

And then, YOU. Don't you dare forget ELECTION DAY. Exercise your right as a free Citizen in a still Democratic Society and cast your vote.

**N.S.A. Executive Board**

Political Advertising Paid for by N.S.A. Executive Board, Harold Getty, Chairman

Thursday, 07 September 1973, Waterloo (IA) Daily Courier, p.10.

Figure 8 NSA Endorsement Ad in the *Waterloo Daily Courier, 1973*

In late July, the WEA – which favored the plan – sponsored a community communications program on behalf of The Consortium, 12 agencies and organizations that had been formed specifically to boost the integration plan. The program included public information dissemination, a rumor control center staffed with trained volunteers, tutorial services for students involved in the integration and interracial education enrichment programs, and a full time coordinating administrator.[91]

By the end of July, there were eight candidates for the three board positions, nine by the end of August, including Sage and incumbent Norma Rehder. A board member since 1949, she'd voted against the board's desegregation plan. Two dropped out before the election, but their names remained on the ballot because, under state law, they had withdrawn after the filing deadline.

The 1973-1974 school year started the last week of August, roughly two weeks before the BOE election and essentially finished any challenge to the desegregation plan, as noted in a Waterloo Daily Courier editorial the week before the board vote.[92]

*With the opening week of school under a controversial desegregation plan now history, the Waterloo school system and this entire community have grounds for great pride and satisfaction.*

*One fact stands out above all others:*

*The city's parents put the education of their children above any disagreement they might have had with the desegregation plan. Waterloo children were in school last week and their education was flawed only by the intense heat wave, not emotional heat.*

*Waterloo has now leaped far ahead of every other Iowa metropolitan area – and probably most similar communities across the nation – in school desegregation.*

*Significantly, Waterloo adopted and implemented its school desegregation plan without a court order – unlike many cities with a similar problem. . . .*

*Nobody claims Waterloo has solved all of its racial problems.*

*Implementation and acceptance of this school desegregation plan, however, indicate good faith and progress by blacks and whites alike. . . .*

*. . .although reasonable people still disagree over the merits of the desegregation plan, the argument is being conducted in a mature, rational, responsible and legal way.*

*These are very good omens indeed.*

The editorial acknowledged the NSA's continuing resistance to the plan, but commended it for adhering to its "policy of resisting the plan only through administrative and court appeals as well as at the polls in the upcoming school board election."[93]

The NSA "scored an overwhelming victory"[94] in the school board election on September 11. Its major objectives were to oust the president who'd cast the deciding vote to approve the desegregation plan and to seat its three endorsed candidates. It did both.

But the election was two weeks after the start of school, and the plan was in place; the new board wasn't going to and couldn't rescind it, according to legal precedence. So, the NSA won, but it lost – it established itself as an influence in the community and its school system, but couldn't stop the inevitable change.

The election results indicated "a majority of voters dislikes the school desegregation plan which went into effect this fall. . . . [And they want] no expansion of desegregation if it involves involuntary busing."[95]

The NSA continued to represent that perspective in board's subsequent decisions adjusting the integration plan, school openings and closings and boundaries and community activism through 1974. In the school board elections that year, both NSA candidates were elected, repeating its success the year before. Six of the seven members of the new board were NSA-endorsed.

# Reflections from the Bridge

*What our city needs more than bridges across the river are bridges between blacks and whites. . . . The Public Speaks*[96]

The Waterloo BOE board desegregation initiatives through the 1960s and first two years of the 70s were minimal. In 1973 – at the behest, if not coercion from the Iowa DPI – it developed a comprehensive desegregation plan to be implemented in the fall at the start of the 1973-74 school year.[97]

ERA 3 wasn't as tumultuous for high school students as ERA2 was. But busing, and the opening of Central High and the closing of Orange created a destabilization of the traditional, comfortable status quo that presented new challenges for the graduates, the school board and the town.

The desegregation plan and its busing component continued to be a major focus of the BOE and the community, especially the NSA, in the summer of 1973 after the last *The Bridge Between* class had graduated.

But after more than a century of East Side-West Side segregation, the resistance of the community and its school board to integrate in the first seven years of *TBB's 1963-1973* story chronology, and five years after the assassination of Martin Luther King, Jr., Waterloo had weathered the storm.

# Endnotes

[1] Schumaker, K.A. (Fall 2013). The Politics of Youth: Civil Rights Reform in the Waterloo Public Schools. State Historical Society of Iowa: The Annals of Iowa, 72(4), 356-357. Retrieved from http://ir.uiowa.edu/annals-of-iowa/vol72/iss4/4.

[2] Walk Together Children. (May 22, 1971). A Report of the Iowa Advisory Committee to the U.S. Commission on Civil Rights on Housing and Education in Waterloo, Iowa, 8.

[3] Student Involvement Idea OK'd by School Board. Voice in Relevant Issues. (October 26, 1971). *Waterloo Daily Courier*, 12.

[4] 1) Enrollment Drop of 500 in 1972-3 Seen; Board Votes to Allow School Use by NSA. Five-year Projection Shows Decrease. (November 09, 1971). *Waterloo Daily Courier*, 13. 2) Early School Attendance Figures Show Pupil Gain. 14,970 Show Up Tuesday. (September 04, 1963). *Waterloo Daily Courier*, 22.

[5] Students Seek Changes. (December 07, 1972). *Waterloo Daily Courier*, 22.

[6] 1) East High Student Is Stabbed. (March 01, 1973). *Waterloo Daily Courier*, 20. 2) Man Sentenced in East High Stabbing Case. (May 31, 1973). *Waterloo Daily Courier*, 5.

[7] A Challenge Change. Waterloo and Plan A. (May 1973). Des Moines, IA: Urban Education, State of Iowa Department of Public Instruction, 3.

[8] Dr. Cunningham – a teacher, principal and deputy superintendent in Waterloo Community Schools for more than 31 years —was Iowa's first African-American high school principal when he started at East High School in 1976. He died at age 58 in 2000 from complications of polymyositis, a rare degenerative muscle disease. Named in his honor, The Dr. Walter Cunningham School for Excellence! is a preschool through fifth grade public school with "state-of-the-art facilities and excellent academic opportunities for all students." Retrieved from http://www.waterlooschools.org/schoolsites/cunningham/about-us/.

[9] Short-Lived Sit-in Held at Central. (February 5, 1973). *Waterloo Daily Courier*, 3.

[10] School Proposal Fails. Open Lunch Hour Move Is Defeated. (February 27, 1973). *Waterloo Daily Courier*, 10.

[11] Central. (March 15, 1973). (High Society. Special Events Filling Schedules. *Waterloo Daily Courier*, 15.

[12] Open Noon Hour to Receive Trial. (March 13, 1973). *Waterloo Daily Courier*, 9.

[13] African Palace was a program in the 1970s which provided a venue for junior high and high school students to make up credit classes. Its Vocational Explorations Program recruited and monitored workers for local employers. Woman of many hats served many hearts in Waterloo. (March 15, 2018). Kinney, P. *Courier*. Retrieved from http://wcfcourier.com/news/local/woman-of-many-hats-served-many-hearts-in-waterloo/article_ea7af715-5184-5bdd-9b68-ee55d6806d6f.html.

[14] Voluntary Integration Praised. Parents Like 'Bridgeway.' (February 18, 1970). *Waterloo Daily Courier*, 2.

[15] Ibid.

[16] Registration is Thursday. Bridgeway Project Enrollment Hailed. (February 18, 1970). *Waterloo Daily Courier*, 1.

[17] Ibid.

[18] Voluntary Integration Praised. Parents Like 'Bridgeway.' (February 18, 1970). *Waterloo Daily Courier*, 2.

[19] School Desegregation in Waterloo, Iowa. (August 1977). Kansas City, KS: A Staff Report of the United States Commission on Civil Rights, 7.

[20] Editorials. Let's Back Diestelmeier in Tough Job. (December 22, 1971.) Opinion Page. *Waterloo Daily Courier*, 4.

[21] Lubera Says Press Should be Muzzled. Stand Repudiated by Board Members. (September 17, 1971). *Waterloo Daily Courier*, 3.

[22] Ibid.

[23] Bill Severin, The Iron Duke. Suffering Illusion. (September 17, 1971). *Waterloo Daily Courier*, 1.

[24] Supt. Lubera's New Contract Under Discussion. (September 20, 1971). *Waterloo Daily Courier*, 5.

[25] Dr. Lubera Out as Sup't of School. (September 21, 1971). *Waterloo Daily Courier*, 1.

[26] Lubera (continued). (September 21, 1971). *Waterloo Daily Courier*, 2.

[27] Editorial. Problems, Opportunities Face New School Supt. (September 22, 1971). *Waterloo Daily Courier*, 4.

354

[28] Diestelmeier Applies. Seeks Elevation to School Sup't. (September 30, 1971). *Waterloo Daily Courier*, 6.

[29] Diestelmeier Applies. Seeks Elevation to School Sup't. (September 30, 1971). *Waterloo Daily Courier*, 6.

[30] Bill Severin. The Iron Duke. Support Diestelmeier. (October 15, 1971). *Waterloo Daily Courier*, 1.

[31] Editorials: Diestelmeier Merits Post of School Superintendent. (October 20, 1970). *Waterloo Daily Courier*, 4.

[32] Schools (continued). (December 21), 1970). *Waterloo Daily Courier*, 2.

[33] Editorial: Let's Back Diestelmeier in Tough Job. (December 22, 1971). *Waterloo Daily Courier*, 4.

[34] Walk Together Children.

[35] Clark Claims 7,500 members. DPI Plan Called NSA's 'Salesman.' (February 11, 1972). *Waterloo Daily Courier*, 6.

[36] NSA Rolls Double Within 2 Weeks. (November 18, 1971). *Waterloo Daily Courier*, 3.

[37] Ibid.

[38] Ibid.

[39] Ibid.

[40] Diestelmeier Reflects on 50 years in school. (May 24, 1983). *The Des Moines Register*, 12.

[41] Common Patterns in an Uncommon Place: The Civil Rights Movement and Persistence of Racial Inequality in Waterloo, Iowa. (2014). Shirey, T.E. Bowdoin College: An Honors Project for the Program of Africana Studies, 44.

[42] The Nation: Speech Defect. (June 12, 1972). *Time*. Retrieved from http://content.time.com/time/magazine/article/0,9171,906012,00.html.

[43] Sit-In Protest at West Jr. of Negro Stereotype Material: Black Parents Demand Teacher Be Fired. (May 24, 1972). *Waterloo Daily Courier*, 5.

[44] Numerous *Little Brown Koko* stories by Blanche Seale Hunt, illustrated by Dorothy Wagstaff, appeared in *The Household Magazine* for a number of years beginning in 1935 when Seale began writing for publication. Six *Little Brown Koko* books sold 600,000 copies. Her stories, by the same title, appeared for 20 years as a monthly feature in the magazine.

[45] The Politics of Youth, 377.

[46] The Nation: Speech Defect. (June 12, 1972). *Time*. Retrieved from http://content.time.com/time/magazine/article/0,9171,906012,00.html.

[47] Sit-In Protest at West Jr. of Negro Stereotype Material: Black Parents Demand Teacher Be Fired. (May 24, 1972). *Waterloo Daily Courier*, 5.

[48] Ibid.

[49] Ibid.

[50] Despite Re-Instatement by Board: Mrs. Hayes Won't Return. May 28, 1972). *Waterloo Daily Courier*, 10.

[51] Black Boycotts Hit Towns in Iowa And Mississippi. (June 29, 1972). Brown, W. Jet, 28. Retrieved from http://tinyurl.com/ycsddk3m.

[52] School Dismissed After Mass Protest. White Students at West Junior Rise to the Defense of Mrs. Hays. (May 25, 1972). *Waterloo Daily Courier*, 3.

[53] Ibid.

[54] Black Boycotts Hit Towns in Iowa And Mississippi. (June 29, 1972). Brown, W. *Jet*, 28. Retrieved from http://tinyurl.com/ycsddk3m.

[55] Diestelmeier Held Hostage: School Protesters Evicted. (May 25,1972). *Waterloo Daily Courier*, Front Page, 2.

[56] Diestelmeier Held Hostage. School Protestors Evicted. (May 26, 1972). *Waterloo Daily Courier*, Front Page.

[57] Ibid.

[58] Superintendent's Office Cleared. Protest (Continued). May 26, 1972). *Waterloo Daily Courier*, p.2.

[59] Ibid.

[60] Ibid.

[61] Ibid.

[62] Ibid.

[63] 1972 Waterloo school sit-in remembered (February 28, 2016). Kinney, The Courier. Retrieved from http://wcfcourier.com/news/local/waterloo-school-sit-in-remembered/article_e2ddd51c-21e5-50f3-83f8-dca81eb1002d.html.

[64] Ibid.

[65] Ibid.

[66] Remember Waterloo schools sit-In. (March 6, 2016). *The Courier*. Retrieved from http://wcfcourier.com/news/opinion/editorial/remember-waterloo-schools-sit-in/article_66d29010-7b62-54a1-a15a-cd0692c6e3bd.html.

[67] Logan Plaza Picket Gets 12-Day Term: [NAME] Found Guilty of Assault. (June 21, 1972). *Waterloo Daily Courier*, 3.

[68] Blacks Demand Quota Hiring. (June 29, 1972). *Waterloo Daily Courier*, 2.

[69] Ibid.

[70] Ibid.

[71] Black Boycotts Hit Towns in Iowa And Mississippi. (June 29, 1972). Brown, W. *Jet,* 29. Retrieved from http://tinyurl.com/ycsddk3m.

[72] Logan Picketing Ends. (July 2, 1972). *Waterloo Daily Courier,* 13, 14.

[73] Mosley Puts Limit on Rights Probe. (July 14, 1972). *Waterloo Daily Courier,* 7.

[74] Change of Venue Okayed in Charge Against Picket. (July 6, 1972). *Waterloo Daily Courier,* 4.

[75] Changes of Venue Pend for Others. (July 7, 1972). *Waterloo Daily Courier,* 6.

[76] Editorials. Waterloo High Schools Are Badly Overcrowded. (August 21, 1968). *Waterloo Daily Courier,* 4. $7.8 Million For Schools Is Proposed. (August 12, 1968). *Waterloo Daily Courier,* 1, 2.

[77] Real Estate City. (July 15, 1969). *Waterloo Daily Courier,* 20.

[78] New High School at Hackett, Huntington. To Build on 53 Acres, Cite Access. (May 27, 1969). *Waterloo Daily Courier,* 1.

[79] History. Waterloo Community School District. Retrieved from http://www.waterlooschools.org/history/.

[80] Board Outlines Reasons for Schools Closing. (March 29, 1973). Waterloo Daily Courier, 9.

[81] Would Close Three Schools. Two Desegregation Plans Recommended. (March 13, 1973). *Waterloo Daily Courier,* 1, 2.

[82] Board Outlines Reasons for Schools Closing.

[83] NSA Asks Board to Drop Plans for Desegregation. (March 13, 1973). *Waterloo Daily Courier,* 5.

[84] Third Public Meeting. Emotions Run High in School Closings. (March 30, 1973). *Waterloo Daily Courier,* 3.

[85] 500 Attend Special Meeting. School Closing Plans Opposed. (March 20, 1973). *Waterloo Daily Courier,* 1, 2.

[86] Board Action Prompts Walkout. School Closing Plan Voted. (April 06, 1973). *Waterloo Daily Courier,* 1.

[87] NSA Appeal on Closing Plan Denied. (June 29, 1973). *Waterloo Daily Courier,* 1.

[88] Lepsch to Run. Rev. Gamb Won't Be Candidate for School Board. (July 18, 1973). *Waterloo Daily Courier,* 9.

[89] School Board Votes New Pay Increases. (August 28, 1973). *Waterloo Daily Courier,* 3.

[90] Goal: Oust Board President. NSA to Back Two in School Election. (July 18, 1973). *Waterloo Daily Courier,* 1.

[91] Communications Program. WEA to Support New School Plan. (July 26, 1973). *Waterloo Daily Courier,* 3.

[92] Editorial. Schools 'Cooled It' Despite Heat. (September 2, 1973). *Waterloo Daily Courier*, 4.

[93] Ibid.

[94] NSA-Backed Slate Sweeps Election. (September 12, 1973). *Waterloo Daily Courier*, 1.

[95] Courier Editorial. Voters Don't Like Involuntary Busing. (September 13, 1973). *Waterloo Daily Courier*, 4.

[96] Labels People Making Demands 'Unreasonable.' (June 21, 1972). *Waterloo Daily Courier*, 4. This letter was selected two years after I titled this book *The Bridge Between*. It turned out not to be a unique theme in my research and discussions with graduates.

[97] School Desegregation I Waterloo, Iowa. (August 1977). Kansas City, KS: A Staff Report of the United States Commission on Civil Rights, 5.

4th Street Bridge at Night. Copyright © 2018 Marvitz Photography. Used with permission.

# Part 3 The High School Afterparty: Adulthood

## TBB 10: What We Know Now We Didn't Know Then

*To people at Iowa State, someone from Waterloo was from the big city. But it wasn't considered a cool town. Compared to other Iowa towns, it's a river town with all the connotations – an industrial town, very much a company town. It had no university. My vision of Waterloo was like the old mining towns in Pennsylvania. Waterloo had that sense to me. [WHS 70 WF]*

*I've never experienced white guilt. But if you're a white heterosexual, you've got it made in society. I feel bad that those characteristics should elevate me above anybody else. The luck of the draw. [EHS 66 WM]*

We obviously don't perceive our teenage years 50 years later as we did when we were living them. Over time, relevant memories and perceptions become stronger, more fixed in our minds. Some are altered for innumerable reasons. And some wane into the "Total No-Recall Zone."

*There's a black homecoming every couple of years in Waterloo, started probably in 1995-96. I took my husband with me a couple of times. Comments made to him were enlightening, especially by the black males. "I want to meet the person that was able to get [me] to marry them. I thought she was hot, but she was just so out of my league . . . ." And I'm thinking, what? Are we talking about the same high school experience? The perceptions that we had when we were in school and then being able to see it a couple of decades away through perceptions of others shared with you [trailed off]. . . . [EHS 68 AAF]*

## Growing Up East or West

*Back in my day the major thing was your name. I'm a [Last Name]. That name better mean something. You can't lie and be a [Last Name]. You can't steal and be a [Last Name]. You have to cherish and respect that name. That's the way it was. [COL 64 AAM]*

*When you get the same messages growing up coming at you from all sides – "your stepdad's shit, you're shit and you ain't ever going to be anything but shit" – you have such a feeling of insecurity. No self-esteem. It shapes you. Shape your psyche. You start to internalize some of those negative messages. To compensate, you act out. I understand that now. Why I was venting my frustration in the manner I was. Why I was involved in such grandiose grandstanding activities and behavior. And I was always the family scapegoat. It was so the attention would be on me and not the dysfunctional family I was in. On one hand, I was under pressure from the guys my mother had relationships with. On the other hand, the guys in the streets – because I was a street kid – protected me at so many different levels. They embraced me, protected me, they loved me. I could have been a kid so easily abused, sexually abused out there in the streets. But there were so many older guys who respected me because of my moxie. I wouldn't take any wooden nickels. I acted out in ways that they admired to some degree. I didn't understand that then, but I do now. [EHS 69 AAM]*

## Would You Take a High School Do-Over?

*When you get to be our age, you all of a sudden realize you are being ruled by people you went to high school with. You all of a sudden catch on that life is nothing but high school. – Kurt Vonnegut[1]*

*Go back to high school and do it over again if I could? In a heartbeat. Said no one ever. – The Author*

High school is arguably one of most important times in our lives in the U.S. Chronologically, we vault from being the at top of the student

360

hierarchy as 9<sup>th</sup> graders in junior high, back in the day, to sophomores at the bottom of the high school pecking order 10 weeks later.

The bar of expectations set by parents, educators and society is raised significantly during the summer. Many of us in *The Bridge Between* story got jobs at our parents' insistence or urging to help with family income or to wean ourselves from pay for family chores and allowances, or both.

Answers to questions we first heard in junior high became a litmus test; "What do you want to be when you grow up?" and "What are your plans after high school?"

Separation from the family as our primary social group became wider as we each dealt with the increasing conflict between the overwhelming influence of peer groups and deciding who we were as people. Driven by testosterone and estrogen, the opposite sex was reclassified in terms other than "platonic" or "indifference."

Educational tracks, course selections, course grades and GPA, passing or failing, standardized test scores were the albatross around the neck for many in high school, hung with unbreakable chains of culture's educational requirements and social conformity.

In Waterloo, there were the added millstones of East or West Side, black or white, segregation, volatile interracial relations in schools and within the community as it, the schools and school district leaders grappled with the present while attempting to assure a future for us.

The perceptions of high school among *The Bridge Between* people range from unhappy recall of a bad experience through "it-was-what-it-was" to happy memories of great experiences.

**'63-'66** *I wasn't focused on school in high school. I was focused on guys. I went to school because I had to. Remember the pimp walk the black guys did? Oh, honey. And some of the older boys would pick up some of the girls after school. They would let you into East then even if you didn't go to school there. I got pregnant in my junior year and got married. You had to get married to stay in school if you were pregnant. I missed the second semesters of both my* *junior and senior years due to pregnancy, but was able to catch up in summer school and still graduate with my class. [EHS 66 AAF]*

*My senior year, my main goal was to graduate and get out of Waterloo, see what else was happening in the world. My dad asked if I wanted to go to college or to go in the military. "I want you out of the house." I didn't really know if I wanted to go to college. I didn't have the money to go to college. My sister's boyfriend, who was five years older, had joined the Navy after he graduated and went to San Francisco. I wanted to be like him. So, I joined the military. I didn't know who was president. Didn't know the difference between a Republican or a Democrat. I always trusted the government. I didn't like what was going on in Vietnam. But I didn't watch the news and really know what was happening. I knew Americans were getting killed. I thought that was the norm when you're protecting your country. If you went to Canada as a draft dodger, you shouldn't be allowed to come back. Everyone was so patriotic, you couldn't believe they had a different viewpoint. Eighteen months after I enlisted, personnel told me I didn't have to serve, couldn't be drafted as the sole survivor of a 100% disabled veteran. I was honorably discharged and went to college. [EHS 66 WM]*

*I wonder how much differently I see my time in high school as the rest of the class. High school wasn't a good time for me. I wasn't one of the jocks or cheerleaders, the most popular kids. I'm not sure I thought about things that much in high school. I was a nerd, as defined now. Which as an okay thing, as it turned out. I don't care if people know I said something for your book or what they would think of me today. [EHS 66 WF]*

**'67-'70**  *At our 10-year reunion at the [former] Holiday Inn on Washington, my buddies who were all white and I got together, had drinks upstairs and then went down for to the reunion dinner. The sense I got from most of the black students was, "Here she comes again with all of her white friends." We were sitting at a banquet table and a lot of the other black students were at the table right behind* *us. The guys were talking back and forth between the tables. Their high school relationships were easier because of sports. It was tougher for the girls, because we didn't have interscholastic sports. We only knew each other from class or choir or band or whatever. Some of the wives started interacting between the tables. After dinner, there was dancing. People from different tables were dancing together, blacks with whites and whites with blacks. And we had a great time. A really, really good time. It was one of the first times I ever felt comfortable in a larger integrated environment at East High. The black people were able to see the whites just as people and not just as white. [EHS 68 AAF]*

*I like to walk around downtown on the East Side when I go back to Waterloo. Drive to see places I used to hang out. I drive by East High. There are good memories. I had a really good time. Part of that was growing up with black kids. We had fun. They would always invite me to their parties and, when I'd go, I'd walk in and all the black girls and guys would say, "Hey, how ya doing?" It's probably because I was social with them. And they loved sports. [EHS 68 WM]*

*We had a full-blooded Navajo in our class, but I never considered asking him how he got to Iowa or if he experience discrimination – or how he viewed the discrimination against blacks. And you still wonder what his answers to those questions might be today. [EHS 69 WF][1]*

*I had a good education and good experiences in high school, which is probably weird. It's just high school. That experience had a greater impact on who I am now as opposed to, "Sure, every kid goes to high school." I had an opportunity to grow up. The whole "how you gonna keep them down on the farm?" It was, "Huh!" I realized I had a choice. That's what the high school experience did. [EHS 70 AAF]*

*I didn't really know what I experienced when I was in high school. Later I did. Conversations with the school counselor who said, "Have you ever thought about a trade school?" when I'm saying I wanted to be*

---

[1] He and I were never able to connect.

*a nurse or a teacher. "But have you thought about . . . ?" And from a distance in time I can ask, "Why would she be able to see me if I couldn't see myself? Why she be able to see me as being a school administrator today?" [EHS 70 AAF]*

*Even after they bused 100 black kids to West in 1968, I had no contact with them while in school. I wanted to like them, but was afraid to say the wrong thing. And I was at the wrestling meet the night of the riot. I was mostly taught to be afraid. Attending West made it seem very difficult, practically hopeless, to overcome fear and prejudice. Maybe if I'd grown up in a neighborhood where you had black people in proximity and a better chance to see them as people, not just a black person . . . . [paused] Even after working in an office in Chicago for nine years where I interacted with African Americans, I'm still afraid of saying the wrong thing. You're afraid you'll accidentally offend someone. One of the typists in our office was black. We reviewed all letters before they were sent out. One time I made a general comment about mistakes made in typing and I said to a typist, "You people. . . ," meaning "you typists." Her back went up and I thought, "Oh, my God, what have I done." [WHS 70 WM]*

**'71-'73** *I'd wanted to be a nurse since I was eight and had been a candy striper junior high. In high school, I was in the co-op program at Allen as a nursing assistant on second shift. That experience had the most impact on me; it got me into the medical field. I saw the difference between LPNs and RNs. RNs worked more with the doctors directly and did more of the paperwork. The LPNs worked more under supervision, directly with the patients, which I prefer. [EHS 73 WF]*

*I had rheumatic fever when I was in kindergarten and was hospitalized for a month. There was a jolly, fat, nice nurse and a really pretty, not-so-nice nurse. I decided to grow up and be a fat, happy nurse. In high school, I got into music because I love playing piano and singing. Then got into the nursing co-op program. Being with the people, talking*

*to them, rubbing their backs and putting them to bed at night. That*
*swung it for me. [WHS 74 WF]*

## Life After High School

It's a timeless cliché: "You can take the student out of Waterloo, but
you can't take Waterloo out of the student."

Our adult lives were influenced by the experiences of our youth.
One-fifth of our waking hours before graduation were spent in a
mandated educational environment interacting with formal and
informal groups, all of whose members had an influence on us and
whom we influenced. Those affects us in adult life for varying lengths
of time as new experiences and perceptions were acquired.

**'63-'66** *Right after high school, I started at John Deere,*
*worked there for a year. Your choice was the foundry*
*or the mill room. I was assigned to the mill room, a nasty, dirty job. And*
*decided that wasn't the career path for me. I enrolled at North Iowa*
*Area Community College [NIACC: nigh'-ack] in Mason City [roughly*
*80 miles northwest of Waterloo]. A lot of my friends would go up there*
*during the week and then run home on weekends. I decided to make a*
*break from Waterloo and made Mason City my home for the next three*
*years. The adjustment was a little easier because my folks belonged to*
*the Knights of Pythias and were known by people in the Mason City*
*area. I made a whole new set of friends there. People just assumed I'd*
*gone to East High school, because I was a black from Waterloo. We*
*didn't have any trouble in Mason City, because those of us from*
*Waterloo hung together. It was a little funny, because up at NIACC,*
*East and West high students – mortal enemies in Waterloo – banded*
*together. I went back to Deere's in 72, got lucky and got into a machine*
*area. I operated a radial drill and learned some other operations. After*
*5-6 years, I went to supervision. I was right-sized out during the*
*cutbacks, but was offered a job back in manufacturing. Nope. [EHS 66*
*AAM]*

*Who would have thought in high school that I would end up where I am and doing the things I have done? I'm not sure many of those I graduated with would understand the trajectory of my life or how I arrived at where I am. I don't know if I was considered white trash at the time, but I was definitely poor. It would be interesting to ask people if they remember me and where they think I ended up. [EHS 66 WF]*

**'67-'70** *I had good social relationships at Orange. However, I've found on Facebook pages in recent years when classmates were sharing memories there were things happening at Orange that I didn't participate in because I didn't know about them. Orange was a rural high school. I saw on Facebook this student or another from the lower academic classes graduated from Iowa State. And some of my Brethren Lutheran Church friends went to [. . .] College. "Really, you graduated from college?" How elitist is that? I think my education would have been better served if the classes at Orange had all different ability levels in them. I was sociable and my social circle would have been larger. I was friends with everybody. At our 25th class reunion someone said, "Oh, I remember you, you were always so nice." [OHS 67 WF]*

*When we first moved to the farm community where my husband and I farmed for 30-plus years, I found there were a lot of people there who had absolutely no contact with the black community. There was one man who was especially bigoted and frequently said the most hateful things. And I thought, "Where does that come from?" One time I had to respond. "My family is biracial. I have black family members. And it really disturbs me that people who've had no experience with black people talk like you are." I didn't see all that much of him after that. He wouldn't be convinced that he might be wrong no matter what I shared with him. And I wasn't going to argue with him. I thought it was unfortunate that he held to those beliefs. [EHS 68 WF]*

*People at Iowa State weren't from racially diverse communities. They'd come into my dorm room during a study break and ask me to share some more stories about high school. Even into my 50s, when people found out that I went to East High school, they'd ask, "Did you carry a knife?" One person told me I couldn't possibly have gone to East because it was all black. The person was from Gilbert, Iowa, a town of about 500 people, all Norwegian, just north of Ames [home of ISU]. [EHS 68 WF]*

*I worked in international admissions at a university. We'd have people over holidays: Africans and Asians, and we had a refugee from Iran living with us for a month. Our church settled a refugee family from Vietnam. At the university, the different ethnic and cultural groups would have country nights. So, we'd go to India nights, for example, and experience the food, culture, singing and dancing. We tried to bring the kids up in as diverse an environment as we could. And my son would say, "But Mom, you're still so prejudiced." [laughs] Because I'll say things. He thinks it's an ethnic bias. My parents and grandparents were terribly prejudiced. It just pops out every now and then. I know it's wrong, but it gets embedded in your brain. I can't erase it. I have black friends and when we see each other, we hug. [EHS 68 WF]*

*When I got into the business world, white men were often very uncomfortable around me at first, because I wasn't what they expected. I didn't fit their stereotype of a black person. I'm smart, articulate, went to a Big 10 school, not an HBCU, and was well-trained. Then they became very protective and the older ones would treat me like their daughter, either because I reminded them of their daughter or I was what they wished their daughter had been. And I had several white men as mentors because I was from Iowa and was proud of being an Iowan. [EHS 68 AAF]*

*One night my husband and I were at dinner one of the fanciest restaurants in Des Moines with the president of a service company my husband's company used. The president and his wife were talking about sending kids to private school, it was "the only way to go, your kids just must go to private school." I didn't say anything. They didn't know me or where I come from. But I remember thinking, "You know, I went to East High School and I'm still sitting here with you." Two months later, their daughter and the governor's son were arrested for driving without a license and having a car full of beer. They went to Dowling, the Catholic high school in Des Moines. [EHS 68 WF]*

*I didn't realize until I went into the service that I had a big chip on my shoulder. I got that chip like most East Side kids going to Columbus. The same kind of chip black kids had about Westsiders regardless of whether they went to Columbus or East. My mother had a nervous breakdown when I was in the 9th grade, and was in and out of mental hospitals. My father died at the start of my senior year. So, I had no money to really go or do anything, like the prom. I couldn't ask any girls out, because I had no place to take them or money to take them out. I hung out with two or three East Side kids and a friend from the West Side. [COL 68 WM]*

*We fought for black civil rights for so many years. And the females and gays and lesbians, that whole group, have received their rights. But we blacks can't get ours. [EHS 69 AAF]*

*There were two reactions when people found out I graduated from East Waterloo. Those who knew football and athletics, and said, "Yeah, you just beat us every time we played you in any athletic event." The other reaction was, "That's the school that was in the North End." Our sports success was a tacit admission that we had an integrated school. At that time, most of the East sports teams were not entirely black or even predominantly black. Sports was a way for a lot of the black kids to get involved in something other than just school work. [EHS 69 WM]*

*In the early 70s, I was promoted from credit manager to office manager for the department store chain I was working for. They needed a new credit manager and quite a few people applied. Store management hired a black man with no experience whatsoever. They were afraid to tell him "no." They were afraid he'd be upset if they hired someone else. He was a nice guy and we got along well, but he wasn't very good at*

368

*credit. He was also a part-time pastor. Had his own little church. He was
very interesting. You could sit and talk to him forever. He and I went out
on collections if we couldn't collect over the phone. It always it had to be
two people and one had to be a man. One time, it was to an apartment
on Main Street in Cedar Falls. We got out of the car, walked up the
street and were standing at a red light. Somebody I knew drove by in a
car, waved and I waved back. And her look was kind of like, "What are
you doing standing there with a black man?" It was kind of funny. I
laughed about it. We were on the East Side another time and I was
trying to talk to this little black lady. When we left, the credit manager
told me, "You made her mad." "What do you mean?" He said, "I could
see it in her eyes." It was quite an education. [WHS 69 WF]*

*When I went to Wharton in the mid-70s, there were a lot of blacks at
the U-Penn campus in Philadelphia. There were maybe 60 blacks in our
class at Wharton. The minority problem was females. There were only
five. It was at the start of when women were just starting to get MBAs.
[COL 69 AAF]*

*I was in the academically advanced classes at West High, so I didn't
have a lot of contact with kids who had issues academically, socially or
whatever. I think that would have happened at East High. I'm guessing I
would have had contact with black kids, but the cohort would have been
those who were skilled academically, had goals to go on to university and
from families with a bit more money. [WHS 69 WF]*

*I worked construction for a while, the only white guy on the labor
crew. I'd heard from a friend they were hiring and it paid 25 to 50 cents
more than my roofing job. There was a labor foreman named Herman,
hired by the construction company, and he brought his own crew who
were local black guys. Herman supplied the old Ford van and one was
the driver – most of the crew didn't have licenses. Herman's job was to
make sure they arrived every day. It was very comfortable, I enjoyed
working with those guys. [WHS 70 WM]*

**'71-'73**    *When I was a freshman at NIACC, a football teammate from East and I went into the locker room for the first time. Three or four sophomores were talking about the conferences they'd played in. They finally asked us where we played and which conference. I said, "Waterloo," and one of them said, "Really. Which school?" We said, "East," and they reacted like, "Oh, WOW, really?" Their boisterousness and talking toned down a bit. It was a respect thing. Teammates wanted to know what it was like playing at East. All the high schools that fed NIACC were basically from one-school towns without minorities. There weren't many players from Cedar Rapids or Des Moines or other schools that had schools with blacks. [EHS 71 WM]*

*I taught $1^{st}$ grade in small, very undiversified rural town of about 2,500 people. The students have no idea what another culture is or that there are people with other colors of skin. And they're afraid of somebody who's different from them. When they found out I'd gone to elementary school with black kids, they asked, "You had those kids in your class?" "Yeah. Sat right next to them. They were my best friends. They're not different than you and I are." Whenever there was an opportunity, I felt it was my job to tell them that that their little town isn't all there is in the world. And it doesn't matter who you are. You have something to give to the world. I was very bold as a teacher. There wasn't anything I wouldn't broach. And I never had any push-back from the parents. [EHS 72 WF]*

*When I started at UNI, people from other parts of the state would ask, "Oh, you went to East High? Were you one of the white kids there?" "Duh!" East was supposedly the school with all the black kids, West High had all the white kids. Talking with my dad, that was the perception through his life, too. "The East side of Waterloo was the ghetto." I was accused of living in the ghetto. "No, I lived in a house." The adjustment at UNI for people who came from small, rural towns where there weren't blacks was tough. Many were terrified of them. And I met kids from*

*West High in my classes who were astounded that I was doing as well academically as I was. Because they thought they'd had everything and that East never had anything. And I was just as smart as they were. [EHS 72 WF]*

*It was a major advantage in life having been able to grow up in the multi-racial environment. I have friends whose children or grandchildren are going to private schools and they're so proud. You can be book smart as hard as you want to study. But you're not going to understand the real world unless you go to school and grow up with different races and religions. I think it's a travesty that parents want to keep their kids in all white private schools. To keep their kids from what they're going to encounter in the world. There were some scary times when I was growing up, but uprisings like we had in Waterloo and at East are necessary for change. Look back at history at women's suffrage and civil rights. There had to be uprisings, incidents for things to change. [CEN 73 WF]*

*After graduating, none one ever said anything negative about my attending East high, but I would hear the stereotypes from others about East High and being scared. People didn't understand. There was always a little stigma. [EHS 73 AAM]*

## We're Not in Iowa Any More, Toto

*My husband and I were on the East Coast visiting friends in the mid-to-late 1980s and they held a dinner party. When everyone arrived, our guests introduced us as "farmers." And everyone wanted to know if we had running water. We were the highlight of the night. My husband typically wore bib overalls around the farm. Our friends joked that he should have worn them that night. [EHS 68 WF]*

*I moved to Louisiana in 1971 and I saw segregation. Waterloo was not segregated. [EHS 69 WF]*

It's a broad generalization, but those of us who grew up in Waterloo were accustomed to the segregation in the schools and the community.

It was what it was. It took agents of change both from within and pressure from the outside to confront and challenge the town's racial comfort zone. That happened in the middle of the 1963-1973 *TBB* chronology.

High school graduation has been characterized endless ways in immeasurable auditoriums in incalculable towns and cities across the country. One constant remains. The ceremony emancipates the graduates, as Dr. Seuss delightfully described in *Oh, The Places You'll Go!*

*You have brains in your head. You have feet on your shoes. You can steer yourself any direction you choose. You're on your own. And you know what you know. And YOU are the one who'll decide to go . . . .*[2]

It was the last Theodore Geisel (Dr. Seuss) book published in his lifetime.

And many of us did go places.

**'63-'66** *I've witnessed a lot of intolerance living in different areas of the country – Kansas, Michigan and Wisconsin. And became more appreciative of my upbringing in Waterloo. Having grown up with the riots, you learned to put black people on an equal basis. We lived in Quad Cities, Iowa, which had never had a civil rights movement. It was like living back in the 1950s. Quad Cities wasn't segregated in terms of where blacks could live. But the whites treated the blacks differently. My son had black friends in college and he'd bring them home. I got to know them well. One year the college was in the conference basketball tournament and one of the black kids he'd brought home a couple of times was a six-foot-eight star. We never had a bed long enough for him. His picture was in the Quad City Times after a game. He'd let his hair grow and had dreadlocks. The local paper was lying on a counter at work and one of the guys said, "Look at that big buck." I couldn't believe it and said, "John, that kid's stayed at my house. Just shut up." He was shocked. Not sure if it was because the kid had stayed at my house or that I'd say something. You heard that* sort of thing there, but not in Waterloo. I worked for a heating & air conditioning company. A black customer came in looking for a part, which I explained wasn't available any more, it had gone to a kit. He said, "I know. I've bought the kits. But I just can't get them to work. I need the original part." I told him there might still be some "out there," and offered to call around to some of our customers and see if any had one. He looked surprised and asked me if I would. I called around, found one and told him where he could go to buy it. He said, "You're not from around here, are you?" "No, I'm from Waterloo." "I knew you weren't from here. You're too nice." [WHS 60 WF]

When I moved to the Pacific Northwest, I was shocked. The first question I asked was, "Where is the diversity around here?" I'd just moved from Waterloo with a huge population of blacks and there was culture shock. That my kids wouldn't experience that diversity in their lives. That's an on-going problem out here. The university in our town has a very popular, wonderful football program. That's where the black population is, at the college. A few years ago, blacks moved into our community. We had a huge problem with them being picked up or stopped by the police for no reason. Prominent people. It's a story in many cities now. We need more people here to make this a community diverse. For me, that allows people to see how easy it is to act and get along. And when you have a community that's predominantly white, that's never going to happen. [COL 63 WF]

I was in culture shock when we moved to Pensacola [FL] in 1966. There were still signs on restaurants, water fountains, restrooms and front lawns which said, "No niggers. Only whites." I thought all that stuff ended after the Civil War. Some of the signs said, "No niggers or sailors allowed." My husband was Navy. At the theaters, black people had to go to the back entrance and sit in the balcony. The admission was $.50 to get in. If you were white, you went in the front entrance and it was $1. My husband and I always sat in the balcony. We didn't care. We were *poor Navy people. My husband had black friends who came to the house all the time. [EHS 66 WF]*

*My husband was a white minority on the football team at Upper Iowa. The university purposely went into Chicago and drafted black players which were good – tough and huge and big, and you were afraid of them. You couldn't beat Upper Iowa. I had trouble living in Fayette [Iowa, 52 miles northeast of Waterloo. The 1960 population was 1,597. Enrollment at UI was 300 students.] Can you imagine what it was like for someone from Chicago living there? But athletes were treated like royalty. They drove Corvettes and were on free rides. [EHS 66 WF]* [Upper Iowa was 23-13-1 during those four years, including an 8-1 season with a shared conference title in an 8-2 season].

*When we moved from California to Virginia, we drove, over 3,002 miles. And we'd stop to eat. I'll never forget the restaurant in Missouri where we had lunch. There was an elderly couple two tables from us. And they stared at my black husband like crazy. It made him, us both uncomfortable. He finally started staring back at them. And it made them so uncomfortable they left. [EHS 66 WF]*

*My husband was stationed at an Army base in Germany in the early 1970s. There were very few people of color. Friends of ours took us and another couple to the home of a German family who were good friends of theirs. There was a lot of racial stuff going on in the U.S. During the conversation, the Germans – who were a little older than we were – asked why Americans treat blacks the way they do. The husband of the other couple was from Mississippi and answered. "I'm not prejudiced, I just don't like them." The Germans didn't perceive black people the way we did. Their prejudice was for Jews and gypsies. [EHS 66 WF]*

*When we lived in England and Germany, I found that people of color are more accepted in those cultures. In the U.S., the impression of an uneducated black person comes from the way they speak. Comes from their environment. It's entirely different when you hear a black person speak with a British accent. It gives the impression that there are no disadvantaged blacks in that culture. And you see more interracial couples overseas. [EHS 66 WF]*

*When people found out I grew up in Iowa, they would stare at me. And I always wondered what was going through their minds. And then they come out with something stupid. "Iowa. That's where they grow potatoes, isn't it?" "No. No. No! We grow corn." Or, "No, we build tractors that you can use to pull your head out." [we both laugh] I'll tell you something else unique about Iowa that I, it seems, am the only one who's noticed. I have eaten steak in many countries. I've paid $142 for a steak dinner at a French restaurant in England. I've eaten steak in Texas. In California, Japan, Alaska, Vietnam, Thailand, Australia and Hawaii. The best steak I ever had was in Iowa. At the Boar's Head in Waterloo. And I think I know why. Iowa grain-fed beef. Other places feed cattle corn for the last month of their lives to tenderize the meat. In Iowa, they're raised on it. And that's the difference. [EHS 66 AAM]*

*My last husband was Jamaican. We had no problems in California. No problems with racism, going to clubs, anywhere. One of my friends once asked, "What's it like being with a black man?" I said, "What?" She asked me again. I went, "Oh, yeah, I guess [my husband] is a black man. I never really thought about it." I was oblivious to that. Then we did a stupid thing and moved to Virginia. It was horrible there, really bad. We had notes put on our car outside our townhouse. "We don't like niggers" and "We don't like nigger lovers, get out of here." All kinds of stuff like that. It hurt bad. I never realized some of the problems our son had in school, because he never told us. They'd call him "Oreo" and "zebra" and a lot of other names which were far worse. It got better in Virginia as the years went on. But it's never totally gone away. [EHS 66 WF]*

*My first introduction to blacks, other than passing them on the street, was in the Navy. I got to know the cooks on the ship, most of whom were black. That's how I got extra fried chicken in my locker, my friendship with them. One night a drunk bosun's mate in my department attacked and tried to kill me because I was antiwar, didn't think like he did and* *wasn't gung-ho. He nearly succeeded. Nobody watching the attack intervened until he hit me in the head with a Coke bottle and I started bleeding profusely from the wound. After the mate was given two weeks' restriction and fined $50 on a charge of attempted murder, I was basically ostracized in my all-white compartment. The cooks must have talked about me to the other blacks on the ship who were radiomen. One took me under his wing, introduced me to his chief and I became a radioman. That moved me from duty at the front of the ship to the back of the ship. The separation made me safer; the bosun's mate was still after me because he said I owed him $50 for his fine. The blacks took me under their arms and literally protected me from this guy. [WHS 66 WM]*

**'67-'70** *When I went to college, whites were, "Oh, you're from Iowa, great." Blacks assumed I would be kind of a rube and was in school under the special support services or the athletic department. In fact, I was the only African American who was on an academic scholarship. [EHS 68 AAF]*

*One of the biggest surprises for people I met in the South after high school at East was when I told them there were only two white starters on my high school football team. These are educated people who truly didn't think there were blacks in the Midwest. [EHS 68 WM]*

*We had some kids at [a prominent white university in Florida] from the South and other parts of the country who really didn't like blacks. They went to segregated or all white high schools and didn't interact or socialize with blacks. That was my first real introduction to people who didn't care for blacks. We had maybe 10-15 minority players on the team, mostly black, and one Hispanic. [EHS 68 WM]*

*I felt little discrimination growing up [a black woman] in Iowa. But when I first went to California in late 1973, I lived in Marin County [a primarily white county then across the Golden Gate Strait from San Francisco.] The racism there took my breath away. I was stunned. It was hostility I had never experienced. People following me. If I went into San*

Francisco and took the bus back, they'd follow me as I walked from the
bus stop to the friends' house where I was saying. Their sons were
biracial and were called names. What I realized was, especially at the
time, Iowans were not particularly open racially. But they weren't
threatening. They were absolutely going to accept you one-on-one at face
value. Marin County was exactly the opposite. It was this supposedly
liberal backstream, but everybody was on the make, everybody was from
somewhere else and living above their means. So, everyone was insecure.
They couldn't trust anybody. Whoever was identified as different
absolutely was beyond the pale. And they weren't willing to give you any
kind of chance to be a person or to show that you were friend material.
They weren't open to integration. Iowans were white and blacks, Jews
and Christians, Catholics and Protestants. Individually, Iowans were
much more accepting. In California, it was "never the twain shall meet."
[EHS 68 AAF]

I was stationed for a while at Warner Robins AFB, Georgia, which
was right at the edge of the town [roughly 20 miles south of Macon, GA].
I didn't see too many blacks. What did surprise me was that most of the
Southern guys I knew had guns in their cars. In Waterloo, it was usually
knives. The county was still a dry county and the base was dry. They
turned wet when I was there. Suddenly, people opened the front rooms of
their houses and had taverns in them. [COL 68 WM]

Around 1990, my husband and I were in a little café in Atlanta. And
this young white waitress warned us, "Y'all be careful. Don't venture too
far." Kind of like, "You know what I mean." We were kind of in disbelief
that she would say that. [EHS 68 WF]

I spent most of the summer of 1970 after high school in the south half
of Georgia working for a feed company. I was in a hardware store in
South Georgia, had inventoried and packed up the garden seed display,
and wrote out an invoice for the customer. I had a company Ford van to
drive with Minnesota plates. And the store owner, who was a decent guy,

*looked out and asked, "Are you from Minnesota? I said, "No, I'm from Iowa." And he said, "Well, that's just as bad." [WHS 69 WM]*

*I spent two years in college at the University of Georgia. Talk about an experience. Left Waterloo on my first plane ride. It was "Football Saturday" when I got there. I'm watching the players walk by, and they're in sports coats and suits. To go play football. Are you kidding me? I really enjoyed my time there. I grew up a lot. People in Georgia called me "Iowa" all the time. I went home with guys almost every weekend. The people in Georgia were awesome. They took care of me. That Southern hospitality is a real thing. They really treated me well down there. [COL 69 WM]*

*I lived in Marshalltown [Iowa, 30 miles southwest of Waterloo and in the same athletic conference as East and West] after high school. I was amazed by the number of people who had never met a black person. Coming from Waterloo, I couldn't understand that. To me, it was so common. [EHS 70 WF]*

*We moved to Huntsville, Alabama, and I was scared. . . to. . . death. [pauses for emphasis] All I ever knew was Selma, Birmingham and Atlanta. Huntsville is a beautiful town and I ended up with temporary work on the line at Chesebrough Ponds [petroleum jelly manufacturer.] I was working hard like an Iowan does putting stickers on. And some of the black girls cornered me and said, "What are you trying to do, show us up?" I said, "No, I was just working." That was scary. I also worked for a black defense contractor in town. One day the black girls and I were talking, and I found out how really prejudiced I was. It wasn't a mean prejudice. I was putting blacks into categories. "You all eat chicken. Eat corn. You eat watermelon." We started talking about things like that. And they started to talk to me about their families having a lot of resentment toward white people because of what they went through and hold against whites. We started being honest with each other and made a breakthrough. That discussion changed my whole life. That was probably in 1990. I'm in a multicultural church now. I used to think biracial couples and them having kids was terrible. We have so many multi-racial couples and kids in our church, I don't even see color any more. [WHS 70 WF]*

*I taught on Navajo Indian reservation. When a white person goes onto a reservation, you go through a test period. They want to know, "Who are you? Why are you here?" The first day you go into the classroom, you're open and you expect interaction. And the students don't say anything. They want proof that you're treating them as human beings and not just as Indians. You can't be there to fulfill your altruism needs. You have to show you're there for them. It takes at least a month, even though you're living with them there on the reservation. [EHS 70 WF]*

*I lived in Salvador, Brazil, which has the largest black population in the country. Brazilians were very proud of the fact that they didn't discriminate. Being from Waterloo, my response was, "Oh, yeah? I've never seen a black teller or a white security guy at a bank." And they'd just look at me . . . . [EHS 70 WF]*

**'71-'73** *When I moved to California, people thought I was a dumb hick since I was from Iowa. And I talked differently. Certain phrases and the way we pronounced certain words. I specifically remember the word "dollar." There was a California way to say "dollar" and an Iowa way. I said "War'-shing-ton" rather than "Wash'-ington." They think of Iowa as this rolling, pastoral landscape with farms, crops growing, tractors in the field and deer prancing. [COL 71 WF]*

*I've lived in the Quad Cities [in southeast Iowa]. It's so cool that blacks are in positions in upper echelons of business and society more than you see in Waterloo. Not that people are going, "Oh, look, there's a black person doing that." But they're in much more advanced positions than what I grew up with in Waterloo. [EHS 72 WF]*

*The first time I was called "nigger" I was 33 and living in Denver, Colorado, on the good side of town. There weren't a lot of blacks there. I had a parking space under my townhome, and sometimes people would park behind me and I couldn't get out. One day I had to go pick my husband up at work. I saw a girl pull in and park where I'd be blocked. I asked her out the window how long she was going to park there, because I needed to leave. She said, "I'm just going to be a minute." I told her if she wasn't back in time, I was going to have her car towed. She left, but the window was still up and I hear this guy – her boyfriend – yelling, "So where does the nigger live?" I went down those stairs so fast I don't even think I touched them. And I asked him, "What did you call me? You called me a nigger? I am not a nigger." My friend, Larry, who was white, and his friends were talking down the way. Larry yelled, "What? You called her a nigger?" And that guy and the girl couldn't get into the car fast enough. [EHS 73 AAF]*

*The more I read and study and find out, we were as bad in the North as things were in the South. When I first moved to Marion, IN, someone asked if I realized the town was famous. I asked why and was told because the town center was the site of the last lynching of a black man in America.[3] And I thought, "What a thing to be famous for." The people there are proud of it. [EHS 73 WF]*

*When people at ISU found out I was from Waterloo, the comment was, "Oh, you were raised in Little Detroit." When I moved to Dallas for my career, I'd be teased about being a hick. They did say Iowans have a great work ethic. If anything was ever brought up about race in Iowa, they were surprised. "Oh, there are blacks in Iowa?" [CEN 73 WF]*

Two weeks after graduating from East High in 1966 I was in Air Force basic training at Lackland AFB, San Antonio, Texas. I didn't know until I was collecting data for this book that two of my classmates were there at the same time.

About 75% of my training flight (a group of enlistees who trained together) was comprised of kids from Georgia or somewhere else in the South. We had a couple of older college graduates from Wisconsin and Minnesota who enlisted to avoid being drafted into the Army. A few from New England and me. There were no blacks in the group. Our lead drill instructors were white, but there were a few black instructors at some of the training phases and some Hispanics.

It was apparent from the first day that the kids from the South were socially different with their "Yes, sir" and "No, sir," even when they weren't addressing drill instructors (DIs). We imitated that during training, which went a long way to smoothing relationships with the DIs. But they were also completely comfortable with the word "nigger," and talked openly about the inferiority of the blacks in their home towns and state, and Jim Crow laws.

It didn't take long to recognize they weren't racist or hateful. They didn't know "better," because culturally and socially in the South, their behavior wasn't "bad."

During our indoctrination into the military, we learned from each other not everyone shared the white intellectual supremacy perspective and to understand behavior rooted in deep social conventions largely not understood outside of Southern culture. Not necessarily tolerant, but more understanding.

## Racial Relationships in Our Adult Lives

One of the original questions that sparked *The Bridge Between* was the effects of having attended and graduated from an all-white or a biracial high school on our adult lives. The insights are a complex kaleidoscope.

**'63-'66**  *The riot in the North End was four years after I graduated from East. I always went to Webbeking bakery on East 4$^{th}$ Street to buy donuts and they made my wedding cake. I saw all this stuff in the news and on TV about what was going on down there. I couldn't believe it was my town going through that. I could understand somewhere else. But I didn't believe people in Waterloo were angry enough to riot. The news was telling people to stay away from the* *area if they don't have business there. That wasn't my style. I decided to go to Webbeking and buy some donuts. I drove down there and East 4ᵗʰ wasn't cordoned off, so I was able to park across the street from the bakery. There were black men of all ages, young to old, standing in front of and leaning against all the buildings. I don't remember seeing any women there. They weren't causing any problems, but they didn't look happy. I got out of the car, a young Sandra Dee-looking⁴ blonde white girl in a blue and white gingham outfit, and walked across the street. I looked the men right in the eyes and smiled. They looked back. Nobody said a word or smiled back, but I knew I wouldn't be harmed. I bought my donuts, came back out and it was the same silent behavior. Nothing changed. Nobody tried to do anything. That's what I expected despite the news reports. And I left. [pause] I wouldn't do that today. [laughs] [EHS 63 WF]*

*There was an older black man in his 70s or 80s in our neighborhood. He was working on his yard one day and I walked down to help. Three older, maybe high school kids, were harassing him. He said he didn't need my help and could handle them "real easy." One of them mouthed off and he told him, "I'll give you three seconds to take that comment back." The kid didn't, and the old man popped him right in the chops and knocked him right on his butt. And then he whipped all three of them. I thought, "Whoa!" When they'd left, he told me he'd boxed semi-pro about 30-40 years before and had been undefeated. Nobody messed with him. [EHS 64 WM]*

*When I was growing up, race wasn't an issue on the basketball court. Whites, blacks and some Mexicans would play pickup games at one of the schools or Gates Park. And we didn't have any problems with each other. I wondered sometimes as I got older why we couldn't go back to when we didn't have race problems with each other. [EHS 64 WM]*

*I had a black friend who lived down the street and worked with me at John Deere. I saved his fingers a few times so they wouldn't get cut off. And I went to school at East with his wife. Whenever they had a new*

382

*baby, he would bring his baby over to my house. I don't know how many white people had that going on back then. [EHS 64 WM]*

*I take the issue of kids today back to the family. A lot of them don't have a male role model in their lives. So, they join a gang for companionship. That's all. They don't even understand life. I think all of us have 15 minutes of life. The first five minutes of your life is everything that mom and dad put into you. The second five minutes is when you're married, working, doing good, trying to live, trying to have money and things. And the last five minutes is getting ready to die. And I tell everybody I'm on my last five. I am a firm believer, if you haven't found something worth dying for, you haven't lived yet. [COL 64 AAM]*

*My kids went to West, but they never heard any of racist crap in our house. My grandson's best friend is a young black man and they got an apartment together last summer. [EHS 66 WM]*

*My sister married a black man she met while a student at the University of Iowa. She was in ROTC and went to OCS after she graduated. She got pregnant and had to resign her commission. My mother was against the marriage and didn't want any part of it. Partly because of his race and partly because my sister had to give up her career. But one of my uncles had married a Japanese woman. [EHS 66 WF]*

*There was a principal I knew in Sioux City who followed high school basketball. In 2003, East Waterloo played West Sioux City in the state championship. The west side of Sioux City has the majority of minority students. East won. And when I pointed it out to him, he said, "Well, that's because they played nigger ball. They were ghetto." Even then, that's how this old, white fat guy regarded East. That reputation still exists in Iowa. [EHS 66 WF]*

*I love the multi-cultural diversity of my family and friends, because it has added so much to my life. I can't imagine not having these experiences or these people in my life – Native American, Hispanic,*

*African American, Asian. It has enriched me and my family. It also allowed me to truly understand white privilege. Most white Americans have no clue. [EHS 66 WF]*

*Coming out of East High and what I grew up with, there's not a person who bothers me, whether it's a black person or a red person or a mentally challenged person. I accept interracial relationships. I'm not against my daughter marrying a black man or a Mexican or. . . . We're all God's people. The only difference may be our skin color. People who haven't been around, been exposed to different races, ethnic groups still have problems with them. The more affluent sometimes. [EHS 66 WF]*

*I have a [white] grandson who graduated from East in 2013. I used to pick him up at school before he had a car because his mother was working. I would see him standing by the commons outside talking with this little black girl. I never asked him about her. You just don't do that with kids. We found out he was taking this girl to senior prom, which was okay. I didn't have any problem with that. I went over to her house that night when she was getting ready so I could take pictures. He'd made reservations for them for supper at 6. I got there about 5. She wasn't ready; her mother was working on her hair. Six o'clock came and went, and her mother was still working on her hair. By the time she and my grandson got going, it was time for the prom to start and she had to be home at 11. They didn't get to go to the post-prom party or anything. I thought that was really strange. Her mother had invited some people out to the casino for the buffet after graduation. We were there, but they didn't show up until about an hour-and-a-half later. I thought it was just being rude. Come to find out, the girl's her mom didn't care for us because we were white and was hoping we'd leave before they got there. A little reverse racism. The girl's mother was never happy about the relationship. Her daughter went to school at Ames and our grandson was in Ankeny, but they still saw one another. About a month after high school, she and my grandson made an agreement to end the relationship. No way it was going to work out. I feel bad because I really loved her. At my grandson's graduation party she came to me and said, "Is there anything that I can help you with, Grandma?" And it just about made me cry. That she felt close enough to me that she would say that. She was always "yes, ma'am" and "no, ma'am," so polite. I'm sorry it didn't work out for them. And I can't do anything about that. [EHS 66 WF]*

---

*I was very different from my parents. Never had a problem with anyone from anywhere. My first husband was part Cherokee Indian, I'm French and Scottish. My dad wasn't happy, but he got over it. And I married a man from LaPaz, Bolivia, and I'm still extremely close to his mother. [EHS 66 WF]*

---

*As an adult, having been where I've been and what I've done, there is and there will always be racial tension. It's how you how you handle and understand it, whether you're talking to a white person and an Indian or someone from Japan or Chinese. East helped me develop a good understanding of racial tension and respect for one another. Because you cannot have understanding without having respect. Mutual respect. If it's not given to me, I'm not giving it to them. [EHS 66 AAM]*

---

*Going what we did through with the riots in the 60s gave me insight into how to treat and not treat people. I didn't think it was right how people treated blacks when they moved into white neighborhoods, even my family. It helped me form my mindset about how I was going to be when I became an adult. [EHS 66 WM]*

---

*My father-in-law grew up in northern Minnesota and they were very prejudiced against the Indians up there. Thought they were a bunch of drunks. That was instilled in him. I didn't know my husband was prejudiced like his father until about a month after we got married. My sister had a friend with a little biracial girl out of wedlock. The little girl was beautiful, so smart and sweet, and I used to babysit with her before I got married. I'd do the little girl's hair, and we played games and stuff. Her mom married a black, and my sister and I were going to visit them one evening after I was married. Her husband was really nice and I liked him. My husband was working second shift and told me I wasn't going over there. I said, "Watch me." And I went. It was probably the first disagreement we had. We had some disagreements about race through the years, but I was finally able to convince him that, just because they're black doesn't mean there's anything wrong with them. They're people just like we are. Through the years we met black people and he liked them. [EHS 66 WF]*

**'67-'70**   *I was disadvantaged many ways attending West High. Not to have a better understanding of the issues that blacks were faced with. My son played sports at Dowling High [in Des Moines], which was basically white. He went to Florida State where there was cultural diversity. FSU recruited kids of color to play sports there from all over the country. He went home with some of the kids to where they were brought up, like Louisiana. "I grew up in such a homogenized world. I had no idea the struggles these kids had and how they ever got to college." [WHS 67 WM]*

*I was in Cedar Falls one Sunday in 1974 or 1975. Needed a new string or pick for my guitar. The store was closed and I was looking in the window. A police car came up with its flashers on. And the young police offer wanted to know what I was doing. I told him I was window shopping. He was so nervous, he had his hand on his pistol. He said, "OK," and I left. But looking back, based on what's happening today, I could have lost my life that day. [EHS 67 AAM]*

*It was a great advantage to attend and come out of East with all its diversity. People might not look like you, may not be as smart or as dumb as you. As a result, you could handle what was thrown at you in life, instead of coming out of a predominantly white background and then going into the military or workforce where there are people who aren't the same color. You don't know how to react to that. I wish my kids could have gone to East. But there were black people that went to their school, too, because we weren't on the elite side of our town. [EHS 67 WF]*

*During the latter part of my career when I was much older, a wonderful old black woman told me a story about when she was a child with her parents in their car. It had broken down, but some white people had stopped and helped. She remembered being terribly afraid of the white faces. Because she'd heard stories about white people. It was an "a-ha" moment for me. Someone being afraid of my color. [OHS 67 WF]*

*I always felt that it would have been so much nicer in high school if we had visited each other's homes. To dispel all the differences that we thought existed. Except for skin color, everyone is pretty much alike. People who live in poverty, whether white or black, have some behaviors and thoughts and attitudes we may not understand. We tend to ascribe social status and hierarchy to skin color. That's even true between darker-skinned and more fair-skinned blacks. But we're all just people. [EHS 68 WF]*

*When I was first married, we lived in an integrated neighborhood with black families around us. One a couple of doors down had three little boys. My oldest was a little girl and she'd go to their house to play with them. One day when she was three their mother called and said, "You're going to be so upset at me. I am so sorry. I don't know what came over me." I asked her what she'd done. She said she was bringing my daughter home and I'd see for myself. She'd put my daughter's hair in cornrows. And it was so funny and so cute. She said she only had little boys and when my daughter was sitting on her on my lap, she just went crazy. Didn't matter to me in the least. [EHS 68 WF]*

*One day my sister went to my biracial nephew's elementary school and he came running out to the car with all these children behind him. She rolled down the window. He pointed at her and said to his friends, "I told you she was white." [EHS 68 WF]*

*My biracial nephew had a daughter out of wedlock; the birth mother was white. His daughter was in foster care and he'd arrange to go get or visit her. There were issues with the foster parents, so he went to court to gain custody. During the trial it became clear that there were some discrimination issues. My nephew is a big man. At that time, he had very long cornrows. He was always immaculately dressed, wore a suit every day in court. Was very well-spoken, well-educated. But black. The judge was an older white male. In the end, my nephew was awarded custody. The mother's family participated in raising the child. She would spend summers with her maternal grandmother. So, she was raised having the best of both worlds. [EHS 68 WF]*

*I was in college when black kids from East surrounded the school bus from Ames [home of Iowa State University] after a football game at Sloane Wallace Stadium [on the West Side] and started rocking it. My mom and her two best friends all laughed about it. We viewed the Ames kids as rich spoiled kids. Years later, I met a person in Ames who said, "I was on that bus and was scared to death." It hit me that my mom and her friends were laughing because these kids had gone through a scary situation we had to go through every day. But life went on and we didn't think anything about it. [EHS 68 WF]*

*Today I think attending West was a disadvantage, partly because the year after I left high school I was married and living in Memphis, Tennessee [where her Navy husband was stationed]. And race wars were still going on. It was the first time I saw drinking fountains which said, "White only." It was jarring. Waterloo was segregated, but it wasn't as overt with the "white only" signs there were in the South. Even in the military, there was a lot of segregation. We didn't associate with any of the black people in the Navy. I'm sure they were there. But my husband had the same prejudiced attitude my dad did, always used the "n-word." Then we moved to Brunswick, Georgia, in the deeper South. We were walking with the baby in the stroller one time. There were three or four young black men walking up the sidewalk toward us, on the same side. My husband said, "We need to cross the street to the other side." I thought, "What? They would have crossed if we hadn't." Those occurrences changed my perception of things because they never made sense to me, even though I knew they made sense to others. People are people. [WHS 68 WF]*

When I went into the service after high school and people found out I was from Iowa, they thought I was a soft white boy. A farmer, some hick. I was at the club drinking one night and I got drunk. The barracks was a condemned WWII barracks with the big open bays and the open toilet rooms with 12 commodes facing each other and a shower area. You had to walk past the commodes to get to the shower, if there was one open. I took a shower and sat on a commode. A bunch of people came in. A small Puerto Rican kid with a lit cigarette walked by me and I felt a burn on my butt. When I jumped up the others took a picture of me. When I got back to the base from tech school, I found the Puerto Rican kid and was going to punch him. His black friends jumped down and said, "You ain't gonna fight him." I said, "I'm gonna kick his ass. Then I'll fight the rest of you guys, too." And they said no, you fight us all at the same time. I started thinking, I might hurt one or two, but the rest will send me to the hospital. They gave me the negative to the photo. After that, everything was smooth sailing. They were testing me. [COL 68 WM]

I've had some white guilt about blacks sometimes. I can understand the frustration among the blacks. But I don't hate Italians because the Romans conquered my Germanic ancestors. Maybe it's a vicious circle. Pull yourself up by your bootstraps and take care of yourself. For example, I'm not that educated about this. But there's an Asian in the black neighborhood working his tail off in the grocery store. Why can't the blacks do that? [WHS 69 WM]

When I worked at a jewelry store downtown after high school, 75% of our customers were black. It was probably because we carried watches, and appliances and plates – what we called our "department-store setup." They came in to buy those things more than expensive jewelry. I met a lot of great people. That's where I learned to relate to them and not be an idiot. [WHS 69 WF]

*One of the East guys I competed against in track four straight years was a fantastic quarter-miler. I always finished the race looking at his back. We knew each other, we competed against each other. If we saw each other in town, we'd speak. But we weren't friends. He was an educator at West High for many years and had my kids in class. I'd drop in, and we talked about how many medals he had and I didn't. We became friends. [WHS 69 WM]*

*A couple of years after graduated from West, I became active in a group in town called the Zebra Golf Group. It's a group of black and white golfers who hold an annual tournament to promote unison in the community. There are two blacks and two whites on each team for the tournament, of which my wife and I are kind of charter members. That tournament is still going on forty-five years later. It's one of the positive things that came out of the turmoil and the race riots of the 1960s. I still play it today. One of the guys that I played with was a John Deere guy. And his son [Quentin Hart] is the mayor of Waterloo now. The first black mayor. [WHS 69 WM]*

*Our family traveled quite a bit in the south. And I'm embarrassed at how little I knew about the racial and civil rights movement in the South growing up. That I was growing up during that time and I really wasn't aware of it. Didn't care about it and see it as relevant. Those issues were just as real for Waterloo. I always thought Waterloo was segregation by choice. That the black families and the black residences were happy to be where they were and what they were doing and whatever. And that we as white people didn't see that was a problem. I hadn't been back to Waterloo for 20 years until five years ago [2012]. And I had a conversation with a friend of my sister who was a couple of years younger and lives in Madison, Wisconsin. I said I felt bad about not having any awareness of the difficulties that black Americans or Native Americans were facing back then. She commented that there has always been racial conflict between the groups and a lot more black dissatisfaction. But during the time we were growing up in Waterloo, the black Americans had been middle class because they had work because it was available. So, there wasn't as much dissatisfaction and the blacks didn't see a need themselves to change things. As much as Madison and other cities had where there were a lot of unemployed or underemployed people. [WHS 69 WF]*

*The first time I had physical contact with black Americans was when I was in medical school in Chicago in the early 1970s. All the black people were security guards, elevator operators, secretaries, cleaners and worked in the cafeteria. Chicago was a scary place and the medical center was near a black ethnic area. Living in the dorm, there were lots of warnings about not walking the streets at night, not going outside the campus. The was a lot of, "Don't go here, don't go there." Ten years later, the head of the school was a black woman with a Ph.D. and there were several black professors. The secretaries were white. Initially, I was surprised, but I was also really thrilled and amazed to think that shift had occurred in just 10 years. It was a false impression that all black Americans had made that jump. There were 30 students in my bachelor's class in '73. There were 30 students in the bachelor's program 10 years later but the proportion of black students had only changed a little bit. I was surprised that, for whatever reason, more black students hadn't been brought in, that it was still very much a white student cohort. [WHS 69 WF]*

*My parents never used and I never use the "n-word." I didn't believe I was a racist. But as I look back now, my thinking was somewhat racist. That segregation was okay. And I was okay with it. I was over here on the West Side of my own little world and, apparently, they were, too, on the East Side. [WHS 69 WM]*

*When I was teaching at East, we had a fight every day at least. I was this white kid who'd graduated from Columbus and UNI whose first teaching job is at East High. A kid gets stabbed to death in the halls a couple of months after I started. Boys fights are so easy to break up, because essentially, they don't want to be fighting. Punches are thrown and the guys are thinking, "That hurts." When you step in, they're usually glad you did. Usually it was whites fighting whites and blacks fighting blacks. A lot of black girls fighting black girls. Girl fights are the worst. Scratching and tearing, and you can't break them up. [COL 69 WM]*

A 16-year-old white East High student was stabbed during a "scuffle" with a black student in the East High student center on September 18, 1974. The victim collapsed as he ran down the hall and was pronounced dead on arrival at the hospital. The assailant was found guilty of second degree murder by a Black Hawk County district judge on February 26, 1975, after he pled guilty to an open charge of murder. He was sentenced to 50 years in prison at the state penitentiary in Fort Madison.

When one of sisters of the young man who had been killed was bused to Central High, she begged her mom to let her attend East. She graduated there in 1982.

*We didn't have the crap going on around us at Columbus they did at East, which was an advantage. We could focus on our education. I'm not sure that Columbus always had the best teachers, but the kids were such good kids that they learned sometimes in spite of the teachers. I became a teacher and I know that there are great teachers in the public schools. Dedicated people trying to deliver education. But there are a lot of distractions in the public schools. You have some idiots in the classroom you have to focus on. And control. You've got a fight going on in the hallway. You've got a whole bunch of things that distract you. But it's not a complete zoo. [COL 69 WM]*

*When people say the "n-word," I ask what do you mean? "Nice? Nauseous?" Just say the word. When it comes to the word "nigger," I'm with Tupac. His take on nigger was not "nig'ger." It was "Nig'ga." To him that meant, "never ignorant, getting goals accomplished."*

*When I say "nigga" it is not the nigga we have grown to fear*

*It is not the nigga we say as if it has no meaning*
*But to me it means Never Ignorant Getting Goals*
*Accomplished, nigga*
*Niggas, what are we going to do?*
*Walk blind into a line or fight*
*Fight and die if we must, like niggas.⁵*

When I talk with young people today, I let them know there's a difference. I also ask, "Who's really the ignorant person?" "Nigger" came from the river Niger. I tell them you must know your history for you to be able to deal with people who must be dealt with. If you know these things, you're bona fide in your feelings and your expressions. And you don't have to worry about looking like a fool and you can stand your ground. The other Tupac thing is "THUG LIFE." It means "The Hate U Give Little Infants Fucks Everyone." Those two statements are powerful words. [EHS 69 AAF]

It's cool to have black friends. We were practicing for the spring alumni swing show at East. The blacks taught us how to dance the way they dance. A lot of the movements we performed were theirs. It was cool to learn to dance how they dance. [EHS 70 WF]

I dated a black guy after high school when I lived in Marshalltown. I don't know whether my family or other people knew I was dating somebody. I never went out of my way to say, "Oh, well, he's black, so watch out for me." I wasn't brought up that way. A person's a person. And color doesn't make a whole lot of difference. [EHS 70 WF]

I can be prejudiced at times. But I've adapted better than some of the people I went to church with from the West Side. Even here in California, when my son was in high school, there were very few blacks. And a lot of his friends were prejudiced, white supremacists. He can't stand that. Doesn't want them around his daughter. I guess he's that way because his dad and I aren't prejudiced. As an Air Force wife, we moved around and you have to adapt. We went to Paris and the first time I heard a black speaking French, I went, "No. No, no, no. Blacks *don't speak French. They speak English." [laughs] It was a shock. [EHS 70 WF]*

**'71-'73** *When we went to Marine Corps boot camp, we all became dark and light green. We couldn't have distinction between black and white. We didn't have time to think about black and white. You have to be a team and think about survival in a war. I had a Spanish drill instructor in boot camp. The first thing he said when he got into my face was, "You're a nigger. You're a nigger." And I guess he thought I was supposed to break down and say, "Yes, sir, I'm a nigger, sir." Every time he came to me with the nigger word, I said, "No, sir, private not a nigger, sir." "Yes, you are. You're a nigger, aren't you?" "No, sir, private not a nigger, sir." So, every time he would say something to me, I'd expand my chest. You're not going to tell me what I am. I knew the game. Manipulation. Trying to make me something I'm not. I'm a lot of things, but not that. Ironic, coming from a short little Spanish guy. I was in at 21 and out at 41. Almost half of my life. My youth was spent in the military in different places and different environments. We had to be uniform, dress alike, had to look alike, light or dark green, there was no black or white. We had race relations classes. We couldn't any afford any distinction among the team. We had walk, talk and fight as one. Racism existed in the ranks in some cases. But regardless of my MOS [Military Occupation Specialty], I was a Marine, a grunt. Trained as a warrior first. [EHS 73 AAM]*

*I worked with a lot of black aides in a Chicago-area nursing home. And the older white women would call them the "n-word." The aides took it very personally and got very upset. I'd tell them that's it's not right for them to do that, but they're of a different generation. That's the way they were raised. You're being paid to take care of them. They're your patients. They can spit on you, swear on you. They can do anything. You must take it because you're an employee. [EHS 73 WF]*

*I started dating my black girlfriend, who's my wife, just before I went into the Navy. She was good friends with my sister. Her parents had no problems with me being white. The only family member who did was her grandmother. It wasn't that I was white. She felt it might be a problem for her granddaughter dating a white boy. She grew up in the South, so she had the perception that maybe us dating wasn't a good idea. "You ought to think about this," she said. But after I met her and sweet-talked her [laughs], we became good friends. She really liked me. We'd go to her house and she'd go out of her way to fix little meals when we came over. And we never had a problem while we were dating. [EHS 73 WM]*

*Most of my workforce during my career were minimum wage blacks. But I knew how to relate to them. I could motivate them. I wasn't fearful of them and didn't think of them as second class. And they knew that of me. They would laugh because I'd bring bagels for the company officers and donuts for the shop. And the workers would say, "You know what we like." [CEN 73 WF]*

*I never thought I was prejudiced, but I am. I'm prejudiced against people who have a job, and sit around and use their color as an excuse not to do their jobs. I have the problem with people who come to work, sleep on the job, don't get the patients up when they're supposed to. I've worked with blacks, Asian Indians, Filipinos. Some nights I was the only white in the building. I kidded about working at the United Nations nursing home. And, yes, there are plenty of whites who probably do the same thing. But I didn't work with many of them. I don't care if they're nurses or at McDonald's. Don't use your race as an excuse for not doing your job. [EHS 73 WF]*

*I met a white brother from Houston while I was in the Marines. The only thing he knew about blacks was basketball, crime and other stuff he saw on TV. He'd never met a black until he joined the military. He became my best friend. He played basketball with us. He became one of us. The black stereotype he grew up with was what he saw on TV. But he recognized that's who we weren't. That happened when he got an opportunity to see us and talk to us and relate to us, became one of us. He's a friend. [EHS 73 AAM]*

## The Racial Divide in Our Adult Lives

**'63-'66**  When I was making service calls on the West Side in the ethnic neighborhoods, I had to go when school was out, because Mom and Dad and Grandma and Grandpa didn't speak English. But the kids could explain in English and show me what they needed. I'd have to go to the same place sometimes three times to catch the kids to figure out what the problem was. [EHS 64 WM]

In the early 1970s when racial tensions were still boiling, I became a conservation officer for Black Hawk County, the first black one in the state. My job was to patrol a lot of the rural areas. If you were black in Waterloo proper, you were safe. You'd go out to the rural areas and try and enforce the laws, and you'd get greeted with a shotgun at virtually every farm house you came to. I got guys telling me, "My grandfather and great grandfather hunted these lands. And just because the county hired a little black guy, you can't come out here and tell me I can't hunt." There were white officers and, yeah, I heard stories about them getting fired on. But not nearly as frequently as I did. I got to the point where I didn't even report it anymore. You're out in the woods and hear something go through the trees, and hear it hit a trunk a second or two later. I started to believe that if they wanted to shoot me, they could have. It was more of a harassment. A lot of my friends who were in Vietnam at the time said, "You never went to the military, you never got shot at." And I just told them, "I was a conservation officer here in Black Hawk County and I guarantee you that I got shot at more frequently than you did." [COL 64 AAM]

It angers me when black people talk about slavery and how the country's indebted to them. That's, excuse me, bullshit. My parents or grandparents never have slaves. I never had anything to do with slavery. Don't tell me I should feel guilty. I don't. If I feel guilty about anything, it's about how our country treated Native Americans. [EHS 66 WF]

*When our son was a little kid, he asked, "Mom, how come Daddy's got really dark skin and you've got really white skin. and mine is kind of in the middle?" That was a hard question to answer. We just explained that his father was from Jamaica and they were a mix of a different kind of people than I was. And he was a mix of us. And I think he got the best of the bargain. Our son ended up with dark, dark brown hair with the most beautiful curls. Now he cuts it down to two inches long. It makes me sick. [EHS 66 WF]*

*I have a friend from Germany also married to an American black man in the Army. We used to talk all the time about sometimes feeling like we had the weight of the world on our shoulders. And if we had married white men rather than black, we wouldn't have had near the problems we had. I think that's true even today. [EHS 66 WF]*

*My husband has had so many problems in his trucking business – he's a black owner operator with six trucks and drivers. I remember the very first truck he bought. All the negotiations were on the phone, so he never saw the people. The day he went to sign the papers, they found out he was black. And everything, everything changed. It was obvious that it was prejudice. That made me so angry. He is the nicest person in the world. Far nicer than I am. How people treat him because he's black drives me crazy. [EHS 66 WF]*

*My son, Jeff [name changed], had several close black friends in school. One had the same first and middle name. The two started at Roosevelt and stayed close throughout school. When he was six, I volunteered there. I asked them, "How does the teacher tell you apart?" My son looked at me like, "What kind of question is that?" "Mom, he's the black Jeff and I'm the white Jeff." "But what does she call you when she calls on you in class?" She called my son "JC" and the other one just "Jeff." [EHS 66 WF]*

*When I was younger and people would use the word "nigger," I would fight. I still don't like it. But I'm hearing it more pervasively in my own* culture. It seems to be a rite of passage for some blacks. "This is my word." And I don't like that. [EHS 66 AAM]

I had a sister-in-law with five kids who lived on the West Side. After busing started, she let every one of those kids drop out of school because "they shouldn't have to go to school with niggers." I was so angry with her. You're going to allow your child not to have an education because you don't want them to go to school with black people? That's stupid and never made any sense. And none of them ever graduated. [EHS 66 WF]

I went to NIACC after high school and rode with three black guys. The guy who owned the car was a friend of mine up until he died. One of the others hated my guts. He didn't like white people. To piss him off, one day we were riding through one of the little towns on the way to Mason City. And just to jack him, I said, "Let's go ride through and integrate that town like Freedom Riders." He said, "Fuck you." [COL 66 WM]

**'67-'70** In 1976, we were going to build a house. One of the other managers at John Deere who lived in the area in which we were interested discouraged me from buying there. He didn't want me in the neighborhood because it already one black family. [EHS 67 AAM]

I can still remember when the first black family moved from the East Side into a house on our street on the West Side. People scattered. Literally. They put their house up for sale and left. Today, you don't see that. We understand that people have a right to be here. They're paying their taxes, too. [OHS 67 WF]

Logan Avenue, Highway 63, that I took home from Allen Hospital would get flooded when it rained. I couldn't get home one day and absolutely didn't know how to get to my house on the West Side. So, I meandered around and ended up going down Idaho Street [on the east side of the North End] under the railroad trestle. The next day at work, our black ward secretary asked me, "What were you doing in my neighborhood yesterday?" [laughs] I told her Logan was flooded and I *couldn't get home. It was kind of a humorous moment. "Like 'What was your white face doing in my neighborhood?'" [OHS 67 WF]*

There's so much divisiveness between the races. People of color, for the most part – not educated people necessarily – but the vast majority of people with color have a lot of anger when it comes to white people. And it doesn't have anything to do with social standing, how much you make, what your job is. In general, it's resentment and anger, and a feeling that because some people are white, they had it easier than black people. Which isn't necessarily the case, because there's an awful lot of poor, underprivileged white people in this country also. Most people that are white are very angry about the race-baiting and believe black people could get ahead if it weren't for their culture which has developed over the past 50 years. A culture of entitlement and a culture of anger. It's gotten worse, much, much worse. Not having lived in the South, I don't know how bad it was for blacks in the South. But I do know we have a lot of reverse discrimination against white people now. Black people today for the most part think we owe them for how badly they or their ancestors were treated. And I don't think it's helping this country at all. We've got to get past that and come together. *[EHS 67 WF]*

I am still fearful when approached by or approaching a group of black males or females. Same with Hispanics. *[EHS 68 WF]*

The black neighborhoods in Waterloo were changing in the mid- to late-60s. The black population was becoming larger. As the black neighborhoods expanded on the East Side, the white people moved to the West Side. When my parents bought their house on the East Side in the mid-1950s, they paid $13,000. They sold it 17 years later to a black family, the first in the neighborhood, for $14,000. *[EHS 68 WF]*

I've been told that when the Bosnians moved to town, the students were put at East High. When it was found out that they could play soccer, they were transferred to a Bosnian education center at West High. *[EHS 68 WF]*

*Both overt and de facto segregation are evil. It's worse to have the rules on the books as opposed to de facto segregation where the rules are clearly understood by everybody. Because it's overt and more visible. The segregation that's not on the books but simply occurs because of the skin color or culture is bad, but not as bad as the overt stuff. A person should be able to make whatever they want to have their life be simply because they are an American or living in America as opposed to being restricted by the color of their skin. [EHS 69 WM]*

*In 1970-75, blacks weren't just moving 50 yards into the West Side of the river. They were moving into the Prospect and Burns Park areas, really nice homes. Educated blacks with double incomes. They had every right to buy any price house they wanted anywhere. I never saw anybody put their house up for sale or move out of a neighborhood. But there were discussions. When the first few homes were sold to blacks and they moved in. Discussion about the value of the homes in the area going down. People mistakenly believed that because an African American bought a home, it would suddenly become run down. The reality was that, because of the upbringing and education, the black family home was one of the nicest on the block. Blacks moving to the West Side erased a lot of frustration. Once white people saw that they want to have a nice home, too, people said, "This isn't so bad. The value of our house didn't go down." [WHS 69 WM]*

*There's no social integration in Waterloo yet. I sponsored several carnivals for three years in a row in Sullivan Park. Rented bounce houses and grilled hamburgers, hot dogs, chips and drinks. And opened it up to the community for free. "Come and meet your neighbors." And barely one percent of the people who showed up were white. [EHS 69 BM*

*Our youngest son was into sports and watching sports. And the black players were his heroes. We used to laugh at him because he'd say, "How come I'm not black?" He was just mad about it. And all I could tell him was that someday he'd understand. [WHS 69 WF]*

*I certainly had a lot of false beliefs about Waterloo. I grew up thinking that the reason we had so many black people in Waterloo was because it was the end of the train line after the Civil War. People got on the train and went as far as they could go and that's where they ended up. The last time I was there, I spent some time at the Grout Museum and discovered, when I was growing up, there were quite a few different ethnic groups that had been in or were in Waterloo. I had absolutely no concept of them being there. And there were a number of reasons for blacks in Waterloo – being brought in as strike breakers much later in history – than the end of the railroad story. [WHS 69 WF]*

*When we moved back to Waterloo, my husband – who wasn't from here – picked a house to buy he wanted me to see. And I'm like, "We can't live here." He was shocked. "Why not?" I said because the kids would have to go to West High. And he looked at me like, "Duh?" Back when I was at East, there were no kids of color at West High. None. Zero. That's not that long ago. It is, but it isn't. Our children did end up at West. [EHS 70 AAF]*

*I worked for the Waterloo schools. It seemed like being black and female the best thing for promotions and such. A black woman with whom I'd worked was promoted to the school district office. We were comfortable enough to joke around with each other and she told me, "You know, they used to call the school district office the White House, but now we call it the Black House." Because so many blacks were getting promotions and going to the admin building. There's still some reverse discrimination in the school administration. That bothers me. Recently, a mom went to the after-school program and her child wasn't there. Nobody knew where he was. He was found sleeping in an annex classroom. Three people had a responsibility for that child, but only one paid the price. The white teacher was fired and the two black workers weren't. Many people and I didn't think that was fair. They should have been treated equally because they all walked away from their responsibility for the child. If one got fired, they should all have been fired. If one got written up, they should have all been written up. The two black ladies are friends with black administrators. It appeared that's why they kept their jobs. That's happened before. I had three co-workers with horrendous attendance records. The white girl was fired, the two black girls kept their jobs. The two were my friends, but as co-workers, they sucked. They were two of the laziest, nonproductive people in the building. [EHS 70 WF]*

*I was happy to see that my son had a mix of friends growing up. And had no fear about racial issues. I think him being at Grant [in the Bridgeway project] when he was five helped. He was comfortable with both black and whites. He was happy at Logan. His black friends would come over to the house. Black friends were the norm for him. And he was a groomsman in one of his black friend's wedding. [EHS 70 WF]*

**'71-'73** *I worked in the foundry at John Deere the year after I graduated. It was probably 50-50 in terms of blacks and whites. I didn't have a chance to have lunch with the guys on the floor because I was hanging upside down in a ladle crane pouring iron. It was so dark in the foundry it was hard to see your hand in front of your face. I couldn't even see the guys on the floor. There were black men who didn't know how to read or write. The foundry clerk would give out the pay checks, they'd put their "X" on the back of the check and the clerk would go cash them. He got fired later for doing that. [EHS 71 WM]*

*We're all Americans. We need to embrace that and be happy for it. When I looked at the class list this past week at Kittrell, most of the names were ethnic names. How lucky are those kids? How fortunate are we to have the exposure to all of that? Which we didn't have when we were growing up? We're a global society. But we don't look at it that way. My hope would be that, as we get more and more different cultures in town, it'll be easier to close the gaps between groups. Because there's just more there. It'll have to happen. We whites are the minority. So, no matter what we think, we're not the people with the majority to do whatever. I don't know that people will really change. I guess that's the job of those of us who have careers that can help mold minds. [EHS 72 WF]*

*I've experienced white rage lots of times. Whenever blacks were yelling about being discriminated against and whites were like, "We didn't have anything to do with your history." Whites want to push against that feeling instead of just acknowledging it and helping everyone move on. [EHS 73 WF]*

*There are other ethnic groups in Waterloo and none is being singled out the way blacks were when we were in school. Someday the white people will take our turn and be the minority. And I think that's good. [EHS 73 WF]*

*For a while, there wasn't much racial tension in Waterloo, not like when we were in school. Over the last several years, there seems to be more than in the past. Because of the immigration. Bosnians and Hispanics moved in. Don't know what's in Waterloo that all these people would want to come here. We don't have Rath's anymore, we don't have Chamberlain, Waterloo Industries or. . . The only big business that's been here forever is John Deere. And they just laid off 155 people. Why would you come to a town that really doesn't have a lot going for it? We talk about this at church. One of the women said – and I don't know where she got her information or whether it's true or not – that Waterloo is a test ground for welfare among minorities. Really? [EHS 73 WM]*

*The bad thing about 1968 the riot was that the blacks were burning up, tearing up their own houses on the East Side. They weren't going on the West Side. And I didn't understand it. You talk about the Civil Rights movement, and you hate the social environment in which you live and the things which you go through as a minority. So, why are you destroying your own neighborhood? Who did they expect was going to rush in and rebuild their houses and replace their jobs and warehouses? That didn't make a whole lot of sense to me. Because someone else is doing it in the country, now you're doing it? You don't really have a cause. And now you're destroying your neighborhood. It defeats the whole purpose. I still don't understand it 50 years later. [EHS 73 AAM]*

*I live in a retirement mobile home court where most people are 70-plus. To move into the court, you must be interviewed by the board and abide by the rules. Someone asked during a discussion, "What if someone black wants to move in here?" A neighbor answered, "We can't have them. That would just bring us down." In this day and age. Someone else pointed out that we didn't have a choice anymore, even as a private development. If they agreed to abide by the rules, you let them in. It's not a big deal for me. But it was a big deal for the older residents. My grandpa thought that anyone who was different from him was Russian. [WHS 74 WF]*

*The average black family will accept a white person or child in their family quicker than a white person would accept a black person in theirs. That's not a prejudiced statement. It's true. I think because black people used to always have this thing, you didn't want to start any trouble because we know who's running everything. So, we don't want to start trouble with them. So, we'd rather get along with them and if they'll be our friends, we'll be their friends. For example, there was only one black cop back then, but he was crooked. Black people never wanted to rock the boat too much because they knew who was running everything. [EHS 74 AAM]*

*Waterloo was seriously damaged by the segregation in the 60s and 70s when I was growing up. I went back to Waterloo about 14 years ago and drove through the area where I grew up, past the house my parents bought in '62. It was a starter house. My mother got the "dramatic," handsome, doctor's wife house four years later. But it's nothing now. I saw black kids on the street. And it was surreal. I felt I was rubbernecking. I was shocked. I never thought I'd see the day. [WHS 74 WM]*

"Steady Eddie" grew up in a small town of less than 15,000 people in the Wiregrass Region in southeastern Alabama. In the mid-1970s, this young black man my age was a fellow employee, the janitor, the only black at the company. The company (details were changed to protect its identity) had some federal contracts that required minority participation. "Steady Eddie" was listed as an African American vice president of facilities.

He was always in a good mood, happy, deferential to the whites to a fault, what would classify as a "Stepin' Fetchit" character.[2] After a couple of months working together, we became friends and I accepted his lunch invitation to what he called "my part of town."

The Steady Eddie who showed up was articulate, well-spoken, confident, educated. The polar opposite of the Steady Eddie I knew at work. Before lunch he took me to three of his businesses in "the quarters,"[3] the black community. He introduced me to his employees and laid out a plan for using the businesses as a springboard to improve the economic situation in the quarters. His idea was a coalition of black businesspeople who could use collective purchasing power to negotiate with local black businesses in the town, county and region. Ultimately, he envisioned products and services of the black businessmen being sold to white buyers.

At lunch, I called him on the dual persona. Why the "Stepin' Fetchit" routine at work, which wasn't obviously who he really was? The explanation was simple. "I know the white rules. I know my place in the white community. People would be threatened if I were me at work, which could cause me to lose my job." So, why work there? "Because I need the income for my family, to support the enterprises. I

---

[2] Stepin Fetchit was a black, a "befuddled, mumbling, shiftless fool" played by Lincoln Perry, "America's first black movie star. Stepin Fetchit, Hollywood's First Black Film Star. (March 6, 2006). National Public Radio, Inc.: News & Notes. Retrieved from
https://www.npr.org/templates/story/story.php?storyId=5245089.
[3] "The Quarters" often refers to the area of a town where the blacks live, thought to be a shortened reference to the "slave quarters." The Quarters was the Negro settlement in Harper Lee's *To Kill a Mockingbird*, which we read in high school.

need to be plugged into the local white community. The time will come when I can be who I am."

## Interracial Relationships: Wisdom from Life Experiences

**'63-'66** *At our 50th reunion, we hosted an event in the Black's department store sky room in the afternoon and current East students attended. I'd created a massive poster for our reunion party and had put it up on a wall. I walked over to kids sitting at one table talking and said, "You've gotta see what it was like 50 years ago so you can see what it's going to be like in 50 years when you have a reunion." They got up and went over the poster, except for one black boy. I asked him to go look at it with me. "I don't think I'm going to even live to graduate," he said. He was serious. And I said, "Please, get through school no matter what. And you will see your 50th reunion." I almost wept because I thought, "These kids, they need another way." [EHS 63 WF]*

*The younger kids today, whites and blacks, have a vastly different way of thinking about and looking at things than we did. I don't know if it's because they weren't brought up right or didn't have a mom or the parents were working all the time and didn't have supervision. The majority really don't want to work. They want somebody to hand them stuff and don't do nothing for it, and walk around with those baggy pants. When we were young, I'd mow yards, shovel snow, babysit, wash windows, deliver newspapers. You don't have kids come by and ask if you want your yard mowed or sidewalk shoveled. They think it's beneath them to do a little work to earn a little money. [EHS 64 WM]*

*I treasure my memories of East High, of Waterloo. I have lasting friendships all over the world because of my learning experiences with different cultures there. And I'm not prejudiced as a result. My son married someone of a different culture and I'm just as proud to say my little granddaughter is mine as I do my daughter-in-law. She and her family are lovely people, and we all get along great. Maybe it's because I didn't agree with racial issues in this big wonderful world of ours. There are just as many bad white people out there. Every little bit I have contributed for my kids to have friends of many backgrounds is an accomplishment for me. Back in my Waterloo life I did fear a great many blacks due to their skin color and crime. I have grown. [EHS 65 WF]*

*I was working in radiology at Allen Hospital [on the northern East Side] transporting patients to be tested. One day I was sent to go get this lady, probably in her 40s or 50s, black. I treat everyone the same way. I made sure she had a blanket and was warm. And I noticed that she had bare feet. So, I got a pair of the footies, took the plastic off, got down and slid them on her feet. And she looked at me and said, "You're not afraid to touch me?" It's on both sides. People are so conditioned for so many years, she couldn't accept the fact that I didn't care if she were black or white. I'm going to treat you as a human being, black or white or whatever. Her reaction shocked the crap out of me. [WHS 66 WM]*

*I got married at Linden United Methodist, which is just a block down from our house and not quite a mile from McKinstry Junior. I didn't have anybody to sing at the wedding, but the minister, who was very young, offered a friend who was the music teacher at McKinstry. I said, "Sure." Turns out she was black. Oh, my God. The church just about closed its doors after they found out a black singer had sung at my wedding. I never realized my church was so opinionated. When the minister adopted a biracial baby, he had a black minister and his wife do the christening ceremony. They all but booked our pastor out of the church. That was pretty sad. [EHS 66 WF]*

*As an adult, having been where I've been and what I've done, there is and there will always be racial tension. It's how you handle it and how you understand it. There are certain integrated suburbs where I live where there is no racial tension and others where there is. I work in a very [emphasis] affluent suburb. I'm usually the first one at work, so I have a routine of going by Starbucks every morning. That's where you're really going to see some cultural diversity. Last week when I was standing in the line, one of the managers, a white woman, came out and called my name and asked, "How ya doing?" I went to give her a fist bump. And she said, "I don't want no fist bump" and hugged me. We're standing there in the middle of all these people and she hugged me. Oh, my goodness. [laughs] [EHS 66 AAM]*

*I worked in the office at Black's Department Store after high school. There were blacks working in the tea room and the coffee shop. But I didn't see a lot of black customers in either. Blacks did shop down in the basement, which was supposed to be a thrift store. The store had chairs on the balcony for the older people who would sit up there. Five years after we graduated, the chairs had to be taken out because rowdy kids would come in, sit up on that balcony and spit over the edge. And these were white kids, not black kids. To get rid of them, Black's took the chairs away and the older shoppers complained. [EHS 66 WF]*

*My daughter worked at Covenant Hospital as a pharmacy tech giving medications one summer college break. She went into a little elderly white woman's room, and the lady looked at her and asked, "Hi, how are you doing?" My daughter answered and asked if there was anything she could get the patient. The woman put on her glasses and said, "Oh, you're a little black girl, aren't you." What do you say? [shaking her head laughing] What do you say? [EHS 66 AAF]*

*Both of my girls worked at Montgomery Ward [downtown on West 4th Street a block from the Cedar River] in high school. Management would tell them to watch the black people when they came in. They were afraid they would steal something. In some of the stores at the mall, I would be trying on something. And the sales person would burst into the fitting room, like she was trying to catch you in the act of stealing or something. I'm not dressed. I mean, come on. Really? [EHS 66 AAF]*

*I live on the West Side in a condo now. I have some great neighbors. If I see them out, I'll say a few words. Other than that, we don't really interact. I grew up as an only child. And I kind of keep to myself. I'm the only black person in the building. Not a lot of people like condos. Me, I don't like mowing grass. I'm all about letting someone else do it. [EHS 66 AAF]*

*I wasn't prejudiced in high school. Never have been. I didn't really have any reason not to like black people, because I never any problems with them. So, I've never considered myself a racist until Obama. [laughs] I hate that guy so much. On the other hand, I like Ben Carson, I like Tim Scott, the black congressman from South Carolina. [EHS 66 WM]*

*We lived in the South for 13 years. There was no river, but there was a good side of town for your elementary kids to go to school and the other side of town where the blacks were. We could afford a nicer home on that "other" side of town so our kids would go to school with the black kids. My kids went to the elementary school that was overwhelmingly black. My youngest was in 2nd grade when my aunt and uncle from Iowa visited. We went to pick her up after school. When my daughter came out, my aunt turned to me and asked, "My gosh, is she the only little white girl in that class?" [EHS 66 WF]*

*East High was an eye-opening experience. It broadened me as a person. It helped me when I had my own family and we moved into a town that had some of the same racial prejudices Waterloo had. It didn't matter to me where our house was located, but it did matter if our kids would get a good education. What they did in school was more important than who they were sitting next to. [EHS 66 WF]*

*It was the late 70s. Black power. Black folks were wearing Afros. I had a gorgeous Afro and was going back into the building where I worked after lunch. There was a little old white lady with me. And she said, "Oh, you have such a lovey tan." And I just did not know what to say. [EHS 66 AAF]*

*People who didn't attend a mixed-race school tend to buy into the stereotypes in their environment, of friends. And never evolve and realize that they can be friends with people who don't look like you or think like you. There are 330 million people in the United States now and no two of us are alike in many ways. [EHS 66 WM]*

*I still carry a picture of Mom and Dad, a biracial couple, in my billfold. When I hear bigotry or racist views, I listen for a while, and then pull out the photo and shut that talk down. As an adult, I've endured enough prejudice to last a lifetime. The picture comes out. [EHS 66 WM]*

*In terms of white guilt, I could see how the way blacks were treated, the violence, did to them. I thought of myself as trying to move against that. Our family didn't have money, but I had received a gift of a very expensive watch from my great-uncle once. It was lost at East and I put up the notices, "Please return, no questions asked." A teacher brought it to me and said someone had turned it in. We took the back off and found a kinky black hair, so it must have been taken by a black person." I had admired that teacher. But I knew no watch, especially that watch, could get a hair into the back of it. I was so, so angry. It was white racism. It was endemic among even those we wanted to admire. [EHS 66 WF]*

*For a long time, I mourned that I had gone to East High. Then when I begin to look back on my life and the person I had developed into, I realized that there were gifts in the experience. I was very comfortable with, not afraid of diversity. Peers were afraid of it. They would put blacks down in private jokes thinking I, being white, would appreciate them. There were a couple of dates I had to tell, "You're not impressing me with your distasteful racist comments. Why don't you take me home?" I can stand up by myself easily in a peer group or with cohorts and say "no" to certain things. And I have a wonderful appreciation of black music. Learning that empathy goes a long way to healing relationships. I had a familiarity with violence. Everyone who's gone to East was marked by violence, unless they were living in a bubble. Not*

410

*necessarily violence against them personally. But by being part of a culture of violence which played out in our school. We all fear violence, but unreasonable fear of violence destroys whole societies and cultures. After cursing that I had to attend East, I realize I've been able to do things and see things, and speak to them and stand up for them in ways I never could have done without having gone through that. Or without having parents to help me process those things. [EHS 66 WF]*

*My friend who lives right across the hall from me is a black woman and we went to massage therapy school together. We used to trade back and forth on our assignments. One time she came to my house to give me a massage and I didn't get to the door right away. My husband came home when she was knocking. He didn't know her and she didn't know him. And she said to him, "I don't know what to do." And he told her, "You could just get back in your car and leave." He thought she was a Jehovah's Witness. When I came to the door, he was really embarrassed when he found out who she was. She was so good natured about it and every time she phoned she'd say, "Tell your husband his little black Jehovah's Witness called." She moved into her apartment across from me about a day after I moved in. We neighbor back and forth all the time. [EHS 66 WF]*

**'67-'70** *When I heard the n-word when I was in school, I was ready to fight. I don't know if that was instinctive or I was taught that. My reaction today? I won't get into a physical confrontation. First, I want to understand the situation, understand my surroundings. When I think about where the n-word was derived from, what it means. It was once the most degrading word ever created. I don't care who's using it, I don't like it. Within the black community it's part of the language, part of the culture, part of the way of life. In my household, my family, we don't use it. I don't know if our kids use it, but we didn't raise them that way. Basically, it's just another word. [EHS 67 AAM]*

*As my older son got into junior high, I watched him start to develop a sense of entitlement. I wanted to make sure that he didn't have the picture everybody grew up like he did, so we talked, a lot. We would talk about the fact there were kids that had come from single-parent homes where there may be several siblings. And all the parents are trying to do is provide a roof over their head, food on the table and clothing. There's no spring break, no vacation. That's life out there. I wanted to make sure he understood that, because I hadn't when I was in junior high school. I thought everyone had a pretty good life like I did. I told him, "You're growing up in this environment by the grace of God. I could go to work tomorrow and not have a job and our life would suddenly change dramatically." [WHS 67 WM]*

*I wish I had done more, but I tried to mentor and back up the very few black employees who worked for me. They were not paid well. My perception was that that the company treated them like pets and I mean, like pets. I tried to treat them the same I would anyone. I hope I did a little bit. But how do you know? [EHS 67 WM]*

*West was an all-white school, but the world isn't that way. You have to deal with people. You might just as well get used to it when you're younger. It would have been more advantageous to have dealt with black folks, folks of other ethnicities when I was growing up. I would have understood them better. [WHS 67 WM]*

*I had the conversations with my kids my parent had with me plus more. They would always tell us basic, common sense things. "Do what you're supposed to do. Follow the rules. We're not third-class citizens." I'd ask my kids, "What are you going to be doing this time next year? How are you going to get there? Don't plan to fail. Be yourself. Use some common sense. Do what's right. Before you do anything, think of the consequences." Things I'd learned in the military, as a professional athlete and as a manager at John Deere. [EHS 67 AAM]*

*My son came home from West with a story which reminded me of East. There were 2-3 black girls in adjacent lockers who got into a fight.*

*He said it took a long time for teachers to come out of their rooms to stop it. And I thought, "Oh my gosh. This is a whole another generation going through the same thing." [OHS 67 WF]*

*We never lost a football game the three years I was at East. And it wasn't because there were black players out there. There was a sense of community when we were at school. Sadly, that sense didn't extend beyond. One of our classmates died in an auto accident some years back. One of the black girls in our class came to the visitation. The only black person there. I was so happy she came. I thought that really spoke to how she felt. That she crossed that racial line. [EHS 68 WF]*

*I've tried to teach my kids to treat everyone as an individual. Find out what they're like. There's good and bad everywhere. If you're lucky, you'll meet more good than bad. And if my son had had a black girlfriend, I'd have gone with the flow. If I raised hell and condemned it, he'd have blown me off and gone the other direction. [WHS 69 WM]*

*People I met after high school knew I went to East because I was black. People thought it was a bad school. That we had fighting all the time. That there were drugs. That was their perception. These perceptions came from the media, quite frankly. Whenever East was talked about, it was from a negative view point. In the sports section, for example, East high can win a game today and they'll be in the back sections of the paper. And they'll have some small town which has just won its first game in five years and they'll be on the first sports page. That's done all the time. So, people don't know how many scholars came out of East High, black or white. We didn't have a lot of discipline problems at East High. The biggest problem came was when we were trying to get our rights as black students in 1968 and '69. [EHS 69 AAF]*

*As long as I live I will always fight for what are called my civil and human rights. They're God-given. God put me down here to live, as he did every other human being. And nobody has the right to take those away. So, as long as I can speak, write or whatever, I will be fighting for what I consider to be injustice. That will never stop for me. You can become really sour and bitter. Or you can do like my dad told me; "Don't let anybody tell you what you can do." I have a friend who says you can be bitter or better. You can be powerful or pitiful. And I've chosen to be better and powerful. [EHS 69 AAF]*

*The math teacher I replaced when I was hired at East taught the advanced classes. But there weren't enough advanced classes to fill my schedule. The other faculty were comfortable teaching the advanced and middle-level classes they were teaching, which meant I had to pick up lower-level classes. The classes were 80% minority students, the opposite of the advanced classes. Teaching these classes was a problem. It's not the kids were less intelligent, but they had all these other things in life they were dealing with. [COL 69 WM]*

*I was totally shocked when the director of a racially mixed summer youth program – a black man – told me there's no such thing as a white who isn't a racist. I don't remember his name, but I'd like to know if he still feels that way. And if so, how carrying that conviction has impacted his life and his ability to interact with whites all of these years. His broad, unfair, statement has affected me at times, making me wonder if some of the blacks I've met feel the same and automatically consider me a racist. [EHS 69 WF]*

*When my son was born I was into drugs and in a lot of other behaviors I'd learned growing up. Not positive and not constructive. I didn't know what it meant to be a father. I never had one. Never saw a positive male or father role model. I grew up as a weed. Like I was thrown out in the field. Without nurturing and nourishment, you grow as a weed. That's what I felt my growing period was. I had to learn manhood. My son and my daughter sat on my lap in prison. Their visits meant something to me. I decided I was going to make a commitment to be a father. I'll never ever be absent. Or allow anyone else to raise them and shape their thinking. I must have an influence. I was more grounded, positive in my blackness because of my studies and my graduate work. I knew the positives of my history and those are the parts*

*I gave my kids. How to be positive and strong. It's amazing what they've done in spite of me being their dad. [EHS 69 AAM]*

*My daughter was three years old the first time we went back to Waterloo. We went back every two years so she could get to know the family. She was the one who started asking questions about race. She knew she was black. In my family on my mother's side, everyone is very light skinned. There's a family story that my maternal grandmother missed being beaten up by the KKK because they thought she was white. The range of colors is from very light-skinned, slightly tanned, to very dark here in Europe. I never really sat down and talked to her about it. It just came up. Her schooling was with all kind of nationalities. She's very comfortable with that. [COL 69 AAF]*

*Our kids were born in Darwin, Australia, which is very multicultural with a lot of Aboriginal people. When they were two-and-a-half and three-and-a-half, we lived in a national park owned by Aboriginal people. Ours were the only white children at the Aboriginal school. They were well-received. A bit of a novelty, because of their white skin. They're both very fair. And one of them absolutely hates sunscreen. He would often say, "I wish I was black," so he wouldn't have to have sunscreen on. He had a dream one night when he was three-and-half and told me the next morning, "I know now why I am white. It's because God ran out of black paint when he got to me." [I laughed] That was at the end of the conversation. When he was five, we moved to Sydney and he was at an all-white school. The darkest kid at the school was one with Italian heritage. A year later he came home from school one day and said, "You know, it's okay that I'm white." I think he realized everybody around him was white. Growing up in Darwin with a lot of Aboriginal and Indonesian people, and then going to a school with Aboriginal or mixed students – half Italian, half Fijian, half-Thai, half Australian – he was surrounded by people of a darker color and that's what he wanted to be. [WHS 69 WF]*

*My UNI classes were multicultural and I became more tolerant. I became a lot more open to ideas like interracial dating, which I saw at the university. When my kids were at West High in the late 1980s, the school needed chaperones at dances. I would volunteer and, of course, there were interracial couples there on the dance floor. I didn't say anything or try to break it up. But in the back of my head I'm thinking, "My gosh, this doesn't look right." I guess even at 35 or so, I certainly had thoughts which probably would be considered racist. Today? My thinking is that we're all human beings, God's creation, and it's not wrong to care for someone of a different race or different culture or nationality. [WHS 69 WM]*

*When I was teaching, I tended to go ballistic when I heard the n-word. I don't feel comfortable with the word when blacks are using it. I know in some circles that's okay. But I still don't feel comfortable with it. [EHS 70 WF]*

*My best friend in the fourth grade was black and I thought she was the coolest, most beautiful girl in the entire school. But I worried about her growing up black, which meant what would now be called a marginal life. Now I think it was maybe elitist to have assumed the worst or worried about her. [EHS 69 WF]*

*We specifically moved to the East Side and put our son in Grant Bridgeway, an experimental school where they tried to get a balance of 50-50, an incubator of some sort. My husband was in the military and I worked in schools. We both worked with black people. It seemed easier, although not always easy. Today, even though I have black friends, there's still a segregation. If we had dinners or potlucks where I worked, the black people always congregated together. I don't know what that's about, honestly. [EHS 70 WF]*

**'71-'73** *It's ironic. White people try to tan. They're not happy with their pale white, so they try to get darker. And be a dark-skinned racist toward people with dark skin. God put* *people in different environments. The people from Africa were subject to the sun, so skin is going to be darker. If you see black and white, that's what you see. Being a believer, if you understand God created us all in his image, then you see a person, a human being. If you cut me, I'm going to bleed the same color as you do. [EHS 73 AAM]*

*Our biracial son and a daughter went to public schools. He went to Central Middle School and East High. Then we moved to the West Side and our daughter went to Hoover Middle and West High. Yes, we talked to them about race. That everybody in the world is different. Different colors. You're a little in between. You got the best of both worlds. My wife was a little more vocal than I was and always told them, "Never be ashamed of who you are." And, "if you ever run into a situation where someone calls you a name, remember that they don't understand the world. They haven't been taught that prejudice is a bad thing. It's ignorance and a sad thing that they don't understand this." [EHS 73 WM]*

*My son had a mix of friends, but mostly black. My daughter had mostly white friends. [They were eight years apart]. Kind of weird for one to go with one group and the other a different group. Moving to the other side of the river unraveled some of the friends my daughter had on the East Side. [EHS 73 WM]*

*Twenty-five years ago, when I was looking to buy a house on the East Side, light years past high school, I went to two different Westside realtors with houses listed on the East Side. They both said, "Don't you want to look in a nice neighborhood?" What they meant was, "You're white, don't you want to live on the West Side?" And I thought, "Racism does exist here." I'd heard stories all my life of blacks applying for jobs and being told no one was being hired, but the next day a "Help Wanted" sign would be in the window. But if you don't look for things like that, you won't see them. [EHS 74 WF]*

*I wasn't disadvantaged by graduating from West, because I was exposed to blacks with busing. This comes up in our family a lot. My daughter is very adamant that her kids go to school with a lot of mixed races. Omaha has a lot of different school districts and she's in the Omaha Public School district, the largest one. It's a very diverse, good school district with an inner-city area and they do very well. She feels the people and some of the other districts are a little bit more segregated, that the multiracial experience for her kids is better. She runs into people a lot who say, "I would never send MY [emphasis] kids to Omaha Public Schools." She doesn't want her kids exposed to segregation. She wants them exposed to people they're going to be working to all their lives. [WHS 74 WF]*

## Reflections from the Bridge

*A man who views the world the same at 50 as he did at 20 has wasted 30 years of his life. – Muhammad Ali*

*The Bridge Between* is the story about the perceptions of and insights from the high school experiences of graduates of the five Waterloo, Iowa, high schools 50 years later. Integral to *TBB* are the interracial relationships or their absence in the high schools we attended. And the impact of racial confrontation in Waterloo on us and our schools as the town and the school district worked to overcome over a century of segregation.

It's the story of our communal transformation from high school sophomore to senior, and ultimately the impact of those three years in that decade on our adult lives.

*The Bridge Between* is a story. This is the end of that story.

## Endnotes

[1] Paul, A.M. (Nov. 18, 2013). Cited in "Does High School Determine the Rest of Your Life?" *Time* magazine. Retrieved from http://ideas.time.com/2013/11/18/does-high-school-determine-the-rest-of-your-life/.

[2] Oh, the places you'll go! (1990). Seuss, Dr. New York: Random House.

[3] Abe Smith, 19, and Tommy Shipp, 18, were lynched on August 7, 1930, in Marion, IN, for the alleged rape of a 19-year-old white Mary Ball and shooting her 23-year-old fiancé, Claude Teeter. Ball was reportedly Smith's girlfriend. A third teenager, James Cameron, 16, was spared. At his trial, Ball testified she hadn't been raped and the all-white jury believed Cameron's story that he had left before the shooting. Cameron was sentenced to 2-21 years for being an accessory before the fact. Paroled from the Indiana State Reformatory after four years, Cameron was pardoned and given a key to the city 58 years later by Gov. Evan Bayh. The father of five, he became an entrepreneur and civil rights activist, and founded the Black Holocaust Museum. "An Iconic Lynching in the North." Kaplan, F. Milwaukee, WI: America's Black Holocaust Museum. Retrieved from http://abhmuseum.org/2012/01/an-iconic-lynching-in-the-north/.

[4] Sandra Dee [real name Alexandria Zuck, b. 1942] "at the height of her fame was arguably the biggest female teen idol of her time. . . . With her squeaky-clean image and girl-next-door charm. . . ." '50s teen queen Sandra Dee dies. (Feb. 21, 2005). The Associated Press. Retrieved from http://www.today.com/news/50s-teen-queen-sandra-dee-dies-2D80555383.

[5] Words of Wisdom. (November 12, 1991). Shakur, T. *2Pacalypse Now,* Shakur's debut studio album. Santa Monica, CA: Interscope Records and EastWest Records America. Retrieved from http://tinyurl.com/ycaa5afp.

West 4th Street, 1910. Retrieved from

# Afterword: The More Things Change...

*Plus ça change, plus c'est la même chose. (The more it changes, the more it's the same thing.) – Jean-Baptiste Alphonse Karr[1]*

*The Bridge Between (TBB)* story ends in 1973. What happened afterward?

"Afterword" includes two updates – one about the school and school system, and the other about Waterloo and the community. What's changed in 50 years in the school system, the schools, the students? What's changed in Waterloo in 50 years? Interpretation of the update data isn't within the scope of *TBB*, so no inferences are offered.

Updates provide context to the contributors' perspectives shared in 2016-17 about the racial relations and tensions, and integration in the schools and school system, and in the town with which you are now familiar.

## Update: The Waterloo Community School District (WCSD) 50 Years Later

The WCSD update in is a "panoramic photo" of key data from the start of this millennium through 2018.

George Diestelmeier, who was overlooked as a replacement for Superintendent George Hohl in 1971, purportedly because he lacked a Ph.D., subsequently served as superintendent for 11 years (January 1972-July 1983). It's the longest tenure since Jack Logan, who served from 1941-1962.

Educated in Waterloo schools, Diestelmeier graduated from East in 1934, started teaching at East Junior and was a teacher, coach, principal and administrator for 45 years.

Betty Jean Furgerson, a member of the school board and director of the Waterloo Human Rights Commission, doubted in 1983 Waterloo or any other town for that matter, "will see a record like Diestelmeier's again" because the job of school superintendent "is becoming Increasingly political and that . . . they'll move on in five or six years.[2] Since then, there have been six superintendents. One served for five years, two for six and two for seven. The sixth is Dr. Jane Lindaman, for whom the 2017-18 school year is her fifth year.

In 1970, there were just over 19,000 students in the WCSD. In 2016-17, there are just over 10,000. East Side school enrollment in 1970 was 16.0% black, West Side was 5.3%. In 2016, the respective percentages are 13.7% and 12.7%. From 1970 t0 2016, percentage of black students in district schools went from 14.2% to 26.4% (Table 1).

| Table 1 Minority Profiles in Waterloo Schools, 1970 & 2016[3] | | | | |
|---|---|---|---|---|
| 1970 | | | | |
| Race (# Schools) | East Side (18) | West Side (21) | All schools (39) | Waterloo |
| Students/Population | 7,652 | 11,614 | 19,266 | 75,553 |
| Oriental (Asian)[a] | 0.0% | 0.2% | 0.1% | 0.2% |
| Negro (Black) | 16.0% | 5.3% | 14.2% | 8.8% |
| Hispanic | 0.1% | 0.2% | 0.1% | NA[b] |
| AmInd/ AlaskaNat[c] | 0.2% | 0.1% | 0.2% | 0% |
| Two or More | Not Collected/Reported in 1970 | | | |
| NatHawaiian/OtherPI[d] | | | | |
| White | 51.5% | 97.1% | 86.9% | 85.4% |
| Waterloo | | | | 98.7% |
| 2016 | | | | |
| Race (# Schools)* | East Side (8) | West Side (10) | All schools (18) | Waterloo |
| Students/Population | 3,963 | 6,136 | 10,099 | 67,934 |
| PCT Change 2970-2016 | -48.2% | -47.2% | -94.8% | -10.1% |
| Asian[c] | 0.5% | 2.0% | 2.6% | 2.6% |
| Black | 13.7% | 12.7% | 26.4% | 10.2% |

| Hispanic | 5.3% | 6.1% | 11.3% | 4.6% |
| AmInd/ AlaskaNat | 0.0% | 0.1% | 0.2% | 0.7% |
| Two or More | 3.0% | 4.4% | 7.4% | 1.5% |
| NatHawaiian/OtherPI | 0.4% | 1.2% | 1.6% | 0.6% |
| White | 15.5% | 32.6% | 48.0% | 83.7% |

*"Oriental" was the designation used by the district in 1970. *Not gathered in 1970 Decennial Census. *Asian: a person having origins in any of the original peoples of the Far East, Southeast Asia, or the Indian subcontinent including, for example, Cambodia, China, India, Japan, Korea, Malaysia, Pakistan, the Philippine Islands, Thailand, and Vietnam.* *No data available. *American Indian or Alaska Native *Native Hawaiian or Other Pacific Islander.*

There are several explanations for the changes in the WCSD minority profile, including integration plans, population shifts as Waterloo neighborhoods city-wide became more accessible to blacks in the mid- to late 1970s and an overall decline in Waterloo population.

It fell by 10% between 1970 and 2016, which resulted in a significant decline in the school district's enrollments.

In 1970, there were three high schools – East, West and Orange. There were seven junior high (grades 7-9) and 31 elementary schools (grades K-6). The map is in *TBB* Chapter 4.

Between the end of *The Bridge Between* in 1973 and 2018, 16 East Side schools closed, five new ones were repurposed or opened. Fifteen West Side schools closed with four repurposed or new schools. Four Catholic schools closed, one new one was opened. And Immanuel Lutheran closed.

In 2018, there are eight East-Side schools, 10 on the West Side and five Catholic schools, all on the West Side of Waterloo.

In 2017-18, there were three high schools (grades 9-12) – East, West and the Expo Alternative Learning Center. (Figure 1) There were four middle schools (grades 6-8) and nine elementary schools (grades PreK-5). (Table 2)

422

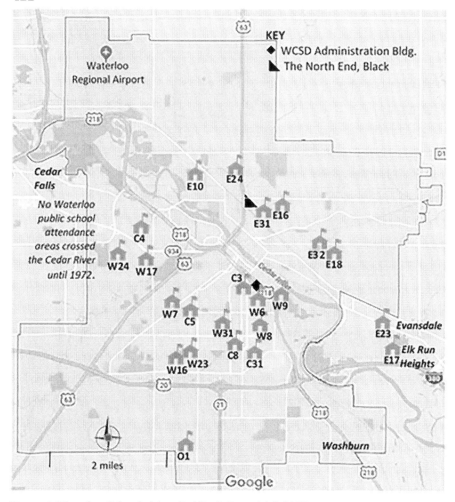

Figure 1 Waterloo Schools Map, Public & Parochial, 2017

| Table 2 Key to Schools in Figure 9 | | |
|---|---|---|
| 2016-2017 Schools Open Key (~~Closed during or after TBB~~) | | |
| East Side Public Schools (8) | West Side Public Schools (10) | Catholic Schools (5) |
| Elementary | Elementary | Grades 1-8 |
| ~~E1 City View Heights, E2 Elk Run, E3 Frances Grout, E4 Grant, E5~~ | O01 Orange Elem ~~W1 Black Hawk, W2 Castle Hill, W3 Edison~~ | ~~C1 Our Lady of Victory Academy (OLVA), C2~~ ~~St. Mary~~ |

| | | |
|---|---|---|
| Hawthorne, E6 Hewitt, E7 Jewett, E8 Krieg, E9 Lafayette | Elem., W4 Emerson, W5 Nellie Garvey | C3 Sacred Heart |
| E10 Lincoln | W6 Irving | C4 Blessed Sacrament |
| E11 Longfellow, E12 Maywood, E13 Roosevelt, E14 Van Eaton, E15 Greenbrier | W7 Kingsley | C5 St. Edward |
| E16 Cunningham (2002) | W8 Kittrell | C6 St. John, C7 St. Nicholas |
| E17 Poyner (2007) | W9 Lowell | C8 Blessed Maria Assunta Pallotta (2012) |
| E18 Highland (Jan2010) | W10 Washburn, W11 Whittier, W12 Cresthaven, W13 Westridge, W14 Cedar Terrace, W15 Devonshire | **High School** |
| **Middle School (Junior High)** | W16 Lou Henry (2005) | C31 Columbus High |
| E21 Logan Jr., E22 McKinstry Jr. | W17 Becker (Jan 2012) | **Lutheran School** |
| E23 Bunger MS | **Middle School (Junior High)** | L1 Immanuel Lutheran |
| E24 Carver Academy (2009) | O21 Orange Jr., W21 West Jr., W22 Edison Jr. | **KEY** Closed Schools |
| **High School** | W23 Hoover MS. | Schools still open |
| E31 East | W24 Central MS (1988) | *(School locations are proximate, but not to scale due to nearness to one another and the size of the icons.)* |
| E32 Expo Alternative Learning Center (2010) | **High School** O31 Orange High | |
| | W31 West High | |
| | W32 Central High | |

Two major criteria reported by the Iowa Department of Instruction for assessing a school's performance are its dropout and graduation rates.

| Table 3 Dropout & Graduation Rates in Seven Largest Iowa School Districts[5] | | | | |
|---|---|---|---|---|
| 2015-2016 | High School Enrollment* | PCT Black* | Dropout Rate** | Graduation Rate** |
| Cedar Rapids | 5,444 | 14.9% | 5.5% | 83.9% |
| Davenport | 4,774 | 17.2% | 6.0% | 83.5% |
| Des Moines | 8,961 | 18.8% | 6.7% | 81.1% |
| Dubuque | 3,776 | 7.8% | 2.2% | 89.8% |
| Iowa City | 4,168 | 17.9% | 1.6% | 93.8% |
| Sioux City | 4,071 | 5.3% | 3.1% | 87.5% |
| **Waterloo** | **3,002** | **24.33%** | **4.45%** | **77.37%** |

| Iowa | 34,528 | 6.5% | 1.9% | 91.3% |

* 2016-17 school year   ** 2015-16 school year

Of the seven largest school districts in Iowa, Waterloo had the fourth lowest dropout rate, but was the lowest graduation rate, which includes Expo Alternative High students. (Table 3)

In 2002, the Dr. Walter Cunningham School for Excellence opened to replace Grant Elementary and half of the Roosevelt Elementary attendance area. Cunningham has maintained a steady enrollment since opening, with 425 students enrolled (33 in PK and 392 students in Grades K-5) in 2014, 406 in 2016-17.

Cunningham's population is high-poverty [89% of students are eligible for free and reduced lunch] and high-minority, 87.93% in 2016-2017. (Table 4)[6] Native languages spoken in the district are English, Spanish and Korean.

| Table 4 Racial Profile Cunningham Elementary in the 2016-17 School Year | | | | | | | | | |
|---|---|---|---|---|---|---|---|---|---|
| A | B | H | I | M | P | W | MIN | PCT | TOT |
| 2 | 272 | 42 | 0 | 34 | 7 | 49 | 357 | 87.9% | 406 |

*TABLE 4 KEY: A, Asian; B, Black; H, Hispanic; I, Native American; M, ; P, Pacific Islander; W, White. MIN, Total Minority Enrollment; PCT, Percentage Minority; TOT, total school enrollment.*

Four [unique] programs were initiated at Cunningham:

1. A continuous year calendar from July through June. A traditional calendar was re-instituted in the 2014-15 school year due to a lack of data to support its effectiveness.

2. A dress code for all students and staff, which was adopted by the entire district in 2009.

3. Single sex classrooms in 2004, which were abandoned in 2010 due to a lack of data to support its effectiveness and the denial of a waiver from the Iowa Department of Education.

4. Enrollment continuity; students could continue at Cunningham, even if moving into a different attendance boundary. [7]

A 2012 Iowa law assuring students read at grade level by the end of third grade included an early warning system to help educators identify and intervene with students at risk for reading failure in kindergarten through third grade. Fifty-three of 398 of Iowa's public school districts and nonpublic schools use the system.

In the 2015-16 school year, a 14.6% increase in WCSD students reading at or above the third-grade level in K-3rd was the largest among the states' urban school districts.

"We are now better equipped than at any point in time to identify which students are on track and which ones aren't, and we have tools to spring into action with instruction that works," Superintendent Jane Lindaman said. "Knowledge is power, and when we know what students need, we are much more effective at providing the right interventions."[8]

In his April 06, 2018, State of the City Address, Waterloo Mayor Quentin Hart cited unique dimensions of the school system – more than 55 languages spoken, one of the state's first dual French-English classes and the Expo Alternative Learning Center, the first exceptional children's program in the state where a child with a disability can showcase their intellectual giftedness.[9]

The center has six educational programs "to provide our students [who may need supplemental and intensive supports]with individualized learning opportunities that address their educational needs in a safe and nurturing environment."[10]

- Expo Alternative High School: designed to educate students in danger of failing and/or dropping out of school for various reasons. Located in the former McKinstry Junior High.
- Graduation Connection (Grad Connect): an individualized credit recovery program for students on a graduation plan who need additional credits to graduate.

426

- WEBC Program: educates students from middle and high schools whose behaviors distract them from the learning environment. Students must demonstrate the ability to responsibly manage their behavior prior to transitioning back to their home school or district.
- Bridge Program: works with 8th grade students from the four area middle schools referred by their home school administrator and/or counselor as at-risk of failing and/or possibly being retained.
- Star-C Program: educates special needs students with significant behavior concerns in grades 6-12 recommended by the home school IEP (Individual Education Program) Team.
- Transition Alliance Program (TAP): increases successful in obtaining, maintaining, and regaining employment by youth with disabilities referred by their home school IEP Team.

Columbus High (9-12)
West Side

(K/1-8)

OLVA (East Side)
St. Mary (East Side)
St. John (East Side/SE)
St. Nicholas (East/Evansdale)
Blessed Sacrament (West Side)
Sacred Heart (West Side)
St. Edward (West Side)
Blessed Maria Assunta Pallotta

Changes in Waterloo's economy, population and family size contributed to declining enrollment in the Catholic schools after 1973. By 2018, OLVA and St. Mary had closed, and St. John and St. Nicholas were consolidated, then closed. had been consolidated. (Figure 2)

Figure 2 Catholic Educational Pathways, 2018

# Perspectives 2016-17: The Waterloo Community School District (WCSD) 50 Years Later

*With wisdom comes age (sic). – Author*

*[By the end of 1999,] some changes had occurred [in the WCSD], but . . . there was still much work to be done to improve race relations. For example, the local public school district was described as unresponsive to cultural differences of African American children while at the same time making special provisions for other children. Because of past incidents of racial harassment and discrimination in student discipline matters, the school district [was] being monitored by the U.S. Department of Education, Office for Civil Rights [as the 20th century arrived].*[11]

The last two questions to which *The Bridge Between (TBB)* contributors responded were about racial relations and tensions, and integration in the schools and school system; were they "worse," "about the same" or "better" than when we were in school? But an open-ended explanation of their responses was also required.

Not all contributors had perceptions about the Waterloo schools in 2016-17, which was expected. Many had migrated from Waterloo and had no basis for any perceptions due to sporadic contact with the town or the schools, if any. And none had children of elementary school age.

But people who stayed and raised families in Waterloo, and have grandchildren attending the schools did.

Many see the Waterloo's schools at the mid-point, "about the same." A number provided a discussion about the cycles through which both the school system and Waterloo had been in dealing with race relations the past 50 years. The other two-thirds split evenly between "better" and "worse."

Perception is reality. Some of the perceptions about the schools were compelling, but weren't included because they were based were second-hand or included information that could identify the contributor. These perceptions are representative.

*East is still segregated because school administrators are more interested in how much money they make and where they live instead of the progress of the black race. Just because you're black doesn't mean you're looking out for the best of your people. And just because you're black doesn't mean that you have the skills to work with any kind of student. We got more discipline problems now than we ever had when we were in school. You've got five times the number of black students who are being disciplined, who are being suspended, who are being kicked out of school at a time when you have all these black administrators, which we didn't have when we were in school. Administrators with supposed expertise. And it's getting worse for our students? It's a plan. It's a plan. I think we're going backwards. I know we're going backwards. [EHS 69 AAF]*

*They did start a program here where individuals from Waterloo could go to Wartburg [College in Waverly, IA, 21 miles northwest of Waterloo]. And they had special training which would allow them to come back and get into the school district. That didn't continue very long. [EHS 69 AAF]*

## Update: Waterloo 50 Years Later

The most dramatic change in Waterloo the last 50 years was the election in 2015 of Quentin Hart as the town's first black mayor.

*Fifty years after the Voting Rights Act and seven years after President Barack Obama won the White House, it may strike some as overblown to note how a Midwestern city of fewer than 70,000 residents, like many others before it, finally reflects modern demographics in its top job and has shed old prejudice at the ballot box. But election of its first black mayor bears special meaning in a city that arguably more than any other in Iowa, has been bitterly divided by race.[12]*

Hart won 34% and Tim Hurley, a former mayor, won 26% of the votes among the five candidates in the regular in November ballot.

Hart won 58.7% of the vote in the runoff. He won the black Fourth Ward, 20 of 30 voting precincts and the absentee balloting by more than 400 votes. His run-off election win was "a shift in the political landscape of Waterloo."[13]

*The vote went beyond the black community. The black community couldn't put him in there. He needed the white votes and he got them. Some things are motivated by race. Nobody is going to come out and say it. But it seems like he gets more criticism a white mayor would. [EHS 60 AAM]*

A product of East Side schools and a 1989 graduate of East High, Hart was Ward 4 Councilman for eight years and the first African American-appointed Mayor Pro-Tem before being elected mayor. He was the Associate Director of Multicultural Affairs for Hawkeye Community College in Waterloo at the time.

In 2016, shortly after moving into the mayor's office, Hart graciously shoe-horned me into his schedule as the newly elected mayor. Attending East was clearly a life advantage.

*I wanted to be at East High. Some of the kids in City View [on the East Side of the North End] went to West High, three miles from East and eight from West. But East High pride. There wasn't anything that could compare to it. A lot of us on the East Side had opportunities during the summer to work with, talk and mix with people from the West Side, Hudson, the surrounding areas. Attending East gave me the opportunity to have experiences which allowed me to become unbiased in judging people. I learned to judge a person on any side of this side of this community over any of the bridges by the content of their character.*

Hart has been described by many and sees himself as a bridge builder.[1] On December 1, 2015, "He [was] in the middle of the [4th Street] bridge – a deeply symbolic spot in this city, as if suspended between

---

[1] *The Bridge Between* became the working title for this book the year before.

two worlds – when he first heard the election results. He had kept this same vigil on at least three previous election nights."[14]

*I think it's good for the community that we have a black mayor. It shows that some people are willing to vote for whoever they think is best, taking race out of the picture. They don't care what color you are. They just want to get the job done. But it seems like he gets more criticism than a white mayor would. [EHS 60 AAM]*

*I've heard nothing but good from people in Waterloo about Mayor Hart. Then they say, "If people would just shut their mouths and let him do his job, things would be going better." There are people who always think they know better or have their own agenda who are always going to be a problem. Kind of like life. That's the way it was when we were in school. [WHS 67 WM]*

*Mayor [Hart] is very qualified. He came out of Waterloo schools and Hawkeye Tech with a good education. He's been on the city council. He's a progressive. I think his color is a good thing. If he'd been a white man with all his qualifications, I would have voted for him. He's young, he has qualifications and I did feel that our community really did need a black mayor. I worked with the mayor's mother, Lillie, at Allen hospital. She was such a fine person. [OHS 67 WF]*

*[Electing a black mayor] shows Waterloo's definitely changed. Older black and white people are gone. We have a younger, more intelligent generation coming up. I think if you polled the black community, the mayor was elected because he's black. If you polled the white community, I think people would say he was elected because he's been in the city government, know what's going on and it's time for a change. [EHS 67 AAM]*

*The relevance of first black mayor in Waterloo is like having the first black Bishop in Georgia. It speaks to the shock some people have that blacks can accomplish something, and are capable and have the capacity to do anything. [EHS 69 AAM]*

Mayor Hart's election was a combination the black vote and the millennials. He won even over in Audubon Park with the $400,000-plus homes. People that want to make it a racial issue are quite literally dying. They're in their 70s. It's a process of attrition. I'm absolutely convinced that in 2016 there's no reason that an African American person who really wants to make something of himself can't. [WHS 69 WM]

It took 50 years to have a black mayor because it took that long for white people to become tolerant. To become tolerant that African Americans can make good leaders. President Obama is a precursor to Mayor Hart's election. I think another factor was that it's finally taken 40 to 50 years to understand that blacks do have a say in how elections come out. That I am going to register, and encourage my kids and friends to register to vote. It's taken that long for them to believe that they can make a difference. [WHS 69 WM]

It's interesting that Mayor Hart was elected while we have a black president. A whole lot of people are going to be watching from the start. Is he only going to do things to help black people in Waterloo? In some ways, Obama is less free to talk about black issues as president. We go tribal so fast. I think Obama has kept himself in check, not going as far that way as sure as I'm sure he'd liked to have. Until it came to the Black Lives Matter issue with the shootings of the black men. Then he tried to use the presidency as somewhat of a pulpit. A lot of people were totally polarized by any tendency or perception of favor. [WHS 70 WM]

Quentin Hart went to East High School. And he was the first black city councilman. The fact that he became the mayor is not unusual. He won the election. It wasn't just the black people who voted. It was a general election. And a lot of people think he was the best man. The uniqueness of having the first black mayor also pushed it. The voters didn't want him to be denied the opportunity just because he was the black. They thought he was the most qualified candidate. The worst *thing that could happen when somebody gets elected is he's a buffoon and looks bad for all African Americans overall. [EHS 71 WM]*

*It's taken so long to have a black mayor because we've had good old boy politics for so long that we kept re-electing the same kind of people all the time. Waterloo wanted a change, but they didn't know what to change for. I think it was really tough for people to vote for a black person as mayor. My mom said he's going to be a good mayor. She knew his mom and remembers when he was born. She worked with Lillie Hart at Allen Hospital. Mom said she was terrified when she got hired as an operating room assistant. Mom was a surgical nurse her whole career and Lillie was afraid that she wouldn't know what to do. Mom said, "You're going to learn and you're going to be fine." She remembers Quentin being born and Lilly having to put all these hours in at work, and raise and get this little boy going. Mayor Hart's going to question things because he's been on the council for so long. He's also going to see Waterloo from a different perspective. He still lives in the North End. He knows what it's like to go through school here. The black community may say, "Here's someone who will listen to us in a different way." I don't think it's going to matter with the white community, since he's so involved already and we've seen him do things on the council. [EHS 72 WF]*

*Being black myself, I think having a black mayor in Waterloo is a good thing. When I was growing up, Mayor (Leo) Rooff was the mayor for years [from 1974-84, one of the longest-serving mayors in the city's history]. A black mayor reflects a change. Waterloo is becoming predominantly minority. Voters are coming together with a common goal and a common purpose. We're going to elect someone who thinks like us, looks like us, and grew up in the same environment so he knows the needs of the community. As Waterloo has expanded, it's been dealing with the same issues which concerns everybody, Jobs, crimes, race relations. Regardless of color, you should come from the environment which you represent. [EHS 73 AAM]*

*I'm glad Waterloo has a black mayor. But it's not going to do any good if he's not going to solve the problems either. They had Rep. Debbie Garry as the state rep for a long time. But I don't see that she's accomplished anything other than taking pictures with the president and his wife. There's still an issue in the city. You need to do something about people coming into town, messing up the city, shooting and stuff. If you're not going to do anything about that, what's your purpose? [EHS 73 AAF]*

*I think it's a great thing myself to have a black mayor. He's trying to do things a little differently than before. He's trying to make a statement by getting out and supporting some of the things being done in the community. The town has had money dropped in our laps to fix University Avenue. And he's wanting to get that taken care of. I understood it was the whole length of University going into Cedar Falls. But right from the starting gate, he was getting opposition from some of the people on the council. Not based on his race. But there are some elder council members who've been in Waterloo politics a long time. Both black and white. And they see things differently than he does. [EHS 73 WM]*

*Waterloo's first black mayor means people are just finally ready to take that step. They are the new minds, younger minds. The younger generation is finally out there to vote. And people want to change because all the crap that's going on. All the shootings. Babies being shot. And it's not one color. It's every color. And the former administration couldn't seem to do anything about it. So, people wanted a change. [EHS 73 WF]*

The mayor's term in Waterloo is for two years. "Mayor Hart is going to have difficulty getting re-elected," was one contributor's observation in 2016.

*The white community is watching him closely. If the black community feels it's more of the same, they won't come out in the next election for him. The black community is jaded. Nothing positive or*

434

*constructive has happened. Just because you're black doesn't mean you have a panacea ideological perspective. We look for instant gratification. Want to see something happening and happening right now. As a politician, he'll have to stay pretty gray. He has to. [EHS 69 AAM]*

Hart won a second term in November 2017 running unopposed. Voters "ousted" two city council incumbents, adding three new members, two of whom are women. The previous council was all male. "New faces and new opportunities. Each person brings a unique set of skills we'll be looking for ways to get them engaged," Hart said.[15]

Table 5 reflects other changes in Waterloo from 1963-1973 and 2016.

| Table 5 Comparative Waterloo Demographic Data, 1970 & 2016 | | |
|---|---|---|
| | 1970 | 2016[16] |
| Total Population | 75,733[17] | 68,357 |
| Median Age | 25.2 | 36.5 |
| Race[18] | | |
| White | 91.2% | 76.2% |
| Black | 8.7% | 15.7% |
| Level of Education[a] | | |
| Graduated high school | 60.1% | 76.6% |
| Graduated college | 8.2% | 9.5% |
| Employment | | |
| Unemployment Rate | 3.9%[b] | 8.3% |
| Income & Poverty | | |
| Median HH Income[c] (in $1970) | $9,920 | $7,163[d] |
| Mean HH income[c] | $5,042 | $9,005[e] |
| Percent persons in poverty | 10.1%[f] | 16.8% |
| Percent families below poverty line | 7. 6% | 12.7% |
| Race Below Poverty Level | | |
| White | 7.6% | 8.4% |
| Black | 26.0% | 34.9% |

[a] *25 and older.* [b] *October 1970. The rate was 3.2% in 1969.*[19] [c] *HH: household. Median: 50% of the household income is above this point and 50% is below.*

*Mean is the average household income. Both are based on people 15 years and older with income. $^d$ $44,146 in 2016 median HH income is equivalent to $9,920 in 1970 dollars. $^e$ $33,190 in 2016 mean HH income is equivalent to $9,005 in 1970 dollars. $^f$ 1969 data.*[20]

The major differences in Waterloo between 1970 and 2016 are:

- the 9.7% decrease in population and a 44.8% increase in the median age [50% of the population is above and 50% is below].
- an unemployment rate that is 112% higher in 2016.
- a 28% drop in median HH income [50% of Waterloo households are above and 50% are below], but a 78.6% increase in mean HH income [the average income for households.]
- the percentages of persons in poverty and families below the poverty line was two-thirds larger in 2016; 10.5% more whites, but 34.2% more blacks below the poverty line in 2016.
- Waterloo remains the most diverse community in Iowa. Its black community is 15.6%, the largest in Iowa, which has a 3.3% black population. The U.S. black population is 13.2 %.

The older median age reflects the failure of Waterloo to keep its younger people after high school. "Young flight," Hart calls it. "More minorities stay in Waterloo than any other group. A minority person goes to college – who, yes, could have gone to Hawkeye – but wants to get away from home. Those who have a bachelor's degree leave because they don't believe they can find the opportunity or the job they need to have here." The lack of jobs for minorities was the major cause for the unrest and riots in Waterloo in the late 1960s and early 70s. "Young flight" is also an Iowa phenomenon.

*Waterloo is still progressing. For example, there's no longer a segregated business district called the North End. There are more people of color in different professions here. It's regressed in the fact that it's still difficult for a black business in Waterloo to have access to funding, for example. It's still not equal economically. There are still not enough black-owned businesses, which would result in more social integration. It would change the perspective of a lot of black people, that economic*

436

*integration is achievable. Our young black elites are leaving the community because there just aren't opportunities for them here. [EHS 66 AAM]*

## WATERLOO – WORST CITY IN AMERICA FOR BLACKS

In October 2015, Waterloo-Cedar Falls was listed as the 10ᵗʰ worst urban area in the country for blacks based on black-white disparities in America on eight key economic and social measures. (Table 6) Des Moines was the second Iowa city to make the "bottom" 10 in the Wall St. 24/7 analysis.[21]

| Table 6 Worst Urban Areas for Blacks in the U.S., 2015 | | |
|---|---|---|
| Comparative Data | #10 Waterloo-Cedar Falls | #9 Des Moines-West Des Moines |
| Population | 169,993 | 611,549 |
| Black residents percentage | 7.0% | 5.0% |
| Black median household income as pct. of white | 54.9% | 57.1% |
| Black unemployment rate | 24.0% | 10.6% |
| Unemployment rate, all people | 4.9% | 4.2% |

*While the data presented aren't consistent with U.S. Census Bureau data, it could be inferred that neither are the data for the other cities. However, the relative comparisons could be valid. It noted the Waterloo area labor market was relatively strong, but "black residents clearly do not have the same job opportunities as their white peers. The unemployment rate among black residents of 24% . . .is in stark contrast with the white unemployment rate of just 3.9%. . . ."[22]*

Waterloo didn't make "The Worst Cities for Black Americans" in 2016. But Des Moines-West Des Moines jumped from number 9 to number 3.[23]

*All I hear about when I visit family in Waterloo is crime. Nobody wants to live in Waterloo any more. It's worse than it was when we were growing up. I was at our 50ᵗʰ reunion a few years ago was riding with some friends from Waterloo to Porky's for dinner and we were meandering through the East Side of town to get to there. It's been a long time since I meandered anywhere in Waterloo and I was totally lost. My friends told me, "We not only have the black population over here on the East Side of town, but we have all of these diverse groups from different countries that are grouped together in different neighborhoods. Some of them are just trouble." I asked what was "trouble" meant and was told it was they'd all gathered in one area. I said, "Do you really find it that hard to believe? You, who lived on 4th Street and went to St. Mary's? Where would they go on the West Side? Who would accept them? Has it changed that much since we grew up?" They couldn't answer the question. "You live in Cedar Falls." I asked the question. "How many black people do you have in Cedar Falls right now?" [COL 63 WF]*

*Waterloo is a melting pot of gangsters from other places trying to survive in a mixed community. You had gangsters when we were growing up – I called them "wangsters" because they weren't gangsters yet but wanted to be. When I go to Waterloo now and meet people, a lot of them aren't from Waterloo. They're from Detroit or Chicago or outside of the environment here in which I grew up. Waterloo has tried to give opportunities to someone with a criminal background. But the drugs and shooting and hopelessness feeds on itself. The environment now is so violent, with the shootings and killings, I'm glad I'm not there. [EHS 73 AAM]*

In May 2017, "Despite a multi-year downward trend in violent crime in the city of Waterloo, Waterloo-Cedar Falls ranks as the most dangerous city in Iowa." The city's violent crime rate was 497 violent crimes per 100,000 people. Iowa's was 286.1 per 100,000, the 18th lowest of 50 states, according to a Wall St. 24/7 report.[24]

An August 2017 crime analytics report by Neighborhood SCOUT placed Waterloo's crime index at nine on a scale where 100 is safest; an index of nine means it's safer than only 9% of other U.S. cities. This is a very interactive, though slightly dated site, which permits looking at crime analytics by neighborhood.[25]

The city averages 47 crimes/mile$^2$ (per square mile) compared to 15 crimes/mile$^2$ in Iowa. The National Median is 32.85. That's the average crimes/mile$^2$ at which 50% of the measured locations are below and 50% are above. Waterloo's index is roughly 15% above the median.[26]

In 2018, however, the National Council for Home Safety and Security identified Waterloo as only the 25th Safest City in Iowa out of 36. (Table 7) The trade association, comprised of home security professionals across the U.S., advocates for safe communities and home safety with a strong focus on community involvement.

"We've had a perception from people around Iowa that it's not safe in Waterloo overall. Coming downtown," Hart admitted in our March 2016 talk. "It's one of safest places in the entire city. We've been doing myriad things,-from Main Street Waterloo[27] to the streetscape program[28] to working with developers to come up with ways to attract people back to downtown." Hart shared an experience a couple of days before.

| Table 7 Safest Cities in Iowa, 2018[29] | | | | | | |
|---|---|---|---|---|---|---|
| Rank | City | POP | Violent crime[1] | Violent /1,000 | Property crime$^2$ | Property /1,000 |
| 10 | Cedar Falls | 41,651 | 66 | 708 | 1.58 | 17.00 |
| 12 | Iowa City | 75,527 | 197 | 2.61 | 1,551 | 20.54 |
| 21 | Dubuque | 59,026 | 210 | 3.56 | 1,832 | 31.04 |
| 25 | Waterloo | 68,470 | 507 | 7.4 | 2,120 | 30.96 |
| 26 | Cedar Rapids | 131,181 | 387 | 2.95 | 5,019 | 38.26 |
| 28 | Sioux City | 82,819 | 365 | 4.41 | 3,247 | 39.21 |
| 31 | Des Moines | 211,501 | 1,497 | 7.08 | 8,881 | 41.99 |
| 34 | Davenport | 103,118 | 750 | 7.27 | 5,001 | 48.5 |

[1]Violent crimes: aggravated assault, murder, rape, and robbery. $^2$Property crimes: burglary, arson, larceny-theft, and motor vehicle theft

*I was coming out of a building and some guys needed change for the parking meter. I said, "Here. Welcome to Waterloo" and gave them quarters. I asked if they were from around here and they were like, "Thank God not." I kind of groaned and said, "Come on guys, you just*

*had the mayor of Waterloo give you change for your parking meter.*
*How often does that happen anywhere?" And they apologized.*

Hart's central theme in his State of the City address in 2018 was Waterloo's strong ties to its past. He's worn bow ties to his office for eight years, at both Hawkeye Tech and the last two (2016-17) as mayor. The clip-on bow tie was patented in 1918 by the United Neckwear Manufacturing Company of Waterloo, which manufactured them in their shop at 310-312 East 4th Street. The site is the location in 2018 of Jameson's Public House, an authentic Irish pub.[30]

That innovation, creativity and forward thinking of Waterloo United Neckwear and John Deere, he stated, "are symbolic of the city of Waterloo. We want to manifest those things [today.] When we talk about our legacy and our history as a community, we are strong because we have an innovative spirit. . . . Waterloo has a rich heritage, strong people, a thriving business community which is investing in Waterloo."[31]

Table 8 *Forbes* The Best Small Places for Business and Careers, 2017[32]

| Ranks[a] | City | POP | COB | Jobs | Education |
|---|---|---|---|---|---|
| | Cedar Rapids | | | | |
| | Davenport | | | | |
| | Des Moines | | | | |
| 49 | Dubuque | 97,000 | 73 | 114 | 53 |
| 6 | Iowa City | 168,800 | 67 | 51 | 6 |
| 62 | Sioux City | 169,100 | 49 | 86 | 129 |
| 46 | Waterloo | 170,300 | 54 | 156 | 63 |

[a] Based on Cost of Business, Job Growth and Education.

This was reflected in Waterloo being ranked among Iowa's "Best Small Places for Business Careers" by *Forbes* magazine in 2017. (Table 8) Three other Iowa cities against which Waterloo is traditionally benchmarked on minority schools and education achievements were also ranked, three weren't. Ames, Iowa, the home of Iowa State University was the fifth Iowa town recognized at #6.

## Perspectives 2016-17: Waterloo 50 Years Later

A lot changes in any town over 50 years even though, as Karr's saying goes, "the more it changes, the more it's the same thing."

The profile of Waterloo in *Walk Together Children*, a 1971 U.S. Civil Rights Commission (USCCR) Iowa State Advisory Committee report, noted that "social and economic segregation isolate the white community from blacks and other minority groups."[33]

*Waterloo is a medium-size conservative Midwestern city with the second largest black population in Iowa. . . . more than 90% [of which] is contained in five of the city's 18 census tracts. The majority . . . live on the East Side of the city, separated by the Cedar River from the white community on the West Side. In Waterloo, there is also a close relationship between the problems of minority housing and school desegregation. Its black population is strong, with a diversity of income, power, and ability. The advantage, however, remains with the established system which can, by the release or suppression of crucial information, frustrate the efforts of volunteer groups seeking to alleviate the status quo.* [34]

The report concluded, "There is a desperate need for a change in the employment and educational structures of the city. . . . Problems of equal education are directly related to open housing. . . . If the housing patterns in Waterloo continue, however, there will be no equal education in Waterloo."[35]

A former Waterloo city council member quoted in a 1977 USCCR staff report said the black community is "particularly hostile to [council] measures to improve the lots of minorities." A council member was president of the local group opposed to busing for desegregation. The low-rent housing commission was abolished by the city council "when it persisted in proposals to establish such housing, which might be occupied by blacks, on the predominantly white [West] side of town."[36]

Twenty-eight years after its 1971 report, the USCCR Iowa advisory committee conducted a forum in Waterloo in 1999 and concluded the situation in Waterloo remained "symptomatic of racial hostilities and strain."

*All we heard in the Waterloo neighborhood coalition was people complaining about how people are treated on the East Side versus the West. Why is the West Side getting their streets cleaned of snow before the East Side? What can be done? How come the people getting arrested are mostly black? Why these kids are dropping out and getting arrested. The Neighborhoods Coalition doesn't exist anymore. It fell apart because all people wanted to do was come with complaints and not solutions or put forth the effort to do something, be part of the solution. [WHS 66 WM]*

From a purely anecdotal perspective, contributors' responses to Waterloo 50 years later were the longest of any of the others. A few offered insights about possible solutions.

## RACE & RACE RELATIONS

For many, race and race relations remain an issue.

**'63-'66** *The racial issues and tension in Waterloo are somewhat better than when I was in school. We can talk across the back-yard fence. But we're not socially integrating. The blacks go to their thing and the whites go to their thing. However, there are more whites going to black churches and some blacks going to white churches. There's more of that than there was 50 years ago. [EHS 60 AAM]*

*I'd like to think racial relations are better in Waterloo than when we were growing up. But there are too many whites who still think all blacks are bad and too many blacks who think all whites are bad. These tensions shouldn't be there. You need to realize that your neighbor may have a different skin color, but you need to get along and make the best of it. Especially the imports who weren't raised here believe that all the white people look down their noses at them, don't want to give them a break or hire them. [EHS 64 WM]*

*To me, race relations in Waterloo isn't so much a black-and-white issue today like it was when we were in school, but a black-on-black issue. I don't have anything to base that on except what I'm doing in my community trying to keep blacks from killing blacks. And that's what I say on Facebook. Or when I get an opportunity to tell the kids. "You're living with Mom and Dad. You have nothing. You have no job and you're killing each other. You're ignorant." These kids, I'm not scared of them. I don't care what they say about me. As long as they don't mess with me. I had a young man call me up when I was on TV a few weeks ago. "I'm going to kill you, you black so and so." I said, "Young man, you called me, now do me one favor. I sit in my yard all day long. When you come by here to kill me, kiss your mama for the last time." And he hung up on me. [COL 64 AAM]*

*It's definitely worse. People are not as free to go wherever they want to in Waterloo because of the racial tensions. Growing up, I never feared going anywhere in the North End. Didn't bother me at all. Maybe I was just stupid. Today there are a lot of people who won't go to the East Side and particularly around the North End because of the attitude, the animosity just because you're white. People look at you like, "What the hell are you doing in our area?" There are places on the West Side around 4th Street down to Western Avenue, that area, that people also avoid. They just don't go there because you just don't know what the hell is going to happen. It's a melting pot ready to burst. You have immigrants that churches have brought in getting jobs that blacks or whites are thinking, "If these people weren't here, I could have a job." [WHS 64 WM]*

*Waterloo is a very racist city, to this day. I hear it all the time when I meet with people there. They're not going around using the n-word, but* when you go around picking out the worst about any social group or any color or any race . . . "all Muslims are this" and it doesn't matter that there are Muslims fighting in Iraq in the American military – that's what you hear in casual conversation. You never hear anything good. You hear, "They're getting all the breaks and all that welfare and the food stamps." And to me that's as racist as wearing a white hood. In many cases they would [emphasizes] NEVER vote for a black person. [EHS 66 WM]

As long as the good-old-boy system is in place in Waterloo, race is going to be an issue. There are others who make race an issue by bringing it up all of the time. They think by doing that, something's going to be done. A diversity study was done through UNI. We brainstormed solutions. Came up with lots of solutions to problems. Unfortunately, nobody wanted to put in the effort to make it happen, although some people tried. [WHS 66 WM]

Our business has a lot of black customers and we have some black friends. Waterloo's better than it was, but it still needs. . . [pause] improving. It bothers me to see the attitude of some blacks that they're owed everything. All of they have to do is look around them. There are a lot of successful black people. They're not being held down as much as they think they are. I don't think they're being picked on as much as they think they are. It does happen. The stories about policemen who are prejudiced make me sick. Why are they not being weeded out? [EHS 66 WF]

Immigrants want to live here, but they want to maintain their cultures. The Burmese are willing to make the changes and still celebrate their own culture with the Burmese festivals. But they're willing to compromise. I don't have any trouble when I pick them up for YWCA English classes. Half are waiting at the door for me. They're there when I arrive. The Congolese will make you wait 5-10 minutes even though you pick them up at the same time every time. You're not changing, you're blending in. In our country, everyone wants the blacks to become white.

*Nobody likes to change. The Native Americans – race is an issue to them because of the way they're treated. Their complaints are more viable than other minorities. They don't have the opportunities the other minorities do. All the minorities have opportunities if they're willing to put forth the effort and do something about it. [WHS 66 WM]*

**'67-'70** *I think the town is more segregated today. In our day, we – meaning white males – could pretty much go wherever we wanted to go. If we wanted to go to the businesses on Upper East 4ᵗʰ Street to get donuts or pizza or whatever. We could go to Gates Park and shoot hoops. But that's way less true now because of crime. Some of my perception has to do with age. Being 20 and prime and 66 is a lot different. I'm not going to put myself in as many risky situations as I did when I was in high school. [EHS 67 WM]*

*I don't know how to say this so that it doesn't sound like sour grapes, so I'm just going to say it. You have to look at both sides of the coin with the problems we've had with so-called blacks or Negroes in Waterloo. There are people in this community, like there are everywhere, who have benefited from the civil rights work and struggles that we and other people have done. Who didn't give a damn about it. Excuse my French. They benefited from it though, because of the people who stood up, stood out, spoke out and made a difference. They were also the ones who were stabbing us in our back and acting like they don't know who we were. But they've obtained high-paying positions as a result. We cannot afford to have that in our culture. Black teachers are still the last hired, first fired. [EHS 69 AAF]*

*The demographics in Waterloo have changed considerably since we were in school. There's still a separation between the black and white communities. I don't know what's causing that looking at it from my Cedar Falls vantage point. The black community in Waterloo still stays very consolidated, together. I had the unfortunate experience of serving as a juror on a first-degree murder trial a year ago, a black-on-black case. It's an experience I'm glad I had, but I'd never care to be on another first-degree murder jury. There were a lot of racial overtones in the trial even though it was black-on-black crime. A lot of the blacks who participated either as a defendant or as witnesses reinforced stereotypes people have about Waterloo. A lot of the females had two or three or four different children from different fathers. They didn't work. A lot of the black males didn't have jobs. The jury was multiracial and there wasn't a person who felt that we should make our verdict based on ethnicity. Everybody was concerned about what had happened. How we would deal with the legalities of the sentence. And what were the things that we had to think about. I would hope that the same would have been true in the late 1960s, but I suspect it would not have been. It would have been more racially tainted than our situation was. [EHS 69 WM]*

*In a lot of ways, Waterloo is the same as it was 50 years ago. We didn't have the overt Jim Crow laws that were present in the South. But there was racism between the blacks and the whites. And I think it worked equally on both sides. In a lot of ways, that hasn't changed that much. I think a lot of the violence that Waterloo is experiencing reinforces stereotypes. It is very, very, very black-on-black violence. [EHS 69 WM]*

*When we were children, we would walk from our house on Newell Street to my grandmother's house on Cottage Street. One time, we were going to walk over to see my aunt. Someone said, "No, you shouldn't walk. Take the car." I said, "But it's just over there." "Take the car. It's become very dangerous." I've heard it's worse now. I've heard that some of the neighborhoods on the black side are really in ruin and nobody's doing anything to keep them up. I looked at a Google shot of our houses on Newell Street and Ankeny Street. And both are really run down compared to what it was before. [COL 69 AAF]*

*This book is about black-white relations, but there's also a large Hispanic and Bosnian population in Waterloo. And they're unnoticed. There's just not a lot of controversial issues. A lot of the violence we read about is Hispanic-on-Hispanic and Bosnian-on-Bosnian. It hasn't become a race issue. It was with the African Americans. [WHS 69 WM]*

*When you're at a social event, the blacks are here and the whites are over there. The most segregated time of the week is Sunday. The blacks are in the black churches, the whites are in the white churches and the Lutherans are in their church. We're Lutherans. [EHS 70 WF]*

*A lot of people in Waterloo say they're not prejudiced. They say that, but they only see blacks in the grocery store, don't attend mixed-race churches, don't socialize with them. A lot of people tell themselves and others that they're accepting of blacks, but that's from a distance. [EHS 70 WF]*

**'71-'73** *Unfortunately, race relations in Waterloo have gotten worse than they were when I was in high school. Not because of anything unique to Waterloo. But everyone, everywhere seems to have lost the ability to discuss, argue and disagree civilly. [EHS 71 WM]*

## CRIME & VIOLENCE

Crime was a major factor in whether Waterloo was perceived as "worse," "about the same" or "better" than 1963-1973.

**'63-'66** *Racial relations got better for a couple of decades in Waterloo during the late 70s into the 80s. Before that, people were scared of the Black Panthers. People harbored a lot of feeling toward the blacks. My brother still lives in the West Parker street area [west of Logan Avenue, west of the North End]. He's not too crazy about blacks. Now the drug gang stuff is getting awful. It's a terrible thing. There's so much gang and drug deals now. All the shootings is crazy. [COL 66 WM]*

**'67-'70** *I was older when I realized there was a perception that Waterloo was the blue-collar town and Cedar Falls was the more educated set. We spend more time and do a lot of things in Cedar Falls now. About three trips a day there for various and* *sundry things. Ride the bike trails. I could move to Cedar Falls and see Waterloo in my rearview mirror because of the violence. I could say "goodbye" to Waterloo. [OHS 67 WF]*

*The violence in Waterloo is really alarming. Where I used to go to church at Trinity Lutheran. . . all of that area. My African-American girlfriend and former co-worker says it's little Chicago over there. The Burmese are a vulnerable group. They would go to Tyson to get their paycheck and they were so happy. Then their homes would be broken into and things would be stolen from them. And the gunfire. It's the violence, the crime. [OHS 67 WF]*

*After our phone interview for your book, I was fairly confident in stating things have changed a lot since high school. I had hoped that had broadened my outlook on racial unrest. But just a couple of weeks ago [September 2017], I had an eerie feeling of days gone by. Signs were posted in area restaurants inviting students who had attended East, but graduated from another school, to a 50th class reunion. I thought about it for a bit, since both my husband and I both graduated from another school. The reunion took place at the Electric Park Ballroom. There had been racial discord and several arrests after a hip hop concert was delayed there in March. Needless to say, we didn't go. I guess I should feel ashamed, but I never was eager to be in anything confrontational and some things never change completely. [OHS 67 WF)*

*When I lived in Chicago, the blacks participated in change. I've been back in Waterloo for 10 years and it's like the clock here hasn't changed. It's like Waterloo is stuck in a time warp. [OHS 68 WF]*

*Waterloo is worse than it was 50 years ago. More drugs and violence. A lot of gang activity all across town. Fights, knifings and gunshot victims. There are many more ethnic groups. [EHS 68 WF]*

**'71-'73** *I think the city's improved quite a bit since we were in school. We still have problems and we have gangs that we didn't have then. Before, a couple guys would get mad at each other, and they'd go out in the street and punch it out. Now they go out* *and shoot each other. You've got to be a little more conscious of that. You could get caught in a bad scenario in a bad area where, before, you might get jumped or hit or something. Now you might get shot. But that's a small minority of us. You go to a school sports event with blacks and whites and Micronesians and so forth sitting together sharing together in the student section. They're hanging out or talking in the hallway or hanging out at lunch, catching a ride home. Before it wouldn't happen because it was like, "I wouldn't have that guy get in my car." It's not that big of a deal right now. [EHS 71 WM]*

*The problem we're having a in Waterloo is violence on the north side of the North End or along church row. Part of the gun-related problems is Waterloo stuff. But you got a lot of traffic coming in from Chicago. If you look at the arrest records, many are from out of town. They come in here and prey upon the poor people who don't have much going for them. They recruit them and get them going in these gangs. [EHS 71 WM*

*I am so glad that I was raised in the 60s and 70s in Waterloo. It was an awesome place. I remember walking the streets at night, never being afraid. From City View to 4th Street. Just young and having fun. We didn't even lock our doors. I loved being raised in Waterloo. Couldn't ask to have been raised in a better place. It's so bad now, so bad. It's gotten crazy in the last 5-6 years. Now it's horrible. All you hear is about people being shot at and being shot. Because so many people have moved from outside Waterloo into Waterloo and bringing thugism with them. The police don't care. They don't do anything. It's sad. [EHS 73 AAF]*

*People from Chicago and other cities get out of jail, and come to Waterloo. They don't want to stay in Chicago. Waterloo is only four hours away. It's an easy town. Since Waterloo is such a small town though, you can't get into crime because you're going to be known. You can't be a drug dealer here. A high-speed chase in Waterloo isn't going to last long. It isn't like the city. I've never seen so many young black kids and 70% of them don't do anything but sell dope. They don't have jobs because I see them all day. What are they doing? Are all the kids in Waterloo selling drugs? There's nothing in Waterloo for black people. If you're from Chicago, Detroit, Kansas City and you come here, there's nothing here, but drinking and getting high. [EHS 74 AAM]*

## THE SOCIOECONOMIC DIVIDE

The socioeconomic divide between the East and the West Side is still an issue.

**'63-'66** *There's much more balance professionally in Waterloo now. I see it in banking on the East Side; it's not all white, it's people. I see more of the young generation of color look at themselves much more as people now. More whites look at people in general as people. The local channel, KWWL-TV, has really made an effort to broaden access to broadcasting for all groups. We're moving on, but it's going to take another generation. I assume it's the same on the West Side, but we don't do much on that side of Waterloo. [EHS 63 WF]*

*When I lived on the East Side of town, I felt happier, like that was a good place to be. We were a happier family, we had fun, we enjoyed playing outside and doing the crazy kids thing you do. We never really got into trouble. It was a fun time. With all the disruptions in our lives, felt like a good time, a home time. Living on the West Side wasn't a happy time. When I go back to Waterloo, I have friends living on the streets I always wanted to live on when I was a kid. Up near St. Edward's (on Mitchell) in some of those beautiful homes where the doctor's kids and all that lived. And I thought if you ever made it in Waterloo, that's where you would live. A couple of my friends who live there have been mayors. And I still get almost a sense of insecurity around some of them, when I go there. I feel like that's not where I belong, I never did belong there, I'm not the country-club type of person. Last year I went back to where we lived on Irving Street and I was shocked. I had a hard time sorting out the neighborhood I lived in and the neighborhood it's turned into. I don't understand it. It's all black. The poverty is shocking. The nature of the homes. How did that happen?*

*Why does a neighborhood get like that? I understand the dynamics of education and jobs. I understand the need to keep what you have as livable. I didn't see that when I was there. [COL 63 WF]*

The economic gap has gotten worse when I think about the shops we shopped when we were in school. The town was divided racially, but it was also divided economically. The ordinary people's department stores – Penny's, Sears and Montgomery Wards – were all on the West Side. The stores which carried merchandise for people who could afford better, higher-priced clothing – Blacks, Palace Clothiers, Zale's and Newton Jewelry, and the two best shoe stores, Walker's and Fox – were on the East Side. The people who spent the most money on the East Side lived on the West Side. The dime stores – S.S. Kresge and Woolworth's – were on the East Side. In 1969, when the first shopping centers were built in Waterloo and Cedar Falls, the one in Waterloo went on the West Side. The downtown stores started moving out to the mall, bankrupting downtown. To this day, there is still no major shopping center on the East Side of town. There used to be an economic balance between East Side and West Side, but the economics shifted to the West side. [WHS 66 WF]

When Paul Simon's "My Little Town" came out [1975], it was immediately a bittersweet reminder for me of Waterloo and why I left.
And after it rains [in my little town], there's a rainbow.
And all of the colors are black.
It's not that the colors aren't there, it's just imagination they lack.
Everything's the same back in my little town.
[chorus] Nothing but the dead and dying back in my little town.
Nothing but the dead and dying. . . .
I don't see much has changed. [EHS 66 WM]

**'67-'70** I travel the state on business and am in Waterloo quite often. The situation in town is much worse than when I was growing up. John Deere has moved its facilities out from downtown. All the buildings have been torn down. Deere had 16,000 people employed back then and now it's 6,500. When we were growing up, we had manufacturing companies like Chamberlain and they're all gone. Technology has taken over. I think the one thing they couldn't get past was the technology and other opportunities out there, and diversify. Waterloo seems like it's stuck in a funk and, when you walk downtown, it's pretty depressing. [WHS 67 WM]

Waterloo is kind of an anomaly. It's always been a one- or two-industry town. Even at John Deere where I worked for 40 years, I see the reluctance to stay in Waterloo. When I got hired by Deere it was like being drafted by the Yankees. What a company. Insurance. Taken care of for life. An unbelievable pension. For just working there. And now, not unlike anyone else, there's no pension. There's a 401k. And if you leave the company, you take that 401k and find another job. Deere has made it easier for Waterloo flight by not making you stay to get your pension, which means a high turnover and flight. One of my kids and his wife live in Brooklyn. The other is in Washington, D.C. One graduated from Iowa and one from Iowa State. They both said, "Dad, Iowa is just not a place where I want to live. There's no culture. There's not a lot to do. We want to live in a big city." For those kind of people, I don't know if they can be kept in Waterloo-slash-Iowa. The ones that are staying are Midwestern people that want to be near family. They're going to make it work even if it means moving to Des Moines. Which our daughter did. [WHS 69 WM]

Waterloo always has been and still is a second-class citizen in the minds of the people from Cedar Falls, which is primarily white. The racial makeup of Waterloo had something to do with that attitude, although there are a lot of ethnicities in Cedar Falls, particularly because of UNI. We live in Cedar Falls on purpose. The Cedar Falls school system is still a better school system and educational opportunities are much better here than they were in Waterloo. [EHS 69 WM]

**'71-'73** When I was at East, Waterloo was a blue-collar community. You had John Deere, Rath Packing,

452

*Chamberlain, Titus and other companies going strong. As time went on, they started downsizing. Rath and Chamberlain closed [1984 and 1994, respectively]. The blue-collar community from East evaporated. The population started to dwindle. Housing was building on the West Side. There was no development or building on the East Side except for Greenbrier [February 1964].[37] That was the last major housing development on that side of the river. [EHS 71 WM]*

## THE GLASS IS HALF FULL

For some, Waterloo's diversity glass is half full.

**'67-'70** *We have a fair number of physicians on our street today from various countries of origin. We have a school administrator who's an African American right down the street. I see all ethnicities walking their dogs and that type of thing in my neighborhood now. My perception is that racial blending into society is accepted in Waterloo. And fine. Things change. Friends have a daughter who married a fine young black man. For baby boomers, I think it's a fine thing. What's not a fine thing is the violence. [OHS 67 WF]*

*I had the privilege of meeting many diverse cultures in Waterloo and Black Hawk County during my career. And it's thoroughly enriched my life. We worked quite a bit with Bosnian senior citizens who had watched their children being murdered and that type of thing. I so enjoyed learning from the Burmese and the Bosnians. I met some wonderful, wonderful people, which I missed when I retired. The county and the community has become very diverse in the last 50 years and I embrace that. I like that. For the most part, the Bosnians are very well educated. There are Bosnian doctors who came here that couldn't work as doctors and they had to do something else. The Burmese came out of Burmese refugee camps. Some knew English. When IBP and Tyson came to town, this workforce was able to meet the hiring criteria, which provided an opportunity for those people to get a job. That is so much better than what they had before. I'll be interested to see how the*

*Burmese community progresses through the next generations. [OHS 67 WF]*

I think Waterloo is better than when we were in school. I try and get back once or twice a year and I don't feel anything in terms of racial tension or discrimination. I still drive through the same neighborhoods I always drove through. I don't have the same day-to-day experience the locals do, but I think the town has straightened itself up somewhat. I hear that there are a lot more Asians in the area, filling a number of the jobs which would normally be taken by black people. If someone isn't going to give you an opportunity to work to provide food for your family, that's always a thing. The blacks are being put in the back seat, which puts a lot of pressure on law enforcement. Waterloo was a good town with a black community. Growing up there really prepared me for life. [EHS 68 WM]

There's more geographic and social integration in Waterloo. More neighborhoods are integrated, nice neighborhoods as well. But I do think there is limited social interaction going on within the neighborhoods. Having said that, there are block parties which take place where it's a multicultural event. I know there's a Zebra Golf picnic. I know there's stuff that happens. But it's very rare or uncommon. The strongest amount of social integration is taking place on the East Side. Leon Mosley is a big driver of this. The African-American leaders are stepping up and saying, "We're tired of this bullshit, we're tired of this violence, we're tired of our kids getting shot over here, shooting each other, and gangs and drugs and all this." We see picnics and so forth on the East Side that are totally diverse. Good things taking place. On the West Side, not so much. Maybe there are no problems to solve there or they're just staying within their homes. [WHS 69 WM]

Waterloo is a lot worse in some areas and a lot better in others. I see more positive interracial relationships among young African Americans and whites. I watch them on the wrestling teams. My youngest son is 23 and I watch how he interacts. One of his very close friends is white, one *is Jewish, one is Mexican, one is bi-racial. It's a hugely diverse group which has been together since kindergarten. That wouldn't have happened when we were in school. What isn't better is relationships with the older black people from my generation. They're set in their ways. Everybody thinks they're right. And nobody's wrong. We can't have a middle of the road. We either have to be all one thing or another. Waterloo's been written up as one of worst places to grow up in. That national reputation is shameful, absolutely shameful. It's there for a reason. Waterloo ranks number one in per capita for incarcerating African-American males. Who would want that reputation and not try to do something about it? But you don't see anything done. We have conferences on disproportionate minority confinement, and we regurgitate these same messages ad nauseum year and year out. We talk about it. But we do nothing about it. [EHS 69 AAM]*

*Waterloo was big-time segregated when I was in school. One of the people my son worked with lived on Patton Avenue on the West Side. When he paid off his house and got the deed, it said right on the deed that the house would never be sold to anyone but a Caucasian. Not today. You see black people living all over now. I don't think they're barred from going anywhere. [WHS 69 WF]*

*I think the race relations in Waterloo have improved, that there's less racial tension. We have a black mayor. Black people have a stronger voice now in the city, in the schools. The Bosnians have integrated very well. They have inserted themselves into the community very well. The perception is that they work really, really hard, drink a lot and beat their women. I work with Bosnian women and they seem to be in good relationships with their husbands. I know Bosnians like their coffee really strong and get more drunk driving tickets than anyone. The Hispanic families I work with have not assimilated because the parents don't speak English a lot of times. That's a big-time barrier. You have to get an interpreter. The schools provide interpreters for Bosnian and Spanish. Lots of Bosnians and Spanish came to Waterloo around the same time. The Bosnian kids generally went to school and learned English, and then helped the parents learn English. And they helped each other. Spanish speakers aren't as apt to learn the language. The kids do in school, but you usually have to have an interpreter when talking with parents. [EHS 70 WF]*

**'71-'73**  *Waterloo is worse than it was when I was in high school. If you look at the neighborhoods that have been integrated, the quality of the housing and safety of the neighborhoods have vastly deteriorated. Safe neighborhoods moved farther south in Waterloo over time. [WHS 72 WM]*

*The neighborhoods are changing. I moved into my aunt's and uncle's house. So, I've known the neighbors on my block from when I was growing up. There's still some of that neighborhood feel. A lot of people on my block are homeowners, grounded, have been there a while, grew up in the neighborhood. We don't necessarily throw block parties, but we do know our neighbors. Home ownership is different than renting. There are more rental-house pockets of the community today. To find someone who's been in a rental house for 15-20 years is less likely than finding a homeowner with that permanence. [EHS 73 AAM]*

*Some of the people I grew up with are still there. But the majority of the others have gone. I don't see the changes that I'm looking for around my old neighborhood. The same houses are boarded up, they're not being torn down, and nothing is there to replace is with some type of positive housing or beautification. The churches are falling down. The black community around the churches is falling apart. People are still living in boarded up houses or houses with trash piled up to the windows. You see a few duplexes coming up. There are still opportunities there. John Deere. What used to be Rath Packing, the packing house. There are opportunities to work if you want to. There are jobs there. If you want one. East and West Waterloo are still there. But people are moving to the rural community. [EHS 73 AAM]*

*Waterloo's totally different now in terms of interracial relationships. There's so many mixed couples and black people in the family nobody trips on it now. If you see a white girl with a black guy, you don't think anything about it. There's a lot less racial tension. The white guys are even acting more like a black male. [laughs] They dress black. They listen to black music. And they like black women. [EHS 74 AAM]*

*I can't say Waterloo is all that much better than we were when I was in school. We don't have the race riots. They've integrated the schools. We've spent so much money busing kids from here to there to everywhere. I'm more aware of it. In high school, I wasn't. I read the news and I see it in life. I can remember my mom talking about blacks coming up from Mississippi and entering the schools, and what a headache it was for the schools because many of them could barely read. As an adult, I'm more aware of the fact that there are problems out there. [WHS 74 WF]*

## A RIOT BY ANY OTHER NAME

There was a consistent tendency for white contributors to define collective actions by blacks as a "riot," which they were in some cases. Many people and sources referred to "riots" in Waterloo occurring within a single time period, even there was only one incident or "riot" at a given time.

*There's still disparity with the police department and blacks. That's a problem. Things are better, but we still have a way to go. It's a combination of both blacks applying and not being accepted, and not being interested in applying. A lot of the blacks of the age bracket where they would want to become policemen have history, have records which would keep them from becoming one. I don't really see a lot of our blacks becoming policemen. It's a difficult one. That disparity is also in the fire department. [EHS 60 AAM]*

In January 2016, the city of Waterloo's insurer paid $2.5 million to the family of a 22-year-old black man who was fatally shot by a white officer in 2013. Six months later, the city settled lawsuits with three black residents who had been "roughed up" by three white officers in separate incidents that occurred between 2013 and 2015. One included a 13-year-old girl. The 17-year-old male plaintiff received $70,000 for two separate incidents, one in 2013 and the other in 2015. The other male plaintiff, 31, received $100,000. A confidentiality agreement existed in the girl's case.[38]

In each case, the charges filed against the suspects were dismissed. Internal investigations found no violations of police department policy or the law, and justified the use of force.[39]

One of the officers had "been sued four times since 2012 over his use of excessive force" and was facing a lawsuit with another officer for shooting a black man in 2015.

Police Chief Dan Trelka said the officer is "one of our most active" and worked in a "special unit" that "responds to our most violent crimes in the city [in] our most challenging neighborhoods. So not necessarily the person, but circumstances can play a heavy dynamic into this."[40]

The officer received a Medal of Valor in December 2016 for blocking a car traveling in the wrong direction on U.S. Highway 20, preventing it from crashing into oncoming traffic. Though injured, he helped the occupants exit their vehicle and guided them to safety away from the roadway. The driver was arrested for driving while intoxicated.[41]

Officers made "honest mistakes" in the cases that were settled due to "deficient training," according to Trelka. "They were errors that we felt we could correct from training, that didn't rise to the level of needing discipline. . . ."[42]

Trelka's Welcome on the department's website calls the department "among the best and most pro-active police departments in the state of Iowa." Its department wide Community Oriented Policing and Problem Solving (COPPS) philosophy is intended "to bring us closer to our citizens and to receive their input and information on crime and disorder in their neighborhoods."[43]

# Reflections from the Bridge

Perhaps in the end, contributors' perceptions are captured by the question one of the women asked and answered.

*Was Waterloo worse than most places? I'm not sure.*

The story of Waterloo schools and the town since 1973, the end of *The Bridge Between,* is another book.

# Endnotes

[1] Retrieved from https://www.merriam-webster.com/dictionary/plus%20%C3%A7a%20change,%20plus%20c'est%20la%20m%C3%AAme%20chose https://en.wikipedia.org/wiki/Jean-Baptiste_Alphonse_Karr.

2 Diestelmeier Reflects on 50 years in school. (May 24, 1983). The Des Moines Register, 12.

3 Hispanics may be of any race, so also are included in applicable race categories. U.S. Census Bureau. "All Schools" in 2016 doesn't include students enrolled in the district's Middle School & High School EDP or Other Programs. Waterloo data sources: 1) Waterloo, Iowa. http://www.city-data.com/city/Waterloo-Iowa.html. American FactFinder. 2) https://factfinder.census.gov/faces/nav/jsf/pages/searchresults.xhtml?refresh=t. (3) Waterloo . Census Bureau Chapter B, General Population Characteristics of Iowa. (February 1973). 1970 Census of Population, 1(17), Part 17 Iowa, 17-77.)

4 Student Reporting in Iowa Data Dictionary 2017-2018. (August 01, 2017). Des Moines, IA: Iowa Department of Education, 13.

5 Iowa Department of Education. District Reports. (May 14, 2018). Retrieved from http://reports.educateiowa.gov/.

6 Enrollment by Race 2015-2016 and Enrollment by Race, 2016-2017. Waterloo Community School District report provided by the district.

7 Cunningham School for Excellence – Waterloo Community School District. (June 26, 2014). LEA School Improvement Grant Application. Retrieved from https://www.educateiowa.gov/sites/files/ed/documents/Waterloo%20Cunningham%20FY%2013%20Iowa%20SIG%20LEA%20App%20FINAL.pdf.

8 Iowa schools' reading efforts are making progress. New brief shows more students on track to be proficient readers by the end of third grade. (March 9, 2017). Des Moines: Iowa Department of Education. Retrieved from https://www.educateiowa.gov/article/2017/03/09/iowa-schools-reading-efforts-are-making-progress.

9 Full Speech: Waterloo Mayor Quentin Hart gives the 2018 State of the City address (video.) (April 06, 2018). Waterloo-Cedar Falls Courier. Retrieved from http://wcfcourier.com/full-speech-waterloo-mayor-quentin-hart-gives-the-state-of/youtube_eed5f8cc-0ba3-5074-95dc-143121446f9f.html.

10 Expo Alternative Learning Center. (March 16, 2012). Educational Services: Waterloo Community School District. Retrieved from http://www.waterlooschools.org/educationalservices/2012/03/16/expo-alternative-learning-center/.

11 Race Relations in Waterloo. Chapter 5 Summary and Observations. (June 2002). Iowa Advisory Committee to the U.S. Commission on Civil Rights. Retrieved from http://www.usccr.gov/pubs/sac/ia0602/ch5.htm.

12 Waterloo's first black mayor a 'bridge.' (January 2, 2016). Munson, K. The Des Moines Register. Retrieved from http://tinyurl.com/y9ulh8gz.

13 Quentin Hart sworn in as mayor of Waterloo. (January 04, 2016). Waterloo, IA: News7KWWL. Retrieved from http://www.kwwl.com/story/30876198/2016/01/Monday/quentin-hart-to-be-sworn-in-as-mayor-tonight.

14 Waterloo's first black mayor a 'bridge.'

15 Two incumbents ousted in Waterloo City Council election. (November 8, 2017). Jamison, T. Waterloo Daily Courier. Retrieved from http://wcfcourier.com/news/local/govt-and-politics/two-incumbents-ousted-in-waterloo-city-council-election/article_bb6c7558-ffe3-503c-972b-9945cc167a9a.html.

16 Waterloo, Iowa. American FactFinder. Washington, D.C.: U.S. Department of Commerce, Bureau of the Census. Retrieved from https://factfinder.census.gov/faces/tableservices/jsf/pages/productview.xhtml?src=CF.

17 Census Tracts. Waterloo Iowa SMSA. Final Report PGC(1)-228 Waterloo, Iowa SMSA. (1972). 1970 Census of Population and Housing. Washington, D.C.: U.S. Department of Commerce, Bureau of the Census, 7.

18 Ibid.

19 Unemployment Rates Still High, But Improve. (November 26, 1970). Waterloo Daily Courier, 3.

20 Poverty Rates Waterloo Iowa, 1969. Report CPH-L-186. (1995). Poverty Rates by MSA. Census of Population and Housing. Washington, D.C.: U.S. Department of Commerce, Bureau of the Census, 11.

21 1) The Worst Cities for Black Americans. (October 6, 2015). Frohlich, T.C., and Stebbins, S. 24/7 Wall Street. Retrieved from http://247wallst.com/special-report/2015/10/06/the-worst-cities-for-black-americans/3/. 2) The Worst Cities for Black Americans. (October 13, 2016). Frohlich, T.C., and Stebbins, S. 24/7 Wall Street. Retrieved from http://247wallst.com/special-report/2016/10/13/worst-cities-for-black-americans/.

22 Ibid.

23 Ibid.

24 The Most Dangerous City in Every State. (May 19, 2017). Stebbins, S., and Comen, E. 24/7 Wall Street. Retrieved from http://247wallst.com/special-report/2017/05/19/the-most-dangerous-city-in-every-state/4/.

25 Waterloo, IA Crime Rates. Neighborhood Scout. Retrieved from https://www.neighborhoodscout.com/ia/waterloo/crime/. NeighborhoodScout is a nationwide neighborhood search engine and provider of location-based analytics for real-estate investors, mortgage professionals and homebuyers. https://www.neighborhoodscout.com/media/top-100-safest-2016-pr.

26 Waterloo, IA Crime Rates. Neighborhood Scout. Retrieved from https://www.neighborhoodscout.com/ia/waterloo/crime/. NeighborhoodScout is a nationwide neighborhood search engine and provider of location-based analytics for real-estate investors, mortgage professionals and homebuyers. https://www.neighborhoodscout.com/media/top-100-safest-2016-pr.

27 Main Street Waterloo is an affiliate of the Main Street Iowa program, using the National Main Street Center's "Four Point Approach" to downtown revitalization. Using this approach, Main Street Waterloo works to strengthen the overall social and economic health of the Waterloo central business district. Retrieved from http://www.mainstreetwaterloo.org/about/.

28 Creating an inviting streetscape is a major part of attracting new businesses and customers for the revitalization of the downtown district, including things likes street furniture as part of a business's curb appeal.

29 National Council for Home Safety and Security. Retrieved from https://www.alarms.org/safest-cities-in-iowa-2018/.

30 Mayor's Strong tie to Waterloo's past. (April 06, 2018). Steffen, A. Waterloo-Cedar Falls Courier. Retrieved from http://wcfcourier.com/news/local/mayor-s-tie-to-waterloo-s-past/article_faa49e30-91c8-5064-9d89-1afb5a1aad6c.html.

31 Full Speech: Waterloo Mayor Quentin Hart gives the 2018 State of the City address (video.)
32 The Best Small Places for Business and Careers, 2017. Forbes. Retrieved from https://www.forbes.com/best-places-for-business/list/small/#tab:overall_state:Iowa.
33 "Walk Together Children" is a poem written by 9-year-old Nadra Dabbagh. Cited in Walk Together Children. A Report of the Iowa State Committee to the U.S. Commission on Civil Rights on Housing and Education in Waterloo, Iowa. (Closed Meeting). (May 22, 1971). Iowa Advisory Committee, 1. Retrieved from http://tinyurl.com/jaxrzyz.
34 Ibid., 1
35 Ibid., 12.
36 School desegregation in Waterloo, Iowa. A staff report of the U.S. Commission on Civil Rights. (August 1977). Washington, V. Kansas City, MO: U.S. Commission on Civil Rights, Midwest Regional Office, 3.
37 Greenbrier Grand Opening, February 22-23. (February 21, 1964). Waterloo Daily Courier, 20.
38 UPDATE: Excessive force lawsuits against Waterloo police settled. (August 11, 2016). The Courier. Retrieved from http://tinyurl.com/y7zbyzpn.
39 Waterloo Settles 3 Police Force Lawsuits. KXEL News. (August 12, 2016). http://www.kxel.com/kxel-news/2016/08/12/waterloo-settles-3-police-force-lawsuits.
40 1) UPDATE: Excessive force lawsuits against Waterloo police settled. 2) Bleeding Heartland. A community blog about Iowa politics. Retrieved from https://www.bleedingheartland.com/2016/08/12/a-disturbing-glimpse-of-police-practices-in-iowas-sixth-largest-city/.
41 Medal of Valor ceremony. (2016). Waterloo Police Department. Retrieved from http://www.waterloopolice.com/press-release/1599-medal-of-valor-ceremony.html.
42 Waterloo settles lawsuits against white police officers. (August 11, 2016). Foley, R.J., Associated Press. Retrieved from http://tinyurl.com/y8cezas9.
43 A Message from Chief Trelka. (2018). Waterloo Police Department. Retrieved from http://www.waterloopolice.com/chief/a-message-from-chief-trelka.html.

# CONTRIBUTORS

*The Bridge Between* contributors are the Waterloo high school graduates whose participation helped write the story. They are "co-authors" in a real sense. Special thanks to *those who went above and beyond.

A   Charlie Aldrich, Jane Henderson Allen, Alice Flener Anders, Mark D. Anderson, Dale Andres, Gary Arms, Diana Babcock, Randy Bearbower, Diane Bohlen, Paula Minor Bortka, *Mariellyn Erickson Bowser, Steve Brase, Kathy Adams Brezinski, Steve Buckles, Norma Caqueline, John Carney, Judy Patrick Castell, Dave Christensen, Wilfried Chust, Pamela Clark, Ralph Clements, Linda Brandt Coan, Linda Schneider Conley, Cheryl Cook, Susan Cox

D   Bonnie Davis, Paula Heacock Davis, Laurie De Bonis, Rus De Bonis, Tony De Bonis, Becky DeLaCruz, Carolyn Allen Derifield, Jeff Dier, Bonnie Brumbaugh Dix, LaVeryl Dlouhy, Janis Eastman, John Elin, Patrice Engstrom, Tony Ferguson, Ronald Fink, Randy Fox, Keith Francis, Sue Sheely Fuhrmann.

G   Donita Gano, Debbie Garcia-Diltz, Lucy De Bonis Garst, Cyndi Geist, Susan Gericke, David L. Graves, Carolyn Green, Rodney Green, Bill Groh, Janet Hagen, Donna Kleppe Hammer, Linda Owen Handy, Denise Hare, Quentin Hart, Jeff Hedrington, Bear Heiple, Kirk Henderson, Barbara Hibdon, Trudy Hoag, Craig Holdiman, Jenny Brooks Hope, Susan Tomkins Huebner, LeAnn King Hughes, Ruth Hughes, Curtis Hundley.

I   Lois Bakarat Ichelson, Kim Isbell, Charlie Jacobs, Donna Jacobs, Sandy Jacobson, Kathy Ravn Jambura, Sue Jans, Jack Jones, Vicki Jones, Pat Kinney, Dick Klemensen, Steve Knipp, Nancy Watson Kollpek, Skeets Lawless, Charles Lemons, Paula Longendyke, Paula Perton Lowry.

M   Jean Maddux, Mike Martin, Dave McPhail, Kriss Schreitmuller Meier, Marlys Messingham, Miles Mondt, Jerry Montgomery, Marilyn Moreland, Leon Moseley, Jennifer Leigh

Mosher, Shirley Muir, Loretta Murphy , *Theresa Nash, Warren Nash, Susan Seeber Ney, Barbara Niebergall Meyer.

N Mike Noland, John Ohrt, Judy Patrick, Tammy Penny, Ron Pepples, Bill Perkins, *Sheryl Petersen, Vicki Stoler Peterson, Suzanne Powers, Jean Purdy, Melodie Quinn, Cathy Strudthoff Robinson, Wally Robinson, Mike Roby, Joan Bedard Ross.

S Terry Sallis, T. Schell, Kathleen Schmidt, Thomas Schmidt, Anne Schoonover, *Kathy Schreitmuller, Dennis Scott, Linda Seeman, Gary Sharp, *Barbara Culpepper-Scheel, Marcia Wier Shields, Laura Haynes Shimek, Steve Sitz, Kathy Lippold Smith, Bev Smith, Rick Smith, Tom Smith, Bruce Spates, Terri Pearson Stevens, Becky Struve.

T Patty Ehrhardt Tann, Jalane Hess Terhune, Anthony Tisdale, Eric Trieweiler, Marilyn Trubey, Linda Tyler, Gary Undisclosed, Canplant Undisclosed, Linda Undisclosed, Nancy Undisclosed, Suzanne Vantluka, Jim Volgarino, Linda Wisecup Wachal, Terry Arnold Walker, A.M. Warnke, Curtis E. Washington, Lois West, Tim Westergreen, Laurel Wheeler, Gene White, Becky Hunemuller Wilharm, Susan Forney Wilson, Nancy Wood, Ken Wymore, Dean Yarrington, Lynnea Young.

*People who contributed without providing a full name or who preferred to be anonymous.

# ABOUT THE AUTHOR

Born in Brookline, MA, Nick De Bonis moved with his parents to his mother's hometown of Waterloo, IA, when he was an infant. He began elementary school on the West Side, attended two others on the East Side, then went to Logan Junior High. He graduated from East High School in 1966, the 100th graduating class.

His 30-year career in marketing combined the professional and academic worlds. He's a global strategic customer value

*Copyright © 2018 Susan De Bonis, flairsouthernstyle.com*

management consultant for more than 20 years and a business owner. De Bonis also taught marketing, advertising and communications at the university level for over 20 years. During this time, De Bonis has co-authored three industry books on Marketing and Management. (URL for his Author's Page on Amazon.com is http://tinyurl.com/zn7e742.)

He earned a B.A. from Flagler College in St. Augustine, FL, an M.S. from Troy State University and a Ph.D. from the University of Tennessee-Knoxville.

He's an Air Force (Vietnam, 1969) and Army veteran with an additional four years of service in the Air Force reserve and Florida Air National Guard.

De Bonis is married to Susan, who has her doctorate in Communications from UT-Knoxville. They have two grown children, Andrew (Colleen) and Gabriela (Josh Frazier). And two beautiful grandchildren, Cayden Jace Frazier (April 2014) and Joanna Kate Frazier (September 2018).

Made in the USA
Columbia, SC
06 June 2018